International Social W~~~
Canadian Perspectives

MW01103494

In memory and gratitude:
Gayle Gilchrist James
April 15, 1940–May 30, 2008

International Social Work
Canadian Perspectives

Edited by:
Gayle Gilchrist James and Richard Ramsay
with **Glenn Drover**

Thompson Educational Publishing, Inc.
Toronto

Information on how to obtain copies of this book is available at:
Website: www.thompsonbooks.com
E-mail: publisher@thompsonbooks.com
Telephone: (416) 766–2763
Fax: (416) 766–0398

Library and Archives Canada Cataloguing in Publication
    International social work : Canadian perspectives / edited by Gayle Gilchrist James, Richard Ramsay, Glenn Drover.

Includes bibliographical references.
ISBN 978-1-55077-169-5

    1. Social service. 2. Social service--Cross-cultural studies. 3. Social service--Canada. 4. Social work education. I. Drover, Glenn, 1935- II. Ramsay, Richard F. (Richard Frederick), 1941- III. James, Gayle Gilchrist

HV40.I557 2008   361   C2008-902585-7

Publisher: Keith Thompson
Production editor: Crystal J. Hall
Production coordinator: Christine Kwan
Cover design: Tibor Choleva
Copyeditor: Gillian Urbankiewicz
Proofreader: Crystal J. Hall

We acknowledge the support of the Government of Canada through the Book Publishing Industry Development Program for our publishing activities.

Printed in Canada. 1 2 3 4 5 6   13 12 11 10 09

Table of Contents

Preface

Gayle Gilchrist James and Richard Ramsay

An eminent Canadian trial lawyer, with every reason for confidence in his preparation and presentation skills, confided to us one day that despite his provincial and national courtroom successes, he always worried en route to any trial about how he might begin his presentation. All he needed, he said, was "the first five words."[1] We have faced the same dilemma in preparing a preface.

The origins of this publication began early in 2005, at what we had thought was a social occasion at the Village Park Inn in Calgary, when our colleague Glenn Drover indicated that he, Eugenia Moreno (Executive Director, Canadian Association of Social Workers), and Gweneth Gowanlock (a former Executive Director of CASW) had mooted having a national symposium, which would invite key individuals to outline their contributions to international social work and also honour our personal contributions.

To this team were quickly added Gayla Rogers (University of Calgary Faculty of Social Work Dean), John Mould (a former Alberta College of Social Workers President and CASW President with a long history on the Executive of the International Federation of Social Workers), and Margot Herbert, a former President of ACSW and representative to the CASW Board. We thank them for their commitment and support.

We also wish to recognize several individuals in significant supportive roles who helped to make the subsequent symposium a success in 2006. In particular, we want to thank Andrea Leffler Hennel (Conference Manager of the University of Calgary Conference and Special Events department), Avernelle Brown (Assistant to the Dean of the U of C Faculty of Social Work), and Lynne Dulaney-MacNicol (Director of Communications for the U of C Faculty of Social Work).

The scholarly contributions of the presenters lie within these pages, expressing a distinctly "Canadian take" on international social work and on those international issues and people, sometimes outside our borders, who have influenced our thinking. But we also had at the symposium, Canadians (and doctoral students in international social work) who work internationally inside and outside our borders, as discussants and facilitators, and who critiqued every major presentation. Thus, we were able to combine theory and practice in a way rarely seen at academic symposia, to the benefit and richness of all.

---

[1] Herein we pay tribute to David C. Day, Q.C., and Executive Member of the Canadian Research Institute for Law & the Family, and with whom we (and John Mould) worked on the *Turner Review and Investigation September 2006*. Further, he has taught the longest running Law & Social Work course in Canada, at Memorial University, and is well-known for his outstanding contribution to the Mount Cashel inquiry, known colloquially as "The Hughes Report."

The discussants and facilitators included the following (with their 2006 professional titles): Lorne Jaques (Senior Director, International Development and Research, University of Calgary International Centre); Evariste Theriault (Former Research Consultant, Social Development Partnerships Program, Human Resources Development Canada); Yasmin Dean (Doctoral Student in Social Work, University of Calgary); Mary Valentich (Professor Emerita of Social Work, University of Calgary); Jean Lafrance (Edmonton Division Head, University of Calgary Faculty of Social Work); Michael Embaie, (Chair, African Community Association of Calgary); Jack McDonald (Professor Emeritus of Social Work, University of Calgary); Francis Boakye (Doctoral Student in Social Work, University of Calgary); Jake Kuiken (Manager, Community and Neighborhood Services, City of Calgary); William Pelech (Associate Professor, University of Calgary Faculty of Social Work); Admasu Tachble (Doctoral Student in Social Work, University of Calgary); Rod Adachi (Executive Director, Alberta College of Social Workers); and Bruce MacLaurin (Assistant Professor, University of Calgary Faculty of Social Work).

In addition to the above, three invited keynote speakers from outside provided case examples of international social work in action. Evelyn Balais-Serrano (Asia Coordinator of the NGO Coalition for the International Criminal Court), based in the Philippines, presented "In Search of Justice," the process of seeking both those persons and evidence that might allow individuals to be charged and brought to the Criminal Court in the Hague. Jim Karls (Clinical Associate Professor, School of Social Work, University of California), presented "Person-in-Environment around the World: A Universal Assessment for Social Work," a data collection and assessment tool which might have universal applicability in social work practice. Frank Campbell (Executive Director, Office of Clinical Research and Consultation, Baton Rouge Crisis Center Foundation) contributed two presentations. The first, "Working Above and Below the Waterline of an Iceberg," delineated the emergency and long-term efforts of that Louisiana community to respond to the devastation of Hurricane Katrina. The title of his second keynote ("An International Approach to Suicide Intervention"), described the long path from treating suicide solely as personal and familial trauma to making it part of the United Nations agenda.

That this excellent assemblage easily came together on short notice over a common cause did not surprise us, given their academic interests and career-long contributions to international social work. They were possessed of a world view long before it was popular. The social work world caught up to them much later. They were folk who realized, perhaps before Eisler[2], that the world historically had advanced better in co-operative societies than in competitive ones, that they favoured linking over ranking, that they sought harmony over conquest, that they sought transformation rather than mere

---

[2] Eisler, Riane, and David Loye. 1990. *The Partnership Way: New Tools for Living and Learning, Healing Our Families, Our Communities, and Our World*. New York: HarperCollins.

"development" or "growth," that they looked for resolution rather than mere closure, and that they recognized "probability" rather than "predictability" as being the operational principle of the universe. Further, these international contributors seemed to understand Eisler's comment, citing John Stuart Mill (*Principles of Political Economy*), that "the way economic resources are distributed is a function not of some inexorable economic laws, but of political—that is, human choices."

Such it has always been in the advancement of human development; i.e. that a band of like-minded persons come together, for reasons in the first instance more attributable to "critical connections" over many years' duration rather than conscious choice. And, despite their being small in number, they may have an effect out of all proportion to the national and international issues at hand. The ease with which they do so is remarkable, but then they have been carrying the same belief system and/or value base, often alone or shared with a precious few, for a long time. In May 2006, in a prairie town, they were able to share it.

For the two of us, who have dedicated a lifetime, publicly but more often privately, to a similar world view and agenda, we express great gratitude to the contributors of this book. They came together as one.

The Contributors

Alean Al-Krenawi
Alean Al-Krenawi is professor, Department of Social Work, Ben Gurion University of The Negev.

Betty Bastien
Betty Bastien is associate professor, Faculty of Social Work, University of Calgary.

Wanda Thomas Bernard
Wanda Thomas Bernard is professor/director, School of Social Work, Dalhousie University.

Glenn Drover
Glenn Drover is a policy consultant to the Canadian Association of Social Workers.

David Este
David Este is professor/associate dean, Faculty of Social Work, University of Calgary.

Don Fuchs
Don Fuchs is professor, Faculty of Social Work, University of Manitoba.

John Graham
John Graham is Murray Fraser Professor, Faculty of Social Work, University of Calgary.

Nina Hayduk
Nina Hayduk is associate professor/head, Department of Sociology and Social Work, Lyiv Polytechnic National University.

Jacqueline Ismael
Jacqueline Ismael is professor, Faculty of Social Work, University of Calgary.

Shereen Ismael
Shereen Ismael is assistant professor, School of Social Work, Carleton University.

Gayle Gilchrist James
Gayle Gilchrist James was formerly professor, Faculty of Social Work, University of Calgary; she passed away on May 30, 2008.

Therese Jennissen
Therese Jennissen is associate professor, School of Social Work, Carleton University.

Linda Kreitzer
Linda Kreitzer is assistant professor, Faculty of Social Work, University of Calgary.

Colleen Lundy
Colleen Lundy is professor, School of Social Work, Carleton University.

Brad McKenzie
Brad McKenzie is professor, Faculty of Social Work, University of Manitoba.

Bob Mullaly
Bob Mullaly is professor/dean, Faculty of Social Work, University of Manitoba.

Richard Ramsay
Richard Ramsay is professor emeritus, Faculty of Social Work, University of Calgary.

Graham Riches
Graham Riches is professor/director, School of Social Work, University of British Columbia.

Gayla Rogers
Gayla Rogers is professor/dean, Faculty of Social Work, University of Calgary.

Wendy Thomson
Wendy Thomson is professor/director, School of Social Work, McGill University.

Maureen Wilson
Maureen Wilson is professor/associate dean, Faculty of Social Work, University of Calgary.

Introduction

Chapter 1

Canadians and International Social Work

Glenn Drover and Gayla Rogers

Since the early days of social work, Canadian social work practitioners and educators have played a leadership role in the international development of the profession. While the contribution of Canadian social workers has been documented, to some degree, in various articles and reports, there has been no recent book in Canada devoted to the topic. This book, therefore, is an attempt to fill the gap by identifying and documenting the role that Canadian social workers currently play in the development of international social work and social policy.

All the contributors to the book have been directly involved in international social work, some in developing countries, some in developed countries, some in both. Their contributions fall broadly into four initiatives: social justice, social development, social work practice, and social work education. These initiatives, in turn, are closely related to Canadian involvement in the International Federation of Social Workers (IFSW), the International Association of Schools of Social Work (IASSW) and the UN Interregional Consultation on Developmental Social Welfare Policies and Programmes (1989).

Internationally, IFSW recently highlighted the importance of protecting basic human rights. In cooperation with IFSW, IASSW developed a report on global standards of social work education as a way of assuring an ongoing commitment to the promotion of social change, problem solving in human relationships, and empowerment of people to enhance their own well-being. The UN Interregional Committee has enunciated new approaches in social welfare to meet specific needs of the family, the advancement of women, and minority groups, as well as addressing ongoing challenges associated with substance abuse, AIDS, poverty, food security, and housing.

The two lead Canadian social work organizations that have played a direct role in the development of international social work are the Canadian Association of Social Workers (CASW) and the Canadian Association of Social Work Education (CASWE—formerly the Canadian Association of Schools of Social Work). These nationally sanctioned bodies have affiliated status with IFSW and IASSW, which, in turn, enjoy varying degrees of consultation status with the United Nations. The CASW was a founding member of IFSW, whose member associations now number approximately 84 national professional social work associations worldwide, representing 470,000 social workers around the world (IFSW 2007).

CASWE is a member of IASSW. Canadian social work educators have played an important part in the international body's global activities by serving on major committees as overseas consultants and collaborating in research and demonstration projects. Additionally, they have helped to find resources to promote social work education and social development training in developing countries, often with the assistance of the Canadian International Development Agency (CIDA). IASSW comprises more than 400 schools and faculties of social work out of 1,700 affiliated schools throughout the world.

The chapters in this book outline a range of ways in which Canadian social workers are, or were, involved in international social work. Before describing the contents of the book, however, we outline the parameters of international social work, the importance of international social work and various models of international development that have been employed by social workers. We also outline how Canadians have been involved in international social work in the past, as well as a range of initiatives and activities in Canadian social work education that influence and have an impact on international social work.

Parameters of International Social Work

Social work, by necessity, is localized. It focuses on the needs of individuals in family and in community. It is funded, in general, by governments to address the concerns of residents and citizens of a particular country. For that reason, social work practice also varies from region to region. In North America, social work has a strong clinical and individualized form of practice. In Western Europe, it is more closely associated with the delivery of public funded social services. In Eastern Europe and South America, as well as in many developing countries of Asia, it is extensively involved in community development and social action. With increasing international linkages created through communication technologies and integrated economies, however, there is a growing sense among social workers of global interdependence.

International migration and large scale movements of refugees have also increased the cultural, linguistic, and religious diversity of developed countries like Canada. They have changed the composition of clientele served by social agencies and consequently have impacted upon established social work practices. There is a growing awareness among social workers that the social problems faced in one country are similar, in many respects, to those of other countries. Increasingly, innovations in practice or changes in policy are likely to occur anywhere in the world and transmitted across the globe through the Internet in a matter of days.[1] The political, economic, and social actions of one country affect another on a regular basis. There is less of a division between

---

[1] An example of Internet connections in social work is Global Social Work, an internet-based community service for social workers that grew out of the crisis occasioned by 9/11. See www.hometown.aol.com/ egeratylsw/globalsw.html

the domestic and foreign affairs. There is less of a communication barrier because of advances in technology.

Because of these changes, appropriate goals for social workers, and social work education, include a renewed understanding of global trends and international development. As Healy (2001, 3) suggests: "it is important that social workers be prepared to (a) address internationally related case and community problems that arise in their domestic practice, (b) contribute to mutual problem solving on global social problems, and (c) monitor the impact of their own nation's policies on other countries' and people's well-being." In considering a definition of international social work, therefore, it is useful to think not only about social work in one's backyard, but also about the interconnectedness between what happens at home and abroad.

In broad terms the definition of social work, developed by the International Federation of Social Workers (IFSW), is inclusive of international social work. It was originally proposed at the IFSW World Conference in Montreal in 2000. It reads as follows: "The social work profession promotes social change, problem solving in human relationships and the empowerment and liberation of people to enhance well-being. Utilizing theories of human behaviour and social systems, social work intervenes at the points where people interact with their environments." (IFSW website 2005). For purposes of this book, however, the IFSW definition is too inclusive. While it is comprehensive and reflects the goals and practice of social work in different parts of the globe, it does not specifically indicate which aspects of social work are international as distinct from those that are primarily national or local in scope.

To assist us in clarifying the parameters of international social work, we turn to social workers in the United States who have grappled with the term. Hokenstad, Khinduka and Midgley (1992, 3–7) state that a narrow but clear way to think of international social work is to associate it only with those services and practices that engage in international activities. In this interpretation, international social work can be considered a distinct area of practice with distinct knowledge and skills. Another way is to specify common roles and activities that social workers perform in different countries—somewhat like the IFSW definition. Still, another approach is to think of international social work as any form of exchange that takes place between social workers in different countries and cultures. In the end, the approach that Hokenstad et al. prefer is to provide a comparative account of social work in the world using three themes that characterize the profession in an international context. The three are commonality, diversity, and challenge.

In our view, a more satisfactory approach to the delineation of international social work is provided by Lynne Healy. She defines international social work as "international professional action and the capacity for international action by the social work profession and its members." (Healy 2001, 7). She then goes on to incorporate four dimensions under the rubric of "international action." The four are: internationally related domestic practice; professional exchange; international practice; and international policy development and advocacy

(Healy 2001, 7–14). The first dimension incorporates social work practice that takes place primarily in domestic settings like those in most regions of Canada. It includes refugee and immigrant settlement, international adoptions, cross cultural practices that involve peoples from other countries and cross-border services. The example that she gives is a service agency in Canada that serves adolescents from Jamaica. Her second dimension—professional exchange— refers to the ways in which social workers improve professional practice by adapting and borrowing from each other. This can be achieved by hosting visitors from other countries (which schools of social work and social agencies regularly do), participating in international conferences (which occur on a frequent basis for both practitioners and academics), and reading foreign periodicals or books (which are available in many locations). Exchange also occurs through the social justice, peace, environmental, and women's movements in which social workers are involved.

The third dimension is the employment of social workers in international development agencies. To be directly employed in international development and relief agencies, social workers typically need to be multi-skilled. In addition to their knowledge of human behaviour, skills in organizing and practice skills, they have to combine a commitment to development, knowledge of international issues, and good cross cultural skills. Many international development agencies in Canada have employed social workers over the years. Social workers have also been extensively involved in international adoptions. Recently, the UK has been seeking to fill vacancies by employing Canadian social workers. Until recently, social workers have also had placements and job opportunities through International Social Service Canada. The agency provided inter-country services related to child placement, child protection, child abduction, and child custody.[2]

The fourth and final dimension identified by Healy is international policy development and advocacy. An example she provides of this type of international action is a symposium held by the International Association of Schools of Social Work (IASSW) on violence against women at the UN Fourth World Conference on Women in Beijing, China, in 1995. Since IASSW and IFSW have consultation status with the United Nations and are also accredited with affiliated organizations like the International Labour Organization (ILO), UNICEF, and the Council of Europe, there are many opportunities for social workers to engage in social policy debates around the world. Canadian social workers, through their national and provincial associations, have been able to participate in international policy debates over the years.

The approach to international social work used in this book incorporates the four dimensions outlined by Healy. While the four dimensions of domestic

---

[2] In Canada, ISS services began in the 1950s as a program of the Canadian Welfare Council (now the Canadian Council on Social Development). In 1979, International Social Service Canada was federally incorporated as a non-profit organization and accepted by the ISS International Council in Geneva as the Canadian Branch of International Social Service. ISS Canada was governed by a national volunteer Board of Directors. In 2007, the government cut its funding.

practice, professional exchange, international practice, and policy development are not necessarily covered in each of the chapters, they are addressed throughout the book. At the same time, the chapters also serve to highlight different skill sets, theories, and values that social workers bring to the table when they are engaged in international social work. This, we believe, is also consistent with the definition of social work promoted by IFSW.

Social work grew out of humanitarian and democratic ideals, and its values are based on respect for the equality, worth, and dignity of all people. "Human rights and social justice serve as the motivation and justification for social work action. In solidarity with those who are disadvantaged, the profession strives to alleviate poverty and to liberate vulnerable and oppressed people in order to promote social inclusion. Social work values are embodied in national and international codes of ethics." (IFSW and CASW websites). Social work is also based on a systematic body of evidence-informed knowledge derived from research and program/practice evaluation, including local and indigenous knowledge. Social work practice ranges from personal or family support to community development, social policy, and social planning. And, as we shall see later on, priorities vary from country to country depending on cultural, historical, political, and socio-economic conditions.

Importance of International Social Work

There are many benefits that flow from the study and practice of international social work. The benefits accrue as much to social workers in developed countries like Canada as they do to social workers in developing countries. Rosemary Sarri, professor emerita of the University of Michigan School of Social Work, identifies three keys reasons for social workers to engage in international social work (Sarri 1997, 390–91). The first is that it widens one's horizon about economic, political, and social welfare systems. Having an understanding of developments outside one's own country opens one to different options for addressing issues and innovative ways of responding to social challenges. Gaining a wider frame of reference than those experienced in North America is particularly important at a time when the privatization and contracting out of established public social services are the norm.

A second benefit is that it introduces a cross-cultural perspective to social work that is very valuable at a time when immigration to North America from Asia, Africa, and Central America is high and our cities are increasingly diverse. Social workers are grappling with the impact of multiculturalism and social exclusion on a daily basis. The third benefit is cross-national collaboration between social workers and other human service professions. By forming teams across countries and across cultures, Sarri believes that it is possible, not only to address human needs caused by periodic crisis such as droughts, floods, or earthquakes, but also to deal with local, national, and international conflict.

Midgley (1997a, 19–25) recognizes that even though international exchanges can be beneficial, there are practical, methodological, and professional challenges. Practical challenges include the cost and demands of international exchanges, which tend to favour social workers from developed countries more than developing countries. Methodological problems arise because social work practices and social work data differ considerably from country to country. Professional exchange challenges occur because it is not always feasible, or even desirable, to transfer practices from one country to another. Some developed countries, like the United States and Great Britain, have tended to dominate such exchanges with a resultant concern about ethnocentrism and Eurocentrism in professional exchange.

Perhaps, however, the greatest value of international social work is that it encourages social workers to come to terms with the forces of globalization.[3] Midgley (1997b) suggests that globalization is leading to greater international collaboration among non-governmental social service organizations in the treatment of refugees and the promotion of the well-being of women. Khan and Dominelli (2000), in a paper presented at an international social work conference in Montreal, outline how globalization has created three sorts of challenges for the profession: external forces, ideological forces, and marginal forces.

Regarding external forces, they point out that market criteria are being introduced into social service delivery in order to encourage efficiency and promote innovation. Market criteria, in turn, lead to increasing frag-mentation of public social services as programs proliferate through various contractual arrangements. They also lead to de-professionalization as management practices reduce professional autonomy (Dominelli 1996). In terms of ideological forces, the main influence is essentially counterfactual, in the sense that governments use globalization to justify the privatization or commercialization of social services. With respect to marginal forces, Khan and Dominelli suggest that globalization has intensified the disadvantages experienced by more and more groups in society, and the diversity of social work clients, without the availability of additional resources.

Jim Ife (2000), in an address to the same conference, highlights the rela-tionship between globalization and social work by recognizing the potential for change. While he is mindful of the dilemmas and concerns raised by Khan and Dominelli, he dwells on the potential for rethinking social work practice in ways that link the global and the local, the personal and the political. Globalization, as he sees it, requires a re-examination of social work knowledge, values, and skills in order to embrace and influence it rather than reject it. In order to understand how social workers are actually responding to globalization, Rowe et al (2000) surveyed social workers in different regions of the world. They reported that globalization increased problems in terms of

---

[3] The next two paragraphs draw on an article by Drover and MacDougall (2002).

economic impacts, but also opened opportunities for international cooperation through global communication, commitments to rights, and participation in international development. Drover and MacDougall (2002) identify how social work is impacted by three forces of globalization: international trade agreements; information technologies; and neo-liberalism. Seen from this viewpoint, the extension of international trade is shifting the justification of professional practice from a foundation based on credentials to one based on competence; information technology is changing the medium of social work education and the forms of social work intervention; and neo-liberalism is modifying the language social workers use to justify and explain their practices.

Models of International Development

For purposes of studying and evaluating the impact of international social work, various models of development have evolved. One of the more salient has been proposed by Jim Midgley (1995). Midgley began his career in South Africa. He worked for a time in England at the London School of Economics, and currently teaches social work at Berkley. He has promoted a social development perspective in the profession. It is used by some of the authors of this book. The essential idea behind a social development model is to demonstrate the close linkage between the economic and the social. Midgley argues that economic development by itself is inadequate to promote human well-being as the enhancement of the standard of living also depends upon social improvements.

The relationship, furthermore, is not unilateral. Economic development has to be evaluated in terms of its impact on social programs, but the reverse is also true. "The integration of economic and social policies with a dynamic process of development is the essence of the development perspective. It requires that economic programs enhance social welfare and, conversely, that social programs contribute to economic development." (Midgley 1997c, 12). Unlike other development models, which Midgley considers to be too negative or vague, he thinks that the social development model has the potential to be used by political leaders, NGOs, and local activists to harness globalization toward progressive ends that would be consistent with social work values.

There are three essential features of the social development model (Midgley 1997c, 17–19). The first is the establishment of international and national organizations and agencies to enable the implementation of policies and programs that systematically integrate economic and social improvements. Existing structural adjustment programs of the International Monetary Fund and the World Bank are counterproductive to the extent that the economic policies override the social and the environmental. The second is a commitment to economic growth that actually benefits the ordinary person as well as the environment. Without this commitment, economic development is likely to be distorted or uneven, which has been the case in Africa, Latin America, and some countries of Asia. To offset the distortion, an important component of the social development approach is the extensive participation of the population in planning and implementation.

Another component is an equitable redistribution of resources in order to meet the basic needs of people. This third essential feature, according to Midgley, is to generate a return on social expenditures rather than to place an emphasis on consumption. Examples of social expenditure that generate an economic return are investments in education, labour market initiatives that encourage employment, and microcredit schemes that promote self-employment. Traditional welfare programs that foster dependency or maintain people in unproductive environments are not considered to be useful and may even detract from development objectives. Social workers can contribute to this sort of social development model by assisting clients to engage in productive employment (Midgley 1997c, 22).

A second model, which complements in some respects the social development model, is a rights-based approach.[4] The rights based approach begins with the assumption that the basic services should be provided to people as a matter of social right. The language is one of rights and obligations rather than concepts of equal opportunities, economic growth, and balanced development (Lindenberg and Bryant 2001). It is also about the importance of people across the globe standing in solidarity with each other to assure basic rights to housing, education, and social security. Following Doyle and Gough (1991), who also use a rights-based approach to development, basic needs include, as a minimum, food, health, and the potential for participation in society. They argue that people have a right to the satisfaction of basic needs and that such needs are a first priority before other goals of development are met.

Drover (2003) has used a rights-based approach to support the alleviation of poverty and the promotion of citizenship. As he sees it, two conditions are required in order to validate a rights-based approach to the alleviation of poverty: institutional justification and normative justification. The former has been achieved by the nearly universal acceptance of the UN Covenant on Economic, Social and Cultural Rights (1966), as well as the increasing acceptance of the UN Convention on the Elimination of All Forms of Discrimination against Women (1981), and the Convention on the Rights of the Child (1990). Normative justification comes, not from the United Nations (which has generally avoided it), but from different cultural traditions (e.g., Liberalism in the West; Confucianism in East Asia). Drover (2000) suggests that a rights-based approach to international development can be used to advocate for a form of international social citizenship that extends beyond the nation-state to include civil society, cultural diversity, and the active engagement of people in the development of policies and programs that affect their lives.

A third model—a feminist perspective on international social development and social work—has been proposed by Lena Dominelli (1997).

---

[4] A rights based approach to development has its roots in the 1948 UN Declaration of Human Rights.

She states that there is a need for a feminist perspective because of the low priority that has been attached to women's roles in the development process. Unlike the previous two development models, feminism incorporates an understanding of power and oppressive relationships, as well as the social divisions that result from those relationships. To avoid treating women as a homogeneous group, however, Dominelli emphasizes that it is important to take into account the diversity of women's experiences, their capacity to build on opportunities, and their potential for change. One way in which that has happened is through the work of DAWN (Development Alternatives with Women for a New Era). The DAWN network covers Africa, Asia, Latin America, the Caribbean, and the Pacific. The aim is to influence mainstream development thinking, to secure gains made through the UN, to work for a radical restructuring of international financial institutions, and to mainstream gender analysis in progressive development organizations.

Within social work, a feminist approach to international development depends, in part, on the validation of anti-oppressive practice at home. In that regard, however, Dominelli believes that social workers are inclined to intervene in emancipatory ways because they are confronted daily in their practice by "poverty, family breakdown, violence against women and children, child abuse and neglect, isolated elderly people, and criminal behaviour. Help for these problems are basic to social development." (Dominelli 1997, 83). By drawing on a growing body of literature on feminist analysis in social work, she recommends a number of feminist elements that can be incorporated into a development framework.

They include the facilitation of the expression of women's voices, the development of partnerships, the turning of private concerns into public issues, the interplay of women's unpaid work and the paid labour market, the validation of women's experiences, and the acknowledgement of the interdependence between domestic and international issues. Because these building blocks of analysis are familiar to social workers in their daily practice, they also provide a basis for moving from the familiar to the unfamiliar, from the local to the global. "In following feminist precepts, social workers are creating spaces in which people can tell and act out their own stories instead of following those that are externally imposed. They are also enabling people to articulate the connections they experience between structural oppression and personal suffering." (Domenelli 1997, 88).

For Canadians, however, a fourth model of development needs to be considered, one that builds on theoretical frameworks extensively used in this country—empowerment, structural social work, and anti-oppressive practice. Two Canadian social workers who have employed this eclectic approach in Latin America are Elizabeth Whitmore and Maureen Wilson, both of whom are represented in this book. Whitmore and Wilson (2005) focus on the role that social workers play in relation to popular movements that have arisen in response to globalization. While they recognize the contribution of theories of social capital and social movements, which provide insights into the important role that civil society can play in international development, they also think that they offer little guidance for social work practice. To assist social workers, they make use of concepts from Gramsci and Freire.

From Gramsci, they draw upon a distinction between structural and conjunctural analysis and a concept of the organic intellectual. Structural analysis allows social workers to look at the more permanent features of society that are difficult to change whereas conjunctural analysis enables us to look at opportunities for action or development in the short-term. The reference to an organic intellectual is Gramsci's way of affirming the importance of leadership in all sectors of society, not just the so-called elite. The essential elements drawn from Friere are a dialogic approach to learning, praxis, and participatory research. Each of those components presupposes a model of development in which social action and social change result from participation wherein social workers are allies with oppressed people. Some of the skills that social workers can bring to a model of development, therefore, are structural and conjunctural, engagement in the process of development (they call it "accompaniment"), the formation of alliances, organizing, and relationship building. In varying degrees, the concepts are employed throughout this book.

Previous Canadian Contributions

Historically, the development of social work in Canada was associated with the rise of Charity Organization Societies in the late nineteenth century. Charity Organization Societies differed from other relief organizations of the time in placing an emphasis on systematic investigation into the causes of human need rather than the simple relief of poverty.[5] About the same time as the Charity Organization Societies developed, the Settlement House Movement also was taking shape in working class urban areas of Canada. Unlike Charity Organization Societies, which focused on individual and family assistance, the Settlement House Movement highlighted the importance of communal and collective responses to need (Drover 1998, 79).

The emergence of Charity Organization Societies and Settlement Houses also demonstrates how, from its beginning, social work in Canada has been associated with international social work, initially as a response to social conditions in Canada, subsequently through the introduction of social work to developing countries and recently through the reintroduction of social work in the former Soviet Union and Eastern bloc countries. In the first stage (the early 20th century), social workers in Canada were closely associated with developments in Europe and the United States. Within a few decades of the initiation of Charity Organization Societies in England and the United States in the late 19th century, similar developments took place in Canada. One of the first was the Protestant Charity Organization of Montreal, founded in 1901. University Settlement in Toronto was started less than a decade later in 1910. Within a few years, the first school of social work

---

[5] Many charity organizations were established in Canada before the Charity Organization Societies. Most of them were rooted in religious and ethnic communities.

was initiated at the University of Toronto in 1914 and McGill University in 1918.[6] These developments, in turn, were followed by the establishment of the Canadian Council on Child and Family Welfare in 1920, with Charlotte Whitton as the first Executive Director, and the Canadian Association of Social Workers in 1926.

About the same time that social work and social work education were taking root in Canada, the United States, and Europe, there were similar developments in Latin America, Asia, and Africa (Healy 2001, 22–24).[7] The first social work school in South America was founded in Santiago, Chile, in 1925 by Dr. Alejandro del Rio. Rio was a physician and sought advice from Dr. René Sand of Belgium, who spearheaded the development of the International Permanent Secretariat of Social Workers in Paris in 1928; Canada was a charter member. Because Sand was an advocate for social medicine, he and Dr. Rio focused on the role that social workers could play in assisting physicians. A similar pattern developed in Argentina.

During the first stage of social work development, Canada was more a recipient than a provider, drawing heavily upon initiatives in Europe and the United States. In the second and third stages of development before and after WWII, Canadians—and Canadian social workers—took more of a leadership role in international organizations. The establishment of the United Nations Relief and Rehabilitation Administration (UNRRA) in 1943, the founding of the World Health Organization and United Nations in 1945, and the adoption of the Universal Declaration of Human Rights in 1948, provided considerable opportunity for Canadians to engage in postwar renewal and development. Canadians, such as John Humphrey of McGill University (who drafted the human rights declaration) and Dr. Brock Chisholm (the first director of WHO) were extensively involved in these initiatives.

In terms of international social work, one of the more prominent Canadians in the early postwar period was George Davidson (Splane 2003, 130–31). Although Davidson was not a trained social worker, he was closely associated with the development of the profession in Canada from the early thirties, initially as superintendent of welfare for the government of British Columbia, subsequently as director of the Vancouver Council of Social Agencies and the Canadian Welfare Council and eventually as deputy minister of National Health and Welfare. In the latter position, he was intimately involved in the development of many of Canada's postwar social programs and also became involved as a Canadian representative on various committees and projects of the United Nations. The International Conference of Social Work (later the International Council on Social Welfare, ICSW) resumed activities after the war and Davidson attended most of the conferences while he

---

[6] The first school of social work in the world was started in Amsterdam in 1899, closely followed by a similar development in Germany. The first school of social work in North America was the New York School of Philanthropy (now the Columbia University School of Social Work). See Healy 2001, 390.

[7] This and the following paragraph draw largely on Lynne Healy (2001).

was deputy minister.[8] He was elected president at the 1956 conference and remained in that capacity for four years. In 1972, Davidson was appointed as Undersecretary General of the United Nations for six years and then as advisor to the United Nations Fund for Population Activities (Splane 2003, 173–94).

Davidson also encouraged senior members of the Department of Health and Welfare, including Richard Splane, to participate in various activities of the United Nations (Billups 2002, 235–52). Splane, a social worker, was initially employed as executive assistant to Davidson, then as director of unemployment assistance, and finally as assistant deputy minister before taking a faculty position at the University of British Columbia School of Social Work. As a consequence of these activities, Splane became increasingly involved in international social work, starting with the International Conference of Social Work in Toronto in 1954 and more proactively at the International Council on Social Welfare (ICSW) in 1970 in Manila and at The Hague in 1972. In 1974, he was elected to the board of ICSW and fostered close relations between ICSW, the International Association of Schools of Social Work (IASSW), and the International Federation of Social Workers (IFSW). He was extensively involved in the organization of the 1984 conference in Montreal that brought all three organizations together in one venue under the International Conferences on Social Development. Over the years, Splane was also active in International Social Services Canada.

In recent years, two other active Canadians involved in international social work were Gayle Gilchrist James and Richard Ramsay. Gilchrist James became president of the International Federation of Social Workers in the 1980s. A lifelong resident of Alberta, she started her career in the mental health field and then worked in educational social work before joining the social work faculty of the University of Calgary in 1975 where she remained until she retired in 2004. Over those years, Gilchrist James was very actively involved in promoting the social work profession, serving initially as the registrar of the Alberta Association of Social Workers (later the Alberta College of Social Workers), then as the president, subsequently as the president of the Canadian Association of Social Workers and eventually as president for two terms of the International Federation of Social Workers (the first Canadian to hold the position). In 2004, she was awarded the Andrew Mouravieff-Apostol diploma and medal for her long-standing and significant contribution to international social work by IFSW.

Like Gilchrist James, Ramsay was associated with social work at the University of Calgary for over thirty years. He also served as the president of the Alberta Association of Social Workers, co-chair of the Canadian Association of Social Workers' national scope of practice task force, treasurer of the International Federation of Social Workers and member

---

[8] The biennial international conferences were paralleled for many years by a biennial Canadian Conference on Social Work. Davidson was involved in the early development of the conference in 1938 in Vancouver and subsequent conferences during the 1940s and 1950s (Splane 2003 174–75).

of the IFSW-IASSW committee on global standards for social work. His outstanding contribution, both nationally and internationally, was in the area of suicide prevention. In the 1980s, he co-developed LivingWorks Education, the world's most widely used suicide intervention training program, with a network of over 3,000 trainers and 600,000 community caregivers in several countries including Australia, Canada, England, Ireland, New Zealand, Northern Ireland, Norway, Scotland, Singapore, and the United States. He was also co-developer of the UN's national suicide prevention strategy guideline and served as an advisor to the WHO.

Internationalizing Social Work Education

As international social work has evolved over time, Canadian schools of social work have played a key role. In some instances, they have led the way with demonstration projects and programmatic innovations that shape policies, programs, and practices. In other cases, they have had to "catch up" to the field and the profession in providing students with the requisite knowledge, skills, and values for the international work they encounter. The need to develop curricula and educational opportunities in international social work and social development has become increasingly important for the successful realization of the mission declaration in most schools of social work, and indeed in most universities in which the schools are housed.

Attempts to explicitly internationalize social work curricula in Western countries are not new. In the United States, Khinduka and Parvis (1969) were early advocates of international content in elective courses. The rationale at the time was that courses were needed to assist foreign students attending American schools while at the same time American students needed a broader understanding of international issues. There was, however, a danger of overemphasizing cross-cultural understanding at the expense of not attending to the importance of political and socio-economic forces. A primary focus on cultural values was a distraction to controversial issues such as land reform and distributive justice facing developing nations.

In the seventies, Anders (1975) criticized American social work educators for the scant treatment they gave international welfare compared to the heavy emphasis on national problems. Students, who became critically appreciative of the dangers of ethnocentrism and xenophobia in liberal arts courses, entered social work and were confronted with a de facto curriculum that was both ethnocentric and xenophobic. Anders was highly critical of "national brand" social work education that assumed local application in disregard of indigenous methods in other countries and contexts. The emergence of generalist and generic social work in the seventies did not do much to help international studies; it tended to define social work practice as a method with a set of generic skills, rather than a broad issue-oriented domain. Anders argued for a curriculum perspective in which students would be directed to a goal of promoting world peace and building effective social relationships among all nations and groups (Anders 1975, 21).

Sanders (1977, 26) pointed to evidence of a world transforming into a more interdependent system juxtaposed with national and political isolationism. He advocated new ways of understanding world hunger and poverty; crises in the world's supply of natural resources and environmental degradation had something to do with the West and were not just problems facing the developing world. Social work educators, in his view, were resistant to calls for international curricula. They were more aligned with an isolationist perspective and generally judged international social work to be a luxury when there were so many problems for social workers to address in their own region and country. Sanders countered the resistance by highlighting the advantages of an internationalized curriculum that would permeate the entire curriculum rather than being confined to one or two optional courses.

In the early eighties, Boehm (1980) reported an increase in the number of international courses in MSW programs in the United States, but the increase seemed to reflect more of an individual contribution than a collective will on the part of the schools. Most of the courses were still electives. Boehm reinforced the advantages cited by Sanders and was critical of course content that narrowly addressed the work of international agencies, professional organizations and comparative methods of service delivery. He believed a much greater emphasis needed to be on the UN approach to social development and the global concerns of population policy and food security. Healy's 1988 study confirmed that few social work educators in the US had adopted an international perspective.

Canada's Version of International Social Work Education

On the Canadian scene, Dennis Kimberley edited a volume published by CASSW titled: *Beyond National Boundaries: Canadian Contributions to International Social Work and Social Welfare* in 1984. It was published in honour of the 22nd International Congress of the IASSW. It begins to expose (but not articulate) a subtle and nuanced distinction between the American and Canadian discourse on international social work that can be seen today as having distinctly different flavours. Kimberley (1984, 1–3) suggests a constructivist stance to the practice and scholarship of international social work and social welfare, allowing the knowledge, definitions, and methods to emerge from the field through considered interpretations, reflections, and praxis.

Canadian concerns about exporting western constructions of social work interventions and education to the non-Western world were a common theme in Kimberley's edited book. Reflecting on social work as a modernizing technology, a former dean of the University of Toronto Faculty of Social Work (Garber 1984, 211–212) wrote the following: "It is disconcerting to visit social work programs outside one's country and find texts that are translated from their North American or European origins, courses, and practica that copy the same labels and forms, while finding so few domestically derived and indigenous materials." Other examples of Canadian concerns were manifest in chapters of the book on power, oppression, social location, and critical analysis—ideas and concepts that became integrated into mainstream social work curricula in Canada in the early nineties.

Through the nineties and into the new millennium, the pervasive impact of globalization moved internationalization from the back burner to the forefront in Canadian universities. Those schools of social work that were already involved in international activities were, all of a sudden, seen as "beacons of light" in their institutions; those schools whose international aspirations were thwarted due to lack of resources, found they now had the institutional support to move forward; and, those schools who had not yet embraced internationalization now had an opportunity. The discourse of partnerships and mutuality replaced an outdated model of "western expert" with notions of mutual agreements, two-way exchanges, joint planning, co-learning, and shared knowledge (Traub-Werner, Shera, Villa, Peón 2000).

Canadian schools have not yet adopted a curriculum policy statement that boldly addresses international knowledge, nor competence requiring programs to prepare students to recognize the global context of social work practice. At present, Canadian standards of accreditation only require schools with international involvement to "delineate policies and proce-dures for meeting standards in these aspects of their programs" (CASSW, 2004). Building upon the early work, however, some Canadian social work educators continue to critique international collaboration and exchanges that are exploitive, give lip service to notions of mutuality, pay nominal attention to power or the dominance of Western hegemony, and dismiss or disregard local and indigenous knowledge (Razack, 2002; Whitmore & Wilson, 1997).

Asamoah (2003), in describing different types of potential international development in schools, identified study-abroad programs and exchanges of faculty and students between academic institutions as the prevalent form. Included in study-abroad initiatives are international field work or practica, faculty exchange, technology-mediated distance education, and consultation regarding specific areas of practice such as child welfare or displaced persons. To further international collaboration, Healy (2003) suggests that educators should draw on relevant inter-organizational theories related to interna-tional exchange, interdependence, and mutuality in order to deepen an understanding about organizational collaboration and provide principles to aid in the conceptualization and implementation of international activity.

Educational Practice and Future Directions

There are currently different models, types, and forms of international activities in Canadian Schools of Social Work. A thematic analysis of inter-national activities of schools of social work in Canada in 2004, and again in 2006, provides a basis for considering the range and extent of activity. There are five themes with many schools involved in at least one. International field education through practicum placements abroad is the most commonly practiced form of international activity. Some schools have well-developed placement partnerships, protocols, and practices while other schools offer international placements in response to individual student circumstances or faculty arrangements. Very few schools mention reciprocity when describing their international field opportunities as they typically take the form of Canadian students going abroad. In a few circumstances, mention is made of managing students coming to Canada as part of the international field program. Issues for consideration include costs, risk management, quality assurance, housing, and course equivalence.

Several schools describe being involved in international social development projects, typically funded by the Canadian International Development Agency (CIDA). These tend to be large in scale, often involving more than one faculty or department within a given university and in some cases, involving more than one Canadian university. The projects offer some opportunities for students and involve a number of both academics and practitioners over a significant period of time. In some cases, the CIDA funded development projects include the creation of social work programs or courses in other countries. In other cases, social work education programs and courses are separate from social development projects. Either way, however, Canadian schools are contributing to the evolution and expansion of social work education in various parts of the world.

Another theme is research. Research projects involving scholars from other countries include activities that extend beyond social development initiatives. These are typically described as multi-site, multi-partnered projects that are often comparative in nature, seeking to build and share knowledge related to policies, programs, and practices in any number of important issues of common concern across the globe. To that end, the Canadian Consortium for International Social Development (CCISD) is an association of scholars, activists, and organizations undertaking and promoting applied research and advocacy on international issues of social policy and social development. Bringing scholars together at international conferences, building networks through technologies, and the dissemination of findings in journals, books, and other formats are all ways to make the knowledge accessible to both practitioners and academics.

The final theme related to international activities in schools of social work can be described in terms of the local application of internationalization through teaching courses within programs in Canada. This is not as widespread as might be expected in terms of required or option courses, although most programs describe content on issues of international import as being infused in core courses to some extent. Most schools report on plans to increase their offerings through new courses and other forms of educational opportunities, such as guest lectures and extra workshops. Other areas of growth include increasing the visibility of visiting scholars in the community and their exposure to students.

The five themes of international activities in schools of social work—field education, social development projects, developing and delivering social work degree programs abroad, research and scholarship on global issues, and internationalized curricula within social work programs—all serve to further Canadian contributions to international social work. Schools of social work and social work educators, researchers and scholars play a vital and critical role in preparing the next generation of activists, advocates, and social development practitioners, generating evidence-informed best practices and policies, and creating the conditions for change on an international level with global impact.

Perspectives in This Book

The remainder of this book outlines international social work initiatives in which Canadian social work educators and practitioners have been engaged in recent years. Following priorities of the International Federation of Social Workers and the International Association of Schools of Social Work as well as the Canadian Association of Social Workers and the Canadian Association of Social Work Education, the chapters are grouped into four categories: Social Justice, Social Development, Social Work Practice, and Social Work Education. The first four chapters under Social Justice illustrate how Canadian social workers have been associated with the promotion of an understanding of social justice issues in Iraq (Jacqueline and Shereen Ismael), the right to food security (Graham Riches), the reform of the public sector in Britain (Wendy Thomson), and the affirmation of the contribution of black men in the diaspora (Wanda Thomas Bernard).

Ismael and Ismael, a mother-daughter team, illustrate how social equity was constructed in Iraq from early times to the development of a modern nation state and how, recently, it has bee deconstructed to suit sectarian interests. Riches, who has been associated with two World Food Summits and co-edited a book of case studies published by the Food and Agricultural Organization of the United Nations, examines how Canada responds, or should respond, to international obligations to assure the right to food within this country. Thomson draws on her experience as head of the Leadership Centre for Local Government and advisor to the office of Prime Minister Tony Blair, to outline the significance of public service reforms in Britain. Bernard's interest in international issues stems from personal and professional experience, as well as comparative study of Black men in England and Canada. She looks at the challenges facing Black men in this country and elsewhere.

The next section of the book, Social Development, records the experience of Canadian social workers who have been working through partnerships with colleagues in Central America (Maureen Wilson), Cuba and Russia (Colleen Lundy and Therese Jennissen), and West Africa (Linda Kreitzer). In general, the purpose of the partnerships has been to explore the challenges facing social workers in developing countries and ways in which social work can be made relevant to development. For Wilson, whose interest is related to women and development in Mexico and Nicaragua, the main objective is to articulate a developmental approach that incorporates gender, dependency, and class analysis. Lundy and Jennissen focus on the impact of development in two socialist countries by outlining the experiences and resilience of women during periods of economic transition. They also look at women's studies and social work in universities. Kreitzer describes how social work has evolved in Ghana and how, as a result of her experience working as a volunteer and teacher, she has come to question her own values and practices.

The third section, Social Work Practice, is composed of four chapters. The first by Richard F. Ramsay draws on his experience with the International Federation of Social Workers and the development of a worldwide suicide prevention program. The next outlines the role that Bob Mullaly played in the promotion of progressive social work in Australia. Subsequently, David Este draws on his experience in working internationally with immigrants and refugees in Canada, and Don Fuchs describes how a Canadian-Russian social work initiative has fostered the inclusion of persons with disabilities in Russian society.

Ramsay is uniquely positioned to talk about the development of international standards of practice because of his involvement in the process. He also is one of the co-founders of LivingWorks Education, an international suicide intervention training program for front-line caregivers/gatekeepers of all disciplines and occupational groups. Mullaly, too, is well-known internationally because of his theoretical articulation of structural social work—a distinctively Canadian contribution to the social work profession. Este, using a different framework based on ecological theory, makes the case for internationalizing social work within Canada. Fuchs, in his chapter, uses a social development model to outline how the Canada Russia Disability Program, of which he has been director, has fostered social inclusion in a period of economic transition in Russia.

The fourth and final section of the book, Social Work Education, illustrates how linkages between educational institutions in Canada and other countries can lead to the development of localized social work education programs in the Negev (Alean Al-Krenawi and John R. Graham) or in Ukraine (Brad McKenzie and Nina Hayduk). It also provides some insight into ways in which social work programs for aboriginal peoples in this country can be indigenized by exploring the ontological and epistemological underpinnings of aboriginal culture (Betty Bastien). The primary contribution of the chapter by Al-Krenawi and Graham is to extend, through international scholarship, the theory of localization or indigenization, as a guide to practice by taking into account the cultural and spiritual context within which practice is exercised. McKenzie and Hayduk describe how joint collaboration between the University of Manitoba and Lviv Polytechnic National University led to a two-tiered social work education program in western Ukraine based on a social development model. Closer to home, Bastien, in the final chapter of the book, contrasts Eurocentric and Aboriginal world views in order to elucidate the potential for reconfiguring social work education to serve the needs of Aboriginal peoples.

References

- Anders, J. 1975. Internationalism in Social Work Education. *Journal of Social Work Education* 11 (1): 16–21.
- Asomoah, Yvonne. 2003. International Collaboration in Social Work Education: Overview. In *Models of International Collaboration in Social Work Education*, eds. L. Healy, Y. Asomoah, and M. C. Hokenstad, 1–14. Alexandria: Council on Social Work Education.
- Billips, James, ed. 2002. *Faithful Angels: Portraits of International Social Work Notables.* Washington: NASW Press.
- Boehm, W. 1980. Teaching and Learning International Social Welfare. *International Social Work* 23 (2): 17–24.
- Canadian Association of Schools of Social Work. 2004. *Standards of Accreditation.* Ottawa: CASSW.
- Council on Social Work Education. 2004. *Educational Policy and Accreditation Standards.* Alexandria, VA: CSWE.
- Dominelli, Lena. 1996. Deprofessionalising Social Work: Anti-Oppressive Practice, Competencies, Postmodernism. *British Journal of Social Work* 26.
- Dominelli, Lena. 1997. International Social Development and Social Work: A Feminist Perspective. In *Issues in International Social Work: Global Challenges for a New Century*, eds. M. C. Hokenstad and James Midgley. Washington: NASW Press.
- Doyal, Len and Ian Gough. 1991. *A Theory of Human Need.* London, Macmillan Press.
- Drover, Glenn. 1998. Our Roots, Our Future. *The Social Worker* 66 (3) (Fall): 79–91.
- Drover, Glenn. 2000. Redefining Social Citizenship in a Global Era. *Social Work and Globalization.* Special Issue. Ottawa: Canadian Association of Social Workers.
- Drover, Glenn and Gail MacDougall. 2002. Globalization and Social Work Practice. In *Social Work Practice: A Canadian Perspective*, ed. Francis Turner. Toronto: Prentice Hall,
- Drover, Glenn. 2003. Poverty Alleviation: A Rights-Based Approach. In *Poverty Monitoring and Alleviation in East Asia*, eds. Kwong-Leung Tang and Chack-Kie Wong. New York: Nova Science Publishers.
- Garber, Ralph. 1984. Social Work Education as a Modernizing Technology. In *Beyond National Boundaries: Canadian Contributions to International Social Work and Social Welfare*, ed. M. Dennis Kimberley, 207–228. Ottawa: Canadian Association of Schools of Social Work.
- Gray, Mel and Jan Fook. 2004. The Quest for a Universal Social Work: Some Issues and Implications. *Social Work Education* 23 (5): 625–644.
- Healy, Lynne M. 2003. A Theory of International Collaboration: Lessons for Social Work Education. In *Models of International Collaboration in Social Work Education*, eds. L. Healy, Y. Asomoah, and M. C. Hokenstad, 15–22. Alexandria: Council on Social Work Education.
- Healy, Lynne M. 2001. *International Social Work: Professional Action in an Interdependent World.* New York: Oxford University Press.
- Healy, Lynne M. 1988. Curriculum Building in International Social Work: Toward Preparing Professionals for the Global Age. *Journal of Social Work Education* 24 (3): 15–22.
- Hokenstad, M. C. 2003. Global Interdependence and International Exchange: Lessons for the Future. In *Models of International Collaboration in Social Work Education*, eds. L.

Healy, Y. Asomoah, and M. C. Hokenstad, 133–141. Alexandria: Council on Social Work Education.

- Hokenstad, M. C., S. K. Khinduka, and James Midgley. 1992. The World of International Social Work. In *Profiles in International Social Work*, eds. M. C. Hokenstad, S. K. Khinduka, and James Midgley. Washington: NASW Press.
- Ife, Jim. 2000. Local and Global Practice: Relocating Social Work as a Human Rights Profession in the New Global Order. Eileen Younghusband Memorial Lecture. IFSW/IASSW Biennial Conference. Montreal. (July 31).
- International Federation of Social Workers. 2007. Information > Membership. www.ifsw.org/en/p38000060.html.
- Khan, Parves and Lena Dominelli. 2000. The Impact of Globalisation on Social Work in the UK. *European Journal of Social Work* 2. (July).
- Khinduka, S. and R. Parvis. 1969. On Teaching of Comparative Social Welfare. *Social Work Education Reporter* 17 (1): 35–38, 65–66.
- Kimberly, M. Dennis, ed. 1984. *Beyond National Boundaries: Canadian Contributions to International Social Work and Social Welfare*. Ottawa: Canadian Association of Schools of Social Work.
- Lindenberg, Marc and Coralie Bryant. 2001. *Going Global: Transforming Relief and Development NGOs*. Bloomfield: Kumarian Press.
- Midgley, James. 1995. *Social Development: The Developmental Perspective in Social Welfare*. London: Sage Publications.
- Midgley, James. 1997a. Social Work in International Context: Challenges and Opportunities for the 21st Century. In *Social Work in the 21st Century*, eds. Michael Reisch and Eileen Gambrill. Thousands Oaks: Pince Forge Press.
- Midgley, James. 1997b. *Social Welfare In Global Context*. Thousand Oaks: Sage Publications.
- Midgley, James. 1997c. Social Work and International Social Development. In *Issues in International Social Work: Global Challenges for a New Century*, eds. M. C. Hokenstad and James Midgley. Washington: NASW Press.
- Razack, Narda. 2002. A Critical Examination of International Student Exchanges. *International Social Work* 45 (2): 251–265.
- Rowe, William, Jill Hanley, Eugenia Repetur Moreno, and John Mould. 2000. Voices of Social Work Practice: International Reflections on the Effects of Globalization. *Social Work and Globalization*. Special Issue. Ottawa: Canadian Association of Social Workers.
- Saari, Rosemary. 1997. International Social Work at the Millenium. In *Social Work in the 21st Century*, eds. Michael Reisch and Eileen Gambrill. Thousands Oaks: Pince Forge Press.
- Sanders, D. Developing a Graduate Social Work Curriculum with an International Cross-Cultural Perspective. *Journal of Social Work Education* 13 (3): 76–83.
- Splane, Richard. 2003. George Davidson: *Social Policy and Public Policy Exemplar*. Ottawa: Canadian Council on Social Development.
- Traub-Werner, B., W. Shera, B. M. Rodriguez Villa, and N. T. Peón. 2000. International Partnerships: A Mexico-Canada Social Work Education Project. *Social Work and Globalization*. Special Issue. Ottawa: Canadian Association of Social Workers, 184–197.
- UN Interregional Consultation on Developmental Social Welfare Policies and Programmes. 1989. General Assembly. (8 December).
- Whitmore, Elizabeth and Maureen Wilson. 2005. Popular resistance to global corporate rule: the role of social work (with a little help from Gramsci and Freire). In *Globalisation, Global Justice and Social Work*, eds. Iain Ferguson, Michael Lavalette, and Elizabeth Whitmore. London: Routledge.
- Whitmore, Elizabeth and Maureen Wilson. 1997. Accompanying the Process: Social Work and International Development Practice. *International Social Work* 40 (1): 57–74.

Part 1: Social Justice

Chapter 2

Social Justice in Iraq: The Construction and Deconstruction of Social Equity

Jacqueline S. Ismael and Shereen T. Ismael

The subject of social justice in Iraq seems counterintuitive to the images of a violent society riddled with sectarian extremism, violence, and repression that appear almost nightly on Canadian and American newscasts. At their best, the images portray Iraqis as a population under siege not only by occupation forces, but also by ancient hatreds run amuck. At their worst, the image portrayed is of the quintessential *Arab*, the essential *other* in chauvinist discourses. This chapter tells the story of social justice in Iraq and the power dynamics that fuelled its deliberate construction and systematic destruction—a process, it is argued, that has become a dominant pattern in the New World Order. The concept of social justice is a fundamental principle of the social work profession, generally couched in a discourse of prescription. By framing the concept of social justice in a discourse of process rather than prescription, this case study of social justice in Iraq provides insight into the epistemological and ontological nature of social justice in the contemporary world order.

Engagement with Iraq has been both a personal and intellectual journey for us. Baghdad was our home in the early 1970s, and remained a second home throughout our family life. Studying Iraq has been a vocation through-out our academic careers in social work. For us, the old dictum "the personal is political" has been interwoven into the fabric of our lives as "the political is personal" for we have had to daily confront the age-old myths and metaphors about the Arab world in general, Iraq in particular, that warped into open hostility since 9/11. It is in this context that our collaboration as a mother-daughter research team was initiated with a research project on a case study of women's search for justice in the Arab world (Ismael and Ismael, 2000).

Framing Social Justice

The metaphor of framing is used to represent a discursive border around a concept that links discourse to action. Prescriptive discourse is based on the (often implicit) assumption of essential states, and that a just society is an ideal state. Framed in prescriptive discourse, the predominant way of thinking about social justice is as a normative description of how society should be, and what elements or dimensions of society are just or unjust—good or bad (Sherwood 2007). As an institutionalized way of thinking about social justice, prescriptive discourse sets a diagnostic boundary around social justice, linking it to ameliorative policies to compensate victims of injustice (Poe 2007), and/or to radical policies to deconstruct unjust social practices. In the framework of prescriptive discourse, social justice is an ideal.

Prescriptive discourse implicitly imbues the pursuit of this ideal with a nobility of purpose, and legitimates it as an end in itself. This link between prescriptive discourse and action is reflected in the International Federation of Social Workers (IFSW) and International Association of Schools of Social Work (IASSW) declarations on the responsibilities of social workers to promote social justice:

1. Challenging negative discrimination—Social workers have a responsibility to challenge negative discrimination on the basis of characteristics such as ability, age, culture, gender or sex, marital status, socio-economic status, political opinions, skin colour, racial or other physical characteristics, sexual orientation, or spiritual beliefs.

2. Recognising diversity—Social workers should recognise and respect the ethnic and cultural diversity of the societies in which they practise, taking account of individual, family, group, and community differences.

3. Distributing resources equitably—Social workers should ensure that resources at their disposal are distributed fairly, according to need.

4. Challenging unjust policies and practices—Social workers have a duty to bring to the attention of their employers, policy makers, politicians, and the general public, situations where resources are inadequate or where distribution of resources, policies, and practices are oppressive, unfair, or harmful.

5. Working in solidarity—Social workers have an obligation to challenge social conditions that contribute to social exclusion, stigmatisation or subjugation, and to work towards an inclusive society (IFSW 2008).

Normative in nature, prescriptive discourse derives its logic from whatever value system is presumed—religious, ideological, aesthetic, cultural. As such, its utility as a tool for understanding a state's social policy is essentially descriptive (of a value system) and evaluative (of actions or empirical conditions in a society appraised against a value system's standards). Considered from a discourse of prescription, the issue of social justice in Iraq might be systematically described and/or evaluated from a (usually implicit) value system perspective, elements or dimensions of injustice diagnosed, and interventions recommended.

Process discourse is based on the assumptions of change and complexity. In process theories, complex "current states" can be explained in terms of the dynamics of change—social systems are dynamical systems whose attributes undergo sequences of change as the social system changes (Buckley 1998). A complex adaptive system has been defined as "a dynamic network of many agents acting in parallel, constantly acting and reacting to what the other agents are doing" (Holland 1998). Framed in process discourse, social justice is an attribute of a value system, and value systems are variable attributes of dynamic social systems. From this perspective, social justice is an attribute of an attribute—that is, one of the values (generally about what constitutes a fair society) embedded in a value system (an inter-connected set of values legitimating action). The meaning of the value derives from the value system in which it is embedded. In other words, the character of social justice does not have essential properties or traits but is value system dependent. Furthermore, in contradistinction to prescriptive discourse, in the framework of process discourse, the pursuit of social justice is not an end in itself but a legitimation for action in pursuit of specifiable ends. Considered from a discourse of process, the issue of social justice in Iraq is about understanding the nature of social justice principles and policies, the ends being legitimated, and their relationship to the dynamics and trajectory of change in Iraq.

Iraq and the Construction of Social Equity

The construction of social equity was the primary principle of social justice that fuelled the dynamic of Iraq's trajectory from feudal-tribal society to modern nation-state. By "construction of social equity," we are referring to the process of constructing a national social infrastructure of health, education, and welfare programs accessible to all citizens, especially the most economically marginalized. The 1958 *coup d'etat* marked a watershed in Iraq's transition. The revolt against the British dominated monarchy not only catapulted Iraq from a backwater outpost of British imperialism into a front line republic in the Third World non-aligned movement; it was also (and perhaps more significantly) transformed from a coup into a social revolution. The social revolution was earmarked by the state's construction of social equity into the framework of state social policy. While the construction of this framework is significant in itself, it is the trajectory of change that reveals the dynamics of transition. Therefore, to understand the role of social justice principles in the dynamics of change, we will explore the trajectory of change, first from cradle of civilization to feudal-tribal society; then from feudal-tribal society to modern nation state.

From cradle of civilization to feudal-tribal society

The territory of today's Iraq is relatively geographically consistent with the ancient land of Mesopotamia. This geographic region is often referred to as the cradle of civilization as it was the birthplace of writing. This was accompanied by advances in the arts and sciences and the birth of complex social, political, and economic institutions. Ancient Mesopotamia introduced the world to a plethora of "firsts": the first recorded epic poem, the first stringed musical instrument, the first written code of law, the first prophet of monotheism (the Prophet Abraham, recognized as the first prophet in Judaism, Christianity, and Islam), the first city-state, and so forth (Teresi 2002). If the history of ancient civilization (c. 2600 BCE to 500 CE) could be condensed by time-lapse cinematography into a 24-hour documentary, for the first three hours we would be watching Ancient Mesopotamia, and for 90% of the remaining 21 hours, Mesopotamia and Ancient Egypt would dominate the picture. The territory of Iraq, in other words, has been a cohesive historical unit and a catalyst to civilization since the dawn of history, with a myriad of patterns of interaction interconnecting the diverse peoples of the area through space and time.

In the medieval period (c. 500 to 1500 CE), Iraq played a central role in the rise of Islamic civilization. The golden age of classical Islamic civilization was initiated under the Abbasid Dynasty, which founded Baghdad in 762 CE. From the 9th to the 13th centuries, Baghdad was the centre of extraordinary cultural and intellectual development and the cultural bridge between ancient and modern civilization. Under the tutelage of the Abbasid Dynasty, Baghdad became a centre of learning and the pursuit of knowledge was championed. In 1184, there were 30 independent schools in Baghdad in addition to an engineering school and three medical schools. Private and public libraries were established and contained tens of thousands of books and manuscripts. From this wellspring bloomed the multicultural, multi-ethnic mosaic of Islamic civilisation fostered from intellectual diversity and cross-cultural synergy (Ismael, Ismael, and Baker 2004).

Following the Mongol destruction of Baghdad in the 13th century, Iraq moved to the sidelines of world history as a backwater region of the Ottoman Empire, where it remained until the collapse of the Ottoman Empire following World War I. Under Ottoman suzerainty, Iraq was politically, socially, and economically localized. Congruent with the provincial feudal social structure established under the Ottomans, social organization was based on segmented agrarian communities. The communities were differentiated by tribal, ethnic, and/or religious affiliation, and held together by the interlocking patterns of exchange, cooperation, and conflict that had evolved through socio-economic and cultural interaction over the millennia (Jabar 1995).

Iraq fell under British occupation in 1917, and from 1918 to 1921 the occupation was legitimated under a League of Nations mandate. Iraq received nominal independence in 1921, but Britain remained in effective control of the state until 1932 when Iraq joined the League of Nations. During its occupation, Britain aligned itself with the conservative tribal and feudal forces advocating maintenance of the status quo, and against the progressive reformist pan-Arab nationalist forces advocating change and modernization. As explained by Philip Ireland (1937, 95), in his definitive study of Britain's role in the creation of modern Iraq in the first quarter of the 20th century, Britain sought to reinforce and strengthen tribal-feudal organization as "a method of control," and sought to exercise control over Iraq through the tribal sheikhs by recognizing their suzerainty over the land.

In effect, the tribal sheikhs were transformed from community leaders into large landowners. At the same time, Iraqi agriculture was coming into increasing contact with the world market, as reflected by the increase of Iraq's grain exports from 65,000 tons in the early 1890s, to 120,000 tons between

1909–13, and to 380,000 tons between 1934–39. The profit associated with this burgeoning export trade stimulated the acquisitive dispositions of the sheikhs, and led them to amass still larger holdings (Warriner 1975, 101–109). Thus, tribal sheikhs joined the class of large landowners and, in effect, become vassals in liege to the British administration. Bedouins increasingly became peasants in liege to their tribal sheikhs as pressures increased for their settlement. Reflecting this, between 1905 and 1930, the Bedouin population of Iraq decreased from 17% to 7%, while the rural population increased from 59% to 68%, but the urban population only increased from 24% to 25% (Hasan 1966, 172).

What emerged in Iraq was a quasi-feudal system composed of large landowners drawn from two distinct strata: (i) Ottomanized urban notables, whose landholdings predated the 20th century (Al-Zâhir 1946: 17–21); and (ii) tribal sheikhs whose landholdings were consolidated through British policy. Hanna Batatu, the premier political historian of modern Iraq, differentiated the landed tribal sheikhs into four categories based on their relationship to the cultivators: "(a) leaders of tribal free-holding farmers; (b) owners of estates or village land tenanted by share-cropping peasants from their own tribes; (c) sheikhs owning estates tilled partly or largely by...client or extraneous tribesmen; and (d) aghas possessing village land cultivated by non-tribal serf-like miskins ("miserables")." (Batatu 1978, 79). Batatu's characterization of the relationship reveals the quasi-feudal nature of land tenure in Iraq:

> The first type of chiefship, which was of infrequent occurrence, rested on kinship, and approached the patriarchal ideal. The authority of the third type of tribal leaders, which grew out of ties of patronship or ties essentially economic in character, could be very arbitrary; but most oppressive was the power of the agha [Kurdish tribal chiefs] of a miskin village (Batatu 1978, 79).

While the quasi-feudal system predated the British, the tribalization of the system occurred under the British, and tribalism was built into the nascent institutions of state from the initiation of the state-building enterprise. In 1918, the British enshrined tribal customary law (al-Sawânî) into the Tribal Civil and Penal Code (Qânûn Da'âwî al-'Ashâ'ir) (Hasanîn 1967, 76) in effect legalizing the imposition on the more progressive urban population of the inherently misogynous and reactionary tribal laws that dominated the lives of the rural population.

From feudal-tribal society to modern nation-state

The political dynamics set in motion by the collapse of the Ottoman Empire on the one hand and British occupation on the other catalyzed the process of structural change in Iraqi society. This was manifested in two interrelated structural dynamics. First, the nominally independent Iraqi state set up by the British in 1921 had, at best, fragile legitimacy and authority within the population. This is because the state was a product of international fabrication and British imposition, not a product of indigenous political processes. Thus, from the outset there was an underlying tension between the state and society. In this fabricated Iraqi state, political elites were empowered by Western symbols of state sovereignty rather than by indigenous cultural symbols of social legitimacy (Lenczowski 1966, 28–29; Cox 1927, 523–525; Salih 1955, 48–78).

Secondly, the fabricated state set up by the British invested rural-based tribal and feudal elites with political authority mediated by external power. Closely related to this, the central mechanism of economic development was tied to the external market of British imperialism, effectively marginalizing locally and regionally oriented economic elites, based primarily in urban centres. Thus, in the economic and political spheres, rural-based elites oriented toward Western economic and political institutions displaced the old-guard urban-based elites of the Ottoman era (al-Zubaidi 1979, 29–38; Lenczowski 1966, 28–29).

The structural tension between state and society on the one hand and between urban based and rural based elites on the other essentially bifurcated Iraq into two solitudes—one, the segmented tribal-rural insular oriented social systems cut off from each other and from the main flow of world history; the other, urban-based outer world oriented social systems populated with a heterogeneous mix of disaffected old-guard elites; emerging middle class of state functionaries, professionals, military staff; and a budding working class largely composed of marginalized peasantry immigrating into the urban centres for work (Ismael 1970, 100–121; Halpern 1963). Caught in the main currents of world history following World War I—collapse of the Ottoman Empire and the retrenchment of Western imperialism—Baghdad became a centre where the ideas of modernity, independence, sovereignty, development, tradition, imperialism, exploitation were all juxtaposed against each other. It was in this tumultuous environment of ideas that the principle of social equity took root in the popular political culture of urban society.

It is useful to draw a distinction between political culture (representing the political values, norms, and interests manifest in a society) and political discourse (representing the political values, norms, and interests of the state) to identify how the principle of social justice as social equity catalyzed the dynamic of change in Iraq. The distinction helps to identify the contradiction between political culture and political discourse manifest in the notion of Iraq as a nation state. The idea of the Iraqi state was manifest in political discourse, a discourse invested by imperialism. However, it was the notion of an Iraqi nation state that gained widespread appeal in the robust political culture of the city, especially among the nascent intelligentsia who vigorously debated the liberal, socialist, communist, and nationalist ideas current in world affairs (Ismael 2008, 1–59). Already ingrained in Islamic culture was the principle of social justice and assumptions of government responsibility for the social welfare of the umma (community) (Khadduri 1984; Qutb 1996). For social activists, the young intelligentsia, and the budding middle and working classes, the construction of social equity had both cultural legitimacy and broad appeal as a means of nation-building in a state fragmented by social inequity and inequality. It was in this context that the call for social justice fuelled the dynamic of Iraq's trajectory from tribal-feudal society to modern nation state.

Construction of social equity

During the inter-war period, ideological politics became a primary mode for the process of value determination and articulation in the political culture of Baghdad (and Iraq's other urban centres). A plethora of nationalist, socialist, and communist groups emerged; all of them espousing the construction of social equity as a principle tool of nation building, but fundamentally differing on the means of its achievement—that is, reform or revolution. In 1926, for example, a nationalist group, *al-Sha'biyyah*, was founded by Iraqi students studying at the American University of Beirut. It characterized itself as "a socio-political liberal movement...which called for the reform of the country, the raising of its people's standard of living, the spread of education, and the eradication of corruption" (Hadid 2006, 67–68). It later merged with the *al-Ahali* group, an influential coalition of progressive liberal intellectuals who agitated for social reform, cultural emancipation, and national liberation. The reformists contrasted with the communist circles which began to appear in the 1920s among Iraq's intelligentsia, and in 1934 formed the Iraqi Communist Party, calling for social revolution, social equality, and nationalization of the means of production (Ismael 2008).

By the time of the 1958 *coup d'etat* led by Brigadier General 'Abd-ul-Karîm Qasim, the ideas of social equity were well entrenched in Iraq's political culture and catalyzed the transition from revolt to social revolution. In the framework of the new republic, "the power of the tribes, clans, sectarian, and feudal forces was severely challenged by progressive policies such as land reforms and legal reforms of family law, and by ideological politics" (Zubaida 2003). Citizenship replaced communal affiliation (tribal, religious, or ethnic) in the identity politics of the state; urban poverty was attacked; workers rights were established; the foundations of a public education system were established in urban areas; and a vibrant civil society emerged. The goals of the social and economic revolution were first, "a desire to be free of foreign —and in particular Western—political and economic control ... Second was the urge for social justice, focussing mainly on a more equitable distribution of income and social benefits. Third, was the drive to achieve greater national unity and integration" (Marr 1985, 169).

The Personal Status Law 188 of 1959 established the legal framework for universal civil rights. Examining the new law, J. Anderson observed that "the Revolutionary regime brought to an end a controversy regarding the codification of the law of personal status which had ebbed and flowed in Iraq for more than twelve years; and it is significant that it produced, in the event, a code which was much more radical than anything which had previously been proposed." (1960, 542–63). A "statement of objects and reasons" that accompanied the code explained that one of the primary aims of the republican regime was the "promulgation of a unified personal status law which will become the foundation on which the structure of the Iraqi family in its new era will be built, and which will guarantee its stability and ensure to women their legal rights and family independence" (Republic of Iraq, Ministry of Justice 1978, 64–65).

The significance of the Personal Status Law to civil rights was in the fundamental limitations it imposed on the subjugation of the individual in general, women in particular, to sectarian tribal authority. This was accomplished by replacing the role of family law based on religious sectarianism and tribal practice with a unified code of law consistent with the Islamic reformist principles of 'Abduh and 'Amîn (Kerr 1966). A major step in Iraq's reform effort was the replacement of Sunni and Shiite courts with the establishment of a Court of Personal Status to adjudicate all claims involving Iraqis, whether Muslim or not. This court had jurisdiction over marriage, divorce, legitimacy, custody, inheritance, succession, and religious endowments (*Awqâf*). As a unified code applicable to all Iraqis, the Code of Personal Status in 1959 established a standardized code of conduct based on citizenship, not religious affiliation.

This code propelled Iraqi citizens into the 20th century. Before its passage, "Iraq was, in fact, the only part of the previous Ottoman Empire … which had been left virtually untouched by the series of legislative enactments in the sphere of the law of personal status which appeared in almost every other country in the Middle East" (Anderson 1960, 543). In effect, with the promulgation of the 1959 code, Iraq leapfrogged from the back of the pack into the forefront in terms of civil rights in the Arab world. Significantly, the new code not only reduced the yoke of tribalism, but also modified two major pillars of patriarchy in the regressive social structural framework of repression—religious sectarianism and feudalism (Anderson 1960, 546).

The passage of the Personal Status Code initiated the dismantling of the legal framework underpinning the feudal structure of the countryside (the 1933 Law of Rights and Duties of the Cultivators, and the Tribal Disputes Code). Passage of the Agrarian Reform Law in September 1958 initiated land redistribution, placing limits on the size of land holdings and ground rents. Qasim, the prime minister of the new republic, proposed that "Agrarian reform by itself … is a revolution against injustice, tyranny, and feudalism" (1959, 394). Lauded as "ambitious in conception," the reform law was criticized for "the amount of land it left to the landlords" (Marr 1985, 170). Nevertheless, the framework of feudalism in Iraq was effectively undermined, though urban/rural disparity remained significant.

As an oil-rich state located in a geopolitically strategic region, Iraq was caught in the currents of Cold War politics and, like many developing countries in Africa and Asia, became a proxy state in the ideological conflict between superpowers. Presaging the US sponsored counter-revolution against the progressive Allende government in Chile by a decade (Klein 2007, 116–127), the ideologically left-leaning Qasim regime was overthrown in 1963 by a vehemently anti-communist nationalist party, the Ba'th, who initiated a nine-month reign of terror against social activists in general, communists in particular, with over 10,000 killed:

> Bands of the National Guard roamed the streets and carried out summary executions, arbitrary arrests and savage torture. Sport grounds, military camps and schools were turned into concentration camps and interrogation centres for tens of thousands of people from all walks of life. At the top of the list were leaders, cadres, and activists of the trade unions and the mass democratic organizations, including the Iraqi Women's League and the General Union of Students of the Iraqi Republic. (Zaher 1986, 31).

Another military coup removed the Ba'th Party from power in November 1963, and for the next four years Iraq was governed by a pragmatic military regime that attempted to pander to both nationalist and tribal affinities. However, a military coup returned the Ba'th Party to power in 1968, and it ruled Iraq for the next 35 years, largely under the dictatorship of Saddam Hussein. Even as the roots of dictatorship spread throughout Iraq's body politic over the next two decades, the basic principle of social equity remained a core principle of social policy. The progressive advancement of social security coverage and benefits from 1960 to 1989 reflects the government's commitment to increase social equity, even in the face of deepening dictatorship and political oppression (Jabber 1989, 203–09); and in 1980, a Law of Social Welfare was enacted to provide a comprehensive social safety net for the entire population (Republic of Iraq, Ministry of Justice 1980). The transformation of society from a tribal-feudal to national structure was fostered by social policies that sought to replace dependency on communal and tribal structures for dependency on the state in the social welfare of the population. The material means for the achievement of this goal was substantially realized with the nationalization of Iraq's oil industry in 1973. By fostering the economic and social dependence of labour on the State, the government in effect bound the welfare of citizens to the national structure of the state.

Thus, the 1958 military coup that marked a watershed in Iraq's trajectory unleashed ideological competition between nationalist and socialist groups for a new development model that emphasized notions of social and political modernization. Substantial investments were made in social infrastructure by the successive military regimes, and by the mid-1980s, Iraq had developed a comprehensive social infrastructure in health, education, and social welfare that ranked as one of the best in the Middle East (United Nations Development Fund for Women c.2006; World Health Organization 2003). Thus, from a rural-agricultural society with 65% of the population living in rural quasi-feudal, quasi-tribal social structures in the inter-war period, by 1970, 58% of the population lived in urban centres, and Iraq was being transformed into a modern urban society with a relatively high standard of living (United Nations Statistic Division).

In 1977, largely due to its immense oil wealth, Iraq's GNP per capita was $1,594, compared to average GNP in the developing world of $548 (Sivard 1980). Basic social indicators reflected the level of public investment in the social well-being of the population. Life expectancy increased from 44 years in 1950 to 62.4 years in 1980 (United Nations Statistic Division). By 1977, 76% of the Iraqi population had access to safe drinking water—well above the world average of 53%, and the developing world average of only 39%; 60% of school-age children were enrolled in school, compared to the developing world average of 50%, and the developed world average of 69% (Sivard 1980).

The dynamics driving Iraq's trajectory from tribal-feudal society to modern nation state were based on the interplay between three forces: the pressure to replace social solidarity based on tribal-feudal bonds with social solidarity based on social citizenship bonds; the compulsion of dictatorship for power; and oil wealth and the unconstrained freedom it allowed the compulsion for power. Along with the construction of a comprehensive social infrastructure in health, education, and social welfare, the seeds of its deconstruction were also being sown. The seeding and sowing metaphor is used here to summarize the complex dynamics between the international political economy of oil and the national political economy of Iraq (Alnasrawi 1994), which marked the shift in Iraq's trajectory from construction to deconstruction of social equity.

Deconstruction of Social Equity

The deconstruction of social equity marked Iraq's trajectory from modern nation state to sectarian dystopia. While the construction of social equity served as a major input in the dynamics of social change fuelling Iraq's trajectory from tribal feudal society to modern nation state, the process of disassembling social equity represented an output of the dynamics of social change in Iraq's reconstruction from modern nation state to sectarian dystopia. Two distinct stages in this reconstruction process can be delineated: first, the transition from modern nation state to subaltern state; and from there the descent to a state of sectarian dystopia.

Modern nation state to subaltern state

Unchecked by financial constraints, and inflamed by a toxic combination of geopolitics internationally, heady nationalism regionally and dictatorial power nationally, the Ba'th in general, and Saddam Hussein in particular, sought self-aggrandizement of the state through extravagant military expenditures. Nationally, the Saddam regime achieved virtually total control first of the Ba'th Party apparatus, then of Iraqi society through a combination of ruthless coercion, financial co-optation, and a complex web of security agencies spying on the population and on each other (Makiya 1989). Regionally, the Saddam regime sought leadership of the Arab world through championing Arab issues, especially the Arab-Israeli question. And internationally, by invading Iran, the Saddam regime sought to fill the geopolitical vacuum created by the collapse of the Shah's regime and emergence of the Islamic state in Iran. This ignited an eight year war that exhausted the state financially and ideologically bankrupted it.

The embroilment of Iraq into a lengthy war with Iran, 1980–88, seems to have been a successful application of the US strategy of "dual containment" (Hadar 1998, 49–59). Both Iraq and Iran posed a potential threat to Israel for various reasons, and Iran represented a direct ideological challenge to US interests, by presenting Islamic revolution as a pathway for the Muslim world out of the Cold War's global competition between the US and the USSR for world hegemony. The economies of both Iraq and Iran were severely damaged during the war. What further aggravated their economic problems was a 75% decline in the value of petroleum revenue by 1986. The war's economic damage to Iraq was at least $120 billion, which amounted to more than the total value of Iraqi oil exports since 1973.

In 1988, Iraq incurred a debt of $90 billion, with about $40 billion from Saudi Arabia and Kuwait. Iraqi oil revenue for the same year was $13–$15 billion, but civilian imports were $12 billion, debt service $5 billion, and another $1 billion for salaries of the army of guest workers required to replace Iraqis conscripted into military service (Ismael 2001, 216–217). Economic loss was perhaps $644 billion, and its GDP per capita declined from $6,052 in 1977 to $2,944 in 1988. Iran suffered even greater economic setbacks than Iraq because it financed its war effort internally, but unlike Iraq, Iran emerged without having developed untenable financial obligations to regional economic powers like Saudi Arabia and Kuwait. Drawn into the vortex of military adventurism by the toxic combination (geopolitics internationally, nationalism regionally, and dictatorship nationally), the Saddam regime hurled the Iraqi state down the path of military adventurism, culminating in the invasion of Kuwait in 1990.

The following table reflects the dramatic increase in Iraq's military expenditures as a proportion of GNP. While social spending registered a small decrease as a proportion of GNP, in terms of the earlier discussion on the state's commitment to social equity, it should be noted that the table reflects proportional budget allocations. Over the period, GNP substantially increased, and in absolute terms, social spending increased substantially as well.

Iraq's Public Expenditures as a Percentage of GNP			
	1960	1987	1990
Health	1.0%	0.8%	0.8%
Education	5.8%	4.6%	5.1%
Military	7.3%	30.2%	27.4%
Source: Sivard, R. L. (1991, 1993). World Military and Social Expenditures.			

The Iraqi invasion of Kuwait in August 1990 resulted in the United Nations Security Council's (UNSC) imposition of the most severe international sanctions regime ever imposed on a country. The stated intent of the sanctions regime was to force a withdrawal from Kuwait. UN Security Council Resolution (UNSCR) 687 called for ending the sanctions when Iraqi compliance was established by the UNSC. However, President Bush (senior) rejected the primary purport of Resolution 687, and opposed any relaxation of the sanctions as long as Saddam was in power. President Clinton later concurred, and Secretary of State, Warren Christopher, announced in 1994 that Iraqi compliance was not enough to lift the embargo, thus, changing the substance of the Security Council ruling unilaterally (Chomsky 2003, 30).

While the US led military attack on Iraq, dubbed Operation Desert Storm, completely destroyed Iraq's civil infrastructure, it left Saddam Hussein's regime intact. In the immediate aftermath of the war, these appeared as unintended consequences. However, the resolute maintenance of the rigid sanctions regime over the next thirteen years supports the contention widely accepted in the Arab world that these were the covert objectives, not unintended consequences (Ismael and Ismael 1999, 70–78). Denis Halliday and Hans C. von Sponeck, both senior international civil servants put in charge of the UN's humanitarian program under the Security Council's Iraq sanctions regime, argued that if the sanctions had been directed against preventing a WMD program instead of targeting the Iraqi population, the direction they assumed under US and UK administration, the Iraqi people might have been able to send Saddam to the fate of other tyrants, like Suharto, Marcos, Ceausescu, Mubuto, and Duvalier (Chomsky 2003, 249).

After the war in 1991, Iraqi per capita income fell from $2,279 US dollars in 1984 to $627 in 1991 and decreased as low as $450 US dollars in 1995. Numerous surveys and reports conducted by the government of Iraq and UN agencies over the decade following the 1991 Gulf War detailed the deepening of the complex humanitarian crisis precipitated by the war's destruction of Iraq's civil infrastructure (especially electricity and water sanitation) and exacerbated by the continuing sanctions regime (Ismael and Ismael 2004, 126–165). The 1999–2000 Report of UN Development Program's Iraq Country Office summarized the situation as follows:

> Iraq's economy has been in crisis since the imposition of economic sanctions in 1990. Despite the Oil-for-Food program, the country continued its decline into poverty, particularly in the south. Food supplies continue to be inadequate in the centre and south of the country; the prevalence of general malnutrition in the centre and south has hardly changed. Although the rates have stabilised, this happened at 'an unacceptably high level'. In the area of child and maternal health, in August 1999, UNICEF and the Government of Iraq released the results of the first survey on child mortality in Iraq since 1991. The survey showed that under-five child mortality had more than doubled from 56 deaths per 1000 live births in 1984 to 131 deaths in the period 1994–1999. At least 50% of the labour force is unemployed or underemployed; a shortage of basic goods, compounded by a drought, has resulted in high prices and an estimated inflation rate of 135% and 120% in 1999 and 2000 respectively … Most of

the country's civil infrastructure remains in serious disrepair. GDP per capita dropped to an estimated US $715 [from US $3508 before the Gulf War], which is a figure comparable with such countries as Madagascar and Rwanda (UNDP 2000).

Food production and availability were major factors exacerbating the problem of increasing morbidity and mortality in Iraq under the sanctions regime. Fuelled by lavish oil income in the 1970s and 1980s, the Ba'th had substituted importation of foodstuffs from the international market for domestic development. As a result, agricultural and domestic industrial sectors were not only undeveloped but languished as the market was deluged with imported goods. Under the embargo imposed by the sanctions regime, oil revenue precipitously declined and food importation was seriously curtailed. In addition, replacement parts for repairs to civil infrastructure destroyed by the aerial bombardment and components essential to increase agricultural production in Iraq were embargoed.

As a result, dietary energy supply fell from 3,120 to 1,093 kilocalories per capita/per day by 1994–95, with women and children singled out as the most vulnerable members of Iraqi society. Against a UN target of 2,463 kilocalories and 63.6 grams of protein per person per day, the nutritional value of the distributed food basket did not exceed 1,993 kilocalories and 43 grams of protein. Reflecting the economic impact of war and sanctions on Iraq's economy, the rate of inflation after the imposition of the sanctions regime increased from 18% in 1975 to 2000 percent in 1992, and the exchange rate of the Iraqi dinar to the US dollar dropped from 1:3 in 1972 to 180:1 in 1993; in other words the dinar was equivalent to 1 cent US (Jabar 1995, 168–169).

Prior to the start of the Oil-for-Food program in 1996, the government of Iraq had been distributing 1,300 kilocalories per day (Office of the Iraq Program 2002) The prevalence of malnutrition in Iraqi children under five almost doubled from 1991 to 1996 (from 12% to 23%). Acute malnutrition in the centre and south regions rose from 3% to 11% for the same age bracket. Indeed, the World Food Program (WFP) indicated that by July 1995, average shop prices of essential commodities stood at 850 times the July 1990 level. While the humanitarian program in Iraq, initiated in 1996 with the Oil-for-Food Program, successfully staved off mass starvation, the level of malnutrition within Iraq remained high and directly contributed to the morbidity and mortality rates (Office of the Iraq Program 2002). In 1999, a UNICEF report estimated that sanctions had caused the death of a half million Iraqi children (UNICEF 1999). The 2003 "Report on the State of the World's Children," which the UNICEF issued, stated "Iraq's regression over the past decade is by far the most severe of the 193 countries surveyed" (Chomsky 2003, 126). The impact of the sanctions regime on Iraq was overwhelming and multifarious. While it pauperized the Iraqi people, it also strengthened the grip of the Saddam regime over the population.

Under the suzerainty of the UNSC, the Iraqi state lost control of its air space in the north and south; nonetheless, it maintained territorial jurisdiction in the centre and the south, and nominal power in the north where the Kurds enjoyed de facto autonomy under American protection. After about a decade under an American protective umbrella, the Kurds appear to have become politically American "clients." In this aberrant context, the Iraqi people, excluding the Kurds, suffered a cynical game of brinksmanship played by the US-UK led Security Council. Bombed back to a pre-industrial stage of development by Operation Desert Storm, the Iraqi population was pushed to the brink of humanitarian disaster by the unrelenting sanctions regime, as detailed in numerous international reports (UNICEF 1993; UNFAO and UNWFP 1997; UNICEF 1999; WHO 2003). With the infrastructure of public health, education, and social welfare programs pauperized, the national institutions of the state were in effect compromised and the structural foundations of social citizenship marginalized.

At the regional and international levels, sanctions served to isolate Iraq politically and economically, in effect reducing it to subaltern state status in the international sphere. The Saddam regime's invasion of Kuwait in 1990 not only exacerbated ideological tensions in the Arab world between the conservative Gulf states, led by Saudi Arabia, and nationalist groups, but also dealt a terminal blow to Arab nationalism as an ideological force in regional politics. The invasion precipitated the collapse of organized Arab opposition to Israeli expansionist policies into the West Bank; and to the expansion of US military bases into Arab territory. Until the Gulf War in 1991, the Ba'th had championed the cause of Arab unity and the "Palestinian Question." They had also kept in the forefront of Arab politics the relationship between the Palestinian question and imperialism. With the collapse of a united Arab front, Israel's right-wing became more politically strident, as reflected in Ariel Sharon's provocative walk on September 28, 2000, to the al-Aqsa Mosque which initiated the second Intifada.

Subaltern state to a state of sectarian dystopia

Structural changes in the global political economy of oil, and the collapse of the USSR in 1991, set the political dynamics in motion that culminated in the US invasion of Iraq (Russell 2005, 283–301). While "the notion of toppling Saddam's regime was championed even before Iraq's invasion of Kuwait by a circle of neo-conservative thinkers" set up by then Secretary of Defense Dick Cheney (Vanity Fair 2004, 232; Leman 2002, 43), the blueprint for a US global strategy that targeted US strategic interests in the Gulf region was drawn up in 2000 by the Project for a New American Century report, Rebuilding American's Defenses: Strategies, Forces, and Resources for a New Century (Donnelly 2000). Arguing that "American power and presence" is essential for Gulf security, the report singled out Iraq and Iran as major threats to US strategic interests in the region (Donnelly

2000: 5). Richard Clarke, who served as National Coordinator for Security and Counter-terrorism for both Presidents Clinton and George W. Bush, reported that "In 2001 more and more the talk was Iraq, of CENTCOM (Central Command) being asked to plan to invade" (2004, 264).

The US invasion of Iraq, initiated on March 18, 2003, reduced Iraq from a subaltern state to a state of sectarian dystopia. While the US vision of transforming Iraq into a utopian free market democracy has been detailed in a number of works (Lennon and Eiss 2004; Packer 2005; Klein 2007; Kaplan 2008), the state of sectarian dystopia actuated by US policy has been fully disclosed in others (Jamail 2007a; Zangana 2007; Chandrasekaran 2006; Rosen 2006; Scahill 2008). A dystopian society may be described as a state in which the conditions of life are characterized by human misery, poverty, oppression, anarchy, violence, disease, and pollution; and this captures the character of life in Iraq since the occupation. The notion of "a state of sectarian dystopia" is used to designate the nightmare scenario of civic breakdown and inter-communal warfare that has emerged with the deconstruction of social equity.

The term deconstruction is used to signify the systematic process of disassembling the social infrastructure of citizenship entitlements in Iraq that were entrenched in Iraq's identity as a modern nation state. For example, Iraq's higher education sector, once vaunted as one of the most advanced and most secular in the Arab world, had been systematically dismantled— first, marginalized with the 13 year long UN sanctions program which embargoed basic supplies and materials (such as pencils, technical equipment, journals); and then, virtually gutted by the unchecked looting and pillaging that accompanied the occupation. "The universities were fundamentally stripped bare—no desks, chairs, equipment, computers, typewriters, copiers, lecterns, paper, pencils, blackboards, fans, wiring, plumbing, or books. And what couldn't be stolen, like libraries, was generally burned," observed John Agresto, the senior US academic administrator, appointed by US Secretary of Defense Donald Rumsfeld to revamp Iraq's universities (Ionnone 2006,38). "A needs assessment we conducted concluded that simply to rebuild and re-supply the classrooms, dorms, bathrooms, labs, and libraries would run into the hundreds of millions of dollars" (Ionnone 2006, 38). Denied the necessary financial support, however, Agresto lamented the fact that "we were able to deliver so little by way of improving the awful physical conditions of the universities"(Ionnone 2006, 42). Instead, USAID funds designated for reconstruction of the higher education system were directed to US universities to provide advice and training for the modernization and reform of Iraq's education sector (Chandrasekaran 2006, 280–282).

The health sector provides another example of this deconstruction process. Prior to the 1991 Gulf War, Iraq's health care delivery system ranked among the most advanced in the Middle East, providing comprehensive publicly funded health care to all citizens. The 1991 war and 13 years of sanctions that followed severely diminished its functioning. The occupation systematically dismantled what was left. Early in 2004, Geert Van Moorter, a Belgian medical doctor, conducted a fact-finding mission to Iraq where he surveyed hospitals, clinics, and pharmacies. He concluded that "nowhere had any new medical material arrived since the end of the war. The medical material, already outdated, broken down or malfunctioning after twelve years of embargo, had further deteriorated (since the occupation)" (Jamail 2007b, 88). In a survey of Iraqi health facilities completed a year later, Dahr Jamail reported on the further deterioration of equipment, supplies, and staffing, compounded by an astronomical increase in both the number of patients and the severity of injury due to the violent nature of the occupation. Dahr's report documented the desperate supply shortages facing Iraqi hospitals, the disastrous effects that the lack of basic services like water and electricity have on hospitals, and the disruption of medical services caused by US military forces (Jamail 2007, 85–117).

The gutting of higher education and health care institutions are examples that illustrate what happened across all sectors of the national social infrastructure of health, education, and welfare programs accessible on the basis of citizenship. Their evisceration is symptomatic of an underlying process of change initiated by US policy in Iraq—that of emasculating the national foundations for social equity that have been at the core of nation-building since the collapse of the Ottoman Empire. Paul Bremer, who served as director of reconstruction for Iraq from May 2003 through June 2004, engineered the deconstruction of the Iraqi state's political and economic infrastructure as the initial stage in his mandate to reconstruct Iraq in the utopian image of a free market economy (2006; Packer 2005). In her seminal book *The Shock Doctrine: The Rise of Disaster Capitalism*, Naomi Klein observed that "in Iraq, this cycle of culture erasing and culture replacing was not theoretical; it all unfolded in a matter of weeks" (2007, 408). As discussed earlier, the construction of social equity was central to Iraq's political culture as a nation state.

From the beginning, the US directed process of state building in Iraq was founded on the political empowerment of sectarian religious forces. The rationale for this was laid out in 1999 in a book by David Wurmser, an affiliate of key proponents of the Iraq invasion in the Bush Administration, and Vice President Dick Cheney's Middle East adviser after the invasion. In *Tyranny's Ally: America's Failure to Defeat Saddam Hussein*, Wurmser argued that Iraqi Shiites could be used to control Iraq by offering them the opportunity to enhance their power in Iraq. However sanctimonious the plan, as noted by Gareth Porter, an investigative journalist, the planners had not anticipated the Sunnis mounting an effective resistance instead of rolling over. Nor had they anticipated that Shi'ite clerics of Iraq would demand national elections and throw their support behind the militant Shiite parties, SCIRI and Dawa, which had returned from exile in Iran in the wake of the US overthrow of Hussein (Porter 2007).

Thus, in the process of its efforts to politically reconstruct Iraq, the US fragmented Iraq into ethnic zones (Arab and Kurdish) and delivered the façade of governance of the Arab area into the hands of sectarian fundamentalist religious elements; and of the Kurdish area, into the hands of sectarian Kurdish tribal elements (Longley 2006; Hersh 2007). Assessing the results of the 2005 elections in Iraq, the International Crisis Group report on Iraq noted that:

> 2005 will be remembered as the year Iraq's latent sectarianism took wings, permeating the political discourse, and precipitating incidents of appalling violence and sectarian "cleansing." The elections that bracketed the year, in January and December, underscored the newly acquired prominence of religion, perhaps the most significant development since the regime's ouster. With mosques turned into party headquarters and clerics outfitting themselves as politicians, Iraqis searching for leadership and stability in profoundly uncertain times essentially turned the elections into confessional exercises (International Crisis Group 2006).

The election installed a National Assembly charged with drafting a new constitution, and in October 2005, under intense pressure from the United States, a referendum was held and the constitution adopted, in spite of bitter sectarian disagreements within the National Assembly and denunciation outside it from human rights advocates and secularists. And the constitution, in effect, delivered the country into the hands of sectarian religious fundamentalism. Section One invokes the primacy of religious law, establishing Islam as "the official religion of the state," in Article 2, and specifying that "no law may be passed that contradicts the undisputed rules of Islam." Article 39 institutionalizes sectarian personal status law in providing that "Iraqis are free in their commitment to their personal status according to their religions, sects, beliefs, or choices." Further establishing sectarianism and its economic foundations in the law of the land, Article 41 guaranteed "the sects are free in the...management of the endowments [*Awqâf*], its affairs and its religious institutions" (UNESCO 2005).

Between June and August 2005, the constitution went through a number of drafts before one acceptable to the US was formulated. The draft of June 30, 2005 explicitly identified social justice as a foundation principle in Articles 5 and 18, and guaranteed the right of citizens to full and free access to health and education services (Articles 6 and 7). In the final draft presented on August 25, all direct or inferential references to principles of social justice or social equity were gone. Thus, the constitution adopted for the reconstructed Iraqi state enshrined the tenets for the organization of a sectarian dystopia politically and for an open free market economy.

Conclusion

The Iraqi case study provides insight into the trajectory and dynamics of change in the construction and deconstruction of social equity and the denationalization of social justice that marks the pathway to sectarian dystopia. The construction of social equity was a major preoccupation of emerging nations in the 1950s and 1960s. The pre-WWII legacy of colonial and imperialist exploitation had left a legacy of social inequity and economic backwardness throughout the Global South. And in the heady days of post-colonial independence, emerging nations tended to confront social inequity head on through national social policy programs to meet basic needs and foster social citizenship through entitlement programs. However, the era of globalization has wrought the deconstruction of social equity and the dena-tionalization of social justice. By denationalization of social justice, we mean a quantum shift in social justice discourse from a universalist doctrine with national scope to a particularistic doctrine with communal scope. In effect, we are arguing that it is not incidental or accidental that a proliferation of sectarian dystopias has accompanied the advance of globalization.

References

- Alnasrawi, Abbas. 1994. *The Economy of Iraq: Wars, Destruction of Development and Prospects, 1950–2010.* Westport: Greenwood Publishing Group, Inc.

- Anderson, J. N. D. A Law of Personal Status for Iraq. *The International and Comparative Law Quarterly* 9: 4.

- Batatu, Hanna. 1978. *The Old Social Classes and the Revolutionary Movements in Iraq.* Princeton: Princeton University Press.

- Bremer, Paul. 2006. *My Year in Iraq: The Struggle to Build a Future of Hope.* New York: Simon & Schuster Inc.

- Buckley, Walter Frederick. 1998. *Society: A Complex Adaptive System.* London: Gordon and Breach Publishers.

- Chandrasekaran, Rajiv. 2006. *Imperial Life in the Emerald City: Inside Iraq's Green Zone.* Toronto: Alfred A. Knopf Books.

- Chomsky, Noam. 2003. *Hegemony or Survival: America's Quest for Global Dominance.* New York: Henry Holt and Company.

- Clarke, Richard A. 2004. *Against All Enemies: Inside America's War on Terror.* New York: Free Press.

- Cox, Percy (Sir.). 1927. *The Letters of Gertrude Bell.* Vol. 2. London: Ernest Benn Ltd.

- Donnelly, Thomas (Principal Author). *Rebuilding American's Defenses: Strategies, Forces and Resources.* Project for a New American Century (September 2000). Accessed January 2, 2008. www.newamericancentury.org/RebuildingAmericas-Defenses.pdf.

- Hadar, Leon T. 1998. Letter From Washinton—Pax Americana's Four Pillars of Folly. *Journal of Palestine Studies* 26 (3).

- Hadid, Muhammad. 2006. *Al-Sira' min ajl al-Dimuqratiyyah fi al-Iraq.* London: Dar al-Saqi.

- Halpern, Manfred. 1963. *The Politics of Social Change in the Middle East and North Africa.* Princeton: Princeton University Press.

- Hasan, Muhammad Salmân. 1966. *Dirâsât fî al-Iqtisâd al-'Irâqî* (Studies in the Iraqi Economy). Beirut: Dar al-Taliah.

- Hersh, Seymour M. Get Out the Vote: Did Washington try to manipulate Iraq's election? *The New Yorker* (April 16, 2007).

- Holland, J. H. 1998. *Emergence: From Chaos to Order.* London: Oxford University Press.

- Hasanîn, Mustapha Mohammad. 1967. *Nidham al-Mas`oliyah 'ind al-'Ashai`r al-Iraqiyah al-Arabiyah al-Ma'asiriah*. Cairo: al-Istiqlal al-Kubra Press.

- International Crisis Group. The Next Iraqi War? Sectarianism and Civil Conflict. *Middle East Report* 52 (February 27, 2006).

- International Federation of Social Workers (IFSW), and International Association of Schools of Social Work (IASSW). *Ethics in Social Work, Statement of Principles*. January 15, 2008. www.ifsw.org/en/p38000398.html.

- Ionnone, Carol. 2006. Disquieting Lessons from Iraq: A Conversation with John Agresto. *Academic Questions* 19:3.

- Ireland, Philip W. 1937. *Iraq: A Study in Political Development*. London: Jonathan Cape.

- Ismael, Tareq Y. 2008. *The Rise and Fall of the Communist Party of Iraq*. New York: Cambridge University Press.

- Ismael, Tareq Y. 2001. *Middle East Politics Today: Government and Civil Society*. Gainsville: University Press of Florida.

- Ismael, Tareq Y. 1970. *Government and Politics of the Contemporary Middle East*. Homewood: Dorsey Press.

- Ismael, Jacqueline S. and Tareq Y. Ismael. 2004. *The Iraqi Predicament: People in the Quagmire of Power Politics*. London: Pluto Press.

- Ismael, Jacqueline S. and Tareq Y. Ismael. 1999. Cowboy Warfare, Biological Diplomacy: Disarming Metaphors as Weapons of Mass Destruction. *Politics and the Life Sciences* 18 (1).

- Ismael, Jacqueline S., Tareq Y. Ismael, and Raymond W. Baker. 2004. Iraq and Human Development: Culture, Education and the Globalization of Hope. *Arab Studies Quarterly* 26 (2).

- Jabar, Faleh A. 1995. *Al-Dawla, al-Mugtam'a al-Madani wa al-Tahawul al-Demokrati fi al Iraq*. Cairo: Markaz Ibn Khaldoun li al-Dirasat al-Inma'iyya.

- Jabber, Sadoon Abbas. 1989. Social Security in Iraq. *International Social Security Review* 42 (2).

- Jamail, Dahr. 2007a. *Beyond the Green Zone: Dispatches from an Unembedded Journalist in Occupied Iraq*. Chicago: Haymarket Books.

- Jamail, Dahr. 2007b. Iraqi Hospitals Ailing under Occupation. In *Barriers to Reconciliation: Case Studies on Iraq and the Palestine-Israel Conflict*, eds. Jacqueline S. Ismael and William Haddad. New York: University Press of America.

- Kaplan, Fred. 2008. *Daydream Believers: How a Few Grand Ideas Wrecked American Power*. Toronto: John Wiley and Sons Ltd.

- Kerr, Malcolm. 1966. *Islamic Reform: The Political and Legal Theories of Mohammad Abduh and Rashid Rida*. Berkeley: University of California Press.

- Khadduri, Majid. 1984. *The Islamic Conception of Justice*. Baltimore: John Hopkins University Press.

- Klein, Naomi. 2007. *The Shock Doctrine: The Rise of Disaster Capitalism*. Toronto: Alfred A. Knopf Books.

- Leman, Nicholas. The Next World Order. *The New Yorker* (April 1, 2002).

- Lenczowski, George. 1966. Radical Regimes in Egypt, Syria and Iraq: Some Comparative Observations on Ideologies and Practices. *The Journal of Politics* 28 (1).

- Longley, James (Director). 2006. Background. Iraq in Fragments. Accessed April 16, 2007. www.iraqinfragments.com/background/index.html

- Makiya, Kanan. 1989. *The Republic of Fear*. Berkeley: University of California.

- Marr, Phebe. 1985. *The Modern History of Iraq*. Boulder: Westview Press.

- Packer, George. 2005. *The Assassin's Gate: America in Iraq*. New York: Farrar, Straus and Giroux Publishers.

- Poe, Mary Anne. 2007 Fairness is not Enough: Social Justice as Restoration of Right. *Social Work & Christianity* 34 (4).

- Porter, Gareth. How Neocon Shi'ite Strategy Led to Sectarian War. *IPS* (Inter Press News Agency). Accessed April 16, 2007. www.ipsnews.net/print.asp?idnews=36461.

- Qâsim, 'Abd-ul-Karîm. 1959. *Mabâdi' Thawrat 14 Tammûz fî Khutab 'Abd-ul-Karîm Qâsim* (The Principles of 14 Tammuz Revolution in Abdul-Karim Qasim's Speeches). Baghdad: Iraqi Government Press.

- Qutb, Sayyid. 1996. *Sayyid Qutb and Islamic Activism: a translation and critical analysis of Social Justice in Islam.* Leiden, Netherlands: E.J. Brill.

- Republic of Iraq. 1980. *Law of Social Welfare.* Baghdad: Ministry of Justice.

- Republic of Iraq, Ministry of Justice. 1978. *Qânûn al-Ahwâl al-Shakhsiyyah wa Ta'dîlâtuh* (The Personal Status Law and Its Amendments). Baghdad: Dâr al-Hurriyyah Print Shop.

- Rosen, Nir. 2006. *In the Belly of the Green Bird: The Triumph of Martyrs in Iraq.* New York: Simon and Schuster.

- Russell, James A. 2005. Strategy, Security, and War in Iraq: The United States and the Gulf in the 21ˢᵗ Century. *Cambridge Review of International Affairs* 18 (2).

- Salih, Zaki. 1955. *Muqdamah fi Tarikh al-Iraq al-Mua'sir al-Iraq.* Baghdad: al-Rabitah Press.

- Scahill, Jeremy. 2008. *Blackwater: The Rise of the World's Most Powerful Mercenary Army.* New York: Nation Books.

- Sherwood, David. 2007. Moral, Believing Social Workers: Philosophical and Theological Foundations of Moral Obligation in Social Work Ethics. *Social Work & Christianity* 34 (2).

- Sivard, R. L. 1980. *World Military and Social Expenditures, 1977–87.* Washington: World Priorities.

- Teresi, Dick. 2002. *Lost Discoveries: The Ancient Roots of Modern Science from Babylonia to Maya.* New York: Simon & Shuster.

- United Nations Children's Fund (UNICEF), *1999 Ira: Child and Maternal Morbidity Surveys* (August 1999).

- UNICEF *Iraq: Children, War and Sanctions* (April 1993).

- United Nations Development Program (UNDP). 1999–2000 Report. *Iraq Country Office.*

- United Nations Educational, Scientific and Cultural Organization (UNESCO). *Iraqi Constitution* (English) c. 2005. Accessed March 22, 2007. www.portal.unesco.org/ci/en/files/20704/11332732681iraqi_constitution_en.pdf/iraqi_constitution_en.pdf.

- United Nations Food and Agricultural Organization (UNFAO) and United Nations World Food Program (UNWFP). *Special Report: FAO/WFP Food Supply and Nutrition Assessment Mission to Iraq* (October 3, 1997). Accessed February 2008. www.fao.org/docrep/004/w6519e/w6519e00.htm.

- United Nations Development Fund for Women (UNIFEM). *Gender Profile of the Conflict in Iraq* (c. 2006). Accessed March 2007. www.womenwarpeace.org.

- United Nations Office of the Iraq Program (UNOIP). Oil-for-Food: Basic Figures (May 18, 2002). Accessed February 2008. www.un.org/Depts/oip/background.

- UNOIP. Oil-for-Food (May 18, 2002). Accessed February 2008. www.un.org/Depts/oip/cpmd/roleofoip.

- United Nations Statistics Division (UNSD) A. Iraq: Population by Sex, Urban and Rural, Census Years. Accessed February 1, 2008. www.unstats.un.org/unsd/cdb/cdb_years_on_top.asp?srID=14910&Ct1ID=&crID=368&yrID=1950%2C1960%2C1970%2C1980%2C1990%2C1995%2C1999.

- UNSD B. Life Expectancy at Specified Ages for Each Sex. Accessed February 1, 2008. www.unstats.un.org/unsd/cdb/cdb_years_on_top.asp?srID=14830&Ct1ID

=&crID=368&yrID=1950%2C1960%2C1970%2C1980%2C1990%2C1995%2C 1999.

- Warriner, Doreen. 1975. *Land Reform and Development in the Middle East: A study of Egypt, Syria, and Iraq*. London: Royal Institute of International Officers.

- World Health Organization (WHO). 2003. *Potential Impact of Conflict on Health in Iraq*, briefing note (March 2003). Accessed March 2007. www.who.int/features/2003/ iraq/briefings/iraq_briefing_note/en/index.html].

- WHO *Briefing Notes on Potential Impact of Conflict on Health of Iraq: March 2003*. Accessed February 2008. www.who.int/disasters/repo/9141.pdf.

- Zaher, U. 1986. Political Developments in Iraq, 1963–1980. In *Saddam's Iraq: Revolution or Reaction?* Ed. Committee Against Repression and for Democratic Rights in Iraq. London: Zed Books.

- Al-Zâhir, 'Abd-ul-Razzâq. 1946. *Al-Iqtâ' wa al-Dîwân fî al-'Irâq* (Feudalism and Bureaucracy in Iraq). Cairo: al-Sa'âdah Press.

- Zangana, Haifa. 2007. *City of Widows: An Iraqi woman's account of war and resistance*. New York: Seven Stories Press.

- Zubaida, Sami. The Rise and Fall of Civil Society in Iraq (May 2, 2003). Accessed March 2007. www.opendemocracy.net/conflict-iraqwarquestions/article_953.jsp.

- Al-Zubaidi, Laith Abdul Hassan Jawad. 1979. *Thawrat 14 Tamuz 1958 fi al-Iraq*. Baghdad: Dar al-Rashid.

Chapter 3

Right to Food Within Canada: International Obligations, Domestic Compliance

Graham Riches

My interest in the right to food first arose in the mid 1980s when I was researching a book on the origins and growth of food banks in Canada (Riches 1986). The first Canadian food bank was established in 1981 in Edmonton, Alberta, and they quickly mushroomed across the country. From a social policy perspective, I became interested in why a country as wealthy as Canada with, at that time, a reasonably well developed welfare state and social safety net (supported by Unemployment Insurance and the Canada Assistance Plan) should be depending on charitable food banks to feed increasing numbers of unemployed persons and welfare recipients. This suggested that peoples' basic needs for food, clothing and shelter were not being met and this in a country that exported grains to feed a hungry world.

In light of this contradiction I was surprised to learn through my research that in 1976 Canada had ratified the International Covenant on Economic, Social and Cultural Rights (ICESCR), which establishes state party obligations to protect such rights including "the right of everyone to an adequate standard of living for himself and his family, including food, clothing and housing and to continuous improvements of living conditions" (Article 11.1); and "the fundamental right of everyone to be free from hunger" (Article 11.2). I was particularly interested to learn that all ratifying member states had core obligations progressively to realize these commitments not only in the international arena, but domestically. Canada, by signing the ICESCR in 1966, and ratifying the covenant ten years later, recognized that the right to food existed in its own society and, as a duty-bearer, accepted significant domestic social policy obligations. Yet, despite these commitments, the rise of charitable food banks were symptoms and symbols of a broken social safety net, pointing to Canada's violation of its ICESCR obligations to meet the basic needs of its most vulnerable citizens. This was a troubling situation twenty-five years ago. It remains more so today following a decade of significant economic growth and massive federal budget surpluses.

Since my early research, my interests in the charitable food bank question have broadened to consider the emergence of food security as an essential component of anti-hunger and anti-poverty strategies in countries of the South and North, including Canada, and, in particular, the role to be played by the right to food in informing and expanding these debates within global and local contexts. This theme was picked up and developed in *First World Hunger: Food Security and Welfare Politics* (New York: St Martins 1997), an edited book that explored the issue of food poverty in five industrialized states: Australia, Canada, New Zealand, the UK, and the US. Again the point was made that hunger and food insecurity affecting the most vulnerable populations were being increasingly left to the charitable sector with wealthy states looking the other way while neglecting their obligations under international law. Evidence for this lay not only in the growth of individual food banks, but in their rapid institutionalization and internationalization. America's Second Harvest was established in 1979, the Canadian Association of Food Banks in 1985, and the European Federation of Food Banks was set up in 1986, thereby reinforcing the view that hunger in first world societies was increasingly perceived as a matter for benevolent community response (similar to international food aid) rather than as a political question and matter of economic, social, and cultural rights requiring the full attention of the state.

The 1996 World Food Summit in Rome drew the attention of the international community to global hunger and led in turn to a commitment to define what was meant by the right to food and how it could be used as a tool to combat global poverty and advance food security. This matter was referred to the UN Committee on Economic, Social, and Cultural Rights whose committee of experts in 1999 issued General Comment 12, which states that "the right to food is realized when every man, woman and child, alone or in community with others, has physical and economic access at all times to adequate food or the means for its procurement" (Eide and Kracht 2005; Kent 2005). This core definition is an elaboration of the right to food as a key component of the right to an adequate standard of living as stated in the ICESCR, and as noted above, signed by Canada in 1966, and ratified in 1976.

At the 2002 World Food Summit five years later, the member nations invited the Council of the UN Food and Agricultural Organization (FAO) to elaborate a set of voluntary guidelines to support the progressive realization of the right to adequate food in the context of national food security. As part of this process five states from the South (Brazil, India, Mali, Uganda, South Africa) and one state from the North (Canada) were chosen as case studies in order to explore the application and benefits of right to food approaches, including that of justiciability, and what could be learned in terms of developing practical guidelines (FAO 2005; Right to Food 2007). I was invited along with three colleagues[1] to prepare the Canadian case study. What was useful about this process was understanding issues of poverty and food insecurity in global contexts and how the human right to adequate food has applications in poor and rich countries alike.

---

[1] Don Buckingham, Adjunct Professor at the University of Ottawa, Faculty of Law, Dr. Rod MacRae, Research Associate of the Centre for Studies in Food Security, Ryerson Polytechnic University, and Dr. Alex Ostry, Associate Professor, Department of Health Care and Epidemiology, University of British Columbia.

In recent years, one pleasing development has been the emergence of Food Secure Canada, which now spearheads Canada's civil society's movement to advance economically viable, socially just, and ecologically sustainable food policies across the country. Through participation in recent conferences and symposia in the UK, Portugal, Australia, Canada, Italy, Germany, and Finland it has been interesting to observe increasing academic, professional and public attention being given to the role of state responsibility for advancing national food and nutrition policy informed by the human right to adequate food. From a social policy perspective, the question of the appropriate balance between the public, market, and charitable distribution of income and/or emergency food aid to vulnerable populations in rich societies remains a central question and shapes the context within which this chapter is written.

This chapter, therefore, examines Canada's domestic compliance with its obligations under international law to "respect, protect and fulfill" the human right to adequate food in one of the better countries in the world in which to live. Its central theme is Canada's commitment to the right to food on behalf of all its citizens. It explores the question of whether the right to food exists in Canada, particularly for vulnerable Canadians. And, if not, what are the implications of such human rights violations for domestic social policy?

International Human Rights

How then might we best understand international human rights as a tool for social policy reform and action? From a social work perspective, Ife contends that by framing social work as a human rights profession, many of the issues and dilemmas that face social work can be looked at in a new light. He argues that the discourse and practice of human rights provide a powerful antidote to economic globalization where "individualism, greed and becoming rich are seen as the most important things in life, and where at the same time the formerly secure moral positions for judging our actions seem to be declining into a morass of postmodern relativism." Indeed as he states "the idea of human rights provides an alternative moral reference point for those who would seek to re-affirm the values of humanity" (Ife 2001). It is a position that would endorse the right to food for all.

Yet, as he also notes, the idea of human rights means different things to different people. Rights are "readily endorsed by people from many different cultural and ideological backgrounds and are used rhetorically in support of a large number of different and sometimes conflicting causes" (Ife 2001). In clarifying the meaning of human rights from an internationalist perspective, Ife refers to the commonly accepted idea that human rights are "universal, indivisible, inalienable and inabrogable" The universality of human rights, as in the right to food, means that they apply to all people, everywhere. Their indivisibility means that you cannot pick and choose which human right should be included in your package and which excluded. In other words economic, social, and cultural rights are equally as important as civil and political rights. What use is freedom of speech if you are hungry or without shelter? Inalienable human rights means they cannot be taken away, though as Ife notes, this is somewhat controversial as clearly the sanction of the law may require the denial of liberty or freedom of association to convicted prisoners. He also notes that given that human rights are inabrogable, they cannot voluntarily be given up or traded for additional privileges.

From the perspective of international law, human rights are best understood within the framework of the UN Charter and their codification in the Universal Declaration of Human Rights (UDHR) in 1948. As Eide has stated "international human rights law provides a constitutional framework for legitimate exercise of authority at the national level: human rights set constraints on, and give direction to, national laws and policies" (2005). Within this context of international law, human rights, according to Eide and Kracht:

> refer to those rights that are inherent to the person and belong equally to all human beings regardless of their race, colour, sex, language, religion, political and other opinion, national or social origin, property, birth or other status. They represent universal values and constitute an ethical imperative to safeguard the dignity of every human being, providing fundamental norms of outcomes and processes of action to this end (2005).

Yet, while human rights are fundamentally concerned with respect for human dignity and a common humanity, and are international in their application in rich and poor countries alike, they raise complex moral, political, and legal questions in their conceptualization and in their enforcement and realization.

Indeed it is important to recognize that if human rights are to have any practical meaning they must not only be understood within a constitutional framework, they must be justiciable and legally enforceable. In other words if a human right is violated (e.g., people are allowed to go hungry in rich societies), remedies must be available. Otherwise, what benefit is it to claim a right?

While in theory or principle human rights may be understood to be universal and indivisible, the division of civil and political rights and economic, social, and cultural rights into two separate covenants underlines the deep divide confronting states in terms of adopting such conventions that are legally binding for a state when ratified (Eide 2005). The 1948 Universal Declaration of Human Rights (UDHR) codified the human rights principles set out in the UN Charter and "extended the human rights platform to embrace the whole range of aspects of life, that is both civil and political aspects and economic, social, and cultural aspects, and that it made the different rights interrelated and mutually reinforcing" (Eide and Kracht 2005). However, as Eide and Kracht, explain "the principles of the Universal Declaration were further elaborated into two major treaties, the 1966 International Covenant on Civil and Political Rights (ICCPR) and the 1966 International Covenant on Economic, Social and Cultural Rights

(ICESCR) constituting, together with the UDHR, what is known as the International Bill of Human Rights.

The adoption of the UDHR by the UN General Assembly and the agreement in 1951 to proceed with the development of two separate covenants, one for civil and political rights and the other for economic, social, and cultural rights (both covenants were not adopted until 1966) was a consequence of East-West tensions and anti-colonialism set in the aftermath of World War II and the ensuing Cold War (Glendon 2001). This division of human rights into two separate categories in 1966 resulted from a controversial and contested decision by the UN General Assembly.

Eide and Kracht note that the division arose from the argument that the two sets of rights were of a different nature and so required different instruments, that civil and political rights were "justiciable" in the sense that they could be applied by the courts and similar judicial bodies, whereas economic, social, and cultural rights were more of a policy nature; and the idea that civil and political rights were understood to be "free" while economic, social, and cultural rights would be costly in their implementation and obligate the state to provide welfare to the individual (Eide 1999). In this context it is interesting to note that while Canada has ratified the ICESCR, the United States has refrained from such action, suggesting it well understands the implications for the state of intervening in the market place on behalf of vulnerable peoples.

The significance of Canada's ratification of the ICESCR is that as a State Party to the covenant and as the primary duty-bearer, all levels of government of Canada are bound by the obligation under international law to achieve the progressive realization of the right of everyone to an adequate standard of living and to be free from hunger. Yet there are complications in the domestic realization and enforcement of the right to food provisions of UN declarations, covenants, and guidelines. On the one hand, although a State Party such as Canada has ratified the ICESCR, there currently exist no sanctions in international law requiring governments to comply with their domestic obligations. Economic and social rights are not constitutionally entrenched and only find, at best, weak support in the Charter of Rights and Freedoms (1982). They are understood as "soft" law and, as such, not justiciable. In other words, the best that can be hoped for is that Canada's welfare state incorporates the right to food in its agricultural, health and nutrition, and income and social policies.

Yet at the same time the ratification of the ICESCR provides opportunities for public education and advocacy. At five year intervals, Canada is required, as are all other 151 ratifying states, to report on its progress in realizing economic and social rights to the UN Monitoring Committee on Economic, Social and Cultural Rights, which sits in Geneva. NGO's have reporting status before this committee and it is a significant arena for examining the degree to which Canada is acting in compliance with its obligations regarding the right to food.

Social Work and Social Policy

Food has rightly been called a Cinderella topic in social policy, barely mentioned in its practice and academic literature. The same could be said of food's relationship to social work. The point is that food is a wonderful metaphor for describing and analyzing social change. While food is rightly thought of as an agricultural and economic commodity, it is also an intimate commodity and a health, social, and cultural good, essential to the nutritional, mental, and spiritual well-being of individuals, families, and communities (Winson 1995). Food is also contested terrain and an intensely political matter (Lang and Heasman 2005). As such, we might expect what is happening, or not happening, to the food system to be a core interest for social policy and social justice.

However, because food is so everyday (Visser 2000) and its distribution is largely an accepted function of the private market, it has largely been ignored by social policy. Yet, to be deprived of food results not only in the loss of nutritional well-being but of personal and social identity, the means to earn one's livelihood and to participate fully in society. To be dependent on food handouts and public begging is to lose one's human dignity and the economic, social, and cultural rights of citizenship in any society. In the context of global hunger and obesity, and of high rates of household food insecurity in Canada, the right to food as a matter of material and distributional justice should be a matter of central concern for social work and social policy. Indeed if, as Ife suggests, social work is a human rights profession, food is clearly a topic that metaphorically and literally should be on its table.

The right to food is a story about the role of the international community, nation states, and civil society seeking to address unmet basic human needs, in this case hunger or food poverty, and the struggle to ensure that all Canadians and impoverished peoples around the world might experience freedom from want. In this sense it links the global with the local. It is about Canada's international recognition of the UDHR (1948) despite its reluctant support for economic, social, and cultural rights as compared to civil and political rights (Arbour 2005). It is also about signing (1966) and ratifying (1976) the ICESCR and its progress in those two decades of advancing these rights (which include the right to food) through its contributions, on the one hand, to international aid and development, and, on the other, to the building of its welfare state including its domestic social safety net, and particularly the Canada Assistance Plan (CAP) (1966). In the 1980s and 1990s it is a different story, given governments' embrace of welfare reform and the recommodification of social rights, that is, the equating of social policy with labour market policy where entitlement to welfare benefits is linked through workfare programs to labour force participation and the consequent abandonment of any pretence that human rights, let alone the right to food, are central commitments informing Canada's social safety net. And, not unexpectedly, within a highly devolved federal state, it is also a story of constitutionally divided jurisdictions, fragmented social policies, the neglect of justiciability, a struggle for social justice, and environmental sustainability by civil society.

The right to food informs tensions between public and privatized welfare provision and between charity and social justice. Recent social history invites consideration of the dilemmas created for the hard-pressed church and voluntary sector as it has struggled over the past quarter of a century to meet the needs of hungry Canadians through charitable works such as food banks. In fact, given the apparent public acceptance and legitimacy of food banks, today, we might wish to ask if they represent the real meaning of "practical compassion" recently espoused by Gerard Kennedy, the recent federal Liberal Party leadership contender and, in 1981, the founding director of Canada's first food bank in Edmonton. While charitable food banks may reflect community values of tolerance, compassion, fair minded-ness and practical help, do they stand in the way of rights based approaches to overcoming hunger while at the same time pointing to indifference by our governments, and their neglect of the economic, social, and cultural rights of vulnerable Canadians?

Put more bluntly, do we, in the social work and social policy community, need to be rethinking our obligations, policies, and strategies towards the needs of the hungry and homeless, whose fundamental human rights are substantially denied because they live outside the labour market, or only cling precariously to it? If rights do not translate into entitlements for welfare claimants, what bedrock values do, and should inform our social policy? What light might a debate, from the perspective of the right to food, throw on these critical questions for social policy and the ability of hungry Canadians to feed themselves?

Food Insecurity in Canada

What, then, do we know about the prevalence of food insecurity in Canada today? Is it a matter that should be of concern to social policy or is it a matter best left to the agricultural sector, to dieticians, nutritionists, and public health, the environmental sector or to charity? Canada's Action Plan for Food Security (1998), adopting international definitions, states that "food security exists when all people at all times have physical and economic access to sufficient, safe and nutritious food to meet their dietary needs and food preferences for an active and healthy life" (CAPFS 1998). The question is whether these conditions prevail for all Canadians. Unhappily, the data indicate that the prevalence of food insecurity is widespread and long-standing.

Despite Canada's cheap food policies, 823,856 people turned to a food bank in one month of 2005, an increase of 24% since 1997 and 118% since 1989. The first food bank opened in Edmonton in 1981. Today they number 650, providing 2.7 million meals a month; 40.7% of food bank users are children and young people (CAFB[2] 2005). Significantly, more than a third of food banks say they cannot meet demand and those who turn to them for food assistance (often referred by government welfare officials) are an underestimate of food insecure Canadians. The 1998–99 National Population Health Survey (NPHS) reports that only 23% of those who are food insecure use food banks (Tarasuk and Power 2006).

The 2000–01 Canadian Community Health Survey (CCHS) reported that 3.7 million Canadians (14.7% of the population) lived in food insecure households: 11% worried about not being able to feed themselves and their families; 12% were unable to purchase the foods of their choice; and 7% were unable to put food on the table (Ledrou and Gervais 2005; Che and Chen 2003). The 2004 CCHS, using a different and more restrictive survey instrument, reported that 6.8% of the population or 2.1 million people lived in households reporting food insecurity (Tarasuk and Power 2006). How tolerant should we be of the fact that "28% of people in low and middle income households had not had enough to eat at some point" in the year 2000? And this during a period of continuing massive Federal surpluses.

Such data should not be a surprise. As Louise Arbour, the former Canadian Supreme Court Justice and current UN High Commissioner for Human Rights has noted, despite Canada's 1990s ranking on the UN Human Development Index as the number one country in the world in which to live, the 2004 Human Poverty Index gave Canada only a 12th place ranking out of the 17 Organisation for Economic Co-Operation and Development (OECD) member countries listed. The eminent justice goes on to say that:

> other reports, studies and indicators, from home and abroad, reveal that First Peoples, single parent families headed by women, persons with disabilities and many other groups continue to face conditions in this country that threaten their fundamental economic, social, civil, political and cultural human rights, the birth rights of all human beings under international law (Arbour 2005).

It should also be noted that the 2005 UNICEF Report on Child Poverty in Rich Countries pegged Canada's child poverty rate at 14.9%—19th out of the 26 countries studied. At the top of the league table are Denmark and Finland where child poverty is less than 3% and, at the bottom, the United States and Mexico with child poverty rates higher than 20%. The UNICEF study makes a telling point: variation in government policy appears to account for most of the differences in child poverty levels between OECD countries (UNICEF 2005).

In this context it is hardly surprising that the incidence and nature of the crisis of food insecurity stretching back a quarter of a century continues to be neglected by all levels of government of all political stripes. In taking for granted the abundance of our food supply and its everyday market availability through imports and local food production, we have failed to notice that for too many Canadians—an estimated 10%—their right to adequate food and nutrition has been consistently neglected by the state.

---

[2] Canadian Association of Food Banks.

Causes of Food Insecurity

Food poverty in Canada springs from a number of interrelated causes: corporate globalization, economic restructuring, and the creation of flexible labour markets; the ascendancy of neo-liberalism with its commitment to market ideology, minimal government, downloading to the provinces and social spending cutbacks. The changes are reflected in the 1996 demise of CAP; Canada's broken social safety net; the recommodification of social rights with eligibility for welfare based, not on financial need, but on attachment to the labour market including stringent work requirements; social assistance benefits below the Low Income Cut-offs (poverty lines), and lack of affordable social housing. In addition, divided agriculture, health and social welfare ministries and jurisdictions result in fragmented food policy (federal and provincial) that is not directed in any comprehensive way at the optimal nourishment of the population (MacRae 1999). The social construction of hunger or food poverty becomes a matter of charity so that the issue is no longer understood as a human rights question demanding state accountability; and, as a consequence, the failure of governments at all levels to comply with their international obligations to "respect, protect and fulfill" the right to food.

Compliance and Non-Compliance[3]

In a general and aggregate sense, Canada is a food secure nation in terms of the production and supply of food (including imports), food safety, and food distribution for the large majority of its population. Since the mid-1990s, the country has been enjoying a period of strong economic growth and employment creation, and the Federal Government has generated six successive budget surpluses. However, while the right to food exists in Canada, its implementation is lacking. The problem is that there are major disconnects between Canada's international support for the right to food, which is ambivalent or lukewarm, and the reality of food insecurity at home. This points to a failure of public policy to connect the dots between ratified international obligations and domestic compliance. In light of the provinces' constitutional powers, this is admittedly a complex affair when Ottawa is reluctant to promote a national social policy agenda in preference for provincial subsidiarity and the transfer of tax revenues and points.

When Canada signed and later ratified the ICESCR, it accepted state party obligations to "respect, protect and fulfill" the right to an adequate standard of living, including the right to food and freedom from hunger. In 1992, Canada ratified the Convention on the Rights of the Child, which establishes rights and obligations for states for children, including nutrition. The Government of Canada has also committed itself to the goals laid out in the World Declaration on Nutrition (1992); the World Summit for Social Development (1995); the Declaration on World Food

---

[3] Refer to G. Riches, D. Buckingham, R. MacRae, and A. Ostry, *Right to Food Case Study: Canada* (UNFAO 2004) on which the section is based.

Security (1996); Canada's Action Plan for Food Security (1998), and the Declaration on World Food Security Five Years Later (2002) as well as the Millennium Development Goals (2000), including the commitment to the halving of global hunger by 2015. Furthermore, in 2004 Canada approved the UNFAO Voluntary Guidelines to support the progressive realization of the right to adequate food in the context of national food security (FAO 2005). Additionally, from the viewpoint of the justiciability of the right to food, it has also been argued that sections 7 and 15 of the Canadian Charter of Rights and Freedoms provide protection for social and economic rights and the meeting of basic human needs, including food (Riches et al. 2004).

Clearly, then, there is evidence supporting the claim that the human right to adequate food finds expression, directly and indirectly, in Canada's agricultural, economic, health, nutrition, and social policy and in its legal instruments, institutions, and international commitments. The fact is that since 1976, Canada has been bound to comply domestically with the implementation of the right to be free from hunger and the right to food. It has also committed itself internationally to realize the right to food generally as well as in specific areas of nutrition, development, women's and children's rights, and those pertaining to indigenous peoples. In terms of domestic law, while the right to food is not explicitly written into existing statutes, bits and pieces of the right can be found in federal and provincial laws and policies regarding agriculture, food safety, nutrition and health, and the welfare state.

From the perspective of justiciability, a former Chief Justice of the Supreme Court of Canada has expressed the view that the Canadian Charter of Rights and Freedoms (1982) should be interpreted in light of Canada's international legal commitments (Public Service Employees Relations Act—Court of Canada (Alta. [1987] 1. S.C.R. 313). Indeed, the Federal Government has stated internationally that the Charter, as interpreted by the Supreme Court of Canada, does protect internationally recognized economic, social, and cultural rights (CESCR, Canada 1998). Also, the Supreme Court has, in recent decisions, recognized the rights of Aboriginal peoples to traditional food gathering and processing practices (Delgamuukw 1997; Thomas 2002).

The Federal Government has pronounced Canada's Action Plan for Food Security (1998) and the Government of Québec, in 2002, passed an *Act to Combat Poverty and Social Exclusion* that also contained an Action Plan. Additionally, the proclamation of food charters by a number of municipalities (Toronto, Saskatoon, Vancouver) is indicative of policy interest by local governments and actions by civil society, including the development of local, provincial, and national food security movements. The establishment of municipal food policy councils are indicative of increasing public interest in creating economically viable, ecologically sustainable, and socially just food systems.

Yet there is compelling evidence that points to serious disconnects between the international claims and the rhetoric of Canada's right to food approaches with the state's domestic compliance and implementation. One set of disconnects can be found in the area of federal, provincial, and territorial policy. Canada's income support programs and social safety net lack domestic, compliance with its international obligations to "respect, protect and fulfill" the right to food of vulnerable peoples. Existing social assistance benefits do not permit the purchase of a sufficient quality and quantity of nutritious food. More stringent eligibility criteria have led to: claimants being denied access to benefits; the reduction of already inadequate benefits; and to benefits being cut off absolutely (Wallace et al 2006).

As a consequence, community based benevolent approaches to meeting the emergency food needs of hungry people in the form of charitable food banks have become institutionalized over the past twenty years in Canada and have relieved the state (federal, provincial, and territorial governments) of its obligations as a duty-bearer to advance the right to food through ensuring adequate social security entitlements. Canadian government reliance on charitable food banking, now established as a secondary part of the welfare system to feed hungry people (Gandy et al 1989), is itself evidence of the lack of a right to food. While demands on food banks have continued to grow, research has shown that charitable food banking has failed to meet the food and nutritional needs of vulnerable populations (Tarasuk et al 1998; CAFB 2006).

A second set of disconnects is evident in the area of justiciability between the dicta of the federal government, the Supreme Court, and the lower courts in Canada, as far as the legal protection of the right to food is concerned, particularly in the case of vulnerable Canadians. While the federal government has explicitly acknowledged that the Canadian Charter of Rights and Freedoms has been interpreted by the Supreme Court of Canada to protect economic and social rights, this protection appears very narrow given the Court's finding in the 2002 landmark case of Gosselin v. Québec (Attorney General) that dismissed a claim against the government of Québec for deficiencies in her welfare entitlement of only $170 per month in the period 1984–89 (since repealed). Gosselin, then under 30 years of age, claimed that her rights under section 7 (right to life, liberty and security of person) and section 15 (rights to equality and freedom from discrimination) were violated as she was entitled to the $460 per month that persons 30 years and older received.

The narrow majority decision (5:4) written by Chief Justice McLaughlin held that the case presented did not merit the protection of section 7 of the Charter. The Chief Justice held that Canadian law did not yet place a positive obligation on the state to ensure this right (Gosselin 2002; SCC per McLachlin). The minority dissent was written by then Madam Justice Louise Arbour, now the UN High Commissioner for Human Rights, who argued that "the concern raised by this justiciability argument is a valid one." In other words, she strongly asserted that a Charter right existed—in this case, to a level of welfare sufficient to meet one's basic needs—and that the courts had a role and responsibility as interpreters of the Charter and guardians of its fundamental freedoms against legislative or administrative infringements by the state to adjudicate such rights-based claims. However, it remained up to the state to determine how much expenditure was necessary in order to secure that right (Gosselin 2002; SCC per Arbour).

A third set of disconnects is apparent in the lack of coordinated federal, provincial, and territorial food policy. Canada lacks a coherent approach to the development of a national food policy (MacRae 1999). The policy infrastructure to ensure a food system (production, processing, distribution, and consumption) that guarantees access to nutrition and affordable food for vulnerable people is highly fragmented. Limited account is taken of the cost of eating nutritious foods in the calculation of welfare benefits or minimum wage (Dieticians of Canada 2006). Despite the declaration of Canada's Action Plan for Food Security and the establishment of a national Food Security Bureau, there is little evidence of support by the different levels of government in Canada, including the Assembly of First Nations, for a national strategy to achieve food security. This would necessitate agreement about policy and purposeful goal setting, indicators, benchmarks and target reductions, accountability and monitoring mechanisms, program funding, and the allocation of resources. The Action Plan lacks concrete legal measures to achieve the stated goals. While Québec is the only jurisdiction in Canada to declare, with all party support, an *Act to Combat Poverty and Social Exclusion* (2002) informed by the Québec Charter of Rights and Freedoms, its Action Plan has yet to be brought forward.

However, the most significant disconnect, or evidence of non-compliance, has been the lack of public debate about the residual burden of welfare falling on the community, families, and women, and the merits of charity versus justice in terms of addressing hunger and destitution. If Louise Arbour (2005) is right, there is little interest in connecting the dots between international obligations, constitutional protection for economic, social, and cultural rights under the Charter, and legislative action. The fact of the matter is that, in terms of food access, Canada's social safety net has been broken. Charity, rather than rights, is now the preferred response to food poverty—this despite the fact that 57% of Canadians see the problem of hunger as the responsibility of government (CAFB 2005). The extensive growth of charitable food assistance has at the same time allowed governments to look the other way while their violation of the right to food condemns growing numbers of impoverished and vulnerable Canadians to the stigma of food handouts, poor diets, and the vagaries of benevolent intentions.

What is to be Done?

In November 2004, the UNFAO Council adopted Voluntary Guidelines (VGs), informed by General Comment 12 (Eide and Kracht 2005) in support of the progressive realization of the right to adequate food in the context of national food security, and presented a framework for right to food approaches. While principally directed at countries of the South, they also have implications for rich societies such as Canada.

The VGs were developed as a human rights based practical tool to advise and assist state parties to the ICESCR to implement the right to food (www. fao.org/righttofood/ 2007). The VGs state that "the progressive realization of the right to adequate food requires states (rich and poor countries alike) to fulfill their relevant human rights obligations under international law. These include guaranteeing: the availability of food in quantity and quality sufficient to satisfy the dietary needs of individuals; physical and economic access for everyone, including vulnerable groups, to adequate food, free from unsafe substances and acceptable within a given culture or the means to its procurements." In other words, the right to food is not about handing out free food, but about enabling people to feed themselves. The VGs remind States Parties to the ICESCR of their obligations to "respect, promote and protect" the right to food (FAO, 2005). State parties should:

- respect existing access to adequate food by not taking any measures that result in preventing such access (e.g., not deny access to welfare benefits nor maintain or cut benefit levels that are insufficient for the purchase of food, clothing, and shelter);
- protect the right of everyone to adequate food by taking steps to ensure that enterprises and individuals do not deprive individuals of their access to adequate food (e.g., ensure food safety as provided for in the establishment of the Canadian Food Inspection Agency);
- promote policies intended to contribute to the progressive realization of people's right to adequate food by proactively engaging in activities intended to strengthen people's access to and utilization of resources and means to ensure their livelihood, including food security (e.g., stimulate employment, adequate minimum wages and benefits);
- and to the extent resources permit, maintain safety nets or other assistance to protect those who are unable to provide for themselves (e.g., act as provider of last resort).

In terms of international comparisons, it is reasonable to assume that the Nordic countries (Denmark, Finland, Norway, and Sweden) with advanced welfare states are more fully in compliance with these three levels of obligations. Norway incorporates the language of the ICESCR covenant into its domestic social policy legislation. However, Finland is interesting in that food banks have begun to appear in recent years though its government is said to be deeply embarrassed by this development. If the existence of charitable food banking is a useful marker of food poverty in rich countries, then it is clear that the residual Anglo-American welfare states of Australia, Canada, New Zealand, and the United States fare poorly as do the 17 countries that belong to the European Federation of Food Banks.[4]

What is important is that "at the national level, a human rights based approach to food security emphasizes universal, interdependent, indivis-

---

[4] National food bank associations belonging to the EFFB are established in: Belgium, France, Germany, Ireland, Italy, Ireland, Luxemburg, the Netherlands, Portugal and Spain, Switzerland, Greece, Czech Republic, Hungary, Latvia, Poland, Slovakia, and Ukraine

ible and interrelated human rights, the obligations of states and the roles of relevant stakeholders" and, in particular, the need to include vulnerable peoples in the processes that determine policies to promote food security (ibid 6). Right to food approaches imply a framework of national law; and in this respect it is instructive to note that countries such as Brazil and South Africa include the right to food in their constitutions. They also imply the adoption of coordinated national plans, strategies, and tools aimed at achieving food security including the setting of targets, monitoring, indicators and benchmarks, justiciable remedies, and actions engaging all aspects of the food system. In Canada, MacRae has argued this should be a nationally orchestrated and coordinated food policy directed at the optimal nourishment of the population (1999). Its first objective would be to ensure that all citizens have access to affordable, nutritious, safe, and culturally appropriate foods for themselves and their families.

For this to occur in Canada there would need to be a profound change in the way in which poverty and food insecurity and economic, social, and cultural rights are understood at the political level. Regarding the right to food, it would require a significant variation in public policy. The Canadian NGO submissions (CNS 2006), in consultation with the Canadian Association of Food Banks and Food Secure Canada for the UN Committee on Economic, Social and Cultural Rights (CESCR) at its 2006 meeting in Geneva to consider Canada's fourth and fifth periodic reviews with respect to its progress on the implementation of the ICESCR (CESCR, Canada 2006; E/C.12/4/Add.15 and E/C.12/CAN/5), set out a rights based agenda for change:

All levels of government in Canada should accept their obligations to recognize and act in compliance with the right to an adequate standard of living for all, including the right to food.

While the CESCR recognized Canada's ranking at the top of the Human Development Index of the UN Development Program and the country's high standard of living, its relatively low unemployment and certain progress in relation to Aboriginal rates of infant mortality and secondary education, pay equity for women and the extension of maternity and parental benefits, it identified a number of items of concern. A major shortcoming was Canada's restrictive interpretation of its obligations under the Covenant, in particular its position that the Covenant sets forth principles and programs rather that legal obligations and the consequent lack of awareness, in the Provinces and Territories, of the State party's legal obligations under the Covenant (CESCR Canada, 2006).

Social and economic rights, including the right to food, should be constitutionally recognized as justiciable rights under the protection of the Charter of Rights and Freedoms as well as under federal and provincial/territorial human rights legislation. In other words, for rights to have practical meaning, remedies must be available.

As former Supreme Court Justice and current UN Commissioner for Human Rights, Louise Arbour, has stated: "Ultimately, the potential to give economic, social and cultural rights the status of constitutional entitlement represents an immense opportunity to affirm our fundamental Canadian values, giving them the force of law" (Arbour 2005). In this respect, it is of more than passing interest to note that in

Norway the full text of the Covenant on Economic, Social And Cultural Rights as well as the Covenant on Civil and Political Rights and the European Convention on Human Rights has been written into Norwegian law and given priority over other Norwegian laws in the case of conflict (CESCR Norway, 2004).

Canada, in conjunction with the provincial and municipal governments and the Assembly of First Nations, should adopt a National Action Plan for Food Security requiring the full partici- pation of all relevant ministries, including federal and provincial justice departments, and with the full representation of civil society. The plan should set verifiable goals, indicators, benchmarks, timeframes and accountability.

While Canada did adopt its Action Plan for Food Security in 1998, it lacked any provisions for implementation and consultations with the provinces and territories.

The erosion of Canada's welfare state must continue to be challenged and reversed, informed by implementation of the proposed Canada Social Transfer, earmarking federal funds for provincial safety net programmes with national conditions and federal monitoring, to ensure the meeting of basic needs. These would include adequate minimum wages and income support, affordable social housing and national day care as prerequisites and provincial food security action plans.

The CESCR report paid particular attention to the absence of an official poverty line, the insufficiency of minimum wage and social assistance benefits, the clawback of the National Child Benefit, the cuts in financial support for legal assistance, the lack of national standards under the Canada Health and Social Transfer and the con- tinuing reliance on food banks.

Food policy councils should be established and food policy charters adopted at the municipal level, recognizing the human right to food and the importance of developing just and sustain- able local food systems and thereby linking food production with equitable food distribution and access.

In this respect it should be noted that food policy councils are now established in Kamloops and Vancouver (BC); Ottawa and Toronto (ON); with Prince Albert and Saskatoon (SK); Toronto (ON); and Vancouver (BC) having adopted food charters.

Civil society organizations from different sectors (anti-poverty, agriculture, education, environ- ment, health, human rights and social development) working to achieve food security within a framework of sustainability and social justice must come together and be adequately funded.

This remains a critical agenda for civil society and is at the forefront of the agenda of Food Secure Canada with its three interconnected goals of zero hunger, a sustainable food system and healthy and safe food.

Conclusion

While the right to food exists in Canada, its full realization in terms of the state's obligations as ratified in the ICESCR, and in other international instruments, leaves much to be desired with respect to meeting the basic needs of vulnerable citizens. While recognizing the complexities of domestic compliance and enforcement in a federal state, significant disconnects exist.

In terms of the compliance of social policy and programs with the Covenant, a key issue is that all levels of government across the country view the obligations as guidelines or principles and programmatic objec- tives rather than as responsibilities for ensuring the legal empowerment of the poor in obtaining their economic, social, and cultural rights. This much is evident if we consider the prevalence of food insecurity in Canada today and the fact that the hungry poor are now left dependent on the vagaries of philanthropic organizations such as food banks, reminiscent of nineteenth century charity. Furthermore, if we consider the lack of a national food policy and the failures of national and provincial welfare policy resulting in Canada's broken social safety net, it is clear that food poverty has become a local, individual, and family responsibility rather than a state obligation or matter of human rights. The social construction of hunger by the media as a charity informs and reflects the Federal and provincial governments' neglect of their obligations to "respect, protect and fulfill" the human right to adequate food.

As far as the issue of the justiciability of the right to food is concerned, the Supreme Court of Canada has to date dismissed the argument that the state has a positive obligation to take responsibility under the Charter to ensure that the basic human needs of vulnerable citizens are met. However, the issue is not dormant given the argument presented by Louise Arbour that economic, social, and cultural rights in Canada should be given the status of constitutional entitlement with the protection of the Charter. Despite the Conservative Government's recent cutting of the court challenges program, it remains essential that human rights' cases continue to be brought before the courts even though such processes are costly, prolonged and have, at least to date, seemingly poor chances of success.

A further course of action is the development of a coherent and coordinated national food policy directed at the optimal nourishment of the population. This requires a national plan of action with the full participation and endorsement of all relevant ministries—agriculture, education, environment, health and social development, as well as justice—to ensure compliance with the ICESCR and the UNFAO Voluntary Guidelines respecting the progressive realization of the right to food. The growth of a national food security movement as well as the development of regional and community food security networks and coalitions across Canada is a hopeful sign that in time such a goal is achievable. The establishment of Food Secure Canada and of food policy councils in Toronto, Kamloops, Ottawa, and Vancouver, as well as the adoption by such municipally based organizations of food policy charters, which incorporate the right to food as a framework for action, points to action by civil society and local governments to advance the case for economically viable, environmentally sustainable and socially just food systems.

Internationally ratified covenants such as the ICESCR and the CRC are intended to be applicable not only to people who live in far away places in the South but as well within the borders of Canada. While the full realization and legal enforcement of such rights are complex matters, this framework of international law provides opportunities and tools for advancing the development of social policy, public education, and advocacy for social justice.

Human rights provide a critical antidote to the excesses and failures of economic growth and greed; they also provide a strong foundation for the social work profession in its historical commitment to social justice with and on behalf of the hungry and homeless. The right to food invites new conversations about why and how we must proceed to shape a new domestic social policy and an inclusive welfare state for all Canadians in a globalized world.

References:

- Arbour, L. 2005. LaFontaine-Baldwin Symposium 2005 Lecture. Québec City.
- CAFB. 2005, 2006. *Time for Action*. HungerCount 2005 and HungerCount 2006, Annual Reports. Canadian Association of Food Banks, Toronto.
- CAPFS. 1998. *Canada's Action Plan for Food Security*. Ottawa: Agriculture and Agri-Food Canada.
- CESCR, Canada. 1998. *Review of Canada's Third Report on the Implementation of the International Covenant on Economic, Social and Cultural Rights: Responses to Supplementary Question*. United Nations Committee on Economic, Social and Cultural Rights (E/C/12/Q/CAN/1).
- CESCR, Canada. 2006. *Consideration of Reports Submitted by States Parties Under Article 16 and 17 of the Covenant*. Concluding Observations of the Committee on Economic, Social and Cultural Rights, Canada (E/C.12/CAN/CO.5).
- CESCR, Norway. 2004. *Implementation of the International Covenant on Economic, Social and Cultural Rights*. Fourth Periodic Reports, Norway (E/C.12/4/Add.14) (State Party Report).
- Che, J. and J. Chen. 2001. Food insecurity in Canadian households. *Health Reports* 12 (4). Statistics Canada, Cat. 82-003.
- CNS, Geneva. 2006. *Compilation of Summaries of Canadian NGO*. Submissions to the UN Committee on Economic, Social and Cultural Rights in Connection with the Consideration of the Fourth and Fifth Periodic Reports of Canada, April 3.
- *Delgamuukw v. British Columbia*. 1997. Supreme Court of Canada, 3S.C.R.1010.
- Dieticians of Canada. 2006. *The Cost of Eating in BC*. Annual Report 2006, Dieticians of Canada and Community Nutritionists Council of BC. Vancouver.
- Eide, A. 1999. Human Rights Requirements to Social and Economic Development, eds. U. Kracht, and M. Schultz. *Food Security and Nutrition—The Global Challenge*. (Spectrum 50), Münster, New York.
- Eide, A. 2005. The Importance of Economic and Social Rights in the Age of Economic Globalization, Ch.1. In *Food and Human Rights in Development*. Vol.1, eds. W. B. Eide, and U. Kracht. Antwerp-Oxford: Intersentia.
- Eide, W. B. and U. Kracht, eds. 2005. The Right to Adequate Food in Human Rights Instruments: Legal Norms and Interpretation, Ch. 4. In *Food and Human Rights in Development*. Vol. 1. Antwerp-Oxford: Intersentia.
- FAO. 2005. *Voluntary Guidelines to Support the Progressive Realization of the Right to Adequate Food in the Context of National Food Security*. Rome: United Nations Food and Agricultural Organization. www.fao.org/righttofood/kc/dl_en.htm.
- Gardy, J. and S. Greschner. 1989 *Food Distribution Organizations in Metropolitan Toronto: A Secondary Welfare System?* Working Papers in Social Welfare in Canada, Faculty of Social Work, University of Toronto: Toronto.
- Glendon, M. A. 2001. *A World Made New. Eleanor Roosevelt and the Universal Declaration of Human Rights*. New York: Random House.
- *Gosselin v Québec (Attorney General)* 2002 S.C.C. S4, File No. 27418 (S.C.C.)

- Heimann, C. 2004. *Hunger in Canada: Perceptions of a Problem.* Toronto: Totum Research Inc.
- Kent, G. 2005. *Freedom from Want: The Human Right to Adequate Food.* Washington: Georgetown University Press.
- Ife, J. 2001. *Human Rights and Social Work: Towards Rights-Based Practice.* Cambridge: Cambridge University Press.
- Lang, T. and M. Heasman. 2004. *Food Wars.* London: Earthscan.
- Ledrou, I. and J. Gervais. 2005. Food Insecurity. *Health Reports* 16 (3): Statistics Canada, Cat. 82-003 (May).
- MacRae, R. 1999. Policy Failure in the Canadian Food System. In *For Hunger-Proof Cities*, eds. M. Koc, R. MacRae, L. Mougeot, and J. Welsh. Ottawa: IDRC.
- NWC. 2006. *Welfare Incomes 2005.* National Council of Welfare: Ottawa, Cat. SD25-2/2005E.
- Riches, G. (1986) *Food Banks and the Welfare Crisis* Ottawa: Canadian Council on Social Development.
- Riches, G., ed. 1997. *First World Hunger: Food Security and Welfare Politics.* Basingstoke: MacMillan.
- Riches, G., D. Buckingham, R. MacRae, and A. Ostry. 2004. *Right to Food Case Study: Canada.* Rome: United Nations Food and Agricultural Organization.
- Robertson, R. E. 1990. The Right to Food—Canada's Broken Covenant. *Canadian Human Rights Year Book, 1989–90:* 6.
- Robinson, M. 2006. *A Voice for Human Rights,* Philadelphia: University of Pennsylvania Press.
- Robinson, M. 2004. *Ethics, Globalization and Hunger: In Search of Appropriate Policies.* Keynote Address, Cornell University (November 18).
- Tarasuk, V. and B. Davies. 1996. Responses to Food Insecurity in the Changing Canadian Welfare State. *Journal of Nutrition Education* 28 (2): 71–75.
- Tarasuk, V. S., G. Beaton, J. Geduld, and S. Hilditch. 1998. *Nutritional Vulnerability and Food Security Among Women in Families Using Food Banks,* Toronto: Department of Nutritional Sciences, Faculty of Medicine, University of Toronto.
- Tarasuk, V. and E. Power. 2006. *The Impact of Income on Healthy Eating in Canada.* Health Canada Policy Forum no. 60. Ottawa (March 23).
- Thomas, K. A. 2002. *The Implications of Delgamuukw to Economic Development on Aboriginal Title Lands.* Toronto: Osgoode Law School.
- UNDP. 2003. *Human Development Report.* United Nations Development Programme. Oxford: University Press.
- UNICEF, Italy. 2005. *Child Poverty in Rich Countries 2005.* Report Card no. 5. Florence: Innocenti Research Centre.
- Wallace, B., S. Klein and M. Reitsma-Street. 2006. *Denied Assistance. Closing the Front Door on Welfare in BC.* Vancouver: Canadian Centre for Policy Alternatives.
- Winson, A. 1993. *The Intimate Commodity.* Toronto: Garamond Press.
- Visser, M. 2000. *Much Depends on Dinner.* Toronto: Harper Perennial Canada.

Chapter 4

Social Justice and New Labour in Britain: An Insider's View

Wendy Thomson

The focus of this chapter is my experience in Britain in trying to make public services work to achieve social justice. The first section positions my local and central government experience in a narrative about British public services, from the Thatcher years through to the election of the Labour government in 1997 and then elaborates my contribution during Prime Minister Tony Blair's period of office. The second connects public service reform and British social democratic politics, as it brought new approaches to the challenge of social justice, human rights, social exclusion, and a new egalitarianism. The approaches were guided by theoretical perspectives about the implications of globalization for the nation state, public services, and social policy. Finally, section three examines some of the key theoretical debates in terms of the British experience and future possibilities for social justice.

I draw upon my experience working inside local and central government in England since the 1980s. In 1982, Health and Welfare Canada financed a doctoral fellowship for me to study at the University of Bristol with Peter Townsend, author of *Poverty in the United Kingdom* (1979). There, I was inducted into the British social administrative tradition at the same time as its hegemony in British social policy circles was being challenged from the New Right and the New Left. At that stage, social service managers, rather than policy per se, were my research interest.

Once out of the university, however, my social work education broadened into wider public policy and service delivery during the Thatcher years when welfare services were under attack ideologically, financially, and politically. I worked in central policy in local government—first at the Greater London Council in the mid-1980s, then at the London Borough of Islington from the mid-1980s to mid-1990s as it transformed radical policies on race, gender, and defending jobs and services into the mainstream. Finally, I was employed as Chief Executive of the London Borough of Newham, in the east end of London—one of the poorest and most racially diverse places in England.

In these positions, I was responsible for trying to make public services work, during some of the more difficult times for public services in the UK. Successive Conservative governments introduced radical changes in economic and social policy in the UK. They pursued policies designed to encourage economic growth through a market free from regulation and transfer formerly collective social responsibilities onto individuals and families. Local government, and many public services, faced large reductions in expenditure, although increased income security spending resulted from high unemployment. A rapid decline in manufacturing and industry resulted in high unemployment. However, at the same time as public spending on income support increased, personal benefit entitlements declined.

As I worked with elected politicians in inner London local authorities, the limits of oppositional politics, however radicalized, became evident. After the collapse of a campaign to oppose rate-capping and the abolition of the Greater London Council in the eighties,[1] local Labour governments in London refocused efforts on providing better public services, addressing the serious problems of low educational attainment, unfit social housing, child abuse, neglect, and dirty streets.

This was, at the same time, both a more positive and a more challenging agenda. The slogan to "defend jobs and services" was not always able to withstand a close scrutiny of the services we were aiming to defend. A commitment to race and gender equality did not always translate into more culturally appropriate services or progressive outcomes. And local democracy did not always find a hospitable environment in the tough social relations common in our housing estates. The views of many of our residents were key in challenging some of long held social policy orthodoxies.

Local State in Transition

The London Borough of Newham, where I was Chief Executive, had voted Labour for decades. Even under Thatcher, it received more than its share of national regeneration and European funding. Increasingly, however, I became skeptical about the value of simply allocating standard goods and services to people as a matter of entitlement. There was growing evidence that a strategy of reliance on the state to make the borough an attractive place to live had its limitations. One indication of the state dependency was our website, which stipulated that: "Newham: Poorest Borough in the UK" was geared to attracting public subsidy for its many needs, rather than presenting its potential for investment. Instead of highlighting deprivation, there was a need to promote our many assets, the diversity and potential of our residents, our proximity to the city of London, and the availability of building sites because of the closing of the Royal Docks and the rail industry in the 1960s.

To inform our strategy for regeneration, we commissioned an analysis of the proportion of the local economy represented by public funds (including personal income support, housing benefits, salaries paid to public sector employees) and found it was over 95%.[2] In spite of a high proportion of public spending in the borough, it was just not generating jobs or local

---

[1] In 1985, the Government instituted a limit on the rates that local authorities could set on domestic and business properties, the primary source of elected councils' discretionary revenues. This bill was opposed by a collation of inner London and metropolitan local authorities, but after a high profile context the bill was passed. In spring 1986, the Government abolished the metropolitan authorities and the Greater London Council.

[2] This analysis was done by Tony Travers from the London Government.

economic activity. Some of our residents had seen two, three, and four cycles of public sector refurbishment of their homes and neighbourhoods. Talking to local people in what became regular council "listening days," people told us: "It will be like this again in a few years; it doesn't matter how much money you put into fixing the place up … it's the people. They will just wreck it."

Some of the neighbourhoods were not socially or economically sustainable. Furthermore, some of our well-intentioned policies seemed to be part of the problem. Like many local authorities, the council had built housing estates to provide needed affordable homes (prior to Thatcher's Right to Buy policy, some borough councils in London owned as much as 80% of the rented housing stock). Social housing was allocated on the basis of the greatest social needs assessed by a point system. As affordable housing became increasingly scarce (as demand outstripped supply), units became targeted to the most in need and its tenants increasingly marginalized. Many estates had families where no one worked, some for generations. A minority of young people would attain educational qualifications. Unskilled jobs were less and less available. The informal economy provided some revenue, but not without insecurity and risk.

The council was part of the dynamic of downward spiral as it tried to address increasing areas of market failure. The local bank and even the ATM closed, then the last post office. What were people to do? The council sometimes stepped in to maintain basic services, optimistically hoping to fill the gap on a transitional basis but the future was at best uncertain. In some areas, there were no shops, making it necessary for local people to take a bus or train to buy milk or bread. The state, even at a local level, is not very good at taking over every function or activity that is "normally" provided through the market. The residents weren't particularly grateful. The council became part of the general dissatisfaction that motivated new generations of residents, as with so many previous ones, to move out of the area as soon as they could afford it.

New local strategy

Faced with a downward spiral, the council worked out a new vision and strategy for the area, rather than accepting its role as one of London's "escalator" boroughs.[3] It decided to use its power and resources to make the borough a more attractive place for people to stay and to move, rather than a destination of last resort. It decided to spend public money more like an investment than a subsidy; particularly on the west side of the borough near the financial district of London (called the City), where land had greater value and investment could be made the most attractive. When faced with a choice between spending on the poorest area or an area where its money might lever sustainable change, it favoured the latter. Rather than rationing

---

[3] From Peter Hall's work on the different roles played by different areas in London. "Escalator" areas were places where people arrived from outside at the bottom and moved out after they had become prosperous enough (i.e., when they reached the top) to move on.

scarce public goods like housing to the most in need, it created incentives to work while not discriminating against couples staying together or parents supporting children. Rather than being an excuse for poor attainment, being poor became an even greater reason for schools to support educational achievement.

Council brought a performance oriented approach to internal management and organization. This involved the introduction of measurement and monitoring results as well as the creation of information systems that could be relied upon to produce the metrics required. The new strategy challenged old welfare thinking and met opposition from some long-standing employees. Making the case, aligning the incentives, and fostering the capacity for change were an explicit task. Cross-sector partnerships were developed to improve service delivery as well as to regenerate the area around the Docks and Stratford. Although the initiatives were "homegrown" to address local issues, this kind of thinking about the state's role in promoting social justice was gaining currency beyond the boundaries of the borough.

When Tony Blair was elected, there was excitement and expectation. The Council leadership actively supported new policies like Best Value, various New Deals (for the Young Unemployed and for Communities), and Action Zones (in Health, Education, Employment). Looking to make progress without waiting for the normal central government mechanisms of new funded programs or legislative powers to kick in, the borough bid to become a "pilot" authority.[4] Newham became known for its innovation and energy, and we turned around some of the poorest services, serving its poorest citizens, into some of the best.

Best Value

Much of what I went on to do was about making sure that public services work. Best Value was a policy developed before Blair took office, to honour commitments to public sector trade unions to abolish the much hated compulsory competitive tendering (CCT) regime, without leaving Labour open to criticism of being soft on public sector productivity and effectiveness. The policy required local authorities to review all of their functions within five years, within a framework of what was called the four "C's": (i) challenge (Is the function necessary any longer? Is it addressing the right needs, in the right way?); (ii) compare (How does the service compare to that provided by other equivalent organizations?); (iii) compete (Does it compete well on costs and quality?); and (iv) consult (What do local people, community groups, and other stakeholders think of it?).

As one of the local authority "pilots," Newham embraced Best Value. It provided an external prompt to service improvement and the motivation for the council to move from defending some of its outmoded services to more openly assess our strengths and address our shortcomings. We could

---

[4] At times, the enthusiasm of central government to initiate new projects had us steering more pilots than City aiport.

determine locally how to group our functions for Best Value reviews, which ranged from conventional service structures (housing benefits, housing management, Child Protection teams) to cross-cutting themes (regeneration, the environment, social exclusion). It brought a more outward-looking focus on what residents thought, and how other sectors did things.

Best Value became law in April 2000 and it became compulsory for all authorities to review their services every 5 years (not just the pilot authorities who were doing it voluntarily). The Audit Commission was made responsible for inspecting the Best Value plans undertaken by local authorities in England and Wales and persuaded me to become their first Director of Inspection. This meant creating an approach to doing these inspections,[5] and setting up an organization, equipping premises, hiring and training several hundred staff. The experience of Best Value was mixed. It introduced challenge, brought about improvements in many services, and provided a national mechanism for turning around "failing" local authorities that were responsible for services to poor people who needed them most. Although local government's reputation for being the opposite of Best Value was often unfounded, inspection provided an independent and public assessment of performance and capacity. Where authorities supported the approach, they made the most of the opportunities for the change that it afforded and the evidence of improvement.

But with compulsion came compliance rather than innovation. Where the council leadership was uninterested, the task was delegated to operations and the focus given to ever smaller units of activity. Where that happened, the process and burden of review became disproportionate to the improvements generated.[6] We began to make the case for a more strategic approach that assessed corporate capacity of the council as a whole. When I moved into Whitehall, we were able to introduce a new policy in the Local Government Act 2001 that became known as Comprehensive Performance Assessment (CPA). By generating improvements in service and strengthening the capacity of local government that had not been performing well, Best Value provided better public services to local people. Residents' access to services became more reliable and secure. And in a way, more just.

---

[5] I was keen that our approach would promote change and retain the local character of services, rather than seek conformity to a uniform national standard. The method we developed marked a departure in many ways from national inspection being done in other areas like schools and social services. This is set out in the Audit Commission publication *Seeing is Believing* (1999). Over time, a more strategic approach characterised the Government's policy on Inspection, which I was instrumental in constructing when in the Office of Public Service Reform (OPSR).

[6] For an assessment of the first year of Best Value see the Audit Commission (2001), *Changing Gear: Best Value Statement 200*, www.audit-commission.gov.uk/reports/NATIONAL-REPORT.asp?CategoryID= &ProdID=D33284C4-1BCF-4b13-BE52-7C85EDC7413F, retrieved January 28, 2008. A longitudinal evaluation was commissioned by the then DETR (now CLGD) and published in November 2006, *The Long-term Evaluation of the Best value Regime*, www.communities.gov.uk/documents/localgovernments/ pdf/153608, retrived on January 28, 2008.

Public Service Reform

Just prior to the 2001 election, the Prime Minister asked me to work with him setting up the Office of Public Service Reform (OPSR) in Downing Street. He wanted a more effective public service, in and outside of Whitehall, building on the experience and progress that had been made in Labour's first term. It was a broad and challenging brief, but one that was hard to refuse. The OPSR articulated the common principles emerging from the Government's approach to reforming public services around the "customer" along with its emphasis on standards in a national framework of accountability, devolution to the front line, flexibility, and more choice for service users. We took on the UK's Citizen Charter standard and brought it in line with contemporary government thinking.

Staffed by people from across Whitehall, including health, education, police, local government, and some private sector, the Office developed networks and facilitated new working relationships across the delivery "landscape." We were charged with service specific projects, considered most critical to the success of reform (on primary care trusts, social care, schools, local government, and criminal justice). As a result, major changes were made in these specific service areas and cross-cutting issues such as public service inspection, pay, workforce, and tackling bureaucracy could be addressed.

The reform of the civil service was high on this agenda, and there was an appetite to involve central government departments in a more radical process of "modernisation" than had been the case in the past. Some of the attributes recognised as great strengths of the British civil service—its drafting, policy-advice, analytic skills, confidence, and enduring sense of culture – were seen as obstacles to the execution of policy that would achieve real change on the ground, in real political time. Whilst no doubt Northcote-Trevelyan[7] was an important basis for a values-driven service, it could also become an obstacle to strengthening the service's accountability for delivery. To address the concern, I designed and piloted the Departmental Change Programme to assess, independently, Whitehall departments' fitness for purpose. This approach was to prefigure the Departmental Capability Reviews introduced by the current Cabinet Secretary.

Emphasis is on delivering results, with government adopting a project management approach as more effective than the traditional bureaucratic hierarchy. Policy and legislation are not the end goal; it is their execution that matters.[8] Changes have been made in how civil servants are recruited,

---

[7] Three characteristics of the Civil Service were laid down in the 1854 Northcote-Trevelyan report, and these remain its touchstone: 1) Permanence—Civil servants do not change when ministers or governments change, they bring stability and continuity allowing new ministers to take up office easily and the process of government is disrupted as little as possible. 2) Neutrality—Permanence makes this necessary, Civil servants must be politically impartial if they are to stay in office while governments change. This does pose questions for some about its loyalty to the government of the day. 3) Anonymity—Politicians are elected to be accountable to the public for their policies, and civil servants must remain anonymous and provide advice in private.

[8] The Home Office expressed this difference when it changed its mindset from producing briefings and

appraised, and rewarded, in order to address some of the problems associated with the way government does business. The clever "amateur generalist" is giving way in some areas to experienced managers and technical or scientific specialists. Across the public service, staff are expected to take personal responsibility and work flexibly to deliver services. It is more common to see services delivered evenings and weekends, with people rewarded for extending their role to get the job done, rather than working to a negotiated job delineation.[9]

In addition, public expenditure is governed by two rules. The "golden rule" is that government only borrow to invest over the economic cycle. The "sustainable investment rule" means that public sector debt is held over the economic cycle at a sustainable and prudent level (HMT 2006, 29). Within this macro-economic framework, public sector debt has fallen from 44% of GDP in 1996–97 to 36.5% at the end of 2005–06 (HMT 2006, 30). Nevertheless, total government spending in the UK is still relatively high at 48% of national income, compared to the European average of 49%, and Canada at 39% (OECD 2006).

In 1997–98, total managed expenditure increased by just under 4% annually, with annual spending in health, education, and transport increasing at a far higher rate (HMT 2006). The priority placed on education, health, and other social services, reflected the Labour government's commitment to a "social investment" state and provided the context for improving public services and reducing social exclusion.

Putting Social Justice into Practice

The Labour government has introduced far-reaching reforms of the services most important to the public. In the short term, this has involved setting specific targets and standards for local services, allocating specific budgets to achieve them, requiring public reporting on performance and introducing independent inspection of all services. Where it was important to deliver visible impacts quickly, we set up dedicated units and allocated funding and staff necessary to deliver specific changes, such as increasing literacy or eliminating rough sleeping. The prime minister took personal leadership for 20 priorities in health, education, criminal justice, and transport, lending their delivery the authority of the office and the scrutiny of high level "stock takes" on progress.

In reality, many public service reforms under Blair, among them changes to the National Health Services, were driven by a pragmatic search for "what works." Nonetheless, some common principles emerged. Services were charged to deliver explicit standards, wherever possible expressed in a way that the public could understand (for example, you could expect to

---

legislation to actually reducing crime (a shift insufficient to save it from its ultimate demise).

[9] Whitehall departments do not directly provide many public services. Local authorities, health trusts, police services, and schools impact more directly on the public, and these were the focus of the Labour government's strategy of Investment and Reform.

see a GP within 48 hours; no one should wait more than four hours to be seen in emergency). Accountability for delivering these standards began with ministers, spelled out in the prime minister's letter of appointment, and then delegated to individual officials in central departments and local service agencies.

The principle of "contestability" probably most distinguishes Blair's thinking from that of some of his colleagues. The goal of contestability is to design systems that will be more open and adaptive to change, in which the needs of a population are assessed and services commissioned from a range of public, private, and voluntary providers. In some cases, the aim is to provide greater efficiencies and innovation; in others, the idea is to provide greater choice for service users, particularly in cases where services are not accessible or of poor quality.

Giving the public a choice of access to services is a controversial principle. It is most often opposed by trade unions and probably most misunderstood here in Canada. Although a tiny portion of public services is provided by the private sector, in health and education, it hasn't changed their fundamentally public character. Services continue to be financed by taxation and free at the point of use. There is evidence of its success with social care clients receiving direct payments to allow them to choose the services and supplier they want, with tenants choosing their social housing rather than having it allocated, and with patients choosing the location and timing of their hospital treatment. If services are to be valued by everyone, they need to be accessible to an increasingly diverse population.

Reducing Poverty

Public services are only one piece of the Labour government's commitment to social justice. There is also an impressive record on reducing poverty. Like the Canadian government, Labour made the commitment to "end child poverty within a generation." But they then executed policies to deliver, and did so in a period that had seen a dramatic increase in poverty. In 1979, 9% of working age households had no member in paid work; by 1997 more than 20% were "jobless" (DWP[10] 1999, chart 4.5) and 24% of all children were living in workless families, compared with 10% in 1979 (Hill & Waldfogel 2004, 768).

Income inequality had also risen during this period, with the proportion of people living in poverty more than doubling (using the relative measure as the proportion of families whose income was below 50% of the average).[11] from a low point of 6% in 1977 to 20% in the early 1990s (Hill & Waldfogel 2004). The increase in relative poverty had a disproportionate impact on children, 8% of whom lived in poor families in 1968 compared to 25% in the 1990s. The UK went from being amongst the more equal of the OECD

---

[10] Department for Work and Pensions.

[11] As in Canada, the UK has no official poverty line, but the relative measure of 50% average income is commonly adopted there and across Europe.

countries, in terms of income distribution, to one of more unequal and hence one of the highest relative poverty rates.

The Labour government committed to "halving the number of children in relative low-income households between 1998–99 and 2010–11."[12] A range of tax and benefit system changes were made to enable people to move out of poverty. Child benefit payments (the universal child allowance) have been increased in real terms. The Child Tax Credit provides a single system of support for families with children, payable to the mother irrespective of work status of the adults in the household. In addition, Working Tax Credit supplements have been introduced for low-income working families (with or without children), with components for disabled workers, lone parents, and couples.

The child care element of the Working Tax Credit offsets the costs of child care for low income parents who work at least 16 hours a week. In 2005–06, it was worth 70% of the first 300 GBP per week per child (in sharp contrast to the Canadian government's $100 a month). Young children in non-working families benefit from increased income support allowances, and Child Trust Funds have been introduced for all children born since September 2002—a step toward an asset-based social policy (Blunkett 2001).

Although some critics lump UK welfare reform with the US's welfare-to-work policies, they are quite different. "Work for those who can and support for those who cannot" is the slogan for combining work and benefits. In contrast to the US programs, UK policy does not involve compulsion for lone parents or any social group, apart from single people under 25. As a result of more jobs, a system of tax credits, and better alignment of income support and employment assistance, more people are in work and fewer on Income Support than at any time since the 1970s.

"Making work pay" has been central to this strategy and the first national minimum wage was introduced in 1999. The impact of the minimum wage is measured by its "bite," that is, the ratio of the adult minimum wage to the median hourly wage. According to the Low Pay Commission, since it was introduced in 1999, its bite has grown from 47.6% of median earnings to 53% (from 1999 to October 2006). As a result of these programs and economic performance, the long-term trend of rising child poverty in the UK has been arrested and reversed, against the trend in most other OECD countries. In all, 700,000 or 17% fewer children were living in poverty in 2006 than in 1998–99.

Social Exclusion

The strategy to reduce poverty has been not only about income, but also about people's opportunity to participate fully in social, political, and economic life. To make an impact on this issue requires "joined-up" government, rather than the traditional silo-based approaches associated with Whitehall departments. One of Blair's first additions to Downing Street was setting up the

---

[12] Her Majesty's Treasury (HMT). *2004 Spending Review*. Ch. 5, A Fairer Society, with Stronger Communities. Para. 5.9, 3. Accessed on May 16, 2008. www.hm-treasury.gov.uk/media/4/7/sr2004_ch5.pdf.

Social Exclusion Unit. Its brief was to develop strategies for preventing social exclusion (rather than just dealing with its effects) by ensuring that mainstream public services are delivered to the most disadvantaged people.

Since its establishment in 1998, the unit has produced over 40 reports, bringing tough social issues to the centre of government thinking. Strategies, such as neighbourhood renewal, recognized the spatial concentrations of poverty and focused investment of over 39 million GBP on areas of less than 4,000 households. Thirty-nine "New Deal for Community" partnerships were each allocated 2 billion GBP, for a 10-year period, to rebuild housing, develop employment and training, renew public infrastructure, and strengthen local services.

Public services were seen as central to neighbourhood renewal and the idea of "floor targets" was introduced to judge performance by how well services performed in the worst neighbourhoods rather than the average. The idea is to target resources and policies to the most deprived areas, shaping services to reflect local needs and "joining up" services across departments and agencies. A study produced in 2005 analyzed the impact on increases in public investment in the most deprived neighbourhoods. It showed that per capita expenditure on public services increased significantly from the least deprived to the most deprived wards. Performance on floor targets also increased, hitting the targets prescribed in previous spending reviews.

The approach to promoting social justice is multi-faceted. It has focused on improving public services, tackling social exclusion through new income security policies, and developing strategies tailored to high priority problems. The strategies are grounded in theoretical debates about how social justice is understood and pursued. Politics have been closely connected to new ways of conceiving the state, poverty, and public administration. Concepts of a risk society, reform as "adaptive work," a social investment state, social exclusion, and even a new egalitarianism lie at the heart of this thinking and bear on the social policy practice of making welfare work.

Britain's adoption of the concept of social exclusion can be understood historically and theoretically. Historically, it is part of the wider language of human rights being employed to develop global strategies to combat poverty. Social rights are enshrined in the Treaty of the European Union (1961) and the European Social Charter.[13] Similar trends can be found internationally, with the IMF, the World Bank's Justice and Human Rights Fund, and the 2005 World Summit commitment to the expansion of the UN's human rights program.[14] Theoretically, UK strategies to tackle social exclusion have

---

[13] The Charter includes a far-reaching set of rights, of which the UK has adopted 60 of its 72 provisions, including the right to adequate and affordable housing, accessible effective health care facilities for the whole population, free primary and secondary education, integration of children with disabilities into mainstream schooling, full employment policies, legal status of the child, protection of ill-treatment and abuse, legal protection of the family, the right to social security, the right to be protected against poverty and social exclusion, and the right of men and women to social treatment.

[14] The High Commissioner for Human Rights, has argued to wider recognition of the legal protection of economic, social, and cultural rights (OHCHR 2006). The Millennium Development Goals are targeted at improving

been important in bridging substantive and procedural concepts of social and economic rights, as well as showing innovation in the governance of public service reform.

The most common distinction made between poverty, as inadequate income, and social exclusion refers to: "the dynamic processes of being shut out, fully or partially, from any of the social, economic, political, or cultural systems which determine the social integration of a person in society. Social exclusion may therefore be seen as the denial (or non-realization) of the civil, political, and social rights of citizenship" (Walker & Walker 1997). This broader sense of deprivation as an absence of rights resonates with T. H. Marshall's classic essays on citizenship and social, economic, and political rights (Marshall & Bottomore 1992).

Social exclusion is systemic and structural; it implies agency and relationship. It is an act that is done by some people to other people (Byrne 1999). In so doing, it reveals the consequences for people who experience a lack of opportunity over the long-term, and allows policy to address spatial and intergenerational dimensions. Perhaps, more importantly, by understanding the problem to be in power relationships, it recognizes the agency of *both* parties. People are neither totally responsible for nor totally victims of their exclusion.

Two forms of exclusion are particularly relevant: One is exclusion at the bottom by being cut off from what societies have to offer; the other is at the top, where there is voluntary exclusion, the "revolt of the elites," a withdrawal from public institutions by more affluent groups who choose to live separately from the rest of society (Giddens 1998, 103). Giddens argues that both groups are important to social solidarity because a "welfare system that benefits most of the population will generate a common morality of citizenship" (Giddens 1998, 108). Although social exclusion at the bottom end of the social spectrum is the primary social policy focus, security of good services and broad political support requires strategies that address both ends of the social spectrum.

The concept of social exclusion is not universally accepted as a positive policy for advancing social justice (Hall 1998; Jordan 2001; Lafontaine 2000) and is seen by some as part of new Labour's abandonment of its socialist heritage. The term is also seen to obscure growing levels of poverty and inequality, and is attributed to Thatcher's period of leadership, when civil servants were forbidden to use the word "poverty" or "low income" in official documents. Others (e.g., Jordan 1996) see the term as too French with an undue emphasis on a republican ideal of social citizenship or too narrowly focused on individual rights and responsibilities rather than on interdependency and collective action.

---

well-being in the developing world and re-introducing a social element to the economic imperatives driving structural adjustment. The international movement advocating social and economic rights through the MDG has placed governance back onto the development agenda. The World Bank's 2004 annual report ("Services for Poor People') showed how little had been achieved in the Millennium Development Goals as a result of market-driven policies, and how there was a need for services (World Bank 2004).

Changes affecting class and social structure associated with globalization demand new ways of analyzing equality, and it is from this perspective that social exclusion has gained currency in the UK. Societies in the West are becoming culturally more diverse, individualistic, and less deferential. More people are employed in service and knowledge-based industries that are casualized and insecure. Though the state may not be entirely obsolete, it is undergoing fundamental change in ways that weaken the powers underpinning Keynesian economic management whilst creating the need for a new kind of governance. Seen in this way, social justice must be pursued by increasing the range of genuine freedoms rather than turning back to a so-called golden era of state collectivism for solutions. The new social democratic politics look for a new relationship between the individual and the community, and a redefinition of rights and responsibilities (Blunket 2006).

Addressing inequality and pursuing redistribution are both important in policy terms; important to reduce the threat of market inequalities that threaten social solidarity and the personal well-being of the most disadvantaged (Miliband 2005). Social justice is central to this political project and is reflected in a commitment to employment and state benefits.

Summing Up

In many respects, the British welfare state represents the golden age of social policy, a reference point for Canadian developments such as (un)employment insurance, pensions, hospital insurance, health care, universal education, child welfare, and our more timid foray into housing and child care. In the mid-nineties, however, Canada abandoned its commitment to universal social provision and federal responsibility for various cost-sharing arrangements, in the interest of reducing the fiscal burden and public debt. What the UK and Canada now share is reasonably positive economic performance. They differ, however, in relation to their social performance. Since 1997, the UK has adopted ambitious social policies to further social justice and reduce social exclusion. Accounts of Britain's track record on the social policy front are inevitably coloured by strongly held views about the Iraq war, but there are lessons that deserve more consideration.

Since its election in 1997, the Labour government has shifted the centre of British politics to the left, securing an unprecedented three terms of office. The importance of the National Health Service, public education, social housing, and even local government is receiving cross-party support as the preferred leaders of place. The Labour government has changed the discourse on public services from one of residual survival in areas of market failure, to positive social investment in universal services. And it has been delivered while improving health and education services, reducing poverty, and tackling social exclusion in the most disadvantaged neighbourhoods in the country.

The UK has enjoyed consistent levels of economic growth in every quarter of the last ten years, generating substantial additional revenues that it has invested in education, health, and other public services. The track record of combining stable economic growth with increasing levels of social investment challenges conventional wisdom that economic and social objectives are incompatible or that increased social spending is a competitive disadvantage. Reversing previous trends, child poverty has been reduced by 17%, which represents about 700,000 children and their families moving into living standards above 60% of the median family earnings. Also, inequality between the top and bottom deciles has decreased (though the very top 1% is continuing to break away from the rest).

Not everything that has been done to deliver these changes has been popular, and not every initiative has worked. Labour politicians have not always persuaded either the public or welfare professionals of their achievements, even though services have improved by any quantitative evidence one would care to consider. Access to health care has improved in waiting times for elective surgery, general practitioners, and treatment for accident and emergency. Educational attainment has increased, as reflected in literacy and numeracy at primary school and pass grades in secondary school qualifications. Violent crime and "anti-social behaviour" has decreased. Children's services have been placed at the top of the political agenda, with impressive results in early education and some improved quality in child protection (admittedly from a pretty poor baseline).

Compared to other developed countries, Britain has differentiated itself, countering theories of both anti-welfare convergence and economic determinism. It also challenges in many respects the future that Esping-Andersen projected in his classification of the UK as a liberal welfare regime. Although some of its services are now being provided through a mix of providers, they remain primarily financed by taxation and are free at the point of use. Further, an emphasis on choice and contestability of supply continues to uphold the British preference for personal freedom.

Politics and leadership matter. The overall strategy of investment and reform was explicit and provided a framework for decision-making. The first two years of fiscal restraint gave way to small initiatives rather than scaled up national programs. Pragmatic in nature rather than part of a great plan, the small initiatives allowed for innovation and provided valuable experience for the largely new ministerial team. Subsequently, as there was revenue available, it was decided to spend on key social investment priorities—education, health, and community safety—guided by benchmarking the UK against its European competitors.

Political decisions also had to be made between the programs traditionally associated with "income security," largely tax and benefit policies introduced by the Chancellor, and investment in public services, for which the Prime Minister tended to be seen as the advocate. The outcome of these decisions is in sharp contrast to the annual drive for incremental expenditure cuts that characterize other English-speaking welfare systems, including Canada.

There were also decisions, sometimes more tacit than explicit, about the pace, focus, and direction of change. A focus on targets, performance management, and independent reporting on progress generates results in the short to medium term. Good politicians recognize a good idea whose time has not come, or whose introduction will benefit the next government. Really good big ideas involving large scale reform, or even more radical new thinking about systems redesign and require time to develop, to execute, and to generate results that the public will recognize. Getting the right balance between short-term and strategic goals, while being conscious of electoral cycles but not limited to them, is a matter of political judgment.

The "Welfare Mix": Creating the Possibility of Choice

In an age where government no longer can act on its own to secure the economic and social welfare of its citizenship, a mature "welfare mix" may be a positive asset. It makes possible flexible and inclusive forms of governance as well as service delivery. Area-based regeneration initiatives, such the New Deal for Communities, require partnerships led by local people involving the whole range of public agencies (local authorities, social housing providers, social services, health care, schools, colleges, police, Job Centre plus), local business and developers, and community groups. Partnerships have also been successful in bringing together people locally to work on specific policy areas such as community safety, child care, children's services and employment.

These partnerships can strengthen communities and give voice to people who would often have no say in the governing of their neighbourhoods. They develop a shared vision for an area and harness efforts across sectors to deliver it. The additional program funds directed to such partnerships provide an incentive for agencies to agree to common priorities informed by local people. Partnerships can be more flexible structures that enable different interests to be brought together, with a specific purpose, dedicated funding, and a fixed time horizon. They provide a way of "joining up" government at a local level, without the costs and disadvantages of restructuring.

In a similar vein, welfare pluralism overcomes some of the problems associated with public monopolies. It requires an active and conscious process of assessing need, designing local policies, and commissioning appropriate services. This is in contrast to doing what we have always done, plus a bit more or a bit less depending on the financial context. This draws attention outward and engages the public and stakeholders. It can provide greater diversity in the way that services are provided, as well as involving a wider range of organizations and providers.

More responsive and better quality services can often result. In areas like residential care, social housing, employment services, neighbourhood management, and schools, a diversity of supply has provided opportunities for different communities to express different preferences and exercise choice. In this way, public services are exposed to different ways of doing things, challenging any expert tendency to see "one right way" (their way). Individual choice in education or health care may give people greater ability to decide what kind of a service they wish to receive, where, when and by whom. Groups of service users may exercise collective choice when they are able to decide the range of services most important to their neighbourhood. This could include the frequency of waste collection, grounds maintenance, or security patrols. In these circumstances, things that were one day considered impossible by one set of service providers are being done the next by others.

The move from welfare "state" to welfare "mix" may be an advance rather than part of a retreat for social justice. The "mix" provides potential to address the critiques of the New Social Movements regarding the discriminatory ideologies embodied in statutory welfare services. Of course, it doesn't resolve the contradictions of care and control, but it does diffuse these conflicts into more differentiated relationships and enriches the scope for advocacy and inclusion.

Pluralism offers benefits to professional staff and managers as well, by offering people a choice of places to work and the opportunity to develop different approaches to practice. They can experience a range of organizations in the voluntary, statutory, or private sectors. Increasingly, the pay and conditions is become more equivalent in each sector as a result of the regulatory environment for public services. There is competition for capable staff in a labour market expanding because of increased public investment and differentiated demands meeting previously unmet needs. That, too, places pressure on professions to attract new entrants (rather than repel them), and requires organizations to offer better conditions of employment. Though in periods of declining resources working inside the bureaucracy may feel more secure, this is more of an illusion than a reality with the decline of "jobs for life," even in the public sector.

Changes that have been characterized as New Public Management or marketization have also yielded progressive results. The commissioning of functions, and charging them with assessing needs and purchasing services, have made for responsive services. The disaggregating of services and the establishment of unit cost provide a reasonable basis for understanding the value of a public provision in a currency of price with which most clients are familiar.

Creating more autonomous units of activity, with budgets and responsibility for delivering a prescribed outcome or target, can establish accountability with fewer rules and bureaucratic procedures. Performance management demands clarity of purpose and measurement that has improved public services, and presses beyond simple compliance. If delivery is an overriding imperative, rather than avoiding risk or demonstrating compliance, professionals have more freedom to focus on outcomes and the best means of doing so. A performance culture has generated an appetite and capacity for better quality data in a format that enables organizational and service comparisons.

There are undoubted improvements in efficiency as a result of competition and resources have been released to reinvest in other services. In developed countries, using the public services for job creation rarely builds popular support for the cause of social justice. The opportunity to grow the service you work for or manage, through successfully competing for contracts, is an incentive.

There have also been unintended consequences and unacceptably high transaction costs as a result of some of these changes, and the right balance has to be struck between action, and recording and auditing action. Too many initiatives dedicated to tackling specific issues have been, at times, counter-productive (the proliferation of "action zones" and "partnerships" being a case in point). And the whole system has been brought into disrepute by the adverse reaction of professionals to the top down systems of accountability and by trade unions opposition to competition. But many will argue that this was a necessary phase to generate quick results and instigate improvement in an inert system.

References

- Adams, J. 2002. PSAs and Devolution Target-Setting Across the UK. *Public Policy Research* 9 (1): 31–35.
- Aucoin, P. 1995. *The New Public Management: Canada in Comparative Perspective.* Montreal: IRPP.
- Alcock, P. and G. Craig, eds. 2001. *International Social Policy.* Basingstoke: Palgrave Macmillan.
- Beatty, C., M. Foden, P. Lawless, and I. Wilson. 2007. *New Deal for Communities National Evaluation: An Overview of Change Data: 2006.* Centre for Regional Economic and Social Research: Sheffield Hallam University.
- Berthoud, R. 2001. A Childhood in Poverty:Persistent versus transitory poverty. *Public Policy Research* 8 (2): 77–81.
- Bogdanor., V., ed. 2005. *Joined-Up Government.* British Academy occasional paper no. 5. Oxford: Oxford University Press for the British Academy.
- Bradbury. B. and M. Jantti. 2001. Child Poverty Across the Industrialized World: Evidence from the Luxembourg Income Study. In *Child Well-Being, Child Poverty and Child Policy in Modern Nations*, eds. K. Vleminckx and T. M. Smeeding. Bristol: Policy Press.
- Canadian Council on Social Development. 2004. What Kind of Canada? A Call for a Debate on the New Social Transfer. *The New Social Architecture Series.*
- Dorling, D. and L. Simpson. 2001. The Geography of Poverty: A Political Map of Poverty Under New Labour. *Public Policy research* 8 (2): 87–91.
- Elson, D. 2004. Social Policy and Macroeconomic Performance: Integrating the "Economic" and the "Social." In *Social Policy in a Development Context*, ed. T. Mkandawire, 63–79. Basingstoke: Palgrave Macmillan.
- Giddens, A. 1998. *The Third Way: The Renewal of Social Democracy.* Cambridge: Polity Press.
- Giddens, A. 2000. *The Third Way and its Critics.* Cambridge: Polity Press.
- Giddens, A. and P. Diamond, eds. 2005. *The New Egalitarianism.* Cambridge: Polity Press.

- Gregg, P., J. Waldfogel et al. 2005. Expenditure Patterns Post-Welfare Reform in the UK: Are Low-Income Families Starting to Catch Up?" *Case papers.* Vol. 42.

- Halpern, D. 2005. Something for Something. Personal Responsibility meets Behavioural Economics." *Public Policy Research* 12 (1): 22–29.

- Harker, L. 2006. Tackling poverty in the UK. *Public Policy Research* 13 (1): 43–47.

- Her Majestry's Treasury (HMT). *Pre-Budget Report.* Ch. 2, Maintaining Macroeconomic Stability. Para. 2.7, 14. Accessed May 16, 2008. www.hm-treasury.gov.uk/media/7/8/pbr06_chapter2.pdf.

- Hills, J. and J. Waldfogel. 2004. A Third Way in Welfare Reform: Evidence from the UK. *Journal of Policy Analysis and Management* 23 (4): 23.

- Larsen, T. P. and P. Taylor-Gooby et al. 2006. New Labour's Policy Style: A Mix of Policy Approaches. *Journal of Social Policy* 35 (4): 629–649.

- LeGrand, J. 1982. *The Strategy of Equality.* London: Allen and Unwin

- Legrand, J. 2006. *Motivation, Agency, and Public Policy: Of Knights & Knaves, Pawns & Queens.* London: Oxford University Press

- Perri 6 Director. 2003. Giving Consumers of British Public Services More Choice: What can be Learned from Recent History? *Journal of Social Policy* 32 (2): 239–270.

- Roche, D. 2004. Choice: Rhetoric and Reality. *Public Service Reform* 11 (4): 189–194.

- H. Rose. 1981. Re-Reading Titmuss: The Sexual Division of Welfare. *Journal of Social Policy.*

- Scott, K. 2005. The World We have: Towards a New Social Architecture. *The New Social Architecture Series* 49.

- Tendler, J. 2004. Why Social policy is Condemned to a Residual Category of Safety nets and What to do About It. In *Social Policy in a Development Context,* ed. T. Mkandawire, 119–142. Basingstoke: Palgrave Macmillan.

- White, S. 2005. A progressive politics of responsibility. What would it look like? *Public Policy Research* 12 (1): 7–14.

- World Bank 2004. *World Development Report 2004: Making Services Work for poor People.* Oxford: Oxford University Press.

Chapter 5

Black Men in the Diaspora: Resilient and Surviving but Still Catching Hell

Wanda Thomas Bernard

Black men throughout the Diaspora have been labelled in the social science literature as an endangered species (Staples 1982, 1987; Gary 1982). Historically, particularly in the post slavery era, Black men have been demonized, criminalized, and perceived as a threat. Although efforts to change the status of Black people in general, and Black men in particular, such as the civil rights and post-colonial movements, have brought about some major changes, I suggest that social justice is still denied to the vast majority of Black men in the Diaspora. They are still catching hell.

This chapter explores the survival strategies used by Black men in England and Canada.

My interest in the topic is rooted in a critical analysis of thirty plus years of social work practice and my research with Black men in England and Canada. As a social work practitioner, I have been a strong advocate of social justice for all marginalized people. As a student of the civil rights and feminist movement, I have also had a special interest in anti-black racism (African Canadian Legal Clinic 2002; Benjamin 2000) and anti-racist social work. My research with Black men is a convergence of my professional work and personal commitment to make visible the plight, and the survival, of Black men in society.

In October 1995, African American Muslims, under the leadership of Minister Louis Farakhan, organized a Million Man March (MMM) on Washington, as a way of calling Black men to action and atonement, to address the "Black men problem" in America. In September, 1995, I completed a three year international study that examined Black men's experiences of survival and success in Canada and England—two countries in which they were expected to fail. In September, 2001, several colleagues and I began a five year study to examine the impact of racism and violence on the health and well-being of Black men, their families and communities, in three Canadian cities. In October, 2005, another March on Washington was organized to review the conditions and experiences of African American men 10 years after the MMM. The challenge is ongoing.

Background

The proportion of Black men in Canadian prisons ranges from two to three times their proportion in the Canadian population. Black men are disproportionately likely to be stopped by police, arrested, held in remand, charged, held without bail, imprisoned, given atypically long sentences, and denied parole (Davis-Wagner and LaVerne 2000; Razack 1999; Canada 1998;

Nova Scotia 1989). The cost to public health and criminal justice systems increases each year (Oliver 2000). The consequences for Black men's well-being and the well-being of their families and communities are inestimable.

Media representations of Black masculinity define the future of Black youth as entwined with the criminal justice system, violence, and addictions (Benjamin 2000; James 1998). This builds an environment where children, youth, adults, and elders are witnessing and surviving the normalization of violence within the community, as well as the violence of racism from outside the community.

With Whiteness as the normative standard, the mass media and popular culture have been consistently implicated in constructions of a hegemonic Black masculinity that centres on violence, addictions, and criminal justice involvement (Barlow 1998; Benjamin 2000; Connell 1995; Ferguson 2000; Gilliam and Iyengar 2000; Hagedorn 1998; Hooks 1994b, 1990; James 1997; Robinson 2000; Schiele 1998; Staples 1982). In part through the racist-sexist construction of Black masculinity, in part through the omnipresence of White racism (Feagin 1995), Black youth may adopt a stance of rebellion or posturing that leads to stereotypes of "uppity Blacks" (Kelly 1998). The prevalent sources of identity for young Black men are infused with aggression and violence (Barker 1998; Bennett and Fraser 2000; Burton 1997). Given the barriers that block full economic participation, some Black men continue to define their masculinity through alternative means—which may include violent activities (Hatchett, Black & Holmes, 1999; Imani, 1998). This violence inevitably affects the lives and life chances not only of Black men, but also of their families and communities.

Although individual experiences of blatant racism may provoke critical incidents or cause immediate trauma, they are less common than the complex intersecting systems of oppression that include institutional and systemic racism, social class relations, gender inequalities, and nationalism (Bolton 1999; Collins 1998; Henry et al. 1999). Philomena Essed's (1991) concept of everyday racism captures the ways these structures of oppression affect the everyday lives of people of African descent. While some may see these everyday acts of racism as trivial, the detrimental impact lies in their overwhelming repetition, and their cumulative burden, both historically and currently. The aggregate burden of everyday racism arises not only from experiences of the individual, but also from the experiences of friends, loved ones, and communities.

Despite these realities though, it is well-documented that some Black men and youth do resist involvement in violence, even if they are less able to resist the violence of racism (Barker 1998; Bernard 1996). This chapter explores the ways in which Black boys and men successfully resist hegemonic representations of masculinity, drawing out the factors that contribute to the strength and resilience of individuals, families, and communities (Barbarin 1993; Fine and Weiss 1998; Hooks 1994a; Miller and MacIntosh 1999; Zimmerman et al. 1999; Bernard and Este 2005). The resilience that helps explain the ability of some youth to resist engagement in violence where it is considered "normal" activity among their peers arises from Africentric values, strong families, and connection to church and school (Miller and MacIntosh 1999; Barker 1998; Bernard and Este 2005; Fine and Weiss 1998; Hill 1998b). Similarly, research has documented the importance of such social and relational networks in healing from witnessing and surviving violence including the effects of incarceration and the grief of losing family members to death or the legal system (Jones 2000; Terrell 1998; Rasheed 1998, 1999; Rasheed and Johnson 1995). The shared vision is that an Africentric framework focues on the strengths of Black communities rather than pathologizing them.[1]

Context

African-Canadians are marginalized in terms of income and occupational status (Mensah 2002; Bernard and Bernard 2002; Este and Bernard 2003). Bernard and Bernard (2002) also argue that the history of marginalization and oppression, in addition to the systemic barriers to social and economic resources and power, has had a devastating impact on the emotional and psychological well-being of African-Canadian people. Similarly, Este and Bernard (2003, 326) assert that: "Poverty, high unemployment, underemployment, and lack of education and marketable skills are symptomatic of the reality of the social, economic, and political exclusion experienced by African Canadians. The unemployment rate for Canadians of African origin is one and a half times higher than that for the total population. This community has the lowest rate of self-employment of all racial groups."

The economic status of African Nova Scotians can be bleak. Este and Bernard (2003, 326) argue that "there is a lack of support for Black businesses and the low business—participation is tied to high unemployment. Although the youth unemployment rate in Canada is high, the rate for African-Canadian youth is even higher, particularly for males, who continue to drop out (or be pushed out) of public school at an alarming rate" (Dei, Mazzucca, McIsaac, and Zire 1997). No business sector exists in the African Nova Scotian community to assist youth who are unemployed and unskilled.

---

[1] Without an Africentric perspective, public health research is typically focused on African-American involvement in interpersonal violence (Farquharson 1995). The public health costs of racial discrimination are unknown. As Krieger and colleagues note, existing epidemiological literature on race, class, violence, and health assumes racial differences in disease can be explained in genetic or economic terms without considering noneconomic aspects of racism, especially the stress resulting from discrimination (Krieger et al. 1993). Yet it is clear that discrimination and violence lead to poor individual health outcomes (Wilkinson et al. 1998). African-American children exposed to community violence report high levels of distress, with untold consequences in their later lives (Li et al. 1998). Thus, if we understand racism as a form of violence, and racism as a "socially induced stress" (Imani 1998) that may lead Black men and youth to resist oppression through their own forms of aggression, we can also assume racism and others forms of violence deleteriously affect the health of Black men and their communities—in spite of the positive effects of the social supports available in Black communities (Brown, Gary, Greene, and Milburn 1992). The impact of the violence of racism on Black communities throughout the diaspora can be seen in the cycle of unequal access (Christensen 1998; Bernard 1996; Small 1994), their economic marginalization, and the persistent high rates of unemployment and underemployment (Pachai 1990; BLAC 1994; Este and Bernard 2003; Mensah 2002).

Christensen (1998) sums up the reality of the African-Canadian experience as a *cycle of unequal access* and argues that extraordinary interventions are required if the *cycle of psychological trauma* that results from such limitations is to be changed. As Christensen (1998) suggests, many get caught in a cycle that leads to low self-esteem, a sense of hopelessness, internalization of oppression and racism, anger, anxiety, and the destruction of self and others. The cycle of exclusion and unequal access has a devastating impact, as Este and Bernard (2003, 236) maintain that "African Nova Scotians are at a greater risk of major health problems such as diabetes and hypertension as well as family and social problems, including violence and abuse."

Similar stories are repeated in other countries. Black men are among the highest of the unemployed, particularly young Black men. In *Racialised Barriers* (1994), Stephen Small reports that the unemployment rate for Black men in America is more than twice as high as White men, and Black men tend to be unemployed for longer periods of time. Furthermore, during the 1980s, White men and women were more likely to be employed than Black men and women. In Britain, African-Caribbeans have higher unemployment rates than Whites and other ethnic groups, other than Pakistanis and Bangladeshis. According to the Labour Force Surveys (1981–89), among African-Caribbeans aged 16–24, the unemployment rate was over 30%, about four times the rate for White youth (Brown 1992). At the time of my study in Sheffield, the unemployment rate for Black men was one third higher than White men.

Given these statistics, what impact does the need and/or desire to work have on the survival of Black men who are unable to find employment? Sivanandan (1982) refers to the young unemployed in Britain as the never employed. He describes their quest for freedom and dignity as a "different hunger." By contrast, in our sample of forty individual interviews, the majority were employed. There is an explanation for this. A strong work orientation was identified by Hill (1971) as one of the strengths of Black families. This view is also evident in British studies. Drew et al. (1990) found that there was a strong tendency for young Black people to stay on at school or college. Regarding continuing studies, Black people have been found to be persistent in the pursuit of qualifications (Eggleston et al. 1986). As a consequence, some Black people are more likely to be underemployed and underpaid than unemployed (Jones-Johnson 1989). While most of the men in my study were employed, many were over-qualified for the jobs they were doing.

Generally, failure for Black men in western society gets defined in terms of how they compare with white men on "success" indicators such as education, employment, and social class position. Failure is perceived as an "under representation" in "successful" positions, and an "over representation" in negative, stereotypical roles and positions. Their overrepresentation in some positions and under-representation in high profile positions have been largely interpreted as their problem. However, the structural barriers imposed by a system of racism, and domination rooted in patriarchy, are rarely examined as the root causes of "the Black men problem." Many Black men internalize such negative stereotyping and work to fulfill the ascribed roles (Farquharson 1995). On the other hand, as Hunter and Davis (1994, 37) argue, although Black males may be at risk for a number of social and economic ills (Hunter and Davis 1994, 37), they also survive.

Survival and Success

Stolenberg (1989) says that one identifies oneself in relation to other men, using some imaginary scale of masculinity. For African descended men, that scale of masculinity is imposed from within, and socially constructed. Normative definitions of masculinity have historically been outside their grasp. Harris (1992) states that African-American men are in multiple jeopardy, and have historically been under attack. As a result, many have argued that Black men have developed highly exaggerated expressions of masculinity, in order to compensate (Staples 1982, 1987; Majors and Billson 1992; Benjamin 2000; Gary 1981; Hooks 1994b; Farquharson 1995). Few studies have actually asked Black men to define themselves, or to assess their strengths.

In my exploratory study with "successful" Black men, I attempt to reveal some of the ways in which Black men survive, using successful strategies and overcoming barriers in an often hostile environment.[2] The study is based on research in two very different locations in the African Diaspora. A total of ten men from Sheffield and Halifax participated in a Research Working Group (RWG) in their home location, and the two groups came together on two occasions. The working groups directed the entire research; they designed, administered, and transcribed the questionnaires; participated in the data analysis; and edited the final report. Forty individual interviews were conducted, twenty in each site, with Black men aged 19 to over 65, the majority between ages 26 to 45. In addition, two focus groups were held in Halifax (HFG) and three in Sheffield (SFG). The RWG members were also interviewed, and collectively worked as two focus groups.[3]

Participatory research, with an Africentric theory base, is an effective tool for exploratory research with Black men of African descent.[4] Participatory research emphasizes the active involvement of "subjects" as key. Ownership of the problems and proposed action strategies rest with them. Through the research, they engage in an exploration of successful strategies they used to

---

[2] The concept of success is discussed in more detail later in the chapter.

[3] The data were analyzed with the assistance of a qualitative data analysis program called *Text Based Alpha*, and the grounded theory method. The focus groups, the conferences, and the joint RWG meetings served as multiple opportunities to conduct member checks to test the accuracy of the data and analysis. Triangulation of data collection and data analysis helped to establish trustworthiness, face validity and catalytic validity (Lather 1991).

[4] For a fuller discussion on Africentric Theory see Asante 1987; Collins 1990; Schiele 1994,1999; Bernard 1996; Akbar 1984).

survive in an often hostile and unfriendly environment. They begin a process of re-defining masculinity and success from an Africentric perspective.

The study builds on my previous work with Black men about survival and success; about their role as fathers; their involvement in the criminal justice system; and about their involvements in their families and communities.[5] The study provides a rare opportunity to engage the African-Canadian community in research that has direct relevance. Using mixed methods, we are investigating the impact of witnessing and surviving individual, collective, and institutional racism and violence on Black men, their families and communities. Our goal is to develop health education materials and policy directions concerning racism as a determinant of health.[6]

Survival Strategies

Eight survival strategies were identified through the data gathered in the *Survival and Success* study: racial identity; positive role models and mentors; strong racial and political consciousness; positive personal values and supportive relationships with family and friends; ability to set and work towards goals; attaining education and marketable skills; finding and maintaining employment; and spirituality. These are each briefly discussed below, augmented by first voice quotations:

1. *Racial identity*: 75% of the research participants from the two sites indicated that the development of positive racial identity, through connecting with African principles and beliefs, and with others in the Diaspora, was a survival strategy that Black men used. This includes: the development of love and respect for oneself and others; a positive value system; and a connection with a Black African community culture:

"... go past slavery and look at our successes in Africa. We have a strong cultural background in our African heritage." (Halifax)

"... this [survival] can only come from a strong inner value system ... staying Black in the white man's arena ... not selling out, and being proud of who you are ..." (SFG)

"The internal network. Black men use friends, brothers, sisters for support and contacts to survive in this society. Black men survive by sticking together ..." (Sheffield)

2. *The presence of positive role models and mentors* was identified by 90% of the participants, in both sites, as a key survival strategy. Role models come from all walks of life, but the critical point is that they must be accessible. Black men want role models whom they can emulate. Mentors are considered special role models who provide a positive influence and standard of

---

[5] The full title of this project was "Caught at the intersection: Working with the impact of witnessing and surviving individual and systemic violence on the health and well being of Black men, their families, and communities."

[6] We are currently completing data analysis from a quantitative survey (900) and in-depth qualitative interviews (120).

conduct for young people (Wilson 1991). Mentors usually have a special relationship:

> "The most significant to be [role] models are those who are visible; those who are readily available, and accessible in the community. Role models are required to be caring and supportive and are expected to be responsible in terms of how they conduct their personal and work lives. ... If role models cannot be mentors, then the relationship does not work." (RWG memo)

> "A role model is someone you can look upon, not to copy, but to know you can get to where they've got ..." (HFG)

> "We can help make a difference by being a mentor and role model for the youth. As young Black men, we must try to encourage the younger ones, by giving back to them." (SFG)

> "If Black men can provide negative influences, then they can provide positive influences by diverting their energies. Even without full opportunity, Black men have potential. Couple that with motivation and you have a positive role model." (Sheffield)

> "If our elders put forward positive images, young people will adopt those ... even though sometimes they appear to resist, especially in their teens." (Halifax)

As is evident from these first voice accounts, role models and mentors are crucial to young Black men on the journey to successful transition to manhood.

3. *The development of a strong racial and political consciousness* was also named as a survival strategy, by the majority of participants. African people in Western societies have had to develop a strong political and racial consciousness and ideology to effectively combat the destruction of colonialism, slavery, racism, and discrimination. This awareness is used to develop strategies for individual and collective action to challenge and change our position vis-à-vis the rest of society. This is evidenced in individual acts of resistance, as well as local and more broad-based collective action and community organizing.

> "Black people ... are strong. Our experience has taught us to be strong, mentally and physically. ...We fight for change, we fight the system and to win things. For example in Sheffield ... we had to fight to get Black workers in the Local Authority ..." (Sheffield)

> "Part of surviving is dealing with racism. I constantly have to deal with racist issues in my work situation ..." (Halifax)

> "Black men forge links with other Blacks or conscious white people... this is an important survival strategy. ...We have to be part of a political struggle ..." (Sheffield)

> "Survival for Black men is the ability to not be suppressed by all the negative connotations that society imposes on Black men. ... Surviving in today's society means reclaiming the ability to be self-sufficient and claiming a structure that will enable Black men to have a voice in the decision making process ..." (Halifax)

Engaging in a political struggle is seen as important as the awareness of the need to do so. Poussaint (1987) argues that the experiences of Black men are unique because they stimulate different responses, such as fear and hostility from white society. Consequently, it is necessary that they organize and take the lead to do something about their situation. He suggests that Black men make themselves a specific targeted issue. Without the framework of an organized civil rights or Black resistance struggle, individual, and collective efforts at Black liberation go unrecognized (Hooks 1988).

Clearly then, there is a need to be part of a larger struggle. While the political organizing for social justice and equality is seen as necessary, most people recognize the challenge and difficulties in being able to do this. Sheffield's Black Community Forum opines that the development of a unified Black political voice is the best way forward. Many of the participants in this study would agree with this argument, which was further developed by Stephen Small who said:

> "We need a Black Agenda for the Black Community. ... A Black Agenda is a statement of intention of our goals, priorities, and actions needed to achieve them. A Black Agenda will enable us to analyze our predicament, conceptualize and write a program to escape from it; draw up a set of policies, short-term, medium-term and long-term, and establish a line of action for implementing this. We must also identify our allies. All of this must be done in the context of the prevailing circumstances. Only in this way, it seems to me, can we move from a situation in which we are struggling for survival, to one in which we can strive for success."

The fight for social justice for Black men is a collective struggle rooted in a clear racial and politicized consciousness.

4. *The development of positive personal values and supportive relationships with family and friends* was also identified by all participants as an important survival strategy. The men who were interviewed stressed the significance of displaying positive values in all aspects of one's life. In addition, the role of the family was probably identified as the most important. Participants named all family members as contributing to their survival, including extended family. However, the role of the mother was undoubtedly the most highly valued by most participants in both sites. As one participant said:

> "My family has been my survival. I would not have made it without them. Beginning with my parents, my grandparents, my siblings, now my wife and our children. They have all helped me tremendously." (Halifax)

> "My family has had an incredible influence on my survival. Overall, they have been extremely positive, and have helped me to negotiate my way through life successfully." (Halifax)

Considering peers and social relationships, the men identified feeling good about being able to relate well socially and with friends; being with positive, like-minded people; being respected, and the ability to be oneself. Racial pride, and satisfaction with oneself and community appear to be common factors here.

> "To be respected. To be recognized as a good friend. Also to be socially conscious. To feel compassion and to understand what is going on in other parts of the world ..." (Halifax)

"At home and socially, I enjoy quality time with other Africans who reflect positive self-images and values. Being able to socially interact with Africans irrespective of education or background. Loving people as they love me, and loving my people." (Sheffield)

Having supportive relationships with family and friends forms a buffer for Black men's survival in an otherwise often hostile and unfriendly environment.

5. *The ability to set, and to work towards goals* was seen as a vital component of Black men's survival. The ability to dream, to set realistic goals, and to work at attaining those was seen as key to survival and success. These men have stated that in order to survive, they have to first have a dream, an ambition, a goal, then work to realize those dreams and goals.

It has been said that one of the most damaging impacts of racism on the individual psyche is that those who are targets of racism are unable to dream, or their dreams are deferred. It has also been stated that those who "fail to plan, plan to fail." In other words, if you have no dreams, no goals, then you will never know if you have reached your full potential. Yet, for Black people, a direct consequence of racism is that dreams, goals, and hopes are frequently outside our control.

"Racism is a very destructive force morally, and emotionally. It stops you from growing, developing as you should, as you are always on the defensive ... it has kept us from achieving our goals. ... Racism destroys our ambition, our will to succeed. Some give up, because they know it is always there ..." (Sheffield)

However, in our examination of Black men who have managed to successfully navigate their way through an unwelcome environment, the ability to dream, to set goals, and to work at attaining those was identified as a survival strategy. This is one of the means used by these men, to help them survive. The emphasis here is on realistic, attainable goals, as the setting of unrealistic goals can be a source of frustration and anger, and can have a negative effect on one's self-esteem. From the data we learned that Black men place a high value on goal setting and attainment, which contradicts Dickson's (1993) thesis that Black men tend to focus on both realistic and unrealistic goals because they take survival issues for granted (my emphasis).

"Black men survive by ... setting realistic goals for themselves." (Sheffield)

"... knowing what one wants out of life and using whatever means necessary, within reason, to survive. Being strong and determined to press on, to get what he wants." (Halifax)

6. *Attaining education and marketable skills* was identified by 90% of the participants as key to survival. However, all participants described their educational experiences as negative in some way, and most have achieved against the odds. Self motivation has been identified as the most significant factor in these individuals experiences. They have identified many blocks

and barriers that they have had to overcome in order to achieve a quality education and marketable skills. Many are overqualified for the jobs they are doing, and many have trained in more than one area. This was more likely to be the experience in Sheffield, than in Halifax. Many described education as "the key to our survival." Hill (1972) has identified this strong orientation to achievement as one of the strengths of Black families.

> "The most important thing is for Black people to get an education; both academic and social, political education." (Sheffield)

> "Education is crucial. I don't think that there is anything greater or more important to the survival of Black men." (Halifax)

> "The school system itself de-motivates them. You spend the largest part of your life there from age four to sixteen and they just destroy you. If you do well, they find ways to kick you out. If you do have a career in mind, they put you down and discourage you. Everything is set up to discourage you, the whole British system. If you are lucky enough to go to a school with a lot of Black children, that school gets a bad reputation; White people take their kids out, and the school gets under-resourced. In England it used to be all White, they never expected us to stay." (Sheffield)

> "The school system itself is a de-motivator for young Black men. Nothing there encourages them ... largely its white teachers who make them feel stupid if they come from a different background with different social skills as compared to their White counterparts. They often don't take an interest in the Black male student, unless he excels in sports. There are not enough positive role models around. There are too many young Blacks who are not going to school, are hanging out. If you leave school you will be amongst your buddies. You are the exception if you stay in school and do well. Peer pressure to "not do well" is probably the worst hurdle ..." (Halifax)

Despite such negative experiences in education, Black men in this study repeatedly emphasized the significance of education and skill building for their survival.

7. Finding and maintaining employment, or creating self-employment were identified as key elements of survival for Black men. Having a job and being able to stay employed was seen as very important. Self-employment was seen as a positive alternative in this economic climate, however, participants also recognized the costs associated with this. Participants also talked of the pressures that Black men have to deal with in employment settings. So, whilst maintaining employment was seen as a survival strategy, participants also identified the barriers to getting employment, those faced when there, the blocks to advancement and the stress that these create, as issues that need to be addressed.

> "The Black man must, in my eyes, work harder than the white man. He must be always covering his back to ensure that everything is done right and not take anything for granted." (Halifax)

> "Being aware and very knowledgeable about the job; being aware of the struggles of Black people; working harder; placing greater expectations on oneself; and engaging in efforts to upgrade the status of all Blacks in the work force." (Sheffield)

Although the majority of the participants identified major issues and factors relating to racism related stress in their employment experiences, they also stressed the fact that having meaningful employment was key to their success.

8. *Spirituality* was identified in the research as a significant survival strategy. Defined in the research as the essence of our survival, our being, participants in the interviews and the two conferences stated that spirituality is that which keeps us sane, whole, and keeps us committed to working through the struggle. Participants stated that it is spirituality that helps Black people cope, resist, survive, and succeed. However, participants also expressed concern that this was becoming lost in the next generation. The older respondents were more likely to name spirituality as a source of strength, than were the younger men. Clearly, the survival strategies named by Black men who participated in this research reflect a caring, sensitive, and goal-oriented focus towards life. These values and qualities are reflective of a much different view of Black men, and Black masculinity.

> "... Spirituality is reflected in all that we do ... in all that we are. ... It is not just about going to Church, but about the belief in a higher power that keeps us strong and keeps us going through even the most difficult times. ... I don't know where I would be if I did not believe ..." (Sheffield)

> "... I thank God every day for keeping me on the right path. I believe that, more and more, Black men are moving away from the spiritual beliefs and teachings, and that is leading to a lot of destruction. We need to do something about this ..." (Halifax)

These eight survival strategies were consistent across the two continents, despite the vastly different histories, origins, and length of time in the respective countries. These are all positive, enabling strategies that help Black men to resist negative stereotypes about Black masculinity and reconceptualize what it means to be successful. The emphasis is on positive identity, values, and responsibility for self, family, and community, rather than competition and domination. Such values are rooted in the definition of success that emerged in the research.

Africentric Definition of Success

One of the more significant findings in this research was the way in which success was redefined by Black men across two continents. At the outset, a successful Black man was defined as one who had achieved, or was working towards a set goal(s), using positive, constructive means and was maintaining these. He was considered to be a man who managed to overcome the barriers in a racist society, and managed to survive. In this research, Black men described success and successful Black men in terms of values, not in terms of the material possessions usually associated with success in white society, particularly the standards set by white men and hegemonic notions of masculinity.

The men who participated in the study adopted a set of positive strategies for survival and re-defined success. They debunked the normative definition of success, and the perception that Black people have to assimilate in order to succeed. David Divine summed it up nicely in his keynote speech at the Sheffield conference when he said: "keys to success are not related to money or influence or sexual conquest, but to common, taken for granted values such as respect, time for self and others, integrity, being open to others, and loving oneself and others" (Bernard 1996, 130).

The way in which Black men have redefined success, by placing themselves in the centre of the discussion, is consistent with the theory of africentricity (Asante 1988), and the Africentric value system as developed by Karenga (1978). Examination of the data from an Africentric feminist perspective revealed that Black men's definitions of success reflect the practice of Africentricity through their lived experiences of the Africentric value system, Nugzo Saba, and their survival strategies. These values are based on the principle of collective struggle, resistance, and unity. These are the models of success that Black people should aspire to, to help break the cycle of psychological trauma from persistent and everyday racism.

A clear picture emerges. We need to let go of class based divisions and categories in our society, and focus attention on those aspects of ourselves that we have ultimate control of: self-respect, identity, and self-image. We have to create filters that are positive and alternative to those offered in society at large. What I am talking about can be compared to what we have done with racial identity, in the shedding of white society's definitions of beauty and cultural ethos ... the movements that have brought us to where we are today, enable us to discard those externally imposed definitions of who we are. The findings in this research suggest that we have to go through a similar process regarding how we define success.

The process must begin with discarding those externally imposed indicators and measurements of success, and create a new image of what success means for African people. An Africentric definition of success is not just about self-achievement and attainment, but a recognition that many contribute to one's success; one is only successful if one is contributing to someone else's success. The African proverb: I am because you are; you are therefore I am, aptly sums up this concept. These Black men are resilient and are surviving; yet, we know that many Black men are still catching hell.

Racism and Violence

One follow-up project that emerged from the study of survival and success is a five year pan-Canadian study on racism, violence, and health that examines the impact of racism and violence, including the violence of racism, on the health and well-being of Black men, their families, and communities. Our initial questions began by asking the following: What is the impact of racism and violence, including the violence of racism, on the health and well-being of young Black men, their friends, families, and communities? How do some resist being drawn into cycles of violence and addictions? And what can we learn from this resistance to develop programs for prevention, intervention, and healing?

Research shows that exposure to racism results in stress, which results in all our physical and psychological systems going on high alert (Wilkinson et al. 1998; Kreger et al. 1993). How an individual, a family, or a community responds to this situation—our coping responses—can either have a positive or a negative effect on our health and well-being (Imani 1998). And, like everything else, our coping responses are affected by our histories of systemic racism.

The largest body of research looking at the effects of racism related stress focus on high blood pressure. We know that high blood pressure, or hypertension, is a major health problem in Black communities. We also know that African descent people in North America have more problems with high blood pressure than European Americans even when family medical history is taken into account. Researchers know that the blood pressure of Black people changes more dramatically in situations of ordinary stress and of racism-related stress than does the blood pressure of non-Black people. And some researchers believe that ongoing temporary instances of heightened blood pressure lead to long-term high blood pressure (Kreger 1998).

Because of historical oppression, many Black people feel they need to be constantly vigilant. In the article about the Jackson Heart Study, the authors say:

> Being guarded or on guard keeps a person safe. It's a kind of listening with one's whole being, a speaking that interprets the intentions of the speaker and gives back what I think you want to hear, and as such keeps me at a distance and assures my safety. The danger lies in [that] seeing even the most innocent, trivial comments or gestures as profoundly racial [places] one at risk for increased reactivity and hypertension. On the other hand, denial of racism as a source of stress may also increase hypertension. (Wyatt et al. 2003, 324)

There are many responses to perceived racism: denial, self-blame or internalized racism, vigilance, resistance, and acceptance. We probably have all of these responses at different times. Research is beginning to look at the consequences of different responses. In general, what has been found to date is that "the more passive or internalized the coping style, the higher the blood pressure" (Wyatt et al. 2003, 325). We can think about it as "daily wear and tear" on all the physical and mental systems. We also know that we can't look just at the biological or just at the social—we have to consider that African-Canadians embody the effects of racism, from birth to death.

Here are some demographic highlights of the sample of the Black population in Halifax, Calgary, and Toronto, looking specifically at education and income levels, and the relation to participants' experience of racism-related stress. Beginning with education, we found that the proportion of the Black population in Toronto and Calgary with less than a high school education is 20% and 18% respectively, which is essentially the same as the total population (22% and 19%). However, the Halifax Black population has 28% with less than a high school education, which is 7% more than the city average. A gender analysis of this data reveals that 32% of the men, compared to 25% of the women, have less than high school. The significantly lower levels of education in Halifax, especially among the men, is understandable once one understands the context of the Black experience in Nova Scotia, as previously discussed in this chapter. It also illuminates the continuing struggle for Black men to resist and survive in societies where they are expected to fail.

In Halifax, although 23% of Black men, and 29% of Black women have some post-secondary education, both are significantly below the city average, which is 35%. In Toronto and Calgary, 31% of the men have some post-secondary education, which is much higher than the Halifax men. We can make certain inferences here about immigration, and who is allowed into Canada. Many immigrants from Africa and the Caribbean come in pursuit of higher education, many pursuing the immigrant dream. How does the experience in education affect employment? In our study we found that for those in the middle aged group (35–45), 40% of the men make less than $20,000 per year or have no reported income. The numbers are a bit better for men in the same age group in Calgary and Toronto, where 25% and 32% respectively make less than $20,000 per year or have no reported income. For those Black men from Halifax in our sample earning $20,000–$39,000, the percentage is the same as the general population. However, those in Toronto, and more so in Calgary, earn significantly less than the general population. Most striking are the higher income groups, where, in all three cities, Black men have significantly less income than the general population.

From these data, we can infer that Black men continue to face systemic barriers in education that has a direct link to their experiences in the labour market. This then sets the stage for an exploration of the experiences of racism and racism-related stress as reported in the study.

Racism-Related Stress

Thirty-two percent (32%) of men report a medium degree of racism-related stress. The same percentage report a low degree of racism-related stress, and 36% report a high degree of racism-related stress. Taken together, 68% report medium to high degree of racism-related stress. Looking at blatant racism, in each of the three sites, there are no significant differences between men and women in the reporting of the degree of stress from blatant racism. Those in the younger age group (18–34) report the highest degree of racism-related stress.

Men in all three cities report a similar level of blatant racism-related stress, 37% to 39% except for one item in the scale, others' reacting as if afraid or intimidated, where Toronto men report significantly higher stress. This is interesting in light of the response to the frequency of this experience. Halifax men report a higher frequency of others' reacting as if afraid or intimidated (20% say once a week or a few times a month) compared to Toronto (15%) and Calgary (15%), but it causes them less stress. Toronto men are sensitized to their being perceived as a threat—perhaps because of racial profiling and the Jamaicanization of crime (Benjamin 2000).

Fifty percent of the young people surveyed say they feel they are treated suspiciously, rudely, and disrespectfully because of their race. Fifty percent say they are being observed, or followed in public, or that they are being ignored or overlooked, or not given service. Fifty percent also say they believe they are being treated as if they are "stupid." Both young men and women say that others react to them as if they are threatening or intimidating. Youth say that racism bothers them "a lot." Youth's most frequent way of coping is by talking to their peers. And yet, despite their rejection of their elders' way of dealing with racism (spirituality, faith, social justice, and political change), the youth who are most likely to succeed in education and employment are those who have some attachment to a spiritual or religious community.

Income has a significant impact on mental health for both Caribbean and Canadian Black respondents, but not African. Those with the highest income do not report the greatest mental health—that comes at the middle income. The racism related stress experienced by Africans in Calgary due to racism-related stress in employment, and financial difficulties experienced by family members, are extremely high and significantly different from that experienced by Caribbeans.[7]

Racism and Health

Racism is a determinant of health, and it's a determinant of health not only for individuals, but also families and communities. Physical health conditions that arise directly from stress are hypertension, heart disease, and poor mental health; indirectly they include diabetes, breast cancer, and prostrate cancer. One man who immigrated to Toronto 25 years ago stated that racism is a "poisonous, chilly, poisoned environment." Without protection from this poison, "you can die." Another man said of the environment in which he lives everyday: "The neighbours look at you differently just because you are Black. On the subway. On the train. As soon as you walk into the train you can see other people giving you a sign of not coming close to them"

An African-born man could not believe the degree of hate he felt directed at him, not anything about him personally: "It's like they are actively trying to exclude me and keep me out of the way or keep away from me or keep their daughters away from me. ... Racism is when somebody hates me so much that they're willing to take action against me ... I think it is more about ignorance ... people just trying to take the easy way out by using a stereotype instead of looking at the person and investigating, 'OK, who's this person?'"[8]

---

[7] Employment: 49% African compared to 31% Caribbean; Financial: 50% African compared to 37% Caribbean

[8] The impact of racism related stress can also be seen in family breakdown. Many of the male participants in

Similar to the Jackson Heart Study (Wyatt 2003), participants who experienced racism in the Canadian study felt there was a strong link between their mental and physical state of health. They reported a major difference in their health status before and after being subjected to racial discrimination. When asked about the impact of racism on their health and well-being, many participants talked about the overwhelming nature of racism, and the effect not only on themselves, but also on others.

One participant said: "Racism has impacted on my health as well as my self-esteem and general well-being. I become angry and feel defenseless. Anxiety, frustration, and stress are what I experience from racism. This stress is not confined to me but passes on to my family and friends. The frustration negatively affects my relationship with my family. Sometimes I lose my motivation and spirit to carry on. In conclusion, racism is a disease that is affecting the Black community in an extraordinary manner."

Another summed up the influence on the health of the community this way: "Racism has not impacted my health, but I am perturbed when I view the lethargy in the African-Canadian community in reference to seeking knowledge of self. Perhaps if African-Canadians had some knowledge of self they would be in a better position to combat racism."

We were repeatedly told that racism was an everyday experience (Essed 1991), and occurred in the workplace, in the educational system, in the streets, and in the popular culture. Among the Black men in our sample, there were 78 reports of racism manifested as their being treated as inferior; 159 reports of being "othered" because of race; and 167 reports of blatant acts of racism. Furthermore, these men reported that the "acts of racism" bothered them a lot, and they were more likely to be extremely bothered by the blatant acts of racism, which had the greatest number of reports in our sample. As previously noted, the burden of racism lies in the repetition and everydayness of the assaults. We have learned from this study that racism is physically, spiritually, and emotionally painful for Black men, their families and communities, and that it has a deleterious effect on the health and well-being of members of the Black community. When internalized, racism can lead to feelings of hopelessness and helplessness, or it may lead to self-destruction, anger, or violence.

Violence does have an impact on Black communities, and in this study we explored verbal, emotional, spiritual, and physical violence. Violence is one of the legacies of racism that we have been examining in the study. To experience, witness, or recall an experience of violence and/or racism is difficult, traumatic, demeaning, painful, and stressful. Furthermore, racism has led to a legacy of silence surrounding violence, with many experiences, especially those in families, being hidden from public view. One participant described

particular talked about the challenge of being qualified, but unable to find employment in their field (Este 2003; Acton 2004). Calgary participants had the highest education levels in our sample, and were more likely to be unemployed or underemployed. The majority of the Calgary participants are first and second generation, which raises many questions about immigration policies in Canada, and has implications for international social work.

the impact of violence on the community as a type of cancer. Participants have stated that they want the cycle of violence and racism, and the silence surrounding it, to end. They have called for a greater effort between, and within, the generations to both name and address violence, including the violence of racism. It has been strongly suggested that the process must begin with healing among those who have suffered racism-based violence.

Conclusion

Are Black Men Still Catching Hell? The short answer is absolutely yes. The structural conditions that they are living with, in Canada, and elsewhere in the Diaspora are indeed changing…they are getting worse. Black men's systemic experiences of racism and exclusion in education and employment continue to be typically below the Canadian average. The effect of racism, violence, and the violence of racism take their toll on Black men, their families, and communities. They want this to change.

For some, the impact of racism related stressful experiences can lead to physical, psychological, and emotional health problems. Although the individual acts may appear trivial, the repetition and cumulative results do the most damage, coupled with the lack of attention to the problem by those in positions of authority who can affect change. Yet, despite the influence on mental and physical health, there is resilience and survival is ongoing … we stand tall on the shoulders of our ancestors, and draw strength and commitment from their legacies, as we continue to fight the everyday battles of racism, in all its forms.

References

- Anderson, James F., Laronistine Dyson, and Terry Grandison. 1998. African-Americans, Violence, Disabilities, and Public Policy: A Call for a Workable Approach to Alleviating the Pains of Inner-City Life. *The Western Journal of Black Studies* 22 (2): 94–102.

- Asante, M. 1987. *The Afrocentric Idea*. Philadelphia: Temple University Press.

- Aylward, Carol A. 1999. *Canadian Critical Race Theory: Racism and the Law*. Halifax: Fernwood.

- Barbarin, O. A. 1993. Coping and Resilience: Exploring the Inner Lives of African-American Children. *Journal of Black Psychology* 19: 478–492.

- Barker, Gary. 1998. Non-Violent Males in Violent Settings: An Exploratory Qualitative Study of Prosocial Low-Income Adolescent Males in Two Chicago (USA) Neighborhoods. *Childhood* 5 (4): 437–461.

- Barlow, Melissa Hickman. 1998. Race and the Problem of Crime in Time and Newsweek Cover Stories, 1946 to 1995. *Social Justice* 25 (2): 149–183.

- Bayne-Smith, Marcia, ed. 1996. *Race, Gender, and Health*. Thousand Oaks: Sage Publications.

- Benjamin, Akua. 2000. The Social and Legal Banishment of Anti-Racism: A Black Perspective. In *Crime of Colour: Racialization and the Criminal Justice System in Canada*, eds. Wendy Chan and Kiran Mirchandani, 177–190. Broadview Press.

- Bennett, M. Daniel Jr. and Fraser, Mark W. 2000. Urban Violence Among African American Males: Integrating Family, Neighborhood, and Peer Perspectives. *Journal of Sociology and Social Welfare* 27 (3): 93–117.

- Bernard, Wanda Thomas. 1996. *Survival and Success: As Defined by Black Men in Sheffield, England and Halifax, Canada.* Unpublished Doctoral Thesis. Sheffield: University of Sheffield.

- Bernard, Wanda Thomas. 1999. Working with Black Men for Change: The Use of Participatory Research as an Empowerment Tool. In *Working with men for change*, ed. Jim Wild, 59–71. London: UCL Press.

- Bernard, C. and W. T. Bernard. 2002. Learning from the Past/Visions for the Future: The Black Community and Child Welfare in Nova Scotia. In *Community Work Approaches to Child Welfare*, ed. B. Wharf, 116–130. Toronto: Broadview Press.

- Bolton, Kenneth Hugh Jr. 1999. *"Everyday Racism" in Policing: Interview with African American Law Enforcement Officers.* Unpublished Dissertation. University of Florida.

- Brown, Diane R., Lawrence E. Gary, Angela D. Greene, and Norweeta G. Milburn 1992. Patterns of Social Affiliation as Predictors of Depressive Symptoms Among Urban Blacks. *Journal of Health and Social Behavior* 33 (3): 242–253.

- Burton, Linda M. 1997. Ethnography and the Meaning of Adolescence in High-Risk Neighborhoods. *Ethos* 25 (2): 208–217.

- Cambridge, Alrick. 1996. The Beauty of Valuing Black Cultures. In *Re-Situating Identities: The Politics of Race, Ethnicity, and Culture*, eds. Vered Amit-Talai and Caroline Knowles, 161–183. Peterborough: Broadview Press.

- Canada. Solicitor General. 1998. *Racism and Social Inequality in Canada.* Toronto: Thompson Educational Publishing.

- Canadian Centre on Minority Affairs. 2000. *Health Promotion Outreach in the Black Caribbean Canadian Community (Ontario and Nova Scotia): Summary report.* Toronto: CCMA

- Christensen, C. P. 1998. Social Welfare and Social Work in Canada: Aspects of the Black Experience. In *Re/Visioning: Canadian Perspectives on the Education of Africans in the Late 20th Century*, eds. V. D'Oyley and C. James, 36–55. North York: Captus Press.

- Cohen, Sheldon, Tom Kamarck, and Robin Mermelstein. 1983. A Global Measure of Perceived Stress. *Journal of Health & Social Behavior* 24 (4): 385–396.

- Cole, Stephen R. 1999. Assessment of Differential Item Functioning in the Perceived Stress Scale-10. *Journal of Epidemiology & Community Health* 53 (5): 319–320.

- Collins, Patricia Hill. 1998. Intersections of Race, Class, Gender, and Nation: Some Implications for Black Family Studies. *Journal of Comparative Family Studies* 29 (1):27–36.

- Collins, Patricia Hill. 1990. *Black Feminist Thought: Knowledge, Consciousness, and the Politics of Empowerment.* New York: Routledge.

- Connell, Robert W. 1995. *Masculinities.* Berkeley: University of California Press.

- Delgado, Richard. 2001. *Critical Race Theory: An Introduction.* New York: New York University Press.

- Dennis, B. P. and J. B. Neese. 2000. Recruitment and Retention of African American Elders into Community-Based Research: Lessons Learned. *Psychiatric Nursing* 14 (1): 3–11.

- Downey, Sandra. 1999. *Bridging the Gap: A Capacity Building Project to Address the Needs of Breast Health and Breast Cancer Support and Information within the Black Nova Scotia Community.* Halifax: Canadian Cancer Society—NS Division. Breast Cancer Action Nova Scotia: Black Women's Health Program.

- Enang, Josephine, with Susan Edmonds, Carol Amaratunga, and Yvonne Atwell. 2001. *Black Women's Health: A Synthesis of Health Research Relevant to Black Nova Scotians.* Halifax: Maritime Centre for Excellence in Women's Health.

- Esposito, Luigi and John W. Murphy. 2000. Another Step in the Study of Race Relations. *The Sociological Quarterly* 41 (2): 171–187.

- Essed, Philomena. 1991. *Understanding Everyday Racism: An Interdisciplinary Theory.* Newbury Park: Sage Publications.

- Este, David. 1999. Cultural competency and social work: An overview. In *Professional Social Services in a Multicultural World*, eds. Gwat Yong-Lie and David Este, 27–48. Toronto: Canadian Scholars Press.

- Este, D. and W. T. Bernard. 2003. Social Work Practice with African Canadians: An Examination of the African Nova Scotian Community. In *Multicultural Social Work in Canada: Working with Diverse Ethno-Racial Communities*, eds. A. Al-Krenawi and J. Graham, 306–337. Don Mills: Oxford University Press.

- Farquharson, Karen. 1995. *Race in the Public Health Violence Discourse.* Paper presented at the Annual Meetings of the American Sociological Association (ASA).

- Feagin, Joe R. and Hernan Vera. 1995. *White Racism.* New York: Routledge.

- Ferguson, Ann Arnett. 2000. Bad Boys: Public Schools in the Making of Black Masculinity. In *Law, Meaning, and Violence Series*, eds. Martha Minow and Austin Sarat. Ann Arbor: University of Michigan Press.

- Fine, Michelle and Lois Weis. 1998. *The Unknown City: Lives of Poor and Working-Class Young Adults.* Westminster: Random House.

- Franklin, Clyde W II. 1994. Sex and Class Differences in the Socialization Experiences of African American Youth. *The Western Journal of Black Studies* 18 (2) 104–111.

- Gary, Lawrence E. 1981. *Black Men.* Newbury Park: Sage Publications.

- Gilliam, Franklin D. Jr. and Shanto Iyengar. 2000. Prime Suspects: The Influence of Local Television News on the Viewing Public. *American Journal of Political Science* 44 (3): 560–573.

- Guy, Talmadge C. 1996. *Africentrism and Adult Education: Outlines of an Intellectual Tradition with Implications for Adult Education.* Paper Presented at the Annual Meeting of the American Association for Adult and Continuing Education, Charlotte (October 29, 1996).

- Hagedorn, John M. 1998. Frat Boys, Bossmen, Studs, and Gentlemen: A Typology of Gang Masculinities. *Masculinities and Violence*, ed. Lee Bowker, 152–167. Thousand Oaks: Sage Publications.

- Hall, Perry A. 1996. Introducing African American Studies: Systematic and Thematic Principles. *Journal of Black Studies* 26 (6): 713–734.

- Hatchett, Bonnie F., Louis Black, and Karen Holmes. 1999. Effects of Citizenship Inequalities on the Black Male. *Challenge: A Journal of Research on African American Men* 10 (2): 65–77.

- Hawkins, Darnell F. 1995. *Ethnicity, Race, and Crime. Perspectives Across Time and Place.* Albany, NY: State University of New York Press.

- Henry, Frances et al. 1999. *The Colour of Democracy: Racism in Canadian Society.* 2nd ed. Toronto: Harcourt Brace Canada.

- Hill, Robert B. 1998a. Understanding Black Family Functioning: A Holistic Perspective. *Journal of Comparative Family Studies* 29 (1): 15–25.

- Hill, Robert B. 1998b. Enhancing the Resilience of African American Families. *Journal of Human Behaviour in the Social Environment* 1 (2/3): 49–61.

- Hooks, Bell. 1990. Representations: Feminism and Black Masculinity. Yearning: Race, Gender, and Cultural Politics. 65–77. Toronto: Between the Lines.

- Hooks, Bell. 1994a. Love as the Practice of Freedom. In *Outlaw Culture: Resisting Representations*. 243–250. New York: Routledge.

- Hooks, Bell. 1994b. Seduced by Violence No More. *Outlaw Culture: Resisting Representations*. 109–113. New York: Routledge.

- Howard, Laura Lee. 1997. *A Report on Delivering Breast Health Information to Ethnic Communities*. Halifax: Atlantic Breast Cancer Information Project. Charlottetown, PEI: Canadian Cancer Society—PEI Division.

- Imani, Nikitah Okembe-Ra. 1998. Development of a Methodology for the Evaluation of "Socially Induced Stress" Among African American Men. *Journal of African American Men* 3 (4): 83–90.

- Jackson, Aurora P. and Andre Ivanoff. 1999. Reduction of Low Response Rates in Interview Surveys of Poor African-American Families. *Journal of Social Service Research* 25 (1/2): 41–60.

- James, Carl E. 1997. The Distorted Images of African Canadians: Impact, Implications and Responses. In *Globalization and Survival in the Black Diaspora*, ed. Charles Green, 307–330. Albany: State University of New York Press.

- James, Carl E. 1998. "Up to no good": Black on the Streets and Encountering Police. In *Racism and Social Inequality in Canada: Concepts, Controversies and Strategies of Resistance*, ed. Vic Satzewich, 157–176. Toronto: Thompson Education Publishing.

- James, Carl E. (in press). Armed and Dangerous: Racing Suspects, Suspecting Race. In *Critical Criminology in Canada: Breaking the Links Between Marginality and Condemnation*, eds. B. Schissel and C. Brooks. Halifax: Fernwood.

- King, Anthony E. O. 1994. An Afrocentric Cultural Awareness Program for Incarcerated African-American Males. *Journal of Multicultural Social Work* 3 (4): 17–28.

- Kirven, Joshua Lorenzo. 1999. *Assessing the Coping Strategies and Well-Being of Young African American Males Through the Lens of Optimal Theory*. Unpublished Dissertation. Ohio University.

- Li, X., D. Howard, B. Stanton, L. Rachuba, and S. Cross. 1998. Distress Symptoms Among Urban African American Children and Adolescents: A Psychometric Evaluation of the Checklist of Children's Distress Symptoms. *Archives of Pediatrics and Adolescent Medicine* 152 (6): 569–577.

- Makrides, Lydia and Shirley Wong. 2001. *Identification of Best Practice Model for Diabetes Prevention Program for African Indigenous and Black Immigrant Communities*. Halifax: Health Canada.

- Majors, Richard and Janet Billson. 1992 *Cool Pose: The Dilemmas of Black Manhood in America*. New York: Touchstone.

- Mensah, J. 2002. *Black Canadians: History, Experience, Social Conditions*. Halifax: Fernwood.

- Messerschmidt, James W. 1997. *Crime as Structured Action: Gender, Race, Class, and Crime in the Making*. Thousand Oaks: Sage Publications.

- Miller, D. B. and R. MacIntosh. 1999. Promoting Resilience in Urban African American Adolescents: Racial Socialization and Identity as Protective Factors. *Social Work Research* 23 (3): 159–169.

- Neighbor, Harold W. and James S. Jackson, eds. 1996. *Mental Health in Black America*. Thousand Oaks: Sage Publications.

- Nova Scotia. 1989. *Royal Commission on the Donald Marshall Jr. Prosecution. Digest of Findings and Recommendations*. Halifax, Province of Nova Scotia.

- Oliver, William. 2000. The Public Health and Social Consequences of Black Male Violence. *Journal of African American Men* 5 (2): 71–92.

- Orbe, Mark P. 2000. Centralizing Diverse Racial/Ethnic Voices in Scholarly Research: The value of Phenomenological Inquiry. *International Journal of Intercultural Relations* 24 (5): 603–621.

- Queener, John E. and Juanita K. Martin. 2001. Providing Culturally Relevant Mental Health Services: Collaboration Between Psychology and the African American Church. *Journal of Black Psychology* 27 (1): 112–122.

- Rasheed, J. M. 1999. Obstacles to the Role of Inner-City, Low-Income, Non-Custodial African American Fathers. *Journal of African American Men* 4 (1): 9–23.

- Rasheed, J. M. 1998. The Adult Life Cycle of Poor African American Fathers. *Journal of Human Behaviour in the Social Environment* 1 (2/3): 265–280.

- Rasheed, J. M. and W. E. Johnson. 1995. Non-Custodial African American Fatherhood: A Case Study Research Approach. *Journal of Community Practice* 2 (2): 99–116.

- Razack, Sherene H. 1999. Making Canada White: Law and the Policing of Bodies of Colour in the 1990s. *Canadian Journal of Law and Society/Revue canadienne droit et societe* 14 (1): 159–184.

- Robinson, Matthew. 2000. The Construction and Reinforcement of Myths of Race and Crime. *Journal of Contemporary Criminal Justice* 16 (2): 133–156.

- Schiele, J. H. 1996. Afrocentricity: An Emerging Paradigm in Social Work Practice. *Social Work* 41 (3): 284–294.

- Schiele, Jerome H. 1998. Cultural Alignment, African American Male Youths, and Violent Crime. *Journal of Human Behavior in the Social Environment* 1 (2/3): 165–181.

- Sharif, Najma R., A. Dar Atul, and Carol Amaratunga. 2000. *Ethnicity, Income and Access to Health Care in the Atlantic Region: A Synthesis of the Literature.* Halifax: Population and Public Health Branch, Health Canada.

- Staples, Robert. 1982. *Black Masculinity. The Black Male's Role in American Society.* San Francisco: The Black Scholar Press.

- Staples, Robert. 1987. Black Male Genocide: A Final Solution to the Race Problem in America. *The Black Scholar* (May/June 1987): 2–11.

- Synnott, Anthony and David Howes. 1996. Canada's Visible Minorities: Identity and Representation, eds. Vered Amit-Talai, and Caroline Knowles. *Re-Situating Identities: The Politics of Race, Ethnicity, and Culture.* 137–160. Peterborough: Broadview Press.

- Small, Stephen. 1994. *Racialised Barriers.* London and New York: Routledge.

- Taylor, Edward. 1998. A Primer on Critical Race Theory. *Journal of Blacks in Higher Education* 19: 122–124.

- Utsey, Shawn O. 1999. Development and Validation of a Short Form of the Index of Race-Related Stress (IRRS)—Brief Version. *Measurement and Evaluation in Counseling and Development* 32 (3): 149–167.

- Utsey, Shawn O. 2000. Development and Initial Validation of the Africultural Coping Systems Inventory. *Journal of Black Psychology* 26 (2): 194–215.

- Wilkinson, Richard G., Ichiro Kawachi, and Bruce P. Kennedy. 1998. Mortality, the Social Environment, Crime and Violence. In *The Sociology of Health Inequalities*, eds. Mel Bartley, David Blane, and George Davey Smith, 19–37. Oxford: Blackwell.

- Williams, Oliver J. 1994. Group Work with African American Men who Batter: Toward more Ethnically Sensitive Practice. *Journal of Comparative Family Studies* 25 (1): 91–103.

- Wyatt, Sharon B., David R. Williams, Rosie Calvin, Frances C. Henderson, Evelyn R. Walker, and Karen Winters. 2003. Racism and Cardiovascular Disease in African Americans. *The American Journal of the Medical Sciences* 325 (6): 315–331.
- Zimmerman, Marc A., Jesus Ramirez-Valles, and Kenneth I. Maton. 1999. Resilience Among Urban African American Male Adolescents: A study of the Protective Effects of Sociopolitical Control on their Mental Health. *American Journal of Community Psychology* 27 (6): 733–751.

Part 2: Social Development

Chapter 6

Gender and Development in Central America: Lessons from the Field

Maureen Wilson

[Because] our world systematically ignores those human issues that are still called "women's issues," millions of human beings of both sexes are deprived of their birthright: the chance to lead healthy, productive, and rewarding lives (Riane Eisler 1987, 179).

R iane Eisler's 1987 statement in *The Chalice and the Blade*, unfortunately continues to hold true in spite of numerous efforts over recent decades to specifically address the issues of women in the context of international development. Drawing on some experiences in working with gender in Central America, this chapter will reflect on the appropriateness of some of these efforts, in relation to the development models and gender paradigms to which they are connected.

In the 1980s, while in Mexico City carrying out my doctoral research, I encountered a poster announcing an upcoming conference of the Latin American Association of Social Workers. I jumped at the chance to attend, and the experience was a profound one. The themes of the conference were health, education, and housing, and the presenters and participants seemed to speak with one passionate voice about the role of social workers in relation to these issues. Speaker after speaker, amid animated discussion, addressed aspects of the role for social workers in accompanying and advocating for popular movements—women's groups, peasant organizations, organized labour, indigenous movements—in their search for social justice. This was my first exposure to the "reconceptualization movement" that was sweeping Latin American social work, as our colleagues there sought to construct a social work more appropriate to the Latin American reality.

Teaching in Mexico after completion of that degree, I accompanied a friend and social work colleague[1] in a visit to Nicaragua. I was inspired, as were many, by the ideals of the Sandinista-led experiment in participatory-democratic socialism underway there. I wondered how I could support and learn from the experience of Nicaraguan colleagues engaged in the transformation of their approach to social work. I will tell some of the story of a development collaboration of some 20 years that began with that original contact, highlighting some of our work with gender issues in that context.

The chapter, following an examination of the development models underlying the well-documented failure of international efforts to improve the

---

[1] Prof. Mona Acker of the University of Regina.

conditions of women, describes a development approach that incorporates gender, dependency, and class analysis, and makes women (and men) subjects rather than objects of development processes. I will then examine an attempt to apply some of these principles in a development project with Nicaragua's national school of social work. Finally, I will reflect on some lessons learned in the course of this experience, and make some recommendations for international practice in the context of the development relationship.

Women Have Been Failed

Given the realities that most people's lives have not improved over the past decades of development efforts and that, indeed, many of the world's poorest countries are doing worse than they were 15 years ago (Social Watch 2006, 64), there is an urgent need for attention to the effectiveness of international development programs. This clearly applies not just to countries of the Global South:[2] the 2005 UNDP Human Development Report observed, for instance, that the infant death rate for African-Americans in Washington, D.C., is higher than that in the cities of the Indian state of Kerala (UNDP, 2005). Some critics have long argued that official development assistance must simply be stopped, "something that might prove to be in the best interests both of the taxpayers of the rich countries and the poor of the South" (Hancock 1991, 193). Others—among whom I would count myself on most days—contend that this work could be done better by employing more appropriate forms of collaboration.

There has been ample documentation in the development literature of the failure of efforts to improve the condition of the world's poor. Virtually from the outset, these failures have spurred a search for more appropriate development models. Also virtually from the outset, it has been recognized by some critics that if "the majority of people in the world have less food than they did in 1945, less care in illness, less useful work" (Swift 1991, 20), women have been those failed most dramatically. In the waning days of the 20th century, Plewes and Stuart noted that the worsening of the lives of poor women in fact has frequently been exacerbated by the very "development" programs supposedly designed to lift these populations out of poverty:

---

[2] Terminology around development issues continues to be troublesome; the terms "Global North" and "Global South" are used here as one of the better of unsatisfactory alternatives. Terms such as "developing," "less developed," and "underdeveloped" reflect the assumptions of modernization theory: that "development" should involve the transition of traditional, "backward" countries to the mass consumption economies of the "developed" countries. "Third World," in its modern usage, incorporates the now outdated implication of the existence of First and Second worlds—industrialized capitalist and socialist, respectively. Noting the growing differentiation process among peripheral societies, Amin (1992) talked about a Fourth World in reference to the African countries that had fallen behind most Latin America and Asian countries. The term "Fourth World" has also been used to describe indigenous peoples as internally colonized groups within nation-states. The terms "core" (or "centre"), "periphery," and "semi-periphery" are frequently used by those favouring dependency or world systems perspectives. Esteva and Prakash (1996) prefer the terms "social minorities" and "social majorities." The "North-South" alternative is inaccurate (Australia and NZ, for example, don't fit) and, based on a geographic dimension, tends to obscure the political and economic parameters.

In many instances, Third World women's workloads in tasks such as gathering fuel and collecting water have increased with development, as wastelands and commons have been privatized for capital-intensive production, and as traditional tree cover has been removed for commercial purposes. The introduction of cash crops or irrigated agriculture may have improved the economic position of some men in rural areas, but it has most often worsened the income and work status of the women with whom they live. Men have increased the area under cultivation with the help of technology, which has increased women's workload of planting, weeding, and harvesting. Women seldom have access to increased revenue from the sale of cash crops. Where women's hand-labour has been replaced by technology—for example where mechanical milling of grain is replacing manual pounding—the newly mechanized jobs have frequently been taken over by paid male labour ... Structural adjustment policies, which drastically cut social services, place an increased burden on poor women to earn money for school fees for their children or medicine for their sick (Plewes and Stuart 1991, 108).

This unfortunate record can probably be traced not just to the inappropriateness of the dominant growth/trickle-down or "modernization" models of development upon which most of these programs have been based, but also to a failure to incorporate gender as a fundamental unit of analysis in this work. With respect to the identification and treatment of "recipient" or "target" groups for Northern largesse, gender has for some time now been acknowledged as a legitimate consideration. There are, however, strongly competing perspectives within the development community on issues of gender and development. Here we will examine and compare some of these competing perspectives in terms of their assumptions about the nature of the problem, and also in relation to what is implied by each set of assumptions in terms of actions needed to address the issues. These alternative approaches represent competing perspectives on development, and they also reflect differing schools of feminist thought.

Women in Development (WID)

By 1970, the contribution of development projects to the deterioration of the status of women had been described by Ester Boserup (1970) in her influential *Women's Role in Economic Development*. A growing awareness and documentation of this negative impact on Third World women was followed in the early 1970s by attention from various quarters[3] to this set of issues, in an approach that came to be known as Women in Development or WID (this perspective as well as WAD and GAD, which follow, are summarized in a table at the end of the text).

This approach has evolved, over time, to an emphasis on addressing issues of equality, poverty, and efficiency with a view that development, to be effective, must involve both men and women. The central problem, from

---

[3] Among these were the UNDP, USAID, CIDA, the World Bank, and several European state development assistance agencies.

the WID perspective, is that women are left out of the development process. Solutions sought involve seeking ways to integrate them "into global processes of economic, political and social growth and change" (Rathgeber 1990, 1). Advanced by liberal feminists, it is an approach that advocates "legal and administrative changes to ensure that women [will] be better integrated into economic systems" (Jaquette 1982, 3). Its goals, strategies, and action programs aim to end discrimination against women and to reduce their disadvantages in the productive sector.

This perspective, reflected in Boserup's 1970 contribution, did not question the dominant development model. Modernization theory, forerunner of the contemporary neoliberal global agenda, viewed development as based in economic growth, with modernization in agriculture and industry producing an increase in exports and wealth that was expected to trickle down to increase domestic consumption on the model of the existing "developed" countries.

By the 1970s, modernization theory was being questioned by many. Not only was it not working in general for those being "trickled" on, but it was having the effect of widening the gender gap. In the industrial sector, "women were being relegated to the lowest-paying, most monotonous and sometimes health-impairing jobs" (Rathgeber 1990, 4). In agriculture, new technologies were directed at men rather than at women. In terms of capacity-building, enrolment in education programs was lower for females than males.

However, with the growing acknowledgement of the legitimacy of WID as an area to address, there came an institutionalizing of the recognition that women's experiences of development and of social change were different from those of men:

> "[WID] became an acceptable area of focus because it was seen as growing out of modernization theory and the notion of development as a process of slow but steady linear progress. Statistics were beginning to show that women had fared less well from development efforts of the 1960s [and] therefore a new strategy was called for. By the mid-1970s, donor agencies were beginning to implement intervention programs to adjust the imbalance of development "payoff" (Rathgeber 1990, 5).

The emergence of WID, then, did not mean a questioning of the development strategies themselves. Focusing on how women could be better integrated into ongoing development initiatives, and on advocacy for more equal participation in education, employment and other spheres of society, WID has avoided questioning the sources and nature of peoples' subordination or oppression. It has focused on women or gender as a unit of analysis without acknowledging divisions and relations of exploitation among women. It tends to be ahistorical, overlooking race, class, and culture. Projects growing out of this perspective typically focus on productive aspects of women's work, ignoring the reproductive side of women's lives. These are often income-generating activities that fail to take serious note of the extent to which women are already overburdened. When successful, they are often appropriated by men. WID, in general, has not made women the architects of its programs. "WID is about poor women in the Third World; it is not a force of those women themselves" (Bandarage 1984, 118). Critics of WID point out that its projects tend to suffer from top-down planning, and that its adoption by major international development agencies such as the World Bank has been "... to promote strategies that incorporate women on exploitative terms into the formal sector ... firms usually benefit from relaxed minimum wages, the absence of trade unions, and weak or non-existent health and safety legislation" (Plewes and Stuart 1991, 118–119).

Thus, while WID unquestionably made the important contribution of documenting and bringing to wide attention the negative effects of the dominant modernization model of development on women, it falls short in its failure to take account of the sources of women's oppression in the nature of the development model itself. Third World feminists have been critical of WID for both its liberal feminist assumptions and its Northern class and race bias, with charges of cultural imperialism when Northern feminists try to impose priorities and strategies for Third World women (Bandarage 1983).

Women and Development (WAD)

A Women and Development (WAD) approach emerged in the late 1970s as a response to the limitations of the WID or modernization theory approach. WAD is informed by both Marxist (class) analysis and dependency theory.

Dependency theory argues that the "underdevelopment" and impoverishment of Third World countries (the periphery) is produced by their dependent relationship with the exploitative rich countries (the centre). Andre Gunder Frank (1969) described this as the "development of under-development." In this view, the centre (the rich countries) has, from colonial times, exploited the periphery (the Global South). The "modernization" or growth/trickle-down approach, which assumes that the Global South can and should go though the same stages of development as did the North Atlantic economies, is seen as not only failing to lead to prosperity, but rather leading to an intensification of poverty. Marxist analysis contributes to this the acknowledgement that both rich and poor countries have class structures with dominating and dominated groups and subgroups, and that "aid" to poor countries does not automatically mean benefits to the poor of those countries.

Drawing on these, WAD argues that the WID strategy of integrating women into development is "inextricably linked to the maintenance of economic dependence of Third World countries on the industrialized countries" (Rathgeber 1990, 8). WAD thus incorporates a recognition of the importance of dependency and class relationships that had been absent in the WID approach.

However, the WAD approach has been criticized on the grounds that it "fails to undertake a full-scale analysis of the relationship between patriarchy, differing modes of production and women's subordination and oppression"

(Rathgeber 1990, 9). It implicitly assumes women's position will improve if and when international structures become more equitable. A further weakness of WAD is seen in its focus on the productive sector at the expense of the reproductive side of women's work and lives. Thus, like WID, its strategies tend to concentrate on development of income-generating activities, ignoring the time burdens on women, with "private domain" work implicitly seen as being outside the purview of development projects.

Gender and Development (GAD)

From the dissatisfaction of Third World women and others with both WID and WAD, there began to emerge another approach—one drawing on the experience of women of the Global South of empowerment through their organization of themselves in grassroots groups.

Leadership in the evolution of this "gender and development" perspective is surfacing in the form of contributions from Third World women, based on the experience of poor women of the consequences of development strategies imposed—through the International Monetary Fund and the World Bank—by the North (Antrobus 2004). Based on this emerging critique from the South of the failure of growth/trickle-down development to recognize the critical links between production and reproduction, and "the negative effect of gender-based hierarchies at all levels on women's access to the resources necessary in support of women's contribution to the well-being and development of their families, communities, and countries" (Antrobus 1991, 74–75), what is called for is the development of a fully articulated alternative development theory and practice.

In the Gender and Development (GAD) view, what is needed is to build on experiences and develop strategies that will address not only the immediate situations in which women find themselves, but also the structures that oppress women. It is an approach, with theoretical roots in socialist feminism, which recognises the need to distinguish between the position (strategic interests) and condition (practical needs) of women, and to incorporate both strategic and practical considerations in development work. That is to say, there is recognition that gender interests must be articulated into, and not subordinated to, a wider strategy of economic development.

This approach attempts to understand why and how women have been systematically assigned to inferior or secondary roles. The social construction of production and reproduction are identified as the bases of women's oppression. Relations of production are related to relations of reproduction. To take into account all aspects of women's lives, there must be a combined analysis of patriarchy and class/dependency. This alternative analysis of the relationship between women's issues and development issues centres not on women alone, but on the relations between women and men as the focus of analysis. It also attends to the processes as well as the goals in development work:

> [GAD] sees poor Third World women and other oppressed groups not as instruments
> or target groups but as architects, agents, and beneficiaries of development ...

[It is] holistic, not segmented, which means that visions, strategies, and actions need to be examined from the perspective both of the world and the hearthstone ...The interactions of gender, class, race, and environmental issues are of concern in a gender and development approach: none is an independent variable capable of being addressed without reference to or impact on the others (Plewes and Stuart 1991, 127).

A GAD approach, then, sees the currently dominant development paradigm as incapable of providing viable solutions for women or other oppressed groups, and thus calls for an alternative paradigm, one that "seeks to transform radically rather than merely reform current social, political, economic, and gender relationships" (Plewes and Stuart 1991, 127). But how can a "gender and development" approach be best advanced by northern and southern partners in "development"? In attempting to respond to the question, I draw on experiences of attempting to apply some of these principles in work with gender issues in Central America, in a development partnership with Nicaragua's national school of social work. I begin with a brief description of the Nicaraguan context for this work in relation both to gender issues and to the practice of social work.

Gender Context

The Sandinista[4] experiment in participatory democracy elicited interest and support from all corners of the globe, and, in or out of power, the Sandinista movement has continued as a significant force in Nicaraguan politics for the past four decades.[5] Before the Sandinistas took power in 1979, to be a poor woman in Nicaragua meant you were probably illiterate, had an average of eight pregnancies beginning in early adolescence, were likely to witness the death of almost half of your children, would be solely responsible for maintaining your household, and would live to be about 50 (Ramírez-Horton 1982).[6] As a result of their poverty, second class status, and the appalling brutality of the Somoza presidency's National Guard, large numbers of Nicaraguan women joined the struggle to overthrow the Somoza dictatorship: almost 40% of the FSLN combat forces were women.[7]

---

[4] The FSLN, or Sandinista National Liberation Front.

[5] How the late 2006 return to power of the Sandinista party will impact the direction of development of Nicaraguan society remains to be seen. The FSLN is now a party rather than a political movement, and leader Daniel Ortega significantly alienated progressive sectors among the Sandinista support base during the election campaign.

[6] The statistics for the population as a whole were stark: 22% unemployment (35% underemployment), 60% illiteracy rate (93% in rural areas), with only 5% going beyond grade 5. University was available to 0.3% of the population. With virtually no medical system, Nicaragua had one of the highest mortality rates in Latin America. The desperate economic situation had a particularly devastating effect on women, for many families were headed by single mothers (Randall 1981, v). Laws under the Somoza regime were paternalistic and discriminatory.

[7] In 1977, a national women's organization, AMPRONAC (Asociación de Mujeres ante la Problemática Nacional: Association of Women Confronting the National Problem) was founded, a first in a country where women's proper place had long been considered to be exclusively in the home. AMPRONAC performed important support and intelligence services for the FSLN (Molyneux 1985, 151).

After the FSLN victory, women played a continuing role in the many changes that occurred over the next few years.[8] One of the most important was the literacy campaign, which not only taught women to read and write, but also encouraged them to work outside the home (Molyneux 1985, 153). The government developed ambitious plans for assisting women's entry into the workforce, including support for collectives and daycare centres. Many far-reaching laws were passed,[9] on the assumption that legal rights constituted an important instrument for equalizing relations between the sexes (Molyneux 1985).

In spite of the ambitious plans, however, there were enormous obstacles to women's gaining equal rights in both the public and private spheres. First, the US-sponsored contra war increasingly monopolized both the attention and the resources of the Sandinista government. As a result, health, education, and housing programs that had particularly benefited women were eroded. The Church hierarchy, strident in its opposition to the revolution, was a powerful obstacle to programs for the emancipation of women (Molyneux 1985, 146). In the private sphere, the attitudes embodied in machismo continued to be pervasive. "Although the revolution offered young people the freedom to participate, in their private lives most girls are repressed by their families and social environment ... 10 years of revolution weren't enough to change a social and cultural structure which oppresses women economically, politically and ideologically" (Wise 1991, 22, quoting anthropologist Mercedes Oliveira).[10]

Following the Sandinista electoral loss in 1990, the new President Violeta Chamorro stated emphatically "I'm not a feminist nor do I want to be one.

---

[8] For many, this was inherent in the revolution. "The option of women's liberation separate from the revolution was not a reality in Nicaragua. The process of the revolution itself created the conditions that made it possible for women to break with the past and mobilize to demand full equality" (Randall 1981:ii).

[9] These included full equality for men and women (Statute of Rights and Guarantees of Nicaraguans, September 1979), a ban on the exploitation of women as sex objects in the media (Article 30, Decree No. 48 of the Statute of Rights and Guarantees), and the Law of Relations between Mothers, Fathers and Children aimed at regulating "equality of rights and duties between men and women with respect to (their) common children" (Molyneux 1985, 154). Others were drafted but never ratified by the Junta, most notably a Law of Nurturing (Alimentos) that strengthened the financial position of women (especially women headed households), and obliged men to take responsibility for child care and housework.

The liberation of women was to proceed in the context of the three priorities for consolidating the revolution and reconstructing the nation: economic development, political activity, and national defence. AMPRONAC was replaced by a new FSLN-based women's organization, AMNLAE (Asociación de Mujeres Nicaragüenses "Luisa Amanda Espinosa"), named after the first women to die in combat against Somoza's National Guard (Collinson 1990, 137), which played a key role in defending women's positions and advocating for legal and social reforms. All major unions developed Women's Secretariats that provided powerful voices in the struggle for women's rights.

The FSLN's 1987 Proclamation, declaring the need to fight specifically against the oppression of women was a direct result of an active campaign, led by AMNLAE, to change the consciousness of the nation's leaders, who were still primarily men (Collinson 1990, 189).

[10] Though there were laws forbidding the objectification of women as sexual objects, the Sandinistas themselves sponsored beauty contests and increasingly engaged young, scantily clad women in their campaigns for popular support. One consequence of women's increased participation in the labour force, in Nicaragua as elsewhere, was the double day. Women continued to be primarily responsible for family and children in their role as caregivers.

I am a woman dedicated to my home, as Pedro [her late husband] taught me" (Wise 1991, 21). The new government began to dismantle many of the specific gains, including sex education, health services (especially birth control), and the prohibition of sexist advertising, made by women over the previous decade. The new governing party, the Union Nacional Opositora (UNO), had made a campaign pledge to the "moral and social recuperation of the family unit," including the restoration of "paternal authority," recognizing the man's right to control the family (Wise 1991, 21). As the economy deteriorated and unemployment increased, the "double day" became a "triple day" as women searched for extra money in informal (black market) activities (Wise 1991, 22).[11]

Social Work in Nicaragua

After the July 1979 victory of the Sandinista forces, social work entered a period of crisis in Nicaragua, with a view temporarily prevailing within the revolutionary alliance that the essential function of social work had been to mediate between the social classes, contributing to the perpetuation of the old regime and class structure. With the revolution then, in this view, the profession would no longer be necessary. Thus, in 1980, the nation's only school of social work was closed to new admissions. The country's social work community quickly mobilized itself in response to this[12] and was successful in persuading authorities of the need for social workers to implement the nation's new social policy.

In fact, while forces had been gathering in Nicaragua to overthrow the corrupt Somoza dictatorship, throughout Latin America social workers had been engaged in a re-examination of their roles and perspectives on practice, in a search for a social work more appropriate to the Latin American reality. Out of the combined influences of dependency theory, Marxist thought, the Cuban and other revolutionary guerrilla movements, liberation theology and the work of Brazilian educator Paulo Freire, there emerged what became known as the reconceptualization movement in social work (Prado and Palacios 2005; Alayón 2005).

This reconceptualization involved a new emphasis on the role of social work in the promotion of social change. In this model, social workers would work more directly with the poor, facilitating groups in analyzing their own positions in the historical moments in which they live, and in determining courses of action for themselves. Thus, social workers would no longer see

---

[11] A study of the impact of structural adjustment policies on women in Nicaragua done by the Fundación Internacional para el Desafío Económico Global (FIDEG 1991), carried out shortly after the 1990 change of government, concluded that, because of their more precarious socioeconomic condition, women are disproportionately affected by the macroeconomic policies of the current government. The survey concluded that women are now forced to abandon whatever progress they have made and spend more time fulfilling the daily tasks of family maintenance.

[12] A national meeting was held in which the social work community deliberated collectively on what should be the content of social work education to prepare professionals to address the new Nicaraguan reality.

themselves as politically neutral, but rather as actively taking the side of the poor. In their search for perspectives more appropriate to their own reality, Nicaraguan social workers and educators were drawn to this perspective.

In Nicaragua, the radical transformation of social work during this time was also strongly rooted in and influenced by the broad-based Sandinista popular movement, which aimed to replace the corrupt US-backed Somoza regime with a more egalitarian society based on social justice, self-determination, and independence from the hegemony of the US. This growing movement united a variety of social sectors, with youth, students and faculty of the universities prominent among these. Nicaraguan social workers—students, professors, and practitioners alike—played very active roles in the prolonged struggle to topple the Somoza dictatorship, with important heroes and martyrs of the popular insurrection coming from among their ranks. This was fertile ground for the ideas of the reconceptualization movement.

By the end of the 1960s, dissatisfaction had begun to manifest itself among Nicaraguan students and teachers with respect to the relevance of their program of social work education. In 1970, faculty members held a first seminar on reconceptualization and between 1971 and 1973, through extensive processes of discussion, significant changes were implemented in the program of study. In 1973, some professors who insisted upon a traditional "social assistance" emphasis in social work were asked to resign and new professors, mostly sociologists, were hired who were to have an important influence in the search for a redefinition of social work for Nicaragua. Then together, students and professors embarked upon the task of a complete review of the program of social work education. After a semester of intensive work a new plan of studies was produced, based upon a dramatically altered conception of the profession. It reflected a marked shift away from the blind *tecnicismo* that had characterized the School's curriculum, and an emphasis on producing social workers capable of the social analysis necessary for the promotion of social transformation. In 1974, this new program received the approval of university authorities.

Following a move from the national university (UNAN) to Managua's Universidad Centroamericana, and a revision of its program, the social work school reopened in 1984. The new mission statement of the School declared that its graduates should be prepared to facilitate the democratic process of popular participation in the structural changes required to achieve a more just and egalitarian society (Wilson and Prado 2007). Basing a new definition of social work on service to the process of social transformation, it observed that intervention at the microsocial level must serve the interests of the popular sectors, involving "... the sensitization and organization of these popular sectors [which] allows them to make themselves subjects of their own transformation" (ETS 1984).[13] The overriding mission of social workers, then, is to enhance "the organized participation of the people in the development of the society ... as the practice of popular democracy" (ETS

---

[13] This and all translations mine.

1984). The methodological keys to this are to be found in the methods of popular education, or "education for critical consciousness" (Freire 1973).

Social Development Project[14]

During the 1986 personal visit to Nicaragua, I was able to make the acquaintance of a number of the faculty members at Nicaragua's only school of social work, the Escuela de Trabajo Social (ETS) at the Universidad Centroamericana. In subsequent correspondence, colleagues there identified some development needs and priorities of the Nicaraguan School: improvement of the qualifications and capacities of teaching faculty[15] and development of a social action documentation centre. Enlisting the support and assistance of colleagues from various disciplines at the University of Calgary, I proceeded to explore ways in which Canadian resources might be mobilized to respond to the development needs identified by our colleagues at the Nicaraguan school. A 1987 planning visit to Nicaragua yielded a proposal, jointly developed by Nicaraguan and Canadian participants,[16] for funding support for the realization of these goals.[17]

The proposal located itself in the context of Nicaragua's need to enhance its ability to effectively plan, implement, and evaluate social policies and community based programs, through the application of its preferred model of popular participation. The broad aim of the project was to assist in the development of the human resources needed to support these functions, through a strengthening of the resources and capabilities of this, the country's only school of social work. Thus, the focus of project activities would be on the upgrading of capacities of teaching faculty, and improvement of programs and of the infrastructure needed to support research and teaching at the Escuela de Trabajo Social (School of Social Work) of the Universidad Centroamericana in Managua.[18]

[14] The support is gratefully acknowledged of the Canadian International Development Agency's Canadian Partnership Branch (University Partnerships in Cooperation and Development) for funding for the Universidad Centroamericana—University of Calgary Collaborative Social Development Project, the development project from which the experience described here is drawn.

[15] In the first years following the Sandinista victory in 1979, there had been a major exodus from the country of members of the educated elite, followed by an exodus of academics from the universities as they moved into government posts. Thus about half of the faculty members at the school of social work were people who had only recently completed their first degrees, having no practice experience other than that obtained during their field education. At the onset of this project there were no faculty members with graduate degrees.

[16] University of Calgary Librarian Sharon Neary participated in this this visit, assisting in facilitating planning for the social action documentation centre.

[17] A more complete description and discussion of this project can be found in Maureen G. Wilson (2003). "South-North Development Partnership: Lessons From a Nicaragua-Canada Experience," eds. Y. Asamoah, Lynne Healy and M. C. Hokenstad. *Models of International Collaboration in Social Work Education* (New York: CSWE Press), 111–123; and in Jocelyne Laforce (1998). *Basic Human Needs Performance Review: Nicaragua Social Development Project Evaluation Report*. Ottawa: Canadian International Development Agency.

[18] The project emphasized the objectives of improvement of levels of knowledge and skill of teaching faculty and the enhancement of the Universidad Centroamericana's capability to produce social practitioners/researchers competent in the popular education/participatory research approaches to practice. This included the aim of developing the school's social action documentation center: building its collection

In 1988, funding was approved by the Canadian International Development Agency for a five-year project and late that year, a process began in which Nicaraguan and Canadian counterparts worked together to determine, prioritize, and carry out means of meeting the project goals. The methodology employed in this project—although it for the most part did not involve direct work with grassroots groups—was one that attempted to be congruent with the principles of a "gender and development" approach. The planning and development of the program were carried out through a participatory process reflecting a shared philosophy of "accompaniment" among the partners. *Acompañamiento,* or "accompanying the process," is an approach to the development relationship that embodies genuine mutual respect and trust, a process of sharing and mutual support, a common analysis of what the "problem" is, and a common commitment and solidarity that comes from an understanding that we all have a stake in what happens in other parts of the globe (Kreitzer and Wilson 2006; Wilson and Whitmore, 2000).[19]

Strategies for achieving the goals and objectives were developed, and amended as needed, jointly by the project partners. The project administrative structure designated the Director of the Nicaraguan School[20] the Project Director; I, as Canadian Coordinator (and through me the Canadian information systems and short-term subject specialists), reported to her. Two advisory committees were established, one based in Canada and one in Nicaragua. The application of the "accompaniment" approach was to be facilitated by the wide participation of all members of the Nicaraguan School in each of the project phases, and by the decision to base the Canadian Coordinator and the information systems specialist[21] on-site in Nicaragua during the first part of the project, gradually reducing this time in the field over the final two years.[22]

---

of learning resources, improving its technical services for more effective organization, documentation, and access to these resources, and providing skill development to enable documentation centre staff and teaching faculty, respectively, to provide technical services and to access these resources. In keeping with the School's philosophy, the social action documentation centre was to be designed to be welcoming and accessible as a resource to grassroots community groups and NGOs as well as students and faculty of the university.

[19] *Acompañamiento* is clear about who owns and controls the process: the Southern partner does. Demanding that collaboration be non-intrusive, and that it be based upon mutual trust, genuine respect, a sense of a common destiny and purpose, and a common analysis of what the issues, it bears strong resemblance to feminist process principles such as mutuality, sharing, honouring each person's experience, the right to be in control of one's own process of understanding and development, and the linking of individual with collective action, the personal with the political, are deeply rooted in progressive feminist praxis (Wilson and Whitmore 2000).

[20] Lic. Iris Prado Hernández, succeeded part way through the project by Lic. Giomar Talavera.

[21] Ms. Sharon Neary of the University of Calgary Library served for two years in this position, following which Ms. Maryon McClary of the University of Alberta Libraries assumed these responsibilities.

[22] During the latter half of this time, the project was also to benefit from the extended on-site presence of two University of Calgary graduate students who were to participate and carry out thesis research in association with the project.

Gender issues were addressed in a variety of ways in the course of this project.[23] The project was one in which both participants and beneficiaries were overwhelmingly female. 90% of the teaching staff of the Nicaraguan program were female, all of the social work students were female, and the Canadian participation was predominantly female as well. Those who benefited from scholarships, workshop attendance, and technical training were all female. During workshops to determine priority areas of content for project development, women's issues emerged as one of the areas in which teaching faculty felt a need to improve their knowledge. It then became my responsibility to identify resource person(s) who might assist the faculty in this.[24]

Our activities related to gender issues included a jointly developed and delivered workshop on gender issues, and a joint presentation at an international women's conference. In our collaborative development of the workshop, there was agreement on the importance of the linking of concrete issues and theory, and a consensus that the Nicaraguan faculty members, while having a high level of awareness of concrete problems, would benefit from a better understanding of alternative theoretical perspectives through which these concrete experiences could be understood. The workshop proceeded with the participation of all eight faculty members, a Canadian content expert[25] and a visiting Canadian library consultant to the project. The content included an overview of gender themes, a discussion of concrete issues related to gender encountered by Nicaraguan social workers, a review of the perspectives of alternative bodies of feminist thought in relation to these, and a discussion of how these might be incorporated into the curriculum. This was followed up by a meeting in which the workshop planning team reflected together and evaluated the experience.[26]

A presentation at an international women's conference (in Washington, DC), made jointly by Nicaraguan and Canadian project members, provided an opportunity for us to share and discuss the experience of collaboration from our differing perspectives in a panel format. This was the first opportunity our Nicaraguan collaborators had had to attend an international gathering focusing on gender issues. North-South politics became central to

---

[23] A file review of Canadian Partnership Branch on Basic Human Needs Programming considered that the Social Development Project was one of the few capacity building projects that "ensured the full participation of women as beneficiaries and made a clear commitment to gender equity and redressing historical inequalities by ensuring that women predominated in training and in the provision of scholarships" (Laforce 1998, 19).

[24] Among other things, the Nicaraguan faculty members had specified as criteria for resource persons that they be fluent in Spanish, and have an orientation to popular education/participatory action research approaches.

[25] Dr. Elizabeth Whitmore of Carleton University.

[26] We carefully documented this process of collaboration, each writing detailed logs describing and reflecting on it. Some of these were in the form of taped conversations, which we later transcribed. To clarify the major themes, we first reviewed the logs separately and then together compared and combined our conclusions. Having two persons (and a third—the Canadian librarian who had participated in the workshop joined us for some of this reflection) participate in this process allowed us a much more complete picture of the situation.

much of the interaction at the conference; Latin American women quickly coalesced around the language issue (the domination of English and the lack of translation) and together mobilized to express their anger and demand change by the organizers.[27]

In our session, since most of those attending understood Spanish, it was agreed that the presentations would be done exclusively in Spanish; for a change, it was the English-speaking minority that was limited to participation through whisper translation. This provided space for the Latin American women not only to share their views about the process of collaboration in their own language, but also to coalesce around their outrage at what was described as "imperialism" in the conference itself. It was a very lively session, as the language issue became a catalyst for mobilizing the Latin American women around other mutual concerns. This conference provided all of us with a valuable opportunity to hear about others' experiences with collaboration, and to network with women doing similar kinds of work—including in Nicaragua—and raised awareness among our Nicaraguan colleagues of the need for improved networking among Nicaraguan women's groups. Two of the Nicaraguan colleagues who participated with us in this conference continue today to be active participants in a cross-disciplinary gender research unit.

Apart from these more structured kinds of activities, gender issues were encountered in many unanticipated ways in the course of the project, as when practicum students placed in a rural agricultural cooperative found that none of the women in the community, for whom their program of literacy training had been planned, appeared for the classes. When the women were asked why they had failed to attend, they informed the students that this was because their male partners would not permit them to participate. The students were stunned and outraged at this information, and the experience precipitated much discussion and a new interest in and awareness of gender issues in these urban-based young women. In another case, the provision of a daycare facility that was also to provide employment for several of the community's women was followed by a significant increase in family violence targeted specifically at the women to be employed in the facility. These experiences provided significant opportunities for reflection and learning on gender issues, and on the utility of various theoretical perspectives on gender and their usefulness in different rural and urban contexts in Nicaragua.

The improvement of faculty members' knowledge of alternative paradigms for understanding issues of gender and development—and of the complex practice implications of these—and the incorporation of these concepts into curriculum were considered significant contributions of this project. These are admittedly small steps, in the context of an overwhelming history

---

[27] All sessions were conducted in English. Conference organizers, given a limited budget, had arranged for a handful of volunteers to do whisper translation for those needing it. This was both disruptive and woefully inadequate.

and environment of *machismo*. In spite of gender equality legislation, well-intentioned national and international agencies found their initiatives to improve the condition of women at the community level often met with disinterest, hostility, sabotage, or even increased family violence. And the Sandinista youth organization continued to stage beauty contests. Perhaps equally important, however, were the lessons learned by both partners in this project, not just about gender and other issues, but about what works in creating an effective and mutually satisfying collaboration for both northern and southern partners.

Lessons Learned

Our attempts to apply principles consistent with a GAD approach to development to this collaborative project yielded significant learning by both Nicaraguan and Canadian participants, particularly with respect to project management and process, and to aspects of North-South relationships.[28] Here are some of the findings:

(i) Project Management and Process

- *Horizontal/participatory management.* The participatory approach and "horizontal management" that characterized the partnership project is considered by local partners as one of the most positive elements of the learning process (Laforce 1998, iii). The structure of the project, with control of the design and process of inputs lying with the overseas partner and "accompanied" and shared by the Canadian partner, was positively evaluated by both partners. Our experience would suggest that such a participatory process, while more time-consuming in the short-run, tends to produce commitment, investment, and "ownership" in the project that pays off over the longer term. However, it would be less likely to be effective if not accompanied by a shared understanding and commitment by both partners to this way of operating. Both Nicaraguan and Canadian participants in this project were of the view that the accompaniment model functions best with an extended on-the-ground presence of the foreign partner.
- *Process goals.* It is recommended for planning and evaluation of such projects that process/empowerment outcomes be identified along with more "concrete" project objectives. With respect to the overall performance of the project ... the participating partners consider that one of the most notable results of this project was related to the collaborative relationship between the partners, team-building supported by a high level of participation, increased self-confidence, and feelings of empowerment and independence on the part of the Nicaraguan partner (CIDA 1998, 29–30).

---

[28] This collaborative project was comprehensively evaluated four times over its life—twice in a participatory, informal process and twice by external, CIDA-funded evaluators.

- *Selection of foreign project personnel.* Our experience would reinforce some of the findings of Daniel Kealey (2001) regarding the importance of appropriate personal characteristics in overseas development workers: empathy, interest in the local culture, flexibility, tolerance, initiative, open-mindedness, and sociability. Given the generally higher rating of women on these indicators, a strengthened presence of women should be expected, including at the level of project/program management.[29]

(ii) North-South Relationships

- *South-North technology transfer.* There is a two-way learning process involved in this kind of an experience. A consequence of the economic globalization process has been the globalization of poverty, and the creation of a "global South" that transcends traditional North-South borders. The creation of a distinguishable global north and south as distinct from the traditional north and south creates the conditions for alliance building amongst like-minded groups. Given the current conjuncture, in which we are seeing an increasing convergence of circumstances between underclasses in the North and in the South, in many ways we in the North have much more to learn than to teach in relation to social work practice in Southern countries.

- *South-South exchanges.* The fruitfulness of opportunities of contact by Nicaraguan participants with other Latin American colleagues was extremely striking in the experience of this project. The richness of

---

[29] Research on the effectiveness of overseas development workers suggests that, in general, women rate higher than men on the skills and attitudes said to be associated with "overseas effectiveness." These results should not be surprising. In arguing for democratic, collaborative development relationships to replace the failed aid programs of past decades, Murphy (1991) has reminded us that "This concept of mutual support has been most clearly developed within the political analysis and empowerment strategies of the feminist movement, which has been the single most influential intellectual and ethical stream in planting the seeds of a transformation" (Murphy 1991, 179). George (1990) also links women's issues with collaborative approaches. Drawing on feminist principles, with their emphasis on process, equality, participation, and valuing of people's experience, she outlines a structural model of analysis. The key elements that she argues must be addressed are structure (how structured inequalities influence the situation of women), ideology (in influencing policies and practices, specifically related to women's lives), power relationships (and the empowerment of women), and the social construction of people's perceptions of reality.

A study by Kealey (1991, 2001) identified a number of pre-departure personal characteristics of effective overseas development workers. These included a set of caring behaviours, such as relationship building, the capacity to build and maintain cooperative, trusting relationships with others, the capacity to show interest in, attentiveness to and respect for others, sensitivity to local social, political and cultural realities, and empathy (the ability to read suffering or discomfort in another person and competence in perceiving the needs and feelings of others). An action orientation is indicated by initiative, being one of the first to act or propose a plan of action, self-confidence and openness in dealing with others. Another important characteristic is other-centredness, seen in self control when confronted by interpersonal conflict or stress, openness to new ideas and other points of view, perseverance in working towards a goal, even when the tasks get overly frustrating, and a preference for working with others rather than alone. Effective workers possess high self monitoring skills, which include reading social situations and adjusting their behaviour to meet the needs of such situations. They are socially adroit, able to persuade others to achieve certain goals, are diplomatic in their work with others, and possess a high degree of social insight. Other characteristics include a low need for upward mobility, and a high tolerance for ambiguity. On overseas assignment the effective worker experiences less difficulty in adjusting to the new environment, expresses a high level of personal and professional satisfaction, learns the local language and makes contact with local people, and derives satisfaction from participating in local culture.

the learning experiences obtaining for project participants though opportunities to travel abroad through this project suggests a need for a reframing of the Northern role in such exchanges. These opportunities for south-south linkages should be maximized in the planning of projects of this kind, through the use of "southern" resource persons wherever possible, and through the facilitation of attendance of overseas participants at conferences, workshops, and formal education institutions in the "south." Rather than thinking about isolated linkages between Northern and Southern partners, it might be more appropriate for comparatively resource-rich northerners to play a facilitating and supportive role also in south-south collaboration.

- *Issues of Dependency.* During the inbound flight on my first trip to Nicaragua, I encountered an acquaintance from Mexico who told me a story about a recent visit to Nicaragua. Begging was at that time virtually nonexistent in Nicaragua, and he witnessed a child beggar being sternly lectured by his Nicaraguan companion on the inappropriateness and lack of necessity for this activity in a society in which people found collective solutions to their issues of need, and then directed the child to a centre where his needs could be addressed. Later my acquaintance was conducted on a tour of a local social project, following which he was presented with a list of things needed by the project. He pointed out the inconsistency of his companion's castigation of the child's attempt at begging with this more sophisticated attempt at essentially the same activity.

When I assumed my role with this project, I was determined that my Nicaraguan colleagues would not be subjected to this indignity. Therefore, when needs were identified for additional resources to carry out some activity, I would quietly go about the "dirty work" of identifying from where resources might be obtained and writing the required grant proposals, letting our Nicaraguan partners know about this only when there had been success in acquiring these resources. This was based on the reasoning that once the war had ended and it was once more possible to redirect state resources to social programs, this kind of "begging" would no longer be necessary.

We all later identified this as having been a mistake. In fact, as the history of Nicaragua evolved, the skill of writing grant proposals was to become more important than we could ever have anticipated in the development and sustainability of social projects. Although the war ended with the change in government, this change also meant drastic cuts to social programs, reinforced by externally imposed neo-liberal policies shifting expenditures from the social sector to the "productive" sector. Thus some important capacity-building was now needed in the skills of writing successful project proposals. The Nicaraguan school later moved to address this issue, even introducing this as part of curriculum content.

- *The issue of language* clearly involves questions of power and control. Had our colleagues been required to interact with us in our language, for them it would have meant working with ideas formulated and expressed within the conceptual framework of that language: another form of cultural imperialism. In this context, we were fortunate in being able to work in Spanish, and also to be able to recruit resource persons able to function in that language. Our having to communicate exclusively in our imperfect Spanish may have had some levelling effect, going some distance in redressing the imbalance created by our greater access to material resources. First-language collaboration may not always be possible, but careful attention should be given to the distortions created by an inability to work in this way.

- *Creating a dream team.* The Nicaraguan women with whom we have collaborated were pretty close to an ideal group with whom to work. They were very clear about the direction in which they wanted to go, what they needed to do to get there, what resources would be helpful to them in this and, most importantly, about who would be driving the bus (not any foreigners). Also critical, for all of us, was the fact that we shared a commitment to similar values and a similar analysis of the problems (writ large) we were confronting. It is important to remember that we have the right to choose our own dance partners.

- *Partnerships.* The theme of inequality pervades all aspects of the North-South development relationship. Many of the foregoing recommendations for development practice are rooted in the need to acknowledge and address this fact; this is the reason for our avoidance of the term "partnership" when describing the relationship.[30] Caribbean development critic Peggy Antrobus succinctly dispatched the subject in the following manner: "I don't want to talk about North-South "partnerships"; partnership implies a relationship among equals. I would like to discuss North-South relations.[31]

Advances and Setbacks

The electoral defeat of the Sandinistas, felt as a betrayal by Sandinista militants, was a devastating blow for many internationalists who had invested themselves heavily in support of this political project. A metaphor employed again and again by individuals among the internationalist community was that it felt "as if someone near to me has died." As one of the (greatly over-represented) Albertans among the Canadian community in Nicaragua, I was hit very hard by this as well.

---

[30] Our attempts to find a Spanish translation for the English term "partnership" as used in the development context yielded only a term used in a narrow legal or business context. We finally settled on the term *alianza* (alliance)—a much more appropriate term in any case—to describe our relationship.

[31] Peggy Antrobus is a Caribbean development critic and former coordinator of Development Alternatives with Women for a New Era (DAWN). This statement was made in her remarks to the opening session of the Fifth International Forum of the Association for Women in Development, Washington, D.C., November 21, 1991.

Then, in the first dark days following this event, a copy of George Orwell's *Homage to Catalonia* mysteriously appeared in our house in Managua.[32] This book tells the story of Orwell's nine months in the Spanish civil war, and it speaks of terrible conditions, betrayals, appalling blunders, and fighting and killing among people who should have been allies. While this may not seem like an uplifting story, it lifted me out of my despondency. First, it made any mistakes made by the Sandinistas seem very small indeed; secondly, it located this experience for me into the longer historical context, reminding me how we are linked across time to our ancestors—and progeny—in these struggles. I had often commented that the Sandinista cause was the Spanish civil war of our generation; this became true for me in a more profound sense.

Only slightly daunted, I have continued to participate in collaborative "development" work in Central America in a variety of ways—through policy research, human resource and water resource management initiatives, and through collaborative writing and speaking on these themes.

Conclusion

How can Northern and Southern partners most effectively collaborate in addressing the human issues cited by Riane Eisler at the beginning of this chapter? After examining some competing approaches to an international development practice to improve the conditions of poor women and their families, I have advanced here an argument for a "gender and development" (GAD) perspective on development praxis. Then, for some clues as to the practicalities of how to effectively implement such an approach, I have examined some experiences in working with gender issues in the context of a development relationship in Central America.

The learning from our experience in attempting to apply these principles in the context of the project would tend to affirm the argument for the appropriateness of a GAD analysis and strategy, informed in its practical application by the principles of *acompañamiento*, in the development relationship. Congruent, mutually informing, and enriching both analysis and action, GAD and *acompañamiento* offer us a means of applying principles inherent in progressive feminism to international collaboration.

There is an urgent need for a radical restructuring of development strategies and the context in which they occur—one that is informed by, and grows out of, a feminist critique of the failed growth-oriented development approaches of the past decades. Incorporating analysis of the interconnections between debt, poverty, and environmental degradation, this requires both short-term (conjunctural) and broader long-term (structural) analysis and strategies. It demands a linking of the household to the macroeconomic structure and, as Henry-Wilson (1990) notes, it will have to involve a substitution of the paradigm of the community for that of the market. It is essential that the critical emphases on grounding in grassroots lived experi-

---

[32] Perhaps not so mysterious: Nicaragua was a popular place for political and solidarity tourism and we had many house guests. It was not unusual for books to appear and disappear.

ence, and the promotion of local self-reliance and participation, be linked to political activity in broader arenas: an exclusive interest in promoting local self-reliance and participation may leave oppressive governments or elites free to shape the larger forces.

In the current conjuncture, the globalization of poverty, and the creation of a "global South" transcending traditional North-South borders, creates a convergence of circumstances between under-classes in the North and South and thus, ideal conditions for alliance building amongst like-minded groups globally. Social workers are well placed, in terms of both ethical commitment and skills, to participate and provide leadership in this, the development and advancement of a praxis that makes our allies in the Global South genuine architects of their own change processes, rather than passive recipients of development assistance.

Perspectives on Gender and International Development			
	WID	**WAD**	**GAD**
Development Model	Growth/trickle-down ("modernization") theory	Draws on both dependency theory and class analysis	Draws on dependency theory, class analysis, and popular education methods
Feminist Stream	Liberal feminism	(Vulgar) marxist feminism	Socialist feminism
Definition of the Problem	Women are left out of the development process (excluded from equal participation in education, employment, etc)	Unjust international structures	Unjust international structures. Development programs have been about, not of, poor women in the Global South
Action Orientation	Integrate women into ongoing development initiatives. End discrimination against women, reduce their disadvantages in the productive sector	Assumes women's position will improve when structures become just and equitable. Development strategies focused on income-generating activities	Builds on Third World women's experience of empowerment through self-organization in grassroots groups, to develop strategies to address not only immediate situations but also structures that oppress women; addresses social construction of both production and reproduction as bases of women's oppression.

Critiques/ Challenges	Fails to question the development strategies themselves, structural sources/ nature of women's subordination, or historical class and race divisions among women Income-generating projects further burden women, with earnings often appropriated by men	As with WID, focuses on productive sector, ignoring time burdens (private domain/ reproductive side of women's work and lives) Fails to address the relationships between patriarchy, modes of production, and oppression of women	Progress may appear slow in the short run Requires exceptional levels of trust and respect on the part of development agencies and national/ international allies.

References

- Alayón, Norberto, ed. 2005. *Trabajo Social Latinoamericano: a 40 Años de la Reconceptualización*. Buenos Aires: Espacio Editorial.
- Amin, Samir. 1996. On Development: for Gunder Frank. In *The Underdevelopment of Development: Essays in Honor of Andre Gunder Frank*, eds. Sing C. Chew and Robert A. Denemark, 59-86. Thousand Oaks: Sage Publications.
- Amin, Samir. 1992. *Empire of Chaos*. New York: Monthly Review Press.
- Amin, Samir. 1997. *Capitalism in the Age of Globalization*. London: Zed Books Ltd.
- Antrobus, Peggy. 1991. Development Alternatives with Women. *The Future for Women in Development: Voices from the South*. Proceedings of the Association for Women in Development Colloquium. Ottawa: The North-South Institute. 74–81.
- Antrobus, Peggy. 1991. *Learning Together/Working Together: A South-North Dialogue*. Paper presented to the Fifth International Forum of the Association for Women in Development, Washington (November 21).
- Antrobus, Peggy. 1991. *A Women in Development Agenda for the Nineties*. Paper presented to the Fifth International Forum of the Association for Women in Development, Washington (November 21).
- Antrobus, Peggy. 2004. *The Global Women's Movement: Origins, Issues and Strategies*. London: Zed Books Ltd
- Asamoah, Y., Lynne Healy, and M. C. Hokenstad. 2003. *Models of International Collaboration in Social Work Education*. New York: CSWE Press.
- Bandarage, Asoka. 1983. Toward International Feminism. *Brandeis Review* 3 (3).
- Bandarage, Asoka. 1984. Women in Development: Liberalism, Marxism and Marxist-Feminism. *Development and Change* 15: 495–515.
- Boserup, Ester. 1970. *Women's Role in Economic Development*. London: George Allen & Unwin.
- Chew, Sing C. and Robert A. Denemark, eds. *The Underdevelopment of Development: Essays in Honor of Andre Gunder Frank*. Thousand Oaks: Sage Publications.
- Close, David. 1988. *Nicaragua: Politics, Economics and Society*. London: Pinter.
- Collinson, H., ed. 1990. *Women and Revolution in Nicaragua*. London: Zed Books Ltd.
- Eisler, Riane. 1987. *The Chalice and the Blade: Our History, Our Future*. San Francisco: Harper Collins.
- Eisler, Riane, David Loye, and Kari Norgaard. 1995. *Women, Men and the Global Quality of Life*. Pacific Grove, CA: The Center for Partnership Studies.
- Escuela de Trabajo Social (ETS), Universidad Centroamericana (1984). *Modelo del Profesional del Trabajo Social*. Unpublished Document.

- Esteva, Gustavo and Madhu Suri Prakash. 1996. Beyond Global Neoliberalism to Local Regeneration: The International of Hope. *Interculture* XXIX (2): 15–52.
- Esteva, Gustavo, and Madhu Suri Prakash. 1997. From Global Thinking to Local Thinking. In *The Post- Development Reader*, eds. Majid Rahnema and Victoria Bawtree, 277–289. New York: Zed Books Ltd.
- Esteva, Gustavo and Madhu Suri Prakash. 1998. *Grassroots Post-Modernism: Beyond the Individual Self, Human Rights and Development*. London: Zed Books Ltd.
- Frank, Andre Gunder. 1969. *Latin America: Underdevelopment or Revolution*. New York: Monthly Review Press.
- Frank, Andre Gunder. 1996. The Underdevelopment of Development. In *The Underdevelopment of Development: Essays in Honor of Andre Gunder Frank*, eds. Sing C. Chew and Robert A. Denemark. Thousand Oaks: Sage Publications.
- Freire, Paolo. 1973. *Education for Critical Consciousness*. New York: Seabury Press.
- George, J. 1990. Women and Development: a Structural Approach. *Acción Critica*. 61–70.
- Goulet, Dennis. 1989. Participation in Development. *World Development* 17 (2): 165–178.
- Hancock, G. 1991. *Lords of Poverty*. London; Mandarin: Atlantic Monthly Press.
- Henry-Wilson, Maxine. 1990. UNIFEM, quoted by Antrobus (1991). 77.
- Hawes, F. and D. Kealey (1980). *Canadians in Development*. Hull: Canadian International Development Agency.
- Hawes, F. and D. Kealey. 1981. An Empirical Study of Canadian Technical Assistance: Adaption and Effectiveness on Overseas Assignment. *International Journal of Intercultural Relations* 5 (3): 239–258.
- Kealey, D. 1991. *Canadians Working Overseas*. Ottawa: Canadian International Development Agency.
- Kealey, Daniel J. 2001. *Cross-Cultural Effectiveness—A Study of Canadian Technical Advisors Overseas*. Ottawa: Centre for Intercultural Learning, Canadian Foreign Service Institute.
- Kealey, Daniel J. and David R. Protheroe. 1995. *Cross-Cultural Collaborations—Making North-South Cooperation More Effective*. Hull: Department of Foreign Affairs and International Trade.
- Kreitzer, Linda and Maureen Wilson. 2006. *Challenging Neoliberal Globalization: International Collaboration to Promote Indigenous Social Work*. Annual Conference of the International Association of Schools of Social Work. Santiago, Chile (August 28–31, 2006).
- Laforce, Jocelyne. 1998. Basic Human Needs Performance Review: Nicaragua Social Development Project Evaluation Report. Ottawa: Canadian International Development Agency.
- Mendoza Rangel, María del Carmen. 1986. *Una opción metodológica para los trabajadores sociales*. Mexico. DF: AMLETS.
- Midgley, James. 1997. Social Work And International Social Development. Ch. 2, eds. M. C. Hokenstad, and J. Midgley. *Issues In International Social Work: Global Challenges For A New Century*. 11–26. Washington: NASW.
- Mies, Maria and Veronica Bennholdt-Thomsen (translated by Patrick Camiller). 1999. *The Subsistence Perspective: Beyond the Globalized Economy*. New York: Zed Books.
- Molyneux, M. 1986. Mobilzation Without Emancipation? Women's Interest, State, and Revolution, eds. Richard R. Fagen, Carmen Diana Deere, and José Luis Coraggio. *Transition and Development: Problems of Third World Socialism*. New York: Monthly Review Press.
- Molyneux, M. 1985. Women, ed. T. W. Walker. *Nicaragua: the First Five Years*. 145–162. New York: Praeger.
- Mueller, Adele. 1991. *The Development Business*. Carleton University, Ottawa (October).
- Murphy, B. K. 1991. Canadian NGOs and the politics of participation. In *Conflicts of Interest: Canada and the third World*, eds. J. Swift and B. Tomlinson, 161–211. Toronto: Between the Lines.
- Orwell, George. 1938. *Homage to Catalonia*. London: Secker and Warburg.
- Peterson, V. Spike and Anne Sisson Runyan. 1999. *Global Gender Issues*. 2nd ed. Boulder: Westview Press.

- Plewes, Betty and Rieky Stuart. 1991. Women and Development Revisited: The Case for a Gender and Development Approach. In *Conflicts of Interest: Canada and the Third World*, eds. Jamie Swift and Brian Tomlinson, 107–132. Toronto: Between the Lines.
- Prado Hernández, Iris and Martha Palacios. 2005. Importancia y Vigencia del Moviemiento de Reconceptualización del Trabajo Social en Nicaragua. In *Trabajo Social Latinoamericano: a 40 Años de la Reconceptualización*, ed. Norberto Alayón, 233–244. Buenos Aires: Espacio Editorial.
- Jaquette, Jane S. 1982. Women and Modernization Theory: A Decade of Feminist Criticism. *World Politics* 34 (2): 3.
- Rahnema, Majid, ed. 1997. *The Post-Development Reader.* London: Zed Books Ltd.
- Ramierz-Horton, S. 1982. The Role of Women in the Nicaraguan Revolution. In *Nicaraguan Revolution*, ed. Thomas W. Walker. New York; Praeger: Westview Press.
- Randall, Margaret. 1981. *Sandino's Daughters: Testimonies of Nicaraguan Women in Struggle.* Toronto: New Star Books.
- Rathgeber, Eva, M. 1990. WID, WAD, GAD: Trends in Research and Practice. *Journal of Developing Areas* 24 (4): 489–502.
- Ruben, B. D. and D. J. Kealey. 1979. Behavioral Assessment of Communication Competency and the Prediction of Cross-Cultural Adaptation. *International Journal of Intercultural Relation* 3: 15–47.
- Sen, Gita and Caren Grown. 1987. *Development, Crises and Alternative Visions: Third World Women's Perspectives.* New York: Monthly Review Press.
- Social Watch Research Team. 2006. *Impossible Architecture: Why the Financial Structure is Not Working for the Poor and How to Redesign it for Equity and Development.* Montevideo, Uruguay: Instituto del Tercer Mundo.
- Swift, Jamie. 1991. Introduction. In *Conflicts of Interest: Canada and the Third World*, eds. Jamie Swift and Brian Tomlinson. 13–24. Toronto: Between the Lines.
- United Nations Development Programme. 2006. *Human Development Report 2006: Beyond scarcity: Power, poverty and the global water crisis.* http://hdr.undp.org/hdr2006/.
- United Nations Development Programme. 2005. *Human Development Report 2005. International Cooperation at a Crossroads: Aid, Trade and Security in an Unequal World.* Cary: Oxford University Press.
- Visvanathan, Nalini, Lynn Duggan, Laurie Nisonoff, and Nan Wiegersma, eds. 1997. *The Women, Gender, and Development Reader.* London: Zed Books Ltd.; Halifax: Fernwood.
- Vulpe, Thomas, Daniel Kealey, David Protheroe, and Doug MacDonald. 2000 *A Profile of the Interculturally Effective Person.* Hull: Canada Department of Foreign Affairs and International Trade.
- Waring, Marilyn. 1999. *Counting For Nothing: What Men Value And What Women Are Worth* 2nd ed. Toronto: University of Toronto Press.
- Wilson, Maureen G. 2003. South-North Development Partnership: Lessons from a Nicaragua-Canada Experience. In *Models of International Collaboration in Social Work Education*, eds. Y. Asamoah, Lynne Healy, and M. C. Hokenstad, 111–123. New York: CSWE Press.
- Wilson, Maureen G. 1993. What Difference Could a Revolution Make? Group Work in the New Nicaragua. In *Group Work Reaching Out: People, Places, and Power*, ed. James A. Garland. 301–314. New York: Haworth Press.
- Wilson, Maureen G. and E. Whitmore. 2000. *Seeds of Fire: Social Development in an Era of Globalism.* Halifax: Fernwood Publishing; Croton-on-Hudson: Apex Press.
- Wilson, Maureen G. and Iris Prado Hernández. 2007. The Liberatory Tradition in Nicaraguan Social Work. In *Radical Social Work in an Era of Globalisation*, eds. Iain Ferguson and Michael Lavalette. Birmingham: Venture Press.
- Wilson, Shamillah, Anansya Sengupta, and Kristy Evans, eds. 2005. *Defending Our Dreams: Global Feminist Voices for a New Generation.* London: Zed Books Ltd.
- Wise, V. 1991. Feminism Must Redefine Itself. *Venceremos*, (Autumn): 21–23.

Chapter 7

Social Development and Human Rights During Economic Transition: Women in Russia & Cuba

Colleen Lundy & Therese Jennissen

S ocial work was borne out of economic and social conditions that accompanied the transformation to industrial capitalist development in nineteenth century Europe and North America. (Woodroofe 1962; Lubove 1965; Wills 1995). The dual processes of industrialization and urbanization, within a market economy, resulted in dramatic increases and intensification of poverty that went well beyond the capabilities of private charities. A social work profession eventually developed, equipped with a set of skills for practice that could effectively be transmitted through education and training, and it embarked on a new approach for dealing with personal and social problems in society. Since the early decades of the twentieth century, cooperative efforts existed among many industrialized nations of the world to share their common experiences and knowledge regarding social work and social welfare.

But while social work is commonly understood as a by-product of industrial capitalism in much the same manner as we understand the welfare state, few comparisons have been made in the social welfare and social work literature between industrial capitalist and industrial socialist societies. The term "industrialization," in fact, has almost become synonymous with capitalist industrialization. Historically in the West there was little understanding of the approaches to social development and social justice that were adopted in socialist countries;[1] it was commonly assumed that there wasn't much development in these areas.

This lack of awareness about life under socialism was largely the result of the propaganda campaigns of the Cold War Era. But as conditions of life during these recent periods of transformation come to light, we are discovering that former socialist societies had highly developed social infrastructures that rival those that exist in private market economies. As these nations struggle to deal with the social dislocation resulting from their transforming economic and political structures, there is an interest in developing social work as a profession that can assist in social reconstruction. As western social workers and social work educators are called on to advise and assist in the development of social infrastructures, including social work education, it is important that we understand both the history and contemporary challenges

---

[1] Comparative studies of social welfare and social work typically deal with an analysis of countries with similar socio-economic systems, such as, countries belonging to the European Union.

that face these societies. Moreover we have an obligation to raise with those we are advising, the challenges to social justice and social development that exist in private market economies as we have experienced them.

Cuba and the Russian Federation have experienced varying degrees of economic transformations from centrally planned socialist economies to private market systems. Over the past several years, we have had the opportunity to be involved with colleagues in these two countries who are struggling with social issues during periods of economic transition. We are particularly interested in how the two countries have dealt with issues of social and economic justice, equality, and human rights as they pertain to women. We examine women's employment opportunities, their economic and health status, and the extent to which they experience violence. While women are only one of many important groups differentially affected during periods of economic transformation, they represent a significant part of the population and constitute a group that consistently carries a disproportionate burden, especially during difficult times (Waring 1999). The status of women, we argue, is an important indicator of a country's commitment, or lack thereof, to social justice, human rights, and equality and almost always is a harbinger of things to come in the social realm.

The chapter draws on secondary sources and is based on primary research that was collected through partnerships with colleagues in Russia and Cuba. Based on research with a team of scholars in the Russian Academy of Science, and two visits to Moscow between 2000 and 2002, we explore the impact on society as a whole, and in particular on women, families and women's organizing efforts to resist and respond to both capitalism and increased patriarchal subordination.[2] In regard to Cuba, the research is based on field visits over a four year period, as well as on secondary sources. While in Cuba we talked with professional women from the Women's Studies Department, the Cuban Women's Federation, and various professional associations. We also met women who were journalists and others who worked in the tourist sector.

Our research was further informed by our participation in the three international women's conferences held at the University of Havana as well as our teaching in the Women's Studies Department at the University of Havana in 1998 and 1999.[3] We also met with a number of Cuban female scholars when they visited Canada in recent years. During these and other visits we have come to know many Cuban women, both as individuals and members of

---

[2] The research project "Social Protection in Russia Under Conditions of Crisis" was a partnership between faculty at Carleton University and the Institute of Socio-economic Studies of Population, Russian Academy of Science in Moscow. The project was funded by the University of Calgary Gorbachev Foundation. The final report and the social welfare strategy was published as a text in Russian with an English summary. Natalia Rimashevskaya (ed.) Social Protection of Population, Institute of Socio-economic Studies: Moscow 2002. Members of the Institute, noted for their feminist analyses and contributions, created the Centre for Gender Studies in 1990.

[3] This research was made possible in part through our involvement in the Carleton University-University of Havana CIDA-sponsored project, "Supporting Cuba's Management of its Transformation: Enhancing the Universities' Contribution."

groups, and have continued to be informed about their experiences in Cuba. As often happens, we came away with more questions than answers as the complexities of Russian and Cuban life was increasingly revealed to us.

We begin with a brief historical context including a discussion of the latest periods of economic transformation that have occurred in both Russia and Cuba and offer an overview of the changes that took place in the economy, politics, state structures, population, and social relations. This is followed by a discussion that compares and contrasts the social conditions of women in the respective countries during times of economic transitions. Particular attention is paid to the status of women as measured by employment opportunities, the prevalence of poverty among women, their health status, and violence against women. We provide a section on how women have been responding to their social and economic circumstances and the resilience that they continue to show in the face of tremendous challenges. In particular, we identify women's studies and social work programs in universities.

Historical and Political Contexts

Throughout history, societies have endured major economic transformations that are accompanied by a reordering of political and social priorities. At the beginning of the last century, some of the most profound economic transformations came in the form of socialist revolutions characterized by efforts to create centrally planned economies, owned and controlled by working people, and social benefits for the entire population. The USSR and Cuba were two of a number of countries that followed this model. By the 1970s, neo-liberal globalization emerged at the head of the world economic order based on an idea that civilization would advance and best grow through global private markets. Globalization carried the blind promise that international trade would create economic growth that eventually would trickle down and lead to a rise in living standards and an improved quality of life for everyone across the globe. The century closed with a "great victory for globalism" (Ralston Saul 2005, 113) when, in 1989, the first socialist country reversed its economic direction and embraced capitalism "of the late-nineteenth-century sort" (Ralston Saul, 112).

The collapse of the Soviet Union had a profound effect throughout the world, but it was felt most acutely in Cuba, a country that had been heavily dependent on the USSR for trade. Although both countries were in periods of economic transition, events unfolded quite differently for each of them. The USSR saw a dismantling of the union of Soviet republics into 15 separate states and a complete overhaul of its economic, political, and social infrastructures. Supported and encouraged by western capitalists, it introduced a ruthless form of capitalism that included the selling off of its resources and an almost complete dismantling of the social infrastructure. Cuba found itself in a different situation. Faced with a severe economic crises unleashed by the fall of the Soviet Union, the Cuban government was compelled to make major modifications to its economic structure. The

Cuban government initiated the *periodo especial en el tiempo del paz* (special period in peace time), which introduced modified capitalism to keep a flow of money entering the country while at the same time retaining elements of socialism, particularly its continued support of its population through social programs. In both Russia and Cuba, these periods of transformation have had profound effects on the population.

Cuba and Russia have many similarities and differences. Russia is the world's largest country, stretching over 11 time zones with a population of 146 million, while Cuba is a small island with a population of 11.4 million. Both countries established socialist societies through political and economic revolutions that had, at their core, a commitment to the distribution of resources within the population. They nationalized major industries, centralized planning, and established publicly funded universal education and health care, daycare, housing, guarantees of employment as well as policies committed to the advancement of women.

But the struggle to build socialism occurred under hostile conditions. The prevalence of the Cold War from the 1940s to the 1980s curtailed the development of socialism in both Cuba and Russia. The paranoia and mistrust that existed between the socialist and capitalist worlds fuelled the development of a military and defence industry in the USA and USSR that is unparalleled in world history. For the USSR, this meant that resources were diverted from the construction of socialism. Pauwels (2002, 243) explains that this lead to a "beleaguered and therefore unattractive and grim kind of socialism." Despite these circumstances, the Soviet people made many important gains in their material, social, and cultural conditions of life. Because of its size and proximity to the USA, Cuba faced different challenges. For over a half century, the American government made repeated attempts to invade the country, sabotage the government, and assassinate its political leaders. Cuba continues to be a victim of economic sanctions and a blockade by the US.

In 1989, with the dismantling of the former Soviet Union, the leaders of the newly formed Russian Federation introduced capitalism and "market fundamentalism," which sent the country into a crisis, unprecedented in peacetime.[4] The introduction of raw capitalism included selling the country's natural resources, at below market prices, to a few well-connected players. These trends and the absence of a civil society created tremendous hardships for the Russian people. The processes of marketization and privatization also included the liberalization of prices, galloping inflation, real unemployment, privatization of industrial enterprises and housing, and a reduction in state funding of science, culture, education, and medical care. Previous social guarantees of employment, medical care and government subsidies for food, clothing, shelter, and transportation were removed or eroded. In

---

[4] While the demise of socialism in 1991 is often viewed as naturally collapsing, Cohen (2000, 24) argues that, prior to this, Gorbachev's reforms had already dismantled socialism and that "The record shows that the Union did not so much 'collapse' as it was disassembled by a small group of ranking Soviet officials, Yeltsin foremost among them, in a struggle over power and property."

1992, when the prices were "freed," consumer prices increased more than 100 times with the "dollarization" of domestic prices, while wages increased by 10 times (Chossudovsky 1997). An example illustrating the dramatic level of inflation is that "before the transition, 7,000 rubles was the price of a car, but in January 1992, at market prices, the same sum would buy only a pair of ladies boots" (Samorodov 1992, 335). Ordinary people were destitute as their savings were wiped out by inflation.

The US Treasury and IMF proponents of this "shock therapy" believed that a rapid process of privatization was needed to counter the threat of a return to socialism. On the other side were the "gradualists" who correctly predicted that such a process would bring disaster, economic failure, and political corruption. Joseph Stiglitz, who has served as chief economist of the World Bank, became disillusioned as he watched the IMF place the interests of financial institutions ahead of the plight of people (Stiglitz 2002). The US administration and IMF advisors' short cut to capitalism created a system of "crony and mafia capitalism" with limited democracy. A capitalist economy without the institutional infrastructure resulted in a cadre of corrupt officials and businessmen who became rich.[5]

The country had been transformed from an industrial power into one with levels of inequality comparable to that of some of the worst in the developing world. The GDP continued to fall year after year resulting in a loss greater than the country had experienced in WWII. Between 1940–46, industrial production fell 24%, whereas in 1990–99 industrial production fell 60%. The GDP in 2000 was less than two-thirds of what it was in 1989. Now natural resources such as oil and gas account for half of all exports. Stiglitz observes: "Russia has gotten the worst of all possible worlds—an enormous decline in output and an enormous increase in inequality" (Stiglitz 2002, 155). Minimum wages in the Russian Federation are currently the lowest in Europe (Titterton 2006, 92).

The transition has produced unemployment and rising income inequality. In the new Russia, 5% of the population is rich or very rich; approximately 5-7 million people hold 72.5% of the general wealth accumulation, whereas the vast majority of the population are poor and hold 3.3% of the wealth. Between 1991 and 2000 the Gini[6] coefficient has increased from .26 to .41. In 1991, the income of the top 10% of the population was 4.5 times

---

[5] The IMF decided on a "rescue package" of $22.6 Billion (IMF $11.2 Billion, WB $6 Billion, and Japan $5.4 Billion) (Stiglitz 2002). And, as the opponents of the rescue package predicted, several days after the loans were made, billions of dollars made their way out of the country into Swiss and Cypriot bank accounts. IMF policies forced Russia deeper into debt—a debt that rests heavily on the backs of the beleaguered taxpayer. The insistence of the IMF that Russia maintain an overvalued currency and the provision of billions of dollars in loans suppressed the economy. Stiglitz outlines how when the ruble was finally devalued in 1998, inflation did not rise rapidly as the IMF predicted and the economy had its first growth.

[6] The Gini coefficient, a common measure of inequality, ranges from 0 (perfect equality) to 1 (perfect inequality). For example, the value for market incomes in Canada in 1998 was .506, a 15% increase from 1980 when it was 441 (Ernie Lightman. 2003. *Social Policy in Canada*, Don Mills: Oxford University Press).

higher than the bottom 10%, while in 2000 it was 14.3 times higher (*Social Protection in Russia Under Conditions of Crisis* 2001).

The most telltale sign of the devastating impact of the changes on the Russian population has been the dramatic decline in life expectancy. Between 1990 and 1994, life expectancy for Russian men dropped from 63.8 to 57.7 and for women from 74.4 to 71.2 (Notzon et al. 1998). By 2003, both increased slightly to 59 for men and 72.1 for women (Human Development Reports 2005). Between 1990 and 1995 there was also a dramatic increase in premature deaths; the mortality rate among men between the ages of 35 and 44, for example, was four times that in Western Europe (Titterton 2006, 93). Such a rapid decline during peacetime in industrial countries has been unheard of.

In recent years, there has been a reappearance of diseases such as tuberculosis, poliomyelitis, and all types of STDs, as well as a sharp increase in hepatitis and HIV/AIDS infections (Titterton 2006, 92). The leading causes of death are heart disease (60% of all deaths), accidents, cancer, drug abuse, and suicide (Titova 2003, 2). Nikolai Gerasimenko, head of the State Duma Committee, reported that "It is a result of a lingering social and economic crisis, characterized by the rise of unemployment; chronic delays in paying salaries, pensions and social aid; worsening nutrition; decreased access to medical care and medicines; and the stress generated by people's lack of confidence in their futures and those of their children" (Titova 2003, 2).

The economic and political changes in the former Soviet Union had a major impact on Cuba. As a key trading partner with the former USSR, Cuba immediately felt the impact of these changes. The drastic decline in imports and exports resulted in severe shortages of basic necessities, and intensified an already difficult situation created by the US economic blockade. During the "special period," the government established an austerity program that included a rationing system for food and essential consumer items. As a strategy for survival, the Cuban government introduced a modified market economy, while maintaining a socialist political and economic structure. This included the decriminalization of the possession of the USD (1993)[7], legalization of self-employment and the promotion of small businesses and foreign investment, the introduction of income taxes, the legalization of the US dollar, and the creation of a convertible peso (in 1995).

Small private businesses began to grow in Cuba; common among them are family-operated restaurants called *paladars,* bicycle repair shops, pastry shops, and lodging arrangements set up in private homes (*casa particulars*). Although such private enterprises or micro-enterprise are permitted, there are legal restrictions placed on their operation. For example, there can be no self-employment in professional work; there is a prohibition on intermediaries ("the middleman"); the public media cannot be used for marketing

---

[7] In November 2004, Cuba stopped circulation of the USD as a response to tighter American sanctions on the county. Tourists that arrive with USD are charged a 10% commission fee to exchange them to convertible pesos.

purposes; and entrepreneurs cannot use the labour of anyone other than family members. Inspectors enforce these laws and violators are fined (Ritter, 1999). The development of "modified" private enterprises creates a complex and contradictory situation in Cuba as the country shifts away from a centralized economy toward a private market model, albeit one that is "modified."

Life for Cubans during the special period is nonetheless a life of increased hardships. Necessary imports were cut off with the demise of the Soviet bloc and this resulted in a growing social inequality in the country. The tourist industry tends to have a preference for young, light-skinned, and "attractive" Cuban men and women when hiring employees (Shakur 2005). Increasingly, tourists arrive expecting the services of prostitutes, and unfortunately, prostitution among young women is prevalent.

Those who are employed in the international capitalist ventures such as the tourist industry and mining, have access to foreign currency and privileges that most Cubans are denied. Frequently, doctors and university professors abandon jobs for which they have had years of training to drive taxis or work as waiters in the tourist sector so that they can access foreign currency and make life easier for their families. These developments have produced a level of entrepreneurs who have lifestyles that are substantially different from the rest of the population (Dilla 1999).

Daily life for the majority of the population includes transportation shortages and scarcity of basic necessities such as food, household items, clothing, and medical supplies. Unofficial estimates in the mid 1990s variously reported that between 10% and 20% of the population had access to the USD and for these Cubans, material life was easier (Granma International 1997; Hurlich 1995). There appeared to be no shortage of food items (including coffee), toiletries, appliances, and clothing in the dollar stores where the currency is the USD. Although the US dollar was replaced by the comparable convertible peso, the privileges remain.

The majority of the populations of both Russia and Cuba have experienced increased hardships during these periods of economic transformation, but there are differences between them. The human development comparisons between the two countries are striking. Most revealing of Cuba's progress compared to Russia are indicators such as life expectancy (age 77.2 v. 65.4), and infant mortality (6 v. 16 per 1000 births). Overall on the Human Development Index (which combines measures of life expectancy, school enrolment, literacy, and income), Cuba ranked 52 and Russia 62 of all countries. Cuba is considered a developing country and on the human poverty index (HPI) ranked 5th among 103 developing countries (Human Development Report, 2005). According to the *World Fact Book* (2006), the mortality rate in Russia is double that of Cuba's—14.65 v. 7.22 per one thousand people (Canada stands at 7.8) and reflects the increase in violence in Russian society. Most disturbing is the documented rise in violence against women and racially motivated killings in Russia (Amnesty

International 2006). Violence against women is also a concern in Cuba, but to a lesser degree.

Marginalization of Women

Women are particularly affected by economic transitions, debt crises, and structural adjustment programs. Their employment is most likely to be threatened and, as living conditions deteriorate, their domestic and caring responsibilities increase (Molyneux 1996; Feldman 1992; Safa and Antrobus 1992). Women are also negatively affected, in disproportionate numbers, by a severe reduction or elimination of state-supported programs following the move to private market economies (Neft and Levine 1997). This combination of circumstances has led to an over-representation of women in the most vulnerable groups (the elderly, single parent households, and low wage workers or the unemployed).

In both the USSR and Cuba, women made major strides towards equality with regard to employment, education, and political participation in government. In both countries the state made efforts to socialize caring work through the institution of maternity benefits and widespread daycare programs to support women's participation in the public sphere. However, these initiatives were unsuccessful in eradicating gender inequalities in the home and while patriarchal beliefs and practices, to some extent, were mitigated, they remained entrenched (Metcalf and Afanassieva 2005; Smith and Padulla 1996). Women continued to be responsible for reproductive labour and the provision of social care: reproducing a supply of labour through child bearing, caring for and nurturing children, cleaning the home, shopping for food and clothing, preparing food, and tending to spouses and extended family members, including ailing family members.

This double or triple workday (some women were also involved in community or political work) presents problems of stress, overwork, health problems, and family problems. The work of caring has been understood as an activity and a set of relations lying at the intersection of state, market, and family (Daly and Lewis 2000). The current situation, in both Russia and Cuba, presents a critical opportunity to examine the impact on women during periods of economic transformation and to revisit the long-standing debate over the relationship between socialism and women's equality.

Russia

The transition, from a centrally planned socialist economy to a private market model, is one where private interests are privileged over public, and collective values are replaced by individualism and competition. While most of the Russian population has been affected by the transition to a market economy, women are negatively affected in unique ways and in disproportionate numbers. Of particular interest to us is the profound and rapid nature of the deterioration of the important gains that women had secured during the Soviet era. During that time, women made major strides towards equality with men. Equal access to higher education, training in almost all trades and professions, equal pay for equal work, publicly funded programs of social protection, universal health care, and guarantees of employment were made available to women (Kalistratova 1989). However, as Western feminists have repeatedly observed, the gains of Soviet women were mainly in the productive realm (McCuaig 1989; Reiter and Luxton 1989). As important as these changes were for women, they did not significantly alter the gendered division of domestic labour and the Soviet Union, despite its socialist orientation, became known as a continent of exhausted women who performed double workdays (McCuaig 1989, 11).

Full employment for women was an important objective during the Soviet era and the participation of Soviet women in the labour market was the highest in the world. This policy was motivated by the belief that full employment was essential for women's emancipation, but it was also driven by the need for labour (Reiter and Luxton 1989, 27). Soviet women were regarded as essentially different from men in their emotional and psychological makeup and in their social responsibilities; women and men were seen as having different, but complementary roles in society (Reiter and Luxton 1989, 27; Waters 1989, 31).

While state-sponsored social programs removed some of the pressures of the double workday for Soviet women, they did little to redistribute domestic labour between men and women. For the most part, men remained uninvolved in domestic work and their roles remained unchallenged. Quite possibly men were placated by the existence of state supports for women since it removed some of the pressure from them and from their partners. The effect of this, however, was that neither Soviet men nor women came to expect that men should play an active role in reproductive labour, specifically, the work of caring. This has resulted in a particularly difficult situation for women in the post-Soviet era when the social support systems have been eroding and the full brunt of reproductive labour falls exclusively to women. Not only are women expected to do this work, but also, because of the erosion of social supports, the care of family interferes with women's ability to participate in the paid labour force.

Cuba

Similar to the USSR, post-Revolution Cuba also directed attention toward improving the status of Cuban women. The dramatic increase in women's participation in the paid labour force, the provision of child care, new educational opportunities, and the encouragement of women's participation in political work made women more independent and less financially reliant on male partners. These positive aspects, however, were contradicted by the fact that women continued to do most of the domestic labour. In fact, Cuban women were also ultimately responsible for triple workloads— paid employment, caring responsibilities in the family, and political work (Allahar 1994). In an attempt to deal with the fact that women were solely responsible for housework and caring, the state introduced the Family Code on International Women's Day March 8, 1975. The Family Code outlines men's responsibility for half of the housework and child care, emphasizes equality between men and women, and equality of all children (Smith and Padula 1996).

Despite the existence of the Family Code, the traditional roles of women in the family have persisted. Stereotypical distinctions between male and female remain strong in Cuba. Carolina Aguilar, a member of the national leadership of the Federation of Cuban Women (FMC[8]) explains the persistence of machismo in Cuban culture as, "a residue of a repressive, macho culture which we've dragged along with us since time immemorial, a characteristic of all former capitalist societies and brought here by the Spanish 500 years ago"(Aguilar and Chenard 1994, 107–108).

In the mid-1990s, as the economic crisis in Cuba intensified the planned electrical blackouts and rotating water cut-offs, transportation shortages, scarcity of basic necessities such as food, fuel, clothing, and soap, shortages of medical supplies and paper products, created a disruption in domestic life and introduced particular hardships for women who not only continue to do the domestic work, but who now need to do it more creatively with fewer resources. Women spent more time going to stores, waiting in lineups at the *bodegas*, searching for scarce items that were often sold out, and regularly waiting for lengthy periods of times for buses that travel on irregular schedules. This situation was compounded by the fact that the universal daycare put into place in 1961 has not been able to keep up with the demand. During this special period, the shortage of money for supplies did not permit much-needed centres to be built and only 20% of women had access to state run daycare services (Rains and Bopp Stark 1997, 84). This was accompanied by a policy to reduce or eliminate subsidies for milk and milk products for children, children's clothes, and school uniforms.

Cuban women freely admit that they continue to do most of the domestic labour in addition to working outside the home. The results of a survey conducted by the *Oficina Nacional de Estadísticas de Cuba* (National Bureau of Statistics) indicate that, among university graduates, working women contribute three times as much time on domestic work as men. An additional factor of interest is that as the cultural level (and possibly educational level) of the man is raised, so is the weight of the household work for the woman (Vasallo 2001, 10). However, there is some indication that there may be some changes occurring. Norma Vasallo points out that the special period has forced men and women to redefine domestic work: " … [domestic labour] has acquired more social and political value; it has become more visible as a supplier to the workforce; and, in many homes, all this has contributed to a redistribution of domestic roles with men assuming tasks that previously they did not perform in order to guarantee the survival of the family" (2004, 94).

---

[8] Federacion de Mujeres Cubanas.

Employment, Poverty, and Health

Russia

During the Soviet period, women's labour market participation was the highest among other economies in the world (Rzhanitsyna 2001). However, the shift from a state supported, community-based system of social protection toward reliance on a private, market-based system drastically changed the society. There is no longer a guarantee of the basic provisions of life such as health care, housing, and employment. With this erosion of the safety net, women often find that their responsibilities within the family are magnified and that their role in society is diminished. This is due to a complex set of factors, some of which are embedded in the history of the Soviet era and are magnified in the current context.[9] According to Natalia Rimashevskaya, it is "the family that protects the person and mitigates the consequences of social and economic shocks caused by liberalization of the economy" (2001, 13). Women now find themselves in situations where their responsibilities to home and family contribute to their inequality in the labour market, and their lack of political and economic power in turn reinforces their subordinate role in the domestic sphere.

Women's reliance on state social supports has engendered, in the post-Soviet era, a backlash against their previous advancements and this further discriminates against women, particularly in the paid labour market. Benería suggests that the "[r]eturn to the market has therefore implied the re-emergence of old male privileges by eliminating mechanisms that decreased gender inequality" (Benería 1989, 332).[10] Related to this is a resurgence of patriarchal ideology and practices; increased violence against women; and the declining participation of women in formal political life. Discrimination against women in employment occurred in two ways: women lost jobs, and they were not hired back once they were laid off work. Between 1991 and 1998, eight million Russian women lost work and represented 67% of the total unemployed over that period (Rzhanitsyna 2001, 52). Unemployment in some professions rose partly because of the sheer numbers of female specialists, such as economists and engineers, who were employed in the state run management organizations that were severely reduced in numbers with the downsizing of the military industrial complex (Koblitz 1995, 54). Many unemployed women are highly educated; overall women constitute 73% of the unemployed population that has secondary or higher levels of

---

[9] Some researchers argue that the contemporary decline in the status of women in Russia was set in motion in the 1970s when there was a steadily increasing support for the notion of male-female biological differences and an increasing public acceptance of the domestic roles of women. "A Liberation from Emancipation? Changing Discourses on Women's Employment in Soviet and Post-Soviet Russia" (R. Kay 2002).

[10] Debates over gender discrimination are not new. For example, there has been a long-standing debate over protective legislation aimed at guarding the physical and reproductive health of women. In the Soviet era, women were excluded from jobs in heavy industry and resource extraction; jobs that were often located in remote communities, but jobs that were also the most lucrative (Luke 1996, 82). The question over whether this constitutes protection or discrimination for women continues to be debated (Rzhanitsyna 2001, 60–61).

education that are registered with the employment service (Rzhanitsyna 2001, 54).

In the new capitalist labour market, workers must be prepared to relocate from one company to another and among the regions. For women, particularly single heads of households, this can present serious problems. Women's labour is often less mobile than it is for men because women's abilities to participate in the labour force depends, among other factors, on the after school programs for their children and their proximity to work.

With an eye to the profit margin, private employers are not willing to hire women because of the extra costs incurred for maternity leave, daycare, and other social protective measures. From a market point of view, the social costs of female labour would have to be lowered before the demand for their labour can expect to increase (Moghadan 1996, 341). This is particularly troubling because private companies rarely comply with existing social legislation, but they continue to justify their actions based on the continued "formal" existence of these policies. These strategies left Russian women vulnerable to layoffs and discriminatory hiring practices (Rzhanitsyna 1995, 41; Koblitz 1995, 54). The very social supports upon which women in the Soviet era came to rely, therefore, served to work against them in the post-Soviet era.

There are a number of other disquieting developments in women's employment. In the last decade in Russia there have been reports of gender bias in hiring, particularly in hiring managers, as well as reports of overt sexism based on women's physical appearances. In some cases women have been required to send in pictures of themselves with their job applications (Kay 2002, 68). Rzhanitsyna reached the following conclusions about women's employment in Russia: wages are lower in sectors where women predominate; at the sector and intersector level, there is a lower range of salaries for men than for women; and women working in predominantly male sector jobs have a chance of getting more than women in the same profession working in "female" sector jobs (Rzhanitsyna 2001, 56).

The overarching conclusion of the study paints a stark picture for Russian women—many employed women are living in poverty and those women with dependents are barely able to survive. Although equal opportunity and equal pay legislation continue to exist on the books, no mechanism for implementation or enforcement exists and the policies are rendered useless. According to Rzhanitsyna, the judicial system is too frail to mount any resistance and the ability of the state to monitor violations of the labour codes is limited. This problem is exacerbated by a declining labour movement and an attitude toward labour relations that features a "balance of interests" between employers and workers (Rzhanitsyna 2001, 60). Moreover, some are willing or compelled to work for low wages; and low wages are better than no wages at all. For other women it makes economic sense to stay at home.

Russia has a high ratio of women to men (111:100) as a result of high casualties in the Second World War and, overall, women live longer than men. This means that there is a concentration of women among Russia's senior population; older women outnumber men by 2:1 (Fong 1993, 3). These older women have seen a rapid and severe deterioration in the quality of life since the onset of capitalism in Russia. Rapid inflation in the early 1990s wiped out savings and left them dependent on small pensions with little or no subsidies for health care, food, and housing. With the removal of a responsive system of social protection, the most vulnerable in the country, particularly the elderly and disabled, cannot survive in the competitive capitalist economy.

Poverty almost always contributes to deteriorating health at some time or other in a person's life. This fact, combined with the erosion of the public health care system, presents a pessimistic picture. The most obvious, but certainly not the only, manifestations of the deteriorating health of women are increased infant and maternal mortality rates (Fong 1993, 1). Termination of milk subsidies for children, escalating food costs, and general impoverishment have led to increased malnutrition among the population overall. Stress and depression are common results of "shock therapy." Another aspect of women's health is the shortage of safe contraceptives that lead to a heavy reliance on abortion as a form of birth control and increases in the risks of contracting sexually transmitted diseases including HIV/AIDS. Russia has witnessed an extensive weakening of its public health system and a tendency toward population decline; the mortality rates far exceeded the birth rates. "Stress, poverty, malnutrition, poor health care, disregard by employees of sanitary norms and requirements of safety precautions have resulted in escalation of disability" (Rimashevskaya 2001, 36).

Another trend that has developed is the trafficking of Russian women for prostitution, particularly in the Nordic countries (Alalehto, 2002). According to a study by Tage Alalehto, the trade in women and children is a booming business that developed with the breakdown of the Soviet Union. "[It] meant that criminal factions that used to be hidden for their own safety could appear openly and run prosperous businesses in a decaying society that demanded radical market-economic solutions. This is where the organized trade of merchandise and services was born, one with whom disreputable consumers from the West would trade" (Alalehto 2002, 97). The state's actions in Russian society support a small segment of the population as it largely abandons its responsibility to the most vulnerable members, namely women, children, and the elderly. Helping to prop up these changes is a resurgence of interest in patriarchal values and attitudes and a return to traditional gender roles (Rzhanitsyna 2001, 60).

Cuba

The circumstances of Cuban women stand in stark contrast. In general, Cuban women do not face the same issues of unemployment, poverty, and an erosion of social services like their Russian counterparts. Since the Revolution, Cuban women have enjoyed the protection of their basic human rights: the right to employment, access to all levels of education without costs to the individual, access to quality health care, and the right to live in a society that officially and actively opposes discrimination on the basis of class, race, and sex.

The impact of the special period, however, had a profound effect on Cuban women. For example, Cuban women were affected by the serious shortage of reliable contraceptives and increasingly were forced to rely on abortions (Aguilar and Pereira 1995). There was a growing concern over the steep increase in teenage motherhood that comprised 25% of all new mothers. This rate was one of the highest in the world, and exceeded the rate of 14% in both Costa Rica and Nicaragua (Neft and Levine 1997, 111).

The female economic activity rate in recent years in Cuba has been about 51%, while in Russia it has been around 59% (Human Development Reports 2005). Since the Revolution, women have made major inroads into non-traditional jobs. For example, in the late 1980s, 41% of all agricultural engineers were women, 35% of all forestry engineers, and 47% of all engineers in a range of fields were female (Smith and Padula, 1996, 111) and nearly 50% of all doctors in Cuba were women (Froines 1993, 236). Yet women comprised only 27 % of those in the managerial positions (Smith and Padula 1996, 114). While women are finding jobs in the burgeoning tourist sector, it is unclear what percentage of the "better jobs" (e.g., management positions) they occupy.

During the special period, transportation problems, a reduction in child care facilities due to the lack of supplies, combined with the pressure of performing domestic work with few resources seriously threatened women's participation in the labour force. Based on her research in Cuba at that time, Ruth Pearson (1997) concluded that:

> ... there has been a considerable shift from the formal sector employment to informal sector income-generating activity as well as a preference for activities linked with tourism and foreign capital. There is a strong suggestion that many women have found it particularly difficult to maintain their place in the formal labour force in the face of the increasing time and effort required to meet the reproductive needs of their household. (698).

Women in both Russia and Cuba have acknowledged that violence against women is a serious concern and is a major factor in women's emotional and physical health. The presence of patriarchy in the context of eroding social welfare and the absence of social cohesion in Russia has resulted in an increase in violence against women. Recent surveys indicate that up to 70% of married women reported violence by their partners (Amnesty International 2006). The first crises centre for women, set up in Moscow by Natalia Rimashevskaya, is a small office with two crisis lines, and a library with many international books on the subject of violence against women. There is a serious shortage of facilities to assist women and there are no shelters for women in Moscow. Given the housing crisis, women have no refuge from abusive relationships and their personal safety is jeopardized.

The spousal homicide rates more than doubled from 1989–1992 to 15% of all homicides and continues to accelerate, making Russian women the most vulnerable among industrialized countries (Gondolf and Shestakov 1997). This increase is attributes to the drastic social disorganization, the overall level of violence in the society, and the rising gender inequality.

In Cuba, violence against women is a subject that is passionately debated and seriously addressed, both in the academy and within the FMC. While the extent of physical and sexual violence against women in Cuba is not well documented, there is clearly an increased awareness of its existence and attempts to address it. This was particularly obvious at the International Women's Conferences (held at the University of Havana in 1995, 1997, and 1999) where interest in the issue was raised in various forums. In 1998, a course on violence against women was approved as part of the curriculum in the Masters Degree program in Women's Studies at the University of Havana, and in December 1999, Colleen Lundy, co-author of this article, was invited to offer a one-week workshop on violence against women at the University of Havana. Twenty-four people (23 women and one man) attended the workshop with representation from the university, local hospitals, and the FMC's women's houses. There is a tremendous interest in developing community responses to the violence that exists and the FMC has established houses/community centres for women and children where a woman can consult with social workers, psychologists, and lawyers around concerns that include violence. Public education campaigns against violence are also apparent in Cuba. For example, there are advertisements that condemn violence against women and point to its consequences—in one case a picture of a remorseful-looking man in prison.

Officially Cuban society does not tolerate sexism or violence against women. It has made attempts to curb male chauvinism and overt sexism and has entrenched equality of the sexes as a fundamental human right. However, violence against women does exist and women we spoke with indicated that "one simply hears these things." And while sexism continues to exist in both Cuba and Russia, the fundamental differences between the two countries is that at the level of the state, Cuba appears to have mechanisms in place to counter sexism whereas in Russia the new order ignores it, or worse, embraces it.

Women's Studies and Social Work

Female academics in both Russia and Cuba have been a visible force in developing social policy and programs and in the delivery of social welfare services. The social achievements of women gained prior to the transitions prepared them well for the challenges that they currently face. Female scholars in the Institute of Socio-Economic Studies of the Population, in the Russian Academy of Science are renowned feminists and well respected researchers. Natalia Rimashevskaya, for example, is a prolific author and participant in the social policy development in the Russian Federation. The aim of our project in Russia, in which we worked with Dr. Rimashevskaya, was to develop a strategy for social protection. The outcome was published in a book that was widely distributed and discussed among government officials, trade unionists, and university faculty and students.

In both countries, university programs in gender studies were introduced and women reached out to the international community. In 1990, an office of gender studies was created at the Institute of Socioeconomic Problems of the Population at the Russian Academy of Sciences and was later called Moscow Gender Studies Centre. In the same year, the first international conference on gender studies was held in Moscow (Khotkina 2002). Similarly, women's studies departments were established in major Cuban universities. For example, the development of the Women's Studies Department (Catedra de la Mujeres) at the University of Havana reflects the responsiveness of the institution to national social needs. The Catedra de la Mujeres is comprised of female professors of psychology, sociology, law, and journalism, as well as representatives of the FMC. Focusing on the study of women and gender relations, the department conducts discussion groups, offers graduate courses at the university, holds international conferences, and invites guest lecturers from abroad.

The Women's Movement of Russia (WMR) has been organized to defend women's human rights and enhance women's participation in the social and political life in Russia. The WMR, founded in 1996, currently has branches in 62 regions in the Federation. It is not known how visible or effective this movement has been in challenging the difficulties facing women. In Cuba, since 1960, the FMC has strived to keep women involved in the revolutionary process by supporting their integration into all levels of education and all parts of the workforce; to advocate for women's rights and equality; to raise the self-esteem of women and to promote the ideas and practices of socialism, not just at the national level, but internationally as well (Allahar 1994).

As the largest organized voice of Cuban women and the major mechanism for ensuring that women's issues are dealt with by the state, the FMC has taken a leadership role in social welfare. In the past, the organization has mobilized women as social workers for every major campaign: literacy, primary health care, voluntary work brigades, and the Committees for the Defence of the Revolution (CDRs) (Rivero y Mendez 1994). The *casas de mujeres y familia* (houses for women and the family), established across the country, offer a wide range of services to women. We visited a centre in Havana and met with the workers there.

Each house is staffed with a team consisting of a psychologist, a lawyer, a health educator, and a social worker, who identify the needs of women and provide help. Most of the women seeking assistance are there because of family problems, but they also seek assistance for health concerns, employment, and housing. Workers also offer outreach and education to women who are involved in the sex trade industry. In addition, the staff carries out research toward developing a methodology for identifying women's concerns and encouraging women's participation in finding answers to these concerns. The women's houses, moreover, offer courses on gender perspectives in literature and the promotion of gender awareness through workshops on subjects related to self-esteem, violence against women, and sexuality.

A renewed consciousness among women has emerged in response to the current economic climate in Cuba. Over the past years, the FMC has started to invite feminist scholars from abroad to meet with Cuban women and it has facilitated the participation of Cuban women in international feminist conferences. Women's studies circles have been organized at some institutions of further education including the University of Havana where new approaches to studying social relationships are being examined, and women are writing about issues such as domestic violence and sexual harassment in the workplace. There have been important initiatives by Cuban women to set up meetings and conferences with women from Latin America, the US, Europe, and Canada. These conferences are held despite tremendous financial adversity. For example, there is little money for printing conference proceedings and for disseminating research reports following major women's conferences.

At the Catedra, students are also beginning to study aspects of women's lives such as violence, women's roles in the family, and prostitution, to further develop participatory research methods for addressing issues of particular concern for women. While Cuban women (including Women's Studies at the University of Havana and the FMC) have initiated projects to respond to the challenges facing them, resources for education, training, and research continue to be in short supply.

Overall, women in Cuba are astutely aware of, and skilled in, economic and political issues and continue to struggle collectively to create a society in which equality based on gender and race is a possibility (Jennissen and Lundy 2001a). These women insist that they want to remain active in the process of constructing a better life for all women. We met women who are interested in a range of topics related to women including: documenting the role that women have played in the initial stages of the Revolution, preparing biographical dictionaries on eminent Cuban women, documenting the role of women in anti-racist work in Cuba, studying and writing about machismo and the continued expectation that women will carry the responsibility for children and housework while working outside the home, understanding the reasons behind high divorce rates, the lack of sexuality education, violence against women, and sexual harassment.

Women in the Russian Federation face a much longer and harsher road to recovery. The dismantling of socialism and the rapid transition to capitalism has had a devastating impact on most women and their quality of life is far below what it was during the Soviet era. What is particularly astounding with the transition to capitalism is that is has wiped out an entire economic and value system and has left Russia with a devastated population. Galena Erincheva (1996) interviewed Russian women about what concerned them most about the changes to a market economy and they reported: fear for the future of their children, concern over the deterioration of their quality of life, fear of unemployment and poverty, rising criminality, concern over the erosion of health care and education, and the violence, anarchy, and lack of sanitation on the streets. The future for Russia appears bleak since there is little political will to hold corporations accountable, and to regain power from the mafia. The state with the richest fuel, energy, and other resources is not willing to provide social support to its population.

Social work, as a profession, has emerged in Cuba and the Russian Federation in the context of these economic transformations and growing social problems. In both countries, the need for highly trained social workers is increasing evident. And in both countries, the profession is at the initial development stage and has yet to take a leadership role in the current program and policy initiatives aimed at ameliorating the social dislocation facing the people of both countries.

In Cuba, while social workers have always worked within organizations such as the FMC, they were not university educated for this work. In 1997, sociology departments in Cuban universities started to offer degrees with a concentration in social work. Then in 2000, the need for a large number of trained social workers was recognized and the development of social work at a lower level became a priority. The government opened its first school of social work for youth between the ages of 16 and 25 in the city of Havana and quickly extended to central and oriental zones of the island. There are currently 15 such schools in Havana. While these are connected to universities they are housed in Municipal Community Centres.

In Russia, the first formal training program for social workers was established in 1991 at the Moscow Pedagogical University (Templeman 2003). While social work in both Cuba and Russia is in its infancy, the conditions for the development of the profession differs significantly between them. Whereas social workers in Cuba will be working within well-established state structures, in Russia, social work "still lacks recognition by public opinion and by other caring professionals" (Iarskaia-Smirnova and Romanov 2002, p.124). Russian social workers in fact, face conditions that are reminiscent of those faced by the early charity workers that characterizes social work in Canada and the US at the turn of the 20th century.

Conclusion

The current economic circumstances present tremendous challenges for women. It appears that both Cuban and Soviet era women gained ground primarily in the public sphere (mainly in terms of labour force participation and political representation) but few gains in terms of altering the sexual division of labour at the domestic level. This historical context and the current crises in reproduction and social caring explain the inordinate burden now placed on women. However, Cuban women have the support of a socially responsive state that is absent in contemporary Russia.

Cuban and Russian women are acutely aware of the dilemmas that confront them and their history of political participation, activism, and grass-roots organizing will, in all likelihood, continue to grow. With increasing opportunities for the exploitation of women, it will be critical that women monitor the changes and advocate for their interests. What we witnessed through discussions with Cuban and Russian women was a renewed commitment to promoting gender equality and a strong interest in linking with women internationally to compare experiences and to develop strategies for negotiating the long road ahead.

Looking ahead with optimism for Cuba, Norma Vasallo emphasizes that in future developments " ... values such as solidarity, equality, and high self-esteem will prevail" (2004, 98–99). In an article, "Social Policy in a Cold Climate: Health and Social Welfare in Russia," Mike Titterton notes that while Russian society is clearly in a state of transition, "what it is moving to is less clear than what it is moving toward" (2006, 89). Clearly the future of the Russian Federation is not determined or decisive at this point in time, and while we remain hopeful that it will move in a more humane and democratic direction, without a clear and concerted focus on its most vulnerable populations, this is not likely to happen soon.

As both Cuba and the Russian Federation move toward private market economies, albeit in dramatically different degrees, the notion of social work, a by-product of industrial capitalism, appears to be assuming a role that previously did not exist in this form under socialism. Currently western social scientists, including social workers, are involved in providing advice and assistance in setting up programs for social work education, and in some cases, providing advice in redesigning aspects of the social infrastructure.

While this can be regarded as an important opportunity to assist in international social development and the promotion of human rights, it must be entered with vigilance. To begin with, as we have attempted in this chapter, we must guard against treating post-socialist societies as though they are newly developing industrial nations seeking to create social programs and services for the first time in their histories. We must acknowledge that they had (and in the case of Cuba, continue to have) highly developed social infrastructures. We need to understand what existed previously and what has been modified or lost in transition. For social work to have a strong and positive role in Cuba and Russia, associated theory and practice must be situated within the context of the countries' long and complex histories.

In our involvement with post-socialist societies, we also must remain committed to the development of a critical knowledge and analysis of the contemporary social, political, and economic contexts of these societies with particular scrutiny of the direction of the transformation. In so doing, we have a chance to avoid the potential of promoting social workers as "stretcher bearers" in society, merely tending to the casualties of a private market economy. As we know from our own history of social work in Canada, this approach does little to alter fundamentally the sources of inequality that persist under capitalism.

References

- Aguilar, C. and I. Moya, eds. 1995. *Reality and Challenges: Cuban Women Toward the End of the Century*. Havana: Federacion Mujeres de Cubanas.
- Aguilar, C., and R. M. Pereira. 1995. The Challenges of Daily Life. *Cuba Update* 16 (2/3): 9–10.
- Alalehto, T. 2002. Eastern Prostitituion from Russia to Sweden and Finland. *Journal of Scandinavian Studies in Criminology and Crime Prevention* 36: 96–111.
- Allahar, A. L. 1994. Women and the Family in Cuba: A Study across Time. *Humboldt Journal of Social Relations* 20 (1): 87–120.
- Amnesty International. 2006. *Russian Federation: Violence Against Women Must Not Be Ignored*. www.amnesty.org/en/library/info/ACT77/006/2006.
- Amnesty International. 2006. *Russian Federation: Racism and Xenophobia Rife in Russian Society*. www.amnesty.org/en/library/info/EUR46/018/2006.
- Antonova, V. 2002. Women in Public Service in the Russian Federation: Equal Capability and Unequal Opportunity. *Review of Public Personnel Administration* 22 (3) (Fall): 216–232.
- Belokonnaia, L. 2001. Gender Statistics in Russia. *Russian Social Science Review* 42 (3): 4–21.
- Benería, L. 1997. Capitalism and Socialism: Some Feminist Questions. *The Women, Gender and Development Reader*. 326–333. London, UK: Zed Books.
- Chossudovsky, M. 1997. *The Globalization of Poverty: Impacts of IMF and World Bank Reforms*. New Jersey: Zed Books.
- Cohen, S. F. 2000. *Failed Crusade: America and the Tragedy of Post-Communist Russia*. New York: W. W. Norton & Company.
- Daly, M. and J. Lewis. 2000 The Concept of Social Care and the Analysis of Contemporary Welfare States. *British Journal of Sociology* 51 (2): 281–298.
- Degitiar, L. 2002. The Transformation Process and the Status of Women. *Russian Social Science Review* 43 (4): 48–60.
- Dilla, H. 1999. Comrades and Investors: The Uncertain Transition in Cuba. In *Socialist Register 1999: Global Capitalism Versus Democracy*, eds. L. Panitch and C. Leys, 227–247. New York: Monthly Review Press.
- Feinsilver J. 1993. *Healing the Masses: Cuban Health Politics at Home and Abroad*. University of California Press: Berkeley.
- Feldman, S. 1992. Crises, Poverty, and Gender Inequality: Current Themes and Issues. In *Unequal Burden: Economic Crises, Persistent Poverty, and Women's Work*, eds. L. Benería and S. Feldman, 1–25. Boulder: Westview Press.
- Fong, M. S. 1993. The Role of Women in Rebuilding the Russian Economy. In *Studies of Economic Transformation, Paper Number 10*, 1–49. Washington: The World Bank.
- Gondolf, E. and D. Shestakov. 1997. Spousal Homicide in Russia versus the United States: Preliminary Findings and Implications. *Journal of Family Violence* 12 (1): 63–74.
- Gvozdeva, G. and E. Gvozdeva. 2002. Women's Path in the Transitional Economy of Russia: From Unpaid Work to Business. *Canadian Women's Studies* 21/22 (4/1): 121–123.
- Human Development Report. 2005. http://hdr.undp.org/en/reports/global/hdr2005/.

- Iarskaia-Smirnova, E., and P. Romanov 2002. 'A Salary is not Important Here': The Professionalization of Social Work in Contemproary Russia. *Social Policy & Administration* 36 (2): 123–141.

- Jennissen, T. and C. Lundy. 2001a. Women in Cuba and the Move to a Private Market Economy *Women's Studies International Forum* 24 (2): 181–198.

- Jennissen, T. and C. Lundy. 2001b. Progress in the Face of Adversity: Cuban Women Entering the New Millennium. In *Cuban Women: History, Contradictions and Contemporary Challenge*, eds. C. Lundy and N. Vasallo Barrueta, 45–69. Ottawa: Carleton University Graphic Services.

- Kalistratova, R. 1989. Legislatively Guaranteed Equality. *Canadian Women's Studies* 10 (4): 38–40.

- Kay, R. 2002. A Liberation from Emancipation? Changing Discourses on Women's Employment in Soviet and Post-Soviet Russia. *The Journal of Communist Studies and Transition Politics* 18 (1): 51–72.

- Khotkina, Z. A. 2002. Ten years of Gender Studies in Russia. *Russian Social Science Review* 43 (4): 4–12.

- Klimantova, G. 2002. The Family Process of the Transformation of Russian Society. *Russian Social Science Review* 43 (5): 16–23.

- Koblitz, A. H. 1995. Women Under Perestroika and Doi Moi: A Comparison of Marketization in Russia. *Canadian Women's Studies* 16 (1): 54–59.

- Lubove, R. 1965. *The Professional Altruist: The Emergence of Social Work as a Career, 1880–1930*. Cambridge: Harvard University Press.

- McCuaig, K. 1989. Effects of *Perestroika* and *Glasnost* on Women. *Canadian Women's Studies* 10 (4): 11–14.

- Meurs, M. 1997. Downwardly Mobile: Women in the Decollectivization of East European Agriculture. In *The Women, Gender and Development Reader*, 333–345. London: Zed Books.

- Metcalf, B. D. and M. Afanassieva. 2005. The Woman Question? Gender and Management in the Russian Federation. *Women in Management Review* 20 (6): 429–445.

- Modlich, R. 1993. Cuba: Struggle for Development is a Challenge for Women. *Women and Environments* 8 (1): 37–38.

- Moghadam, V. M. 1996. Patriarchy and Post-Communism: Eastern Europe and the Former Soviet Union. In *Patriarchy and Economic Development: Women's Positions at the End of the Twentieth Century*, ed. V. M. Moghadam, 327–353. Oxford: Clarendon Press.

- Molyneux, M. 1990. The "Woman Question" in the Age of Perestroika. *New Left Review* 183 (September/October): 1–25.

- Molyneux, M. 1996. *State and Institutional Change in Cuba's "Special Period": The Federacion de Mujeres Cubanas*. London: University of London.

- Neft, N. and A. D. Levine. 1997. *Where Women Stand: An International Report on the Status of Women in 140 Countries*. New York: Random House.

- Norton, F. C., Y. M. Komarov, S. P. Ermakov, C. T. Sempos, J. S. Marks, and E. V. Sempos. 1998. Causes of Declining Life Expectancy in Russia. *JAMA* 279 (10): 793–800.

- Pearson, R. 1997. Renegotiating the Reproductive Bargain: Gender Analysis of Economic Transition in Cuba in the 1990s. *Development and Change* 28: 671–705.

- Pauwels, J. 2002. *The Myth of the Good War: America in the Second World War*. Toronto: James Lorimer & Company.

- Rains, R. H. and A. E. Bopp Stark. 1997. The Role of Women in Cuba: Cuban Women's Equality in the Context of Articles 24–28 of the Family Code Enacted in 1975. *Social Development Issues* 19(2/3): 71–86.

- Reiter, E., and L. Meg 1989. Soviet Women—A Canadian View. *Canadian Women's Studies* 10 (4): 27–30.

- Rimashevskaya, N., ed. 2001. *Social Protection in Russia Under Conditions of Crisis,* Final Report. Moscow: Institute of Socio-Economic Studies of Population. Translated by Tatyana Kislitsina.

- Ritter, A. 1999. Is Cuba's Economic Reform Process Paralyzed? *World Economic Affairs* 2 (3): 13–20.

- Isel, R. and M. 1994. Cuban Women and Politics. *Women in Action* 1: 22.

- Robinson, N. 2002. *Russia: A State of Uncertainty.* London: Routledge.

- Rzhanitsyna, L. 2001. Working Women in Russia at the End of the 1990s. *Russian Social Science Review* 42 (4): 52–63.

- Rzhanitsyna, L. 1995. Women's Attitudes Toward Economic Reforms and the Market Economy. In *Women in Contemporary Russia,* ed. V. Koval, 34–46. Oxford: Berghahn Books.

- Safa, H. and P. Antrobus. 1992. Women and the Economic Crisis in the Carribbean. In *Unequal Burden: Economic Crises, Persistent Poverty and Women's Work,* eds. L. Beneria and S. Feldman, 49–83. Boulder: Westview Press.

- Samorodov, A. T. 1992. Transition, Poverty and Inequality in Russia. *International Labour Review* 131 (3): 335–353.

- Santibanez, S. S., A. S. Abdul-Quader, L. N. Broyles, N. Gusseynova, R. Sofronova, V. Molotilov, R. S. Garfein, and L. A. Paxton. 2005. Expansion of Outreach through Government AIDS Centres is Needed to Prevent the Spread of HIV in Russia. *Drugs: Education, Prevention and Policy* 12 (1): 71–74.

- Saul, J. R. 2005. *The Collapse of Globalism and the Reinvention of the World.* Toronto: Viking Canada.

- Shakur, A. 2005. Transnational Blackness: Africa and the African Diaspora, Asia, and Globalization. *The New Black Renaissance,* ed. M. Marable, 231–240. Boulder: Paradigm Publishers.

- Silverman, B. and M. Yanowitch 2000. *New Rich, New Poor, New Russia: Winners and Losers on the Russian Road to Capitalism.* Armonk: M.E. Sharpe.

- Smith, C. G., S. M. Hills, and G. Arch. 2003. Political Economy and the Transitions from Planned Market Economies. *European Business Review* 15 (2): 116–122.

- Smith, L. M. and A. Padula. 1996. *Sex and Revolution: Women in Socialist Cuba.* New York and Oxford: Oxford University Press.

- Stiglitz, Joseph E. 2002. *Globalization and its Discontents.* New York: W.W. Norton.

- Temkina, Ana and Elena Zdravomyslova. 2003. Gender Studies in Post-Soviet Society: Western Frames and Cultural Differences. *Studies in Eastern European Thought* 55: 51–61.

- Templeman, Sharon B. 2003. Social Work in the New Russia at the Start of the Millennium. *International Social Work* 47 (1): 95–107.

- Titterton, Mike. 2006. Social Policy in a Cold Climate: Health and Social Welfare in Russia. *Social Policy and Administration* 40 (1): 88–103.

- Titova, Irina 2003. Russian Life Expectancy on Downward Trend. *St. Petersburg Times.* January 17th. Also available at www.cdi.org/russia/johnson/7023-14.cfm.

- Toksanbaeva, M. 2001. The Social Vulnerability of Women. *Problems of Economic Transition* 43 (9): 72–83.

- Vanoy, Dana, Natalia Rimashevskaya, Lisa Cubbins, Marina Malysheva, Elena Meshterkina, and Marina Piskalova. 1999. *Marriages in Russia: Couples During the Economic Transition.* London: Praeger.

- Vasallo, Norma Barrueta. 2004. Women's Daily Lives in a New Century, eds. Max Azicri, and Elsie Deal. *Cuban Socialism in a New Century.* Gainsville: Tallahassee.

- Vasallo, Norma Barrueta. 2001. Women's Studies in Cuba. In *Cuban Women: History, Contradictions and Contemporary Challenges*, eds. Colleen Lundy and Norma Barrueta Vasallo. Carleton University: Ottawa.

- Waters, E. 1989. Reading Between Novosti Lines. *Canadian Women's Studies.* 10 (4): 31–34.

- Waring, Marilyn. 1999. *Counting for Nothing: What Men Value and What Women are Worth.* Toronto: University of Toronto Press.

- World Factbook. 2006. www.cia.gov/cia/publications/factbook/index.html.

- Wills, Gale. 1995. *A Marriage of Convenience: Business and Social Work in Toronto. 1918–1957.* Toronto: University of Toronto Press.

- Woodroofe, Kathleen. 1962. *From Charity to Social Work in England and the United States.* London: Routledge and Kegan Paul.

- Young, Kate, Carol Wolkowitz, and Roslyn McCullagh, eds. 1984. *Of Marriage and the Market: Women's Subordination Internationally and its Lessons.* 2nd ed. London: Routledge.

- Zaslavskaia, Tatiana. 2002. The Structure of Social Change in Russia. *Russian Social Science Review* 43 (3): 24–35.

Chapter 8

Social Work in Africa: With Special Reference to Ghana

Linda Kreitzer

The purpose of this chapter is to provide an overview of social work in Africa through a consideration of its past, present, and future. I wish to highlight how social work has evolved in West Africa and issues that are presently affecting positively and negatively on its growth and development. The chapter concludes by highlighting important themes that need to be addressed in order for social work to gain future influence in Africa.

To begin, however, it is important to note that Canada has a long tradition of development work in Africa and, in particular, Ghana. Due to its early independence in 1957, and stable conditions since 1980, organizations like the Canadian International Development Agency (CIDA) have supported many projects there. In fact, CIDA's longest running program has been in Ghana (CIDA, 2006). The Canadian International Development Research Centre (IDRC) has also supported some 2,500 research projects in Africa (IDRC, 2007) including Ghana. In addition, the Canadian University Services Organization (CUSO) and World University Service of Canada (WUSC) have been active in Ghana for many years (CUSO 2006; WUSC 2006).

In my case, it was a sister organization of CUSO, Voluntary Services Overseas (VSO), that took me to my first overseas volunteer job in Ghana teaching social work at the University of Ghana. While teaching there, I began to question why I was teaching western social work values, knowledge and skills to a country whose values and beliefs were not particularly western. Midgley's (1981) ideas and my own experience fuelled questions concerning social work and development. In 1996, the only program available to pursue these questions was through the MSW International Social Work Concentration at the University of Calgary. I was in the first cohort of students of the program. I completed my MSW thesis degree after collecting data and doing a field practicum at Buduburam Refugee Camp in Ghana (Kreitzer 1998; Kreitzer 2002).

After graduation, I had my first international social work job with the American Red Cross in Armenia. In 2000, I started a Ph.D. program at the University of Calgary and in 2002, I went back to Ghana to facilitate a research project looking at social work curriculum (funded by IDRC and the Social Science and Humanities Research Council (SSHRC)). During my Ph.D. program I helped run the MSW International Social Work Concentration at the University of Calgary by preparing students to do their practicum overseas and supporting them throughout their practicum experience. Some of the students go to Africa and Ghana for their student practicum. Equally,

Ghanaians and other Africans are taking the opportunity to study for the MSW and Ph.D. through the University of Calgary. The African connection is growing. Since 2000, I have attended and presented at the International Federation of Social Workers (IFSW) conferences and more recently have attended the International Association of Schools of Social Work (IASSW) conferences. I also attend the IFSW African regional meetings.

In November 2002, a Participatory Action Research project was facilitated at the University of Ghana looking at the relevance of the social work profession to present day Ghana (Kreitzer 2004). A group of students, faculty, former students, a Queen Mother, and myself from Canada met for nine months to look specifically at issues surrounding the indigenisation of social work training and practice in Ghana. As part of the preparation for developing a more appropriate curriculum for Ghana, the group looked at social development issues through the eyes of the history of social work education in Ghana/West Africa. The group discussed how colonization, modernization, and globalization affect Ghanaian society, its social development, as well as social work education and practice. This chapter highlights the analysis and reflection that the group undertook, in particular looking at the profession of social work in Ghana.[1]

Social Context

Africa is a continent with vast resources, human and material, which continues to be challenged by many historical and contemporary influences. Colonized by Europe as far back as the 1500s (McFarland 1985), the continent has been a source of wealth for the growth of industrialized countries in the world (Busia 1951; Hochschild 1998; Jones 2003; Satre 2001; Smith 1999; Willinsky 1998). Colonization (Memmi 1965) has results in what Freire (1997) speaks of as a culture of silence. The effect on Africa has been a loss of identity as well as an African culture that has silenced its people and greatly affected their psyche. What is human and not human, what is civilized and primitive have been defined, in considerable measure, by colonial discourse (Willensky 1998).

Through modernization, colonization continued on the assumption that western knowledge and thinking was "civilized" and that traditional knowledge was "uncivilized" (Kreitzer 2004; Mosha 2000; Semali and Kincheloe 2000; Smith 1999; Willensky 1998). Today, the hegemony of western knowledge influences all aspects of African life. Another form of colonization has been the establishment of the new world economic order. Borrowing money from international financial institutions, many countries in Africa cope with debts that devastate their chance for growth (Boahen 1975; Konadu-Agyemang 2000; Rimmer 1992). Also, as others have pointed out in this book, theories of development have favoured a modernization

---

[1] What is clear is that in order to understand the future of social work education in Africa, the past and present social development factors need to be understood (Asamoah and Beverley 1998; Payne 2000; Venkataraman 1996).

approach to growth with the assumption that economic growth alone would alleviate poverty and that all countries would eventually experience economic and social prosperity (Prigoff 2000; So 1990; Wilson and Whitmore 2000).

To some, globalization signifies interdependence, prosperity and progress (Martin 2000) while others see it as an advanced stage of colonization/modernization causing poverty, fragmentation, corruption and marginalization (Lechner 2000; Midgley 2000). Under the present form of globalization, that of globalism (Wilson and Whitmore 2000), countries in Africa are struggling to provide for their own people in their own land. "These rigid fundamentalist policies did extraordinary damage to African economics from which they have yet to recover" (Lewis 2005). Many countries in Africa suffer from poverty, starvation, and famine and millions of Africans are dying of HIV/AIDS each year (Bar-On 2001; Lewis 2005; United Nations 2005). Economic and social prosperity are still a future goal for these countries and only a concerted effort by African governments and the international community will change this situation.

However, there are positive initiatives happening at the local level that are changing the circumstances in many countries of Africa. Michaëlle Jean, Governor General of Canada, on her recent visit to Africa pointed out that there are many women and men who are on the ground building sustainable and dynamic communities. Some of these projects were, and continue to be, established by social workers trained in Africa and in Europe (Kaseke 2001) and funded by Canadian agencies. With people and institutions working towards the millennium goals, the social work profession in Africa has an opportunity and responsibility to work toward alleviating poverty through strengthening the profession in different countries, and in the continent as a whole. The reality is that for many African countries social work is on the periphery and has little or no influence in social policy and development. The dynamics of this reality are complex and historical factors have contributed to its success and failure over the years.

The Past

The influence of the colonizer and modernizer plays an important role in the development of social work in Africa (Asamoah 1995). These influences began with the missionaries who came to Africa to evangelize, civilize, and provide charity to the continent (Apt and Blavo 1997; Willensky 1998). Although traditional social systems and mechanisms for social development were already established, an introduction to a more formal approach to social welfare was needed due to the effects of colonialism, the World Wars, and capitalism, which broke down the extended family networks and traditional ways of society (Burke and Ngonyani 2004; Kreitzer 2004). European welfare systems were exported through colonial administrations. Africans were trained, through Schools of Social Work, to work in and uphold these structures (Ajayi, Goma, and Johnson 1996; Berstein and Gray 1991; Kaseke 2001;

Lebakeng 1997; Memmi 1965; Wicker 1958). The profession of social work in Africa was firmly established during the 20th century (Asamoah 1995; Hampson 1995; Kaseke 2001; Kendall 1995; Midgley 1981; Ntusi 1995).

Through modernization, western social workers and social work institutions, working under the assumption that western social work knowledge (theories, methodologies, and practices) was universal, exported this knowledge to non-western countries (Haug 2000; Kendall 1995; Midgley 1981; Nagpaul 1995; Smith 1999). However, colleagues from some of these countries question western social work knowledge and its appropriateness in solving problems confronting the consequences of colonialism, poverty, government corruption, religious practices, and other philosophical orientations (Lebakeng 1997; Midgley 1981; Noyoo 2000; Osei-Hwedie 1990; Shawky 1972; Walton and Ebo El Nasr 1988).

Social work training in Africa was influenced by the United Nations (UN) in order to encourage the growth of social work education and to encourage African people to train in the US, the United Kingdom, Canada, and Australia. The United Nations began a series called "Training for Social Work" and completed five surveys between the 1950s and 1970s concerning social welfare training worldwide (K. Healy 2001; Midgley 1981). The purpose of the first three surveys was to provide a detailed description and analysis of training methods in educational institutions that train social workers worldwide (UN 1950, iii) and to identify "trends and problems that appear to be significant for the further development of training for social work" (UN 1955, 2). The fourth international survey was "designed to identify significant developments and trends in training for social work at all educational levels" (UN 1964, 1) ten years after the first survey.

The importance of these surveys was: 1) the affirmation and justification of the profession worldwide; 2) the depiction of social work throughout the world through the identification of trends; and 3) the assumption that it was the responsibility of the international organizations to establish, coordinate, and improve training in social work (UN 1955). Over time, the assumptions were challenged and a more focused approach "drew attention to the unintended consequences of development and the critical role that social welfare personnel must play in ensuring that the social objectives of national development are kept in focus" (Asamoah 1995, 227). During this time, the UN also sponsored personnel to study in Africa and Europe in community development (Bar-On 2001).

Along with the surveys, the United Nations published monographs between 1964 and 1971 concerning various themes related to social welfare in Africa (Appendix 1). One theme was the need for a published directory of social welfare activities. Other themes included the historical aspect of social work in Africa (UN 1964, No. 3), issues around urbanization (UN 1966, No. 5), the status and role of women (UN 1967, No. 6), youth employment, national development (UN 1969, No. 7), and rural development (UN 1971, No. 8). More importantly, however, the UN also acknowledged that little or no consultation occurred with local people concerning social welfare services in the past. Instead, it was recognized that earlier services reflected "the differences in structure, traditions, intellectual values, and concepts of the colonizing countries and not of the indigenous African societies" (UN 1964, No. 2, 7). These same issues continued to emerge in other literature throughout the next 36 years.

With the growing understanding of the need for Africans to determine their own social work education and training, the United Nations, The Organization of African Unity (OAU), CIDA, the International Association of Schools of Social Work (IASSW), the Economic Commission for Africa (ECA), and other organizations supported a continental organization to unify social work training. The Association for Social Work Education in Africa (ASWEA) heavily influenced the development of the profession (Yimam 1990). Many conferences led to the establishment of ASWEA; in particular, the 1962 conference held at the University of Ghana for the purpose of "discussing problems confronting social workers throughout West Africa" (Drake and Omari 1962, 2). At the conference, culturally appropriate recommendations were made by Africans themselves in relation to the creation of a journal of social work, the analysis of professional training, an understanding of the professional status of social work and the identification of legislation concerning social issues, research, and vulnerability in society. Another conference was held in Lusaka, Zambia in 1963; it identified a shortage of trained social workers, a lack of indigenous literature or curriculum and a lack of financial backing for social work education in Africa (Tesfaye 1973). In 1971, ASWEA was formally established (Asamoah, 1995, 226) in order to "serve, among many other functions, as a forum where social work educators [could] discuss and resolve common problems [facing] schools of social work in Africa" (Tasfaye 1973, 20).[2]

Alongside the ASWEA conferences were the Conferences of Ministers. They served to challenge "the international social work community to pursue a dynamic agenda that would put social work out front on issues of development and make it, as a profession, more relevant to current realities" (Asamoah 1995, 225). It was eventually renamed the Conference of African Ministers of Social Affairs and "continued to press the issue of re-orienting social welfare services to a developmental model and training key personnel

---

[2] Appendix 2 describes the documents of the conferences sponsored by this organization from 1972–1989. The documents provide historical documentation on the evolution of social work education and practice directly after independence and issues surrounding the residue colonization (ASWEA 1973, Doc. 6). Conference participants were informed on the role of ASWEA, the objectives of the Organization of African Unity (OAU), and the idea of pan-African solidarity (ASWEA 1977, Doc. 12; ASWEA 1974). They highlight similarities and differences between Francophone and Anglophone social work issues (ASWEA 1975; ASWEA 1976; ASWEA 1978; ASWEA 1979; ASWEA 1989). They identify resources, opportunities, limitations and constraints when planning for the future of social work in Africa (ASWEA 1978, Doc. 15, 7). Unfortunately, they are in danger of becoming extinct through lack of awareness of them by Africans and western social workers (only one copy survives in some cases). The only analysis completed was by Arega Yimam (1990) in his book on Social Development in Africa. From 1971–1985 ASWEA held an impressive twenty-one conferences, produced extensive documentation of these conferences, and established a social work journal that published eight issues (1986, 62).

accordingly" (Asamoah 1995, 226). Eventually, the African Centre for Applied Research and Training in Social Development (ACARTSOD) was formed out of these conferences. Together, ASWEA and ACARTSOD worked for change, growth, and development of African social work practice and training through their work and publications.

At the same time, the Ghana Association of Social Workers (GASOW) was active in planning its own seminars and publishing these seminars as part of indigenous teaching material for teachers and students. The purpose of GASOW was to: promote activities that strengthen and unify the social work profession; stimulate sound and continuous development of various areas of social work practice; and contribute effectively to the improvement of social conditions in the country (GASOW 1972, v). GASOW demonstrated the importance of a professional association in promoting indigenization while learning from others. Issues identified by association were similar to the ASWEA (Appendix 3).

The Present

Unfortunately, the momentum to continue the social work agenda developed by ASWEA and GASOW has decreased over the past fifteen years and social work continues to struggle to keep a professional identity. Many of the countries involved in the development of social work in Africa have experienced instability, civil war, economic hardships, and political upheavals. In Ghana, although there has been relative stability since the 1980s, it was not until 2000 that a sense of freedom to speak out has been felt by Ghanaians. In the past 30 years, Ethiopia, where ASWEA was located, has experienced upheaval, revolutions, famine, and war with Eritrea (Africanet 1997). Also, many countries have been affected by Structural Adjustment Programs and the added burden of hosting refugees. South Africa continues to struggle with the task of "drawing together social workers with diverse and seemingly irreconcilable moral and political ideologies" (Mzaibuko and Gray 2004, 140). By the end of the 1980s, ASWEA ceased to exist and GASOW became dormant.

Given this background, the research group, of which I was a part, attempted to undertake a critical examination of the issues facing social work in Ghana today.[3] One of the important contributions that earlier organizations made to social work was to "sensitize African governments on the importance of social development training at all levels ... to involve ministries and departments of social affairs ... and to obtain financial support for the work" (Yimam 1990, 286). Even with this sensitization, however, social work continues to be an unknown profession in many parts of Africa including Ghana. Where it is known, the colonial legacy of welfare systems remain despite their increasing inappropriateness, as they breed negativity toward the profession.

---

[3] We identified themes that highlighted these issues. They are as follows: 1) social work in relation to Ghanaian society; 2) an effective professional association; 3) access to written indigenous material, western literature and technology; 4) the development of indigenous social work models; 5) appropriate curriculum; 6) consequences of globalism and structural adjustment programs; and 7) a need for a new ASWEA to coordinate curriculum development in Africa.

During our research, we had a media person come to talk to us about making a video on social work. His perception of a social worker in a social welfare office was a person with his head on a desk taking a nap. In Ghana, social workers themselves have a negative attitude toward their profession and many are embarrassed by their association with it. One pioneer of social work says "I am telling you the enemies of social work are the social workers themselves" (Kreitzer 2004, 204). On a positive note, however, non-government organizations (NGOs), International Governmental Organizations (IGOs), and the United Nations are acknowledging the importance of social work training for social development. Approximately half of the trained social workers in Ghana are employed by NGOs.

Associations are important to a profession. When effective, they can be an important voice to the government for the poor and vulnerable in society. GASOW was very progressive in understanding social development, advocating for the term social worker to be replaced by social development worker, promoting dialogue with other non-western countries, dealing with internally displaced peoples, and hosting interdisciplinary workshops. After a grand beginning, GASOW slowly deteriorated to a point where it became ineffective and needed to be reorganized. Its influence also diminished in the eyes of the government (Kreitzer 2004). In South Africa, with five separate associations formed during apartheid, there is a struggle to establish an association that will "unify the profession and reach consensus on the tasks and functions of a united professional association" (Mzaibuko and Gray 2004, 140). Professional associations grow when political and social stability prevail and the survival of a nation is not threatened.

One of the constant themes in ASWEA documents and literature surrounding social work in Africa is a lack of indigenous material for teaching (Asamoah 1995; Yimam 1990). Access to African social work articles is a problem. There are few places to publish in Africa. Consequently, many articles and books, written by Africans about Africa, are published in the western world. Although ASWEA produced two documents giving case examples from West Africa (ASWEA 1974) and East Africa (ASWEA 1973) social workers are still reading western books and having to adapt the examples to their own context. As one research member in our project said: "We are tired of reading about urban Chicago and having to adapt it to rural Ghana" (Kreitzer 2004). African social work libraries are full of western social work textbooks and there is little effort to collect indigenous materials for teaching and research. Viewing and printing articles from the Internet is expensive. [4]

According to Bar-On (2001), social work books in Botswana are also western and in English, even though the social work agencies speak in Swetswana. The cost to African social work is great. The practice perpetuates a dependency on western social work literature and frustrates students who

---

[4] In Ghana, there are no Ghanaian social work textbooks and few articles available. As part of the research action initiative, I downloaded African social work articles from libraries in the western world and sent them to Ghana in binders for the social work library in 2004.

are continually adapting the material to their own culture. Our research group also was concerned about the potential loss of African social work history. The people involved in the emergence of social work in Ghana are now in their 70s and 80s. If care is not taken to collect and publish their stories and experiences about the evolution of social work, it will be too late. With the lack of indigenous writing comes a lack of culturally appropriate social work models.

President Kenneth Kaunda of Zambia once said: "Our great need is to educate people for Africa and not merely to educate people from Africa." ASWEA was committed to making social work training culturally appropriate. Ghana, like many African countries, tries to balance traditional and western knowledge and practice in all areas of culture including law, social policy, education, and social welfare. However, an awareness of the value of traditional knowledge and practice is not encouraged in educational institutions. In Ghana, very little critical thinking has taken place regarding the development of social work models that incorporate traditional practices to create an African approach to intervention. Our group suggested collaboration in teaching and writing with the Institute for African Studies and with traditional authority to look at traditional social practices before colonization (Kreitzer 2004, 168).

Still, the cycle continues as foreigners come and teach in the universities, thus perpetuating western knowledge hegemony and dependency. Poverty continues to prevail and is an accepted condition, particularly in rural areas. Poverty reduction, through community economic development, is essential. Social work training needs to encourage critical thinking in understanding the issues surrounding poverty and the constant reduction of funds for health, education, and social welfare in the context of world institutions and events. Social workers, through their associations, need to be a voice for the poor using the media and social protest to create public awareness of the challenges facing many in Ghana.

Until recently, no continental association for social work education existed. This has had the effect of leaving African social work training to the individual countries where professional associations and training institutions struggle to survive. In April 2005, however, a new Association of Schools of Social Work in Africa (ASSWA) was launched at the Nairobi International Federation of Social Workers (IFSW) regional conference. The major challenge for the association is to promote collaboration between countries in Africa concerning social work education, practice, and research.

The Future

Social workers in Africa are struggling to find their way in the modern world. They are searching for new ways of being proud of their profession and advocating for themselves, as well as the people whom they serve. Professional associations can be strengthened through support from local social workers and encouraged to develop ethical guidelines. Corruption within the associations needs to be eliminated in order to gain respect from governments of these countries. This strengthening can be done, in part, through collaboration with the International Federation of Social Workers (IFSW) and the International Association of Schools of Social Work (IASSW), as well as with other associations. An example of strengthening professional associations is an action plan that came from our research project. Through the project, we were able to provide an opportunity for social workers throughout Ghana to come together and address their discontent with GASOW. As a result, the old executive was disbanded; free and fair elections were held. The new executive represents a more varied social work committee and the president is on the regional executive of IFSW.

In order to advocate for good social policy, social workers, in the future, will have to be educated in their own social work history. Curriculum becomes relevant when it addresses issues and situations in which social workers are engaged in everyday life. It involves the development of curriculum that is culturally appropriate and developmental (Burke and Ngonyani 2004; Kaseke 2001; Mupediziswa 1996) as well as anti-oppressive and anti-discriminatory. In addition, it needs to deal with ethnic diversity (Berstein and Gray 1991). Combination degrees, like social work and African studies, or social work and religion, can be promoted. Research and graduate studies can challenge current social work practice and social policy. To that end, it will be important for African students to have free access to journal articles in and around Africa and the western world. Student and faculty educational exchanges can also be developed within Africa. Country and continental conferences need to be organized and financed through international and continental groups like IFSW, IASSW, OAU, and governments of different countries.

With the imbalance of access to knowledge, economic conditions, and research money, collaboration between western social work researchers and African researchers remains vital. Resources are available in the western world not available in Africa, particularly for research and development. Until the imbalance is addressed, collaboration between western and non-western partners provides some potential for development.[5] Collaboration between countries within Africa is also important. Through collaboration, schools of social work will be able to share successes and failures; faculty and students will be able to undertake fieldwork in other African countries; and networking will take place across the continent.

Conclusion

Africa is a continent with rich material and human resources. Confronted by colonization, modernization, and globalization, it struggles to gain an identity within the new world. At the same time, it continues to be plagued by colonial debris, modernization's assumptions concerning the relevance of particular

---

[5] Examples of collaboration are outlined in this book and also in Al-Krenawi and Graham 1999; Drower 2000; Kreitzer 2004; J. Nimmagadda, and C. D. Cowger 1999; Tesoriero and Rajaratnam 2001; J. Venkataraman 1996; Wilson and Whitmore 2000.

knowledge bases, and economic disadvantages through Structural Adjustment Programs. The HIV/AIDS pandemic, famine, civil wars, bad governance, and exploitation continue to have an effect on African people and their ability to rise above their current condition. Social development is affected by historical and contemporary factors, which have slowed progress.

Social work in Africa had a good beginning through the work of the United Nations, ASWEA, ACARTSOD, and GASOW. They provided "a valuable exchange of information and experience that took place, enabling institutions to strengthen their pan-African solidarity" (Yimam 1990, 186). Funding came from many sources, including Canada through CIDA. That beginning needs to be built upon if social work is to play an important part in the re-creation of African identity by recreating and revisiting the historical heritage in social work curriculum. Currently, ASWEA publications are not available to people in Africa. If African social work is to move forward, however, the availability of these documents to African social work educators and researchers is essential. Strengthening the professional association, critically examining colonial welfare systems, evaluating social work curriculum and publicly advocating for the lifting of constraints that affect African progress can help re-create a new sense of identity.

Our research work has had a small impact on social work in Ghana. Our action plan produced a document with recommendations for curriculum change at the University of Ghana. We produced a 30-minute documentary in Ghana that can be shown on public TV and used in the classroom for educational purposes. We challenged GASOW to make changes in the way it worked. As a result of the project, several Ghanaian social workers have attended international conferences as well as the IFSW regional African meetings. Our research is like a pebble thrown into a still pond; it challenges that stillness and makes people critically reflect on social work education. Ripples continue to develop that may have a lasting effect on the whole pond.

Appendix 1: United Nations Monographs		
Name of Monographs	Year of publication	Themes
M1 Directory of Social Welfare activities in Africa	1964	Provides a Directory of Social Welfare activities in Africa.
M2 Patterns of social welfare organizations and administrations in Africa	1964	Acknowledges that social welfare services are western and no consultation with indigenous elements were completed.
M3 Training for social work in Africa	1964	Over fourteen African countries produced information concerning the history of their schools of social work and their curriculum.

M5 Family, child, and youth welfare services in Africa	1966	Emphasizes the mother and the family, health problems, food and nutrition and social welfare for children and youth, including the issue of the rural exodus of youth.
M6 The status and role of women in East Africa	1967	Looks at all aspects of women's issues including education, family life, work, community development, legal and political rights of women, and the participation of women in community life.
M7 Youth employment and national development in Africa	1969	Concentrates on the problems of youth unemployment and youth training schemes.
M8 Integrated approach to rural development in Africa	1971	Brings out factors influencing rural development, problems of rural development, and present strategies for rural development.

Appendix 2: ASWEA Documents			
Document	Year	Place	Main themes
1	unknown	Lakota	An effort in community development in the Lakota Sub-prefecture.
2	1972		Community Services, Lakota Project Methodology.
3★	1972	Ethiopia	The important role of supervision in Social Welfare Organization.
4	1972		The use of films in social development education.
5	1973	Ethiopia	Guidelines for making contact with young people in informal groups in urban areas.
★Compilation of case studies	1973		Compilation of case studies in social development in East Africa.
★Compilation of case studies	1974		Compilation of case studies in social development in West Africa.
6★	1974	Lomé, Togo	Relationship between social work education and national social development plan. 2nd ASWEA conference.
7★	1974	Ethiopia	Curricula of Schools of Social Work and Community Development Training Centres in Africa
8★	1975	Ethiopia	Directory of social welfare activities in Africa. 3rd Edition.
9★	1975	Ethiopia	Report of ASWEA's workshop on "Techniques of teaching and methods of field work evaluation." Proceedings of the Debre Zeit Workshop.

10★	1976	Doula, Cameroon	Techniques d' Enseignement et methods d'evaluation des travaux pratiques.
11★	1976	Ethiopia	Social realities and the response of social work education in Africa. 3rd ASWEA conference.
12★	1977	Ethiopia	The role of social development education in Africa's struggle for political and economic independence. 3rd ASWEA conference.
13★	1978	Ethiopia	The development of a training curriculum in family welfare. From the ASWEA expert group.
14★	1978		L'Elaboration d'un programme de formation en benetre familial
15★	1979	Lusaka, Zambia	Guidelines for the development of a training curriculum in family welfare.
16★	1979	Lomé, Togo	Principes directeurs pour l'etablissement d'un programme d'etude destine à la formation aux disciplines de la protection de la famille.
17★	1981	Ethiopia	Social development training in Africa: Experiences of the 1970s and emerging trends of the 1980s. 4th ASWEA conference.
18★	1982	Ethiopia	Survey of curricula of social development training institutions in Africa. 2nd edition.
19★	1982	Minia, Egypt	The organization and delivery of social services to rural areas.
20★	1985	Ethiopia	Training for social development; Methods of intervention to improve people's participation in rural transformation in African with special emphasis on women.
21★	1989	Ethiopia	Social development agents in rural transformation in Africa.

Association for Social Work Education in Africa (1986). Addis Ababa: ASWEA Publication. Dates are the published dates and not the dates when the seminars were given.

Appendix 3: Ghana Association of Social Workers (GASOW) Seminars			
Document	Year	Place	**Theme**
1	1972	Ghana	Social welfare education and practice in developing countries

2	1973	Ghana	Social planning in national development
3	1974	Ghana	The role of agriculture and rural technology in national development
4	1975	Ghana	Popular participation and the new local Government system

References

- Africanet. 1997. *Ethiopia—History.* Accessed May 19, 2004. www.africanet.com/africanet/country/ethiopia/history.htm.
- Ajayi, J. F. A., L. K. H. Goma, and G. A. Johnson. 1996. *The African Experience with Higher Education.* Athens: Ohio University Press.
- Al-Krenawi A. and J. R. Graham. 1999. Social Work and Koranic Mental Health Healers. *International Social Work* 42 (1): 53–65.
- Apt. A.A. and E.Q. Blavo. 1997. Ghana. In *International Handbook on Social Work Theory,* eds. N. S. Mayadas, T. D. Watts, and D. Elliott. Westport: Greenwood Press.
- Asamoah, Y. W. 1995. Africa. In *International Handbook on Social Work Education,* eds. N. S. Mayadas, T. D. Watts, and D. Elliott. Connecticut: Greenwood Press.
- ASWEA. 1974. *Relationship Between Social Work Education and National Social Development Planning.* Doc. 6. Addis Ababa: ASWEA publication.
- ASWEA. 1975. *Techniques of Teaching and Methods of Field Work Evaluation,* Doc. 9. Addis Ababa: ASWEA publication.
- ASWEA. 1976. *Social Realities and the responses of social work education in Africa.* Doc. 11. Addis Ababa: ASWEA publication.
- ASWEA. 1977. *The Role of Social Development Education in Africa's Struggle for Political and Economic Independence.* Doc. 12. Addis Ababa: ASWEA publication.
- ASWEA. 1978. *Guidelines for the Development of a Training Curriculum in Family Welfare.* Doc. 15. Addis Ababa: ASWEA publication.
- ASWEA. 1981. *Social Development Training in Africa: Experiences of the 1970s and Emerging Trends of the 1980s.* Doc. 17. Addis Ababa: ASWEA publication.
- ASWEA. 1982. *Seminar on the Organization and Delivery of Social Services to Rural Areas in Africa.* Doc. 19. Addis Ababa: ASWEA publication.
- ASWEA. 1985. *Training for Social Development: Methods of Intervention to Improve People's Participation in Rural Transformation in Africa with Special Emphasis on Women. Document 20.* Addis Ababa: ASWEA publication.
- ASWEA. 1986. *Association for Social Work Education in Africa.* Addis Ababa: ASWEA publications.
- ASWEA. 1989. *Social Development Agents in Rural Transformation in Africa.* Addis Ababa: ASWEA publication.
- Bar-On. 2001. When Assumptions on Fieldwork Education Fail to Hold: The Experience of Botswana. *Social Work Education* 20 (1): 123–136.
- Berstein, A. and M. Gray. 1991. Introducing the South African Student to the Social Work Profession. *International Social Work* 34 (3) (July): 251–264.
- Boahen, A. 1975. *Ghana: Evolution and Change in the Nineteenth and Twentieth Centuries.* London: Longman Group Limited.
- Busia, K. A. 1951. *The Position of the Chief in the Modern Political System of Ashanti.* London: Oxford University Press.

- Burke, J. and B. Ngonyani. 2004. A Social Work Vision for Tanzania. *International Social Work* 47 (1) (January): 39–52.
- CIDA. 2006. CIDA Home Page. www.cida.org.
- CUSO. 2006. CUSO Home Page. www.cuso.org.
- Drake, S. C. and T. P. Omari. 1962. *Social Work in Africa*. Accra: Department of Social Welfare and Community Development.
- Drower, S. J. 2000. Globalisation: An Opportunity for Dialogue Between South African and Asian Social Work Educators. *The Indian Journal of Social Work* 60 (1): 12–31.
- Freire, P. 1997. *Pedagogy of the Oppressed*. 20th ed. New York: Continuum.
- GASOW. 1972. *Social Welfare, Education and Practice in Developing Countries*. Accra: Ghana Association of Social Workers.
- GASOW. 1973. *Social Planning in National Development*. Accra: Ghana Association of Social Workers.
- GASOW. 1974. *The Role of Agriculture and Rural Technology in National Development*. Accra: Ghana Association of Social Workers.
- GASOW. 1975. *Popular Participation and the New Local Government System*. Accra: Ghana Association of Social Workers.
- Gray, M. and F. Mazibuko. 2002. Social Work in South Africa at the Dawn of the New Millennium. *International Journal of Social Welfare* 11: 191–200.
- Hampson, J. 1995. Zimbabwe. In *International Handbook on Social Work Education*, eds. N. S. Mayadas, T. D. Watts, and D. Elliott. Westport: Greenwood Press.
- Haug E. 2000. *Writings in the Margins: Critical Reflections on the Emerging Discourse of International Social Work*. Unpublished Master's Thesis, University of Calgary: Calgary, Alberta, Canada.
- Healy, K. 2001. Participatory Action Research and Social Work: A Critical Appraisal. *International Social Work* 44 (1): 93–105.
- Hochschild, A. 1998. *King Leopold's Ghost*. New York: Houghton Mifflin.
- IDRC. 2007. IDRC Home Page. www.idrc.ca.
- Jones, J. 2003. *The Congress of Berlin (1884–1885)*. http://courses.wcupa.edu/jones/his312/lectures/ber-cong.htm.
- Kaseke, E. 2001. Social Work Education in Zimbabwe: Strengths and Weaknesses, Issues and Challenges. *Social Work Education* 20 (1): 101–109.
- Kendall, K. A. 1995. Foreword. In *International Handbook on Social Work Education*, eds. N. S. Mayadas, T. D. Watt, D. Elliott. Westport: Greenwood Press.
- Konadu-Agyemang, K. 2000. The Best of Times and the Worst of Times: Structural Adjustment Programs and Uneven Development in Africa: The Case of Ghana. *Professional Geographer* 52 (3): 469–483.
- Kreitzer, L. 1998. *The Experiences of Refugee Women in the Planning and Implementation of Programmes at Buduburam Refugee Camp, Ghana*. Master's Thesis, University of Calgary, Calgary.
- Kreitzer, L. 2002. Liberian Refugee Women: A Qualitative Study of Their Participation in Planning Camp Programmes. *International Social Work* 45 (1): 45–58.
- Kreitzer, L. 2004. *Indigenization of Social Work Education and Practice: A Participatory Action Research Project in Ghana*. Unpublished Ph.D. Thesis. Calgary: University of Calgary.
- Kreitzer, L. 2005. *Queen Mothers and Social Workers: A Potential Collaboration Between Traditional Authority and Social Work in Ghana*. Chieftain, 1, 2004–present. D-space at the University of Calgary.
- Lebakeng T. J. 1997. Africanisation and Higher Education. *Sapem* (July 15–August 15). 4–7.

- Lechner, F. J. and J. Boli. 2000. Introduction. In *The Globalization Reader*, eds. F. J. Lechner and J. Boli. Oxford: Blackwell Publishers.
- Lewis, S. 2005. *Race Against Time*. Toronto: House of Anansi Press.
- Martin, P. 2000. The Moral Case for Globalization. In *The Globalization Reader*, eds. F. J. Lechner and J. Boli. Oxford: Blackwell Publishers.
- McFarland, D. M. 1985. *Historical Dictionary of Ghana*. Metuchen & London: Scarecrow Press Inc.
- Memmi, A. 1965. *The Colonizer and the Colonized*. Boston: Beacon Press.
- Midgley, J. 1981. *Professional Imperialism: Social Work in the Third World*. London: Heinemann Publication.
- Midgley, J. 2000. Globalization, Capitalism and Social Welfare. In *Social Work and Globalization*, ed. B. Rowe. Ottawa: Canadian Association of Social Workers.
- Mosha, R. S. 2000. *The Heartbeat of Indigenous Africa: A Study of the Chagga Educational System*. New York & London: Garland Publishing Inc.
- Mupedziswa, R. 1996. The Challenge of Economic Development in an African Developing Country: Social Work in Zimbabwe. *International Social Work* 39: 41–54.
- Mzaibuko and M. Gray. 2004. Social Work Professional Associations in South Africa. *International Social Work*. 47 (1) (January): 129–142.
- Nagpaul, H. 1993. Analysis of Social Work Teaching Material in India: The Need for Indigenous Foundations. *International Social Work* 36: 207–220.
- Nimmagadda J. and C. D. Cowger. 1999. Cross-Cultural Practice: Social Worker Ingenuity in the Indigenization of Practice Knowledge. *International Social Work* 43 (3): 261–276.
- Noyoo, N. 2000. Preparing South African Social Workers for Social Development Praxis. *Social Development Issues* 22 (1): 35–41.
- Ntusi, T. 1995. South Africa. In *International Handbook on Social Work Education*, eds. N. S. Mayadas, T. D. Watts, and D. Elliott. Westport: Greenwood Press
- Osei-Hwede, K. 1990. Social Work and the Question of Social Development in Africa. *Journal of Social Development in Africa* 5 (2): 87–99.
- Payne, M. 2000. *Is Social Work Sustainable?* Paper presented at the International Federation of Social Workers Conference, Montreal.
- Prigoff, A. 2000. *Economics for Social Workers: Social Outcomes of Economic Globalization with Strategies for Community Action*. Belmont: Brooks/ColeThomson Learning.
- Rimmer, D. 1992. *Staying Poor: Ghana's Political Economy, 1950–1990*. Oxford & New York: Pergamon Press.
- Sacco, T. and W. Hoffmann. 2004. Seeking Truth and Reconciliation in South Africa: A Social Work Contribution. *International Social Work* 47 (2): 157–167.
- Sartre, J. P. 2001. *Colonialism and Neo-Colonialism (1964)*. London: Routledge.
- Semali L. and J. Kincheloe. 2000. Series Editors' Foreword. R. S. Mosha *The Heartbeat of Indigenous Africa*. New York & London: Garland Publishing Inc.
- Shawky, A. 1972. Social Work Education in Africa. *International Social Work*. 15 (3): 3–16.
- Smith, L. T. 1999. *Decolonizing Methodologies: Research and Indigenous Peoples*. London: Zed Books.
- So, A.Y. 1990. *Social Change and Development: Modernization, Dependency and World-System Theories*. London: Sage Publications.
- Tesfaye, A. 1973. Social Work Education in Africa: Trends and Prospects in Relation to National Development. In ASWEA *Relationship Between Social Work Education and National Social Development*. Addis Ababa: ASWEA publication.

- Tesfaye, A. 1985. Welcome Address. In ASWEA *Training for Social Development: Methods of Intervention to Improve People's Participation in Rural Transformation in Africa with Special Emphasis on Women*. Addis Ababa: ASWEA publication.
- Tesoriero, F. and A. Rajaratnam. 2001. Partnership in Education: An Australian School of Social Work and a South Indian Primary Health Care Project. *International Social Work* 44 (1): 31–41.
- United Nations. 1950. *Training for Social Work: An International Survey*. Lake Success: United Nations Department of Social Affairs.
- United Nations. 1955. *Training for Social Work: Second International Survey*. New York: United Nations Bureau of Social Affairs.
- United Nations. 1958. *Training for Social Work: Third International Survey*. New York: United Nations Department of Economic and Social Affairs.
- United Nations. 1964. *Training for Social Work: Fourth International Survey*. New York: United Nations.
- United Nations. 1964. Patterns of Social Welfare Organization and Administration in Africa. *Social Welfare Services in Africa*, No. 2, December. New York: United Nations Social Development Section of the Economic Commission for Africa.
- United Nations. 1964. Training for Social Work in Africa. *Social Welfare Services in Africa*, No. 3 (December). New York: United Nations Social Development Section of the Economic Commission for Africa.
- United Nations. 1966. Family, Child and Youth Welfare Services in Africa. *Social Welfare Services in Africa*, No. 5 (December). New York: United Nations Social Development Section of the Economic Commission for Africa.
- United Nations. 1967. The Status and Role of Women in East Africa. *Social Welfare Services in Africa*, No. 6 (June). New York: United Nations Social Development Section of the Economic Commission for Africa.
- United Nations. 1969. Youth Employment and National Development in Africa. *Social Welfare Services in Africa*, No. 7 (November). New York: United Nations Social Development Section of the Economic Commission for Africa.
- United Nations. 1971. Integrated Approach to Rural Development in Africa. *Social Welfare Services in Africa*, No. 8 (July.) New York: United Nations Social Development Section of the Economic Commission for Africa.
- United Nations. 2005. U.N. Millennium Development goals. http://www.un.org/millenniumgoals.
- Venkataraman, J. 1996. *Indigenization Process of Alcoholism Treatment from the American to the Indian Context*. Unpublished Doctoral Thesis. Urbana-Champaign: University of Illinois.
- Walton, R. G. and M. M. Abo El Nasr. 1988. Indigenization and Authentization in Terms of Social Work in Egypt. *International Social Work* 31: 135–144.
- Wicker, E. R. 1958. Colonial Development and Welfare, 1929–1957: The Evolution of a Policy. *Social and Development Studies* 7 (4): 170–192.
- Willensky, J. 1998. *Learning to Divide the World: Education at Empire's End*. Minneapolis & London: University of Minnesota Press.
- Wilson, M.G. and E. Whitmore. 2000. *Seeds of Fire: Social Development in an Era of Globalism*. Nova Scotia: Fernwood Publishing.
- WUSC. 2006. Home Page. www.wusc.ca.
- Yimam, A. 1990. *Social Development in Africa 1950–1985*. Aldershot: Avebury.

Part 3: Social Work Practice

Chapter 9

International Social Work Practice: Frameworks and Suicide Prevention

Richard Ramsay

This chapter is set in the context of the early beginnings and evolution of the International Federation of Social Workers (and, its sister organizations the International Association of Schools of Social Work (IASSW) and the International Council of Social Welfare (ICSW)). The founding members of these organizations understood the international scope of social work long before it was given serious attention in practice or scholarship. When the International Permanent Secretariat of Social Workers was founded in Paris in 1928, social work was in its infancy. The secretariat was an active and evolving organization of social work practitioners until its suspension at the outbreak of World War II.

The beginnings of a successor organization emerged in 1950 at the international social work conference in Paris, when seven national organizations agreed to re-establish the former organization as the International Federation of Social Workers (IFSW). The federation was formally launched in 1956 at the International Conference on Social Welfare in Munich, Germany. It has been active ever since providing leadership and advocacy to advance the international scope of social work, especially regarding values, ethics, standards, and human rights. Munich was again the host for the 2006 international social work conference, celebrating the 50th anniversary of IFSW.

My introduction to the global nature of the profession occurred in 1978 during my early years in social work academia, after several years in social work practice and near the end of five years as president of the Alberta Association of Social Workers (AASW). I was awakened to the international perspective at a meeting with the President of IFSW, Mary Windsor from the UK, during the first visit to Canada (and Alberta) by a IFSW president. Her appeal to the importance of broadening one's awareness to include international social work was compelling to the extent that two AASW members— Gayle Gilchrist James and Gweneth Gowanlock (who subsequently became executive director of the Canadian Association of Social Workers)—attended their first IFSW world conference in Israel that same year.

Gilchrist James returned as the newly elected Vice-President for the North America region and the beginning of her unwavering leadership to international social work for more than two decades, culminating in two terms as Canada's first President of IFSW (1988–1992) and founding president of IFSW's Human Rights Commission. Gowanlock became the executive director of the Canadian Association of Social Workers and a staunch supporter of Canada's participation in international social work.

Their combined leadership was instrumental in Canada hosting its first world conference on social work in 1984, which turned out to be one of the most successful conferences ever sponsored by the three sister organizations: IFSW, IASSW, and ICSW.

My international involvement happened somewhat later, beginning in 1980, as Canada's representative on a six-country IFSW committee to prepare the first international definition of social work statement for the general meeting and world social work conference in Brighton, UK in 1982. It served as a significant guide for social workers until its replacement at the 2000 Montreal world conference with an updated definition, which was also approved by the International Association of Schools of Social Work. I was elected to the IFSW executive committee at the Montreal meeting and then as its treasurer from 1985 to 1992. In 2000, I was Canada's IFSW representative on the joint IFSW-IASSW committee to develop a global standards guideline for education and practice. During my years with IFSW, I was actively engaged in the search for a common conceptual framework standard to underpin the diverse manifestations of social work wherever it is practiced, locally or internationally (Ramsay 1985; Ramsay 1988).

Conceptual Framework for Social Work

My interest in a common conceptual framework for social work practice started about the same time as Mary Windsor's visit to Alberta. I joined a search that has a long history in North American social work. Although the profession is deeply connected to charitable and philanthropic foundations, the development of a scientific foundation was a major concern in the early years of the 20th century. The distinguishing "person in his environment" domain of the profession was clearly emerging but there were duality conflicts about the primary entity of concern (person or environment) and concerns about proliferating fields of practice specialties.

By the 1920s, the first of several conceptual framework meetings started with the Milford Conferences (1925–1929) to examine the question: Is there a generic social casework method? The final report concluded that social casework was a common method and that method differences across fields of practice were primarily descriptive rather than substantive. Although there was great progress in social work after the Milford Conferences, the next conceptual framework meeting was almost 50 years later. In 1976 (Madison, Wisconsin) and 1979 (O'Hare, Chicago, IL), the National Association of Social Workers in the United States sponsored two meetings on the topic.[1] The Madison meeting asked a basic question. Is there a common conceptual framework for the social work profession? (Briar 1977, 415). The meeting discussed the whole of social work, not just social casework. Several prominent social workers (including Anne Minahan, Allen Pincus, and William Reid) were commissioned to write conceptual framework papers. Reaction papers were also commissioned.

---

[1] Subsequently published in Special Editions of *Social Work* (NASW 1977; NASW 1981).

Issues that were raised included the value of having a broad social work orientation before advancing to a specialist form of practice and critical concerns about over identification with the uniqueness of the individual as a contributing factor in social work's drift away from social activism. Bernice Simon's reaction paper was blunt about the failure of the commissioned papers to present a common conceptual framework. Their collective efforts were akin to blind people trying to describe an elephant based on which part of the animal they handled: "None could describe the elephant as a whole" (Simon 1977, 394). She was concerned the papers reflected a growing proliferation of personal practice frameworks in social work. Nonetheless, she was optimistic that a common conceptual framework likely existed even though its time had not arrived. Another critic, Alexander (1977, 407) felt that social work had yet to develop a "unitary conception reflecting a consensus of practitioners." He was concerned the papers had "reconstructed and repeated the dichotomies and perceptions that have continued to spread doubt and dissension in the profession. He proposed the need for a unitary conception that incorporated Bartlett's, *The Common Base of Social Work Practice* (1970).

The O'Hare meeting continued with concerns about the absence of a common conceptual framework. Morales (1981) supported Bartlett's common base model, arguing for a model informed by ecology and general systems theory to frame the focus of social work practice on interactions between person and environment. Meyer (1981) addressed the profession's reliance on casework and other methods at the expense of addressing broad social problems. She too wanted a conceptual framework that had a greater emphasis on the person-in-environment domain of social work.

After these early meetings, it was 20 years before another meeting on the topic was held at the University of Kentucky in 2001. Following a competition for five keynote and five discussant papers, my submission was selected as one of the keynote papers.[2]

The Kentucky paper advanced the usage of a minimum whole system framework as the underlying structure that was needed to develop a common conceptual framework. When Bertalanffy's general systems theory (GST) was introduced to social work in the 1950s and 1960s, it was thought to be the answer to a (w)holistic conception of social work (Stein 1974). GST identified the central importance of interconnected relationships between all parts of a system. However, no one was able to use it to provide an objective understanding of what constituted a minimum whole system or to develop a common conceptual framework. At about the same time, Buckminster Fuller, a contemporary of Bertalanffy, was working on geometric systems and discovered that nature's minimum whole system was a tetrahedral structure consisting of a minimum of four components and

---

[2] The other papers were by Jerome Wakefield (New York University), Ann Weick (University of Kansas), Roberta Greene (Indiana University), and Dale Albers (University of Kentucky). My discussant colleague was Theora Evans (2001) from the University of Tennessee (Memphis).

six interconnected relationships that had a dynamic capacity to unfold (or return) to increasing and decreasing complexity (Fuller 1969).

This understanding of a whole system structure offered the potential of constructing a (w)holistic conceptual framework, common to social work, anywhere in the world. Bartlett (1970) came close, but she was not guided by an underlying systems structure to help her determine the minimum number of interrelated components needed to develop a whole system conception of social work. She nonetheless had advanced social work beyond the specialized method frameworks that had dominated social work for most of the first half of the 20th century. Bartlett's "common base of social work" described three core components: a central focus on social functioning relationships in a person-interaction-environment context; a broad orientation to people being served, directly or indirectly; and a repertoire of interventions. She addressed the significance of the professional use of self in social work but it was not conceptualized as a core component.

Transforming Bartlett's components to common global concepts was aided by Wilber's (1990) views on the minimum conceptual requirements for something to be considered a science and Kuhn's (1970) views on the conceptual nature of like-minded communities engaged in common work. Wilber argued that any discipline or profession could be a science provided it had a distinguishable domain (or central area of concern) for its work and a method(s) of arriving at (or applying) knowledge claims that are open to challenge and refutation. Kuhn used the paradigm concept as a way to identify like-minded groups engaged in any discipline or professional endeavor. Together, they identified three common concepts: domain, paradigm, and method. When the professional use of self in social work is included as a conceptual component, an additional domain for practitioners is identified that has the same distinguishable area of concern. This led to a development that advanced Bartlett's common base to a whole systems framework with four common conceptual components: (i) Domain of Social Work; (ii) Paradigm of Social Work; (iii) Method(s) of Practice; and (iv) Domain of Social Worker. Each is elaborated below.

Domain of Social Work

Bartlett identified three critical elements that characterized the domain of social work: person, interaction, and environment or more commonly described as person-in-environment (PIE). The distinguishing feature of this domain is its unifying and central focus on relational interactions between personal and environmental elements, rather than the traditional dual-focus on either the person or environment elements of the domain. From a World Health Organization (WHO) perspective, the social well-being of health is the primary concern of the social work profession. Central to this concern is a vision of just and civil societies throughout the world (Witkin 1999). The person element in varying configurations generally refers to the developmental, demographic, and social functioning status of individuals in family, groups, and communities. The environment concept includes elements in societies that enhance or impede the development of individual and collective social well-being. In particular, the elements generally include natural support networks and societal resource structures that are shaped by a variety of societal norms and expectations in the form of influential attitudes, beliefs, customs, policies, and laws, all of which contribute to the kind of just and civil societies in which people live.

Paradigm of Social Work

Bartlett's broad orientation becomes part of the paradigm of like-minded social work people who have an agreed-on domain of practice, common values and ethics, and common modes of intervention, regardless of national boundaries or adherence to particularized bodies of knowledge. The paradigm component provides generalist-specialist and micro-macro social workers a broad base of practice options to work directly or indirectly with different size client groups and/or work on behalf of non-client groups or populations in their person-in-environment contexts.

Methods of Practice

The interventive repertoire becomes part of the method component that accommodates the use of multiple intervention methods that are deemed appropriate to the domain of social work assessments and practice option decisions.

Domain of Social Worker

This domain recognizes that social workers, like the people with whom they work, function in their own relevant person-in-environment system. Inclusion of this component requires social workers to be professionally aware of their own personal PIE influences that may affect the way they use the other components in practice situations. The disciplined use of self requires social workers to constantly monitor their personal lives in relation to the natural support networks and societal resource structures that are shaped by a variety of societal norms and expectations in the form of influential attitudes, beliefs, customs, policies, and laws.

The four interrelated components and their underlying minimum whole system structure constitute a common conceptual framework for social work. The social worker uses the interconnections between the components to make practice decisions. Once a domain of social work assessment is completed, the social worker selects a paradigm practice option before deciding on the selection of a generalist-specialist and/or micro-macro method of intervention. After domain assessment and paradigm option decisions are made, the methods component is activated with the selection of an intervention. When the intervention is selected, each decision to that point can be double-checked to make sure the interconnected components are appropriately aligned. For example, if a social worker's assessment identified a social functioning problem between a parent (client) and the operator of their child's daycare centre (societal resource), the social worker (in agreement with the parent) might appropriately select a case advocacy option to address the operator's role in the problem. This plan would require an intervention designed to influence the daycare operator to respond more positively to the client's concerns.

If a counselling intervention for the operator was selected, on the other hand, the social worker would be able to confirm the congruence between the person-in-environment assessment and the selected practice option, but discover that something is amiss with the planned intervention when a double-check between components is made. If the original assessment is confirmed, then either the practice option or intervention choice is out of line. If the practice option decision is confirmed, the counselling method must be reconsidered in favour of a more appropriate case advocacy intervention. To complete the process, the social worker would monitor her or his own domain to assess the person-in-environment factors that might affect their professional judgment and practice decisions.

Person-in-Environment

About the same time that work was beginning on the common conceptual framework, a small group of dedicated volunteers in California were concerned about the absence of a social work classification system for social functioning problems. Their concerns peaked with the inclusion of psychosocial stressors and publication of the third edition of the Diagnostic and Statistical Manual of Mental Disorder (DSM-III) in 1980. Although the inclusion of psychosocial factors was welcomed, it was quickly recognized that if social work didn't develop its own classification system, it would eventually end up relying on the language of another discipline (e.g., psychiatry) to describe the focus of its work.

In 1981, the National Association of Social Workers (NASW) of the United States funded a 2-year project and commissioned a small task force of prominent California academics and practitioners, led by Jim Karls and Karen Wandrei, to develop a prototype classification system to describe, classify, and code problems of social functioning (Karls and Wandrei 1994). The task force adopted person-in-environment as the foundation construct for the system. A four-factor PIE classification system was developed to provide comprehensive descriptions (problems and strengths) of social role and relationship interactions, environmental, mental and physical health dimensions of social functioning.

The environment factor included a problem statement on discrimination to identify social justice issues that affect individual social role functioning or larger categories of affected groups. Its intent was to provide a common language for all social workers to use in describing problems of social functioning and determining appropriate interventions. A pilot reliability study was conducted in 1984 using videotaped cases with generally positive results. Coincidently, one video case was from a social work interviewing series that I had produced at the University of Calgary in the late 1970s. International interest led to a number of informal validity tests of PIE in Italy, Netherlands, Japan, Canada, and Australia.

Karls and I became aware of our overlapping interests in conceptual frameworks and classification systems at a meeting in 1989, which led to an ongoing collaboration to integrate our respective work.[3] In 1997, with the support of a Learning Enhancement grant from the University of Calgary, a computer-assisted learning prototype was developed to instruct students and practitioners in a whole systems model of social work and how to apply the holistic, four-factor PIE classification system to the domain of social work, and facilitate its use as an assessment tool in method of practice interventions (Ramsay and Karls 1999).

Interest in the development of a common classification system for social work continues to grow within the profession in North America and beyond to other nations, but the adoption of an international classification system has yet to materialize. The recent adoption by IFSW and IASSW of global standards for the education and training of the social work profession recognized person-in-environment and the need for social workers to be prepared within a holistic framework (Sewpaul and Jones 2004). Although the need for an international classification system to guide assessment and practice decisions in social work was not included, the possibility is embodied in the standards.

Global Standards

Following the IFSW and IASSW joint adoption of the updated International Definition of Social Work in 2000, the two organizations agreed to further their collaborative initiatives. A Global Minimum Qualifying Standards Committee was formally sanctioned as a joint initiative of the IASSW-IFSW Conference in Montreal in July 2000. Representatives from 12 countries were named to the committee. The vision of an achievable set of global standards was ambitious and resisted by some skeptics who saw it becoming an exercise in reinforcing the hegemony of Western views of social work. Yet, there was wide support from member nations to pursue the goal of a global standards guideline for the profession.

The committee undertook their work with several objectives in mind. One was to develop a set of standards that had sufficient flexibility to "allow for interpretations of locally specific social work education and practice, and take into account each country or region's socio-political, cultural, economic, and historical contexts while adhering to international standards" (Sewpaul and Jones 2004). The standards were developed as a "dynamic process" to encourage critical debate and be open to review and revisions as

---

[3] Publication of the Person-in-Environment System book and manual (Karls and Wandrei 1994) was a best seller for NASW and expanded international interest in the PIE system.

needed. Nine sets of standards were established for education and training programs: 1) core purpose and mission; 2) program outcomes and objectives; 3) program curricula including field education; 4) core curricula; 5) professional staff; 6) social work students; 7) structure, administration, governance and resources; 8) cultural, ethnicity, and gender inclusiveness; and 9) values and ethical codes. I was particularly interested in efforts to avoid Western dominance and further develop the core curricula standard. In early drafts, core curricula items were presented in list form with little recognition that they might be organized within a globally acceptable conceptual framework to guide curriculum development and integrate with practice applications.

Following a submission in which members were asked to consider the possibility of a common conceptual framework at the international level, the final draft of the core curricula standard was reorganized into the four components of the proposed common conceptual framework with slightly revised names for each component after a post-conference ratification proviso was completed. The respective general assemblies of IASSW and IFSW adopted the standards document at their joint international conference in Adelaide, Australia, in 2004 with a proviso that the concerns of instructors from some of the newer member nations be incorporated into the document with language to be inclusive of their professional work. As a result, the scope of the document was broadened and all reference to "social work" was revised to read the "social work profession." The curricula items that are aligned with each of the core conceptual components in the standards document are open to ongoing review and critical debate to determine the relevance of their allocation and allow for different cultural and regional manifestations of these items to be developed within the structure of a common conceptual framework.

Suicide Prevention

Part of my introduction to the international scope of social work and subsequently to suicide prevention at an international level is linked to the 1987 UN meeting of Ministers Responsible for Social Welfare and subsequent General Assembly approval of the *Guiding Principles for Developmental Social Welfare Policies and Recommendations in the Near Future* (United Nations, 1987). The Canadian delegation to this meeting included Gayle Gilchrist James, Chair, Canadian Council of Social Welfare, at the request of the Minister of Health and Welfare, and IFSW's Vice-President (North America). Four years later in 1991, the Secretary General asked government and non-government organizations and universities (for the first time) to help with a global review of national and local progress toward achievement of the social welfare recommendations set forth in the 1987 document. The request to the University of Calgary was passed to the dean of social work. I was assigned the task of preparing the university response.

At the time, I was beginning to use the whole system structure to develop a parallel conceptual framework for crisis intervention and suicide prevention that emerged from several years of volunteer experience in training volunteers for new crisis lines. On the policy side, my experience with crisis line training contributed to my appointment as a charter member of Alberta's provincial suicide prevention advisory committee responsible for the implementation of the province's first suicide prevention strategy (Boldt 1985). Part of the strategy called for the development and dissemination of a standardized, province-wide suicide intervention training program for a broad cross-section of professional and community caregivers. Evidence at the time indicated that the young science of suicidology had established a significant knowledge base that wasn't sufficiently disseminated by educators and trainers to those most likely to encounter persons at risk of suicide in their community and professional positions (Maris 1973).

Almost ten years after the release of the report, *Suicide Prevention in the Seventies*, there was little evidence of progress to address the dissemination problem. The challenge was taken up in Alberta with development support from the advisory committee and a multi-disciplinary group of practitioners and mental health volunteers interested in program development. I was part of the group that evolved into a core of four developers. Following a three year development and field trial period (1982–85) using Rothman's social R&D model (Rothman 1980), a first of its kind, two day suicide first aid training workshop (ASIST—Applied Suicide Intervention Skills Training) and a five day training for trainers (T4T) course was ready for dissemination in Alberta through the Canadian Mental Health Association (CMHA) and a small cohort of community-based trainers. The core developers were part of CMHA's dissemination network and later became out-of-province providers of the training to the California Department of Mental Health (Ramsay, Cooke, and Lang 1990). By 1991, with investment support from the University of Calgary's venture company, University Technologies International, the developers were aided in establishing LivingWorks Education as a university start-up company to standardize the T4T course and disseminate the training outside Alberta, nationally and internationally.

The scope of the university response to the UN's extensive survey questions was narrowed to overview the Alberta suicide prevention strategy with a primary focus on the development and dissemination progress of the training program. The Secretary General's report to the General Assembly on local applications of the 1987 policy recommendations highlighted suicide prevention as a social welfare challenge in need of more policy and practice attention at all levels. The UN reply to the University of Calgary acknowledged that suicide was a "problem we have neglected hitherto, and we are grateful to you for having stimulated the idea that this neglect should not continue" (personal communication, Michael Stubbs, Developmental Social Welfare Unit, August, 1991). The social welfare unit of the United Nations had long held the assumption that suicide was a mental health problem and therefore the exclusive domain of the World Health Organization (WHO).

In acknowledging their "neglect," the UN became a policy leader in recognizing and promoting that the prevention of suicide should not be treated as the exclusive domain of any group, locally or internationally. All domain groups need to be involved including public health, injury prevention, social welfare, and mental health. As more commonly described, "Suicide is everybody's business" and should not be treated as a phenomena that only certain specialists can address. As a concrete response to this "confessed" error, the UN invited LivingWorks Education and the Canadian Mental Health Association's (CMHA) Suicide Information and Education Centre (SIEC) to work with them to host a week long interregional "experts" meeting with suicide prevention representatives from all regions of the world. With UN strategy development guidance, the task was to develop a national suicide prevention strategy guideline that the UN could endorse and distribute to interested national governments and NGOs around the world.

With funding support from Health and Welfare Canada and two Alberta government departments, a meeting was convened in Banff in 1993, attended by 15 representatives from 12 countries: Australia, Canada, China, Estonia, Finland, Hungary, India, Japan, the Netherlands, Nigeria, United Arab Emirates, and the United States. Representatives from the WHO and UN were present along with observers from Sweden and Australia. The resulting strategy development guideline was a first-of-its-kind policy that was widely distributed by the UN to national governments and other interested groups (UN 1996). The community-based perspective of the guideline included both government-initiated and citizen-initiated steps to achieve broadly supported and collaboratively developed national strategies.

The impact of the UN guideline was almost immediate. Jerry Weyrauch, the father of a young physician daughter who had died by suicide in 1987, obtained an early draft of the guideline. The document moved him beyond the private grief that he and his family had been struggling with for almost five years to a heightened awareness of suicide as a serious public issue in the United States. When he realized that the US did not have a national strategy, he vowed to use the UN guideline to mobilize a grassroots, citizen-initiated movement of suicide survivors to advocate for a national strategy. With determined persistence, mushrooming support from survivors throughout the nation, and the significant influence of political leaders in the US Congress, the public policy groundwork for a national strategy was in place in less than three years.

Led by the country's Surgeon General, Dr. David Satcher, and the collaborative involvement of federal department administrators, interested professionals and academics, concerned citizens and supportive corporate partners, the US approved a comprehensive national suicide prevention strategy in 2001 (US 2001). It was a short seven years from the time that the UN guideline came into Weyrauch's possession and the time that the entire country had an approved citizen-initiated national strategy. The UN document has since served as a guide or reference for a growing number of countries that have developed and implemented national suicide prevention strategies in the past ten years, including Australia, England, Estonia, New Zealand, Northern Ireland, Norway, Republic of Ireland, Scotland, and Slovenia. The irony is the absence of Canada on the list of countries with a national strategy.

While nations were becoming more aware and concerned about suicide as a serious community problem, the Alberta-initiated training program was expanding internationally. A government-supported field trial was conducted in Australia to test the international portability of the program (Turley and Tanney 1998). Its success paved the way for its implementation in several countries that now includes Australia, Canada, England, New Zealand, Northern Ireland, Norway, Republic of Ireland, Scotland, Singapore, the United States including the territory of Guam, and Wales. Currently, with an international network of more than 3,000 trainers, the suicide first aid training (ASIST) program is annually presented to over 50,000 community level participants toward the goal of helping to create suicide-safer communities around the world.

Conclusion

The contributions of Canadian social workers to the development of international practice, social justice, social development, and social work education have been numerous and varied since the International Permanent Secretariat of Social Workers was founded in 1928. For its successor organization, IFSW, Canadian contributions became prominent after 1978 when Gayle Gilchrist James became Vice President, North America. Since then, Canadian social workers have provided continuous leadership to the IFSW executive, contributing to the international definition of social work, Canada's hosting of two international social work conferences, the IFSW human rights commission, UN developmental social welfare recommendations to the General Assembly, ethical declarations, policy positions on international social welfare issues, global standards in education and training for the social work profession, and much more.

Working with colleagues from different regions of the world afforded many opportunities to discuss and reflect on the scope of international social work and the many variants that have to be addressed in formulating internationally relevant policy positions, practice statements, conceptual frameworks, classification systems, and global standards for education and training. In particular, my involvement with IFSW inadvertently led to significant connections between the growth of international practice activities in suicide intervention training and development of UN policy guidelines for national strategies to prevent suicide. At the time, the interconnections between IFSW's submission to a meeting of UN ministers responsible for social welfare, the social welfare recommendations submitted to the General Assembly, and the Alberta-based suicide prevention training would appear to have had little connection with each other.

This changed dramatically with the UN's inclusion of university organizations to its circulation request for practical applications of the recommendations endorsed by the General Assembly. The University of Calgary's request of an IFSW member who reported on an innovative suicide prevention program and the UN's decision to recognize suicide as more than a mental health problem brought the connections to the fore. Further connections surfaced when the survivor parent of a daughter who died the same year as the UN meeting of ministers championed the UN national strategy guidelines to spearhead a citizen movement resulting in a breakthrough national suicide prevention strategy for the United States. Without the unfolding of these connections, international guidance in suicide prevention and development of several national strategies may have taken a decidedly different turn and slower evolution in addressing one of the worlds most underrated community health problems.

References

- American Association of Social Workers 1929. *Social Casework, General and Specific: A Report of the Milford Conference*. New York: AASW (Reprinted by NASW in 1974).
- Alexander, C. 1977. Social Work Practice: A Unitary Conception. *Social Work* 22 (5): 407–414.
- Bartlett, H. 1970. *The Common Base of Social Work Practice*. New York: NASW.
- Boldt, M. 1985. Toward the Development of a Systematic Approach to Suicide Prevention: The Alberta Model. *Canada's Mental Health* 30 (2): 12–15.
- Briar, S. 1977. In Summary. *Social Work* 22 (5): 415–416, 444.
- Evans, T. 2001. *The Time is Right for a Conceptual Framework: A Response*. Paper presented to Reworking the Working Definition: The Kentucky Conference on Social Work Practice and Education. Lexington: February 8–10.
- Fuller, R. B. 1969. *Utopia or Oblivion: The Prospects for Humanity*. Woodstock: The Overlook Press.
- Kuhn, T. 1970. *The Structure of Scientific Revolutions*. 2nd ed. (enlarged). Chicago: University of Chicago Press.
- Meyers, C. 1981. Social Work Purpose: Status by Choice or Coercion? *Social Work* 26 (1): 69–77.
- Morales, A. 1981. Social Work with Third-World People. *Social Work* 26 (1): 45–51.
- NASW. 1977. Special Issue on Conceptual Frameworks. *Social Work* 22 (5).
- NASW. 1981. Conceptual Frameworks II: Second Special Issue on Conceptual Frameworks. *Social Work* 26 (1): 5–96.
- Ramsay, R. 1985. A Conceptual Framework for Teaching the Practice of Social Work: A New Approach to an Old Problem. In *The Teaching of Social Work Methods: Discussions and Innovations*, ed. M. Rodway. Calgary: Faculty of Social Welfare, University of Calgary.
- Ramsay, R. 1988. *Is Social Work a Profession? A 21st Century Answer to a 20th Century Question*. Unpublished Manuscript. Calgary: University of Calgary.
- Ramsay, R., M. Cooke, and W. Lang. 1990. Alberta Suicide Prevention Training Program: A Retrospective Comparison with Rothman's Developmental Research Model. *Suicide and Life-Threatening Behavior* 20 (4): 7–22.
- Ramsay, R. 1994. Conceptualizing PIE within a Holistic Conception of Social Work. In *Person-in-Environment System: The PIE Classification System for Social Functioning Problems*, eds. J. Karls and K. Wandrei, 171–195. Washington: NASW Press,

- Ramsay, R. and J. Karls. 1999. Person-in-Environment Classification System: Adding CD-ROM Options to Social Work Learning. *New Technology in the Human Services* 12 (3/4): 17–28.

- Ramsay, R. 2001. *Revisiting the Working Definition.* Paper presented to "Reworking the Working Definition," The Kentucky Conference on Social Work Practice and Education, Lexington, February 8–10.

- Rothman, J. 1980. *Social R&D: Research and Development in the Human Services.* Englewood Cliffs: Prentice-Hall.

- Sewpaul, V. and D. Jones. 2004. *Global Standards for the Education and Training of the Social Work Profession.* Adopted by IASSW/IFSW General Assemblies, Adelaide, Australia.

- Simon, B. 1977. Diversity and Unity in the Social Work Profession. *Social Work* 22 (5): 394–400.

- Stein, I. 1974. *Systems Theory, Science and Social Work.* Metuchen: Scarecrow Press.

- Turley, B. and B. Tanney. 1998. *SIFTA Evaluation Report.* Melbourne: Lifeline Australia.

- United Nations. 1987. *Guiding Principles for Developmental Social Welfare Policies and Programmes in the Near Future.* Vienna: Centre for Social Development and Humanitarian Affairs.

- United Nations. 1996 *Prevention of Suicide: Guidelines for the Formulation and Implementation of National Strategies.* New York: U.N. Department of Policy Coordination and Sustainable Development, ST/ESA/245.

- Wilber, K. 1990. *Eye to Eye: The Quest for the New Paradigm.* Expanded ed. Boston: Shambhala Publications.

- Witkin, S. 1999. Editorial: Identities and Contexts. *Social Work* 44 (4) (July): 293–297.

Chapter 10

Wombats and Dingos: Contributions To Progressive Social Work Down Under[1]

Bob Mullaly

Consistent with the overall theme of this book of looking at Canadian contributions to international social work, this chapter focuses on Canadian contributions to progressive social work in Australia. A major difference in this chapter and most of the others is that whereas they focus mainly on contributions to developing countries, I focus on Canadian contributions to a developed country. In particular, but not exclusively, I present my own experiences of contributing to Australian progressive social work during the 1990s and the first few years of the current decade. Although this may sound somewhat self-indulgent, I base my claims in this paper on several years of activity in Australia.

I wrote a book on structural social work, published in 1993, that immediately became popular in Australian social work programs. I spent one year as a visiting scholar where I was invited to speak at most major social work programs in the country, six years as the head of the social work program at the University of Victoria in Melbourne, and one year as a professorial fellow at the University of Melbourne (a position that I still hold). I wrote two major social work books while I was in Australia; and I was the editor of the major social work journal in Australia, *Australian Social Work*, during the last year I lived there (2002–03). More importantly, however, is the fact that my work has been cited in the Australian social work literature more than any other Canadian writer over the past decade.

I will first present a brief introduction to the subject of international social work in which I frame the chapter. The second section will explain the meaning of "progressive social work" and provide an historical overview of its development in Anglo democracies. This section will also provide the context for Canadian contributions to progressive social work in Australia. The third section will provide a brief look at social work in Australia and

---

[1] Wombats and dingos are two animal species indigenous to Australia. The wombat is an herbivorous marsupial mammal that is stout and sturdy and is the largest burrowing animal on earth. The dingo is a wild dog that has lived in Australia for the past 3,500 years. These two animals (and many others) live no other place on earth. Just as there are flora and fauna that are indigenous to Australia, so too is its social work. Although not extensively different than social work in other Anglo democracies, its geographical location, context, culture(s), and history have made its configuration of social work perspectives, theories, methods, and practices uniquely Australian. Other countries, most notably Britain and the United States, have played major roles in the development of many of Australia's social institutions including its welfare state. And, of course, because social work is a major player within the welfare state, it has been influenced by social work in these same two countries as well. However, as I argue in this chapter, Australia's unique brand of social work has been influenced by Canadian social work as well.

some of the factors that influenced it during its formative years. The fourth section will identify some Canadian contributions (including my own) to the development of progressive or critical forms of social work in Australia. The chapter ends with a brief conclusion in which some of the major themes are highlighted.

International Social Work

There is, by now, a substantial literature on international social work and I will not attempt to summarize it here. Instead, I will present a brief overview of some of the significant commonalities and differences with respect to social work around the world. I will then look at some of the meanings or definitions of "international social work" as found in the literature from which I adopt a particular definition as a framework and point of departure for this chapter. Other chapters in this book may have adopted different notions or understandings of the meaning of international social work.

Healy (2001, xiii) comments on the global nature of social work in the following manner: "As the 21st century begins, the reality of global inter-dependence is widely appreciated. The profession of social work, having entered its second century as an organized profession, is now a global profession. Social work practice and policy are increasingly shaped by global phenomena, and there are many opportunities for social work to make an impact on the world scene. These are exciting times for international social work." Two other prominent international social work writers, Cox and Pawar (2006, 7), identify a few commonalities that exist among most countries with respect to social work. They are:

- Organized professional social work exists in varying degrees in the majority of countries (many least developed countries being the exceptions), and the various national social work structures recognize each other as sharing much in common and as being part of a global profession.
- Social work everywhere shares the same ethical underpinnings as evidenced by similar Codes of Ethics, joint ethical statements, and shared ethical concerns.
- Social workers are dealing with similar social problems in many, if not most, countries and programs, and discussions at international social work conferences underscore this point.

To this list, Hokenstad, Khinduka, and Midgley (1992, cited in Healy 2001, 99) add the following:

- Social work in most countries has a broad range of roles and responsibilities.
- Social work defines itself as an agent of social change.
- Work with poor people is a part of social work in all countries.
- There are shared values of "promoting human dignity and social justice, empowering poor and vulnerable peoples, and encouraging intergroup harmony and goodwill" (182).

As well as commonalities, there is also significant variation in social work on an international level. Cox and Pawar (2006) identify differences in social work from country to country that could be anticipated within any global profession and that reflect the social, economical, political, and cultural differences in prevailing environments, along with historical factors. Social work in Latin America, for example, has been influenced by liberation theology and the conscientization (consciousness-raising) pedagogy of Paulo Freire, resulting in a strong social justice and social action focus with a commitment to revolutionary change (Healy 2001; Kendall 2000, cited in Cox and Pawar 2006). In many parts of Africa, social work has been influenced by recent ideas on social development that emphasize social structure, community, and social change rather than theories of individual change (Healy 2001; Midgley 1995; Midgley 1999). Social work in India has a strong focus on rural social work and in China the need for culturally sensitive social work education and practice is increasingly being recognized (Cox and Pawar 2006). A final example of difference lies in the birth or rebirth of social work in Eastern Europe following the Cold War (1989) and the collapse of communist regimes, which stresses social reconstruction and the building of a free and democratic civil society (Constable and Mehta 1994, cited in Cox and Pawar 2006).

Given the above commonalities and differences, what exactly is "international social work"? The literature is pretty clear that there is no standard definition. Healy (2001, 5) contends that international social work is a complex concept comprised of a number of related ideas such as "comparative social welfare, international practice, cross cultural knowledge, and understanding, intergovernmental work on social welfare, concern and action on global social problems, a worldwide collegiality among social workers, professional exchange activities, and a general worldview". *The Social Work Dictionary* (Barker 1995, 194) defines international social work as a term "loosely applied to: (1) international organizations using social work methods or personnel; (2) social work cooperation between countries; and (3) transfer between countries of methods or knowledge about social work." Some definitions are very narrow referring to one or another of the above concepts, while other definitions are very broad.

Given the wide array of social work activities and the nature of globalization, I favour a broad and inclusive definition such as that developed by Cox and Pawar (2006, 20): "International social work is the promotion of social work education and practice globally and locally, with the purpose of building a truly integrated international profession that reflects social work's capacity to respond appropriately and effectively, in education and practice terms, to the various global challenges that are having a significant impact on the well-being of large sections of the world's population."

Some of the important features of this definition include the need for action to address social work education and practice at global and local levels, links between education and international practice, and an integration of diverse practices rather than domination by one country or culture. This chapter focuses on a particular social work perspective (i.e., structural social work), which originated and was developed mainly in Canada and transported to another country, Australia, where it has become part of the curriculum in many social work programs and part of social work practice in many places in Australia. Given the above brief précis of international social work, this chapter then clearly fits into any concept and/or definition of international social work. With respect to Healy's definition, this chapter is congruent with most of the concepts in her definition, but in particular with "concern and action on global social problems, a worldwide collegiality among social workers, [and] professional exchange activities."

The chapter also includes two of Barker's three areas of international social work, "social work cooperation between countries, and transfer between countries of methods or knowledge about social work." And, it epitomizes Cox and Pawar's definition. Also, because progressive social work, in general, and structural social work, in particular, focus on social structures rather than individuals as the source of social problems, progressive social work is consistent with many of the social change approaches adopted by social work in other regions of the world such as liberation theology and Freire's conscientization in Latin America, the social development model in Africa, the emphasis given to cultural sensitivity in social work in China, and the social reconstruction approach of many Eastern European countries.

Progressive Social Work

Although progressive forms of social work date back to the Settlement House movement of the late nineteenth and early twentieth centuries, the modern formulation of progressive social work began with the 1975 publications of Roy Bailey and Mike Brake's *Radical Social Work* in Britain, Jeffry Galper's *The Politics of Social Services* in the United States, and Harold Throssell's *Social Work: Radical Essays in Australia*. Despite being written independent from one another and in three different English-speaking continents, they contained a number of common themes (that had emerged in the radical sixties). Each criticized capitalism as a social and economic system that was antithetical to human need; each criticized mainstream social work for being an unwitting agent for capitalism; and each called for emancipatory/ radical (i.e., progressive) forms of social work practice that would contribute to the transformation of capitalism to some form of socialism. This early form of progressive social work was called "radical social work" because it radically departed from the mainstream "reform the person" approach to social problems and emphasized social change or "reform society" as the solution to social problems.

A flood of progressive social work writings appeared in the late 1970s and early 1980s focusing mainly on class struggle (Bolger et al. 1981; Brake and Bailey 1980; Carniol 1979; Corrigan and Leonard 1978; Galper 1980; Jones 1983; Longres 1986; Moreau 1979; Pritchard and Taylor 1978; Wagner and Cohen 1978). From these writings, the progressive social work agenda was clear. The critical analysis of capitalism would be further developed to show not only its oppressive effects, but also its contradictions, which would provide the levers and latitude for the practice of radical social work. The critique of mainstream social work practices would also be further developed to show how they actually covered up many of the oppressive features of capitalism by helping people to cope with it, adjust to it, or fit back into it.

These critical analyses of capitalism and mainstream social work would, in turn, be used to develop radical or progressive theories and practices of social work at both the personal and political levels. This would include raising the awareness of social services users of how capitalism exploited them and encourage them to organize and mobilize against it; joining with the trade union movement, which was seen as the major vehicle for over-throwing capitalism; building up the welfare state that had need rather than profit as its criterion for production and distribution; and electing social democratic political parties that were viewed as more committed to social justice than were bourgeois parties. Also, radical or progressive social work in the 1970s was responding to the criticism of feminist social workers that it was gender-blind and in the early 1980s to the criticism, mainly from black social workers, that it was colour-blind. In varying degrees, most social work educational programs incorporated some of these progressive ideas and analyses into parts of their curriculum, but for the most part, they occupied marginal or token positions alongside mainstream social work ideas and practices.

By the mid-1980s it was clear that the progressive project of radical social work was being undermined by the worldwide economic crisis and right-wing social policies brought about by the oil crisis in 1973. Led by "big business" and bourgeois governments, economic restructuring occurred to address a worldwide recession and inflation (i.e., stagflation). Capitalism was transformed from its rigid and centralized postwar form to a flexible (for the capitalists at least) and global form (Harvey 1989), thus making much of the earlier critical analyses of capitalism outdated and irrelevant. We witnessed, as Leonard (1997) pointed out, the ascendancy of neo-conservatism on a global scale and the virtual collapse of Left politics, a reduced welfare state, increasing disparities between rich and poor, national trade unions in disarray, and massive economic uncertainty. Given the irrelevance of much of its analysis of capitalism, the diminished political power of the trade union movement, continuous cutbacks in the welfare state, and the election of neo-conservative governments, the development of radical social work came to a halt and the whole radical social work movement seemed to go underground.

Though never dead, there was a period of inactivity and virtual invisibility (roughly during the 1980s) for radical social work before an important book was published in Britain in 1989. *Radical Social Work Today* (Mary Langan and Phil Lee, eds. 1989b) contained articles from various radical writers and practitioners that reassessed the need for radical social work in its new social, economical, and political context. These authors identified what they believed to be the essential elements of a radical social work strategy in the 1990s. In my view, this book breathed new life into progressive social work. The title of its opening chapter, "Whatever happened to radical social work?" addressed the questions that so many progressive social workers had. What did happen to radical social work? To what extent is it still relevant? Which aspects should be modified or rejected, given the events of the previous decade and the new realities facing social work? Langan and Lee called attention to several factors that, in their view, would have to be considered and addressed before radical social work could move on.

One of these factors was the changed practice context in which social work operated: dramatic increases in workloads of social workers; criticism and condemnation of social workers from conservative politicians and a mainstream media; the drive to push social workers into more a more coercive and interventionist role in policing "deviant" families; and a growing criticism from members of oppressed groups, such as women, people of colour, persons with disabilities, and older people, that their interests had not been adequately articulated by the radical social work movement. A major criticism of the 1970s radical social work was that it was strong on critique, but short on practice. Although such objection seemed to underestimate how necessary this critical stance was, as well as the constructive role it played, by 1989 it was obvious that radical social work had to translate its critical analysis into practice if it were to move on. A few other books around this time furthered the critical analysis of social work and the social welfare state—Fiona Williams's 1989 book from Britain, *Social Policy: A Critical Introduction: Issues of Race, Gender, and Class*; Ben Carniol's second edition of *Case Critical* (1990) from Canada; and George Martin's *Social Policy in the Welfare State* (1990) from the US—but none of these really addressed the practice of radical social work.

It was shortly after the publication of *Radical Social Work Today* that I wrote the first edition of *Structural Social Work* (1993). In the first edition, I attempted to address many of the criticisms made of radical social work in Langan and Lee's book, but in particular I focused on the inconsistent treatment that radical social work had received in the literature up to that time and the criticism that it had not moved much beyond a critique of conventional social work. I chose critical social theory as my theoretical base and, as my framework, a particular school of radical social work pioneered in Canada by Maurice Moreau, which he termed "structural social work." I chose critical social theory because it, unlike mainstream social theory, goes beyond merely attempting to explain and understand social phenomena to a political purpose of changing social conditions and challenging oppression. I chose "structural social work" for several reasons. First, the term "structural" is descriptive of the nature of social problems in that they are an inherent part of our neo-conservative/liberal, capitalist society and do not reside in the individual. Second, the term is prescriptive, as it indicates that the focus for change is mainly on the structures of society and not on the personal characteristics of the individual. Third, structural social work has more potential for integrating various theoretical concepts and political practices because it does not establish hierarchies of oppression, but is concerned with all oppressed groups. Fourth, it is a dialectical approach to social work practice and, therefore, does not get trapped within false dichotomies or binary opposites. Finally, most of the development of structural social work had occurred in Canada and it was increasingly becoming a major social work perspective.[2]

Coincidentally, another radical social book was published in Australia in the same year as the first edition of *Structural Social Work*. Jan Fook's *Radical Casework* focused primarily on the practice (at the micro level) of radical social work and de-emphasized theory, whereas my *Structural Social Work* was stronger on theory than it was on practice. Many radical social work instructors in Australia and Canada used the two books together as each supplemented the other. As well, these two books are credited by many as representing an important milestone in the development of radical forms of social work theory and practice, as evidenced by the plethora of progressive social work books published a few years after 1993. However, *Radical Casework* is still one of the best books written on the practice of radical social work.

In 1996, I began writing the second edition of *Structural Social Work*, which was published in late 1997. It was also in 1997 that I moved to Australia to assume the position of head of the social work program at the University of Victoria in Melbourne. In the 1997 edition, among other changes, I attempted to address the limitations of the first edition and in doing so to further the development of structural social work theory and practice. I also included a chapter on "oppression" and argued that it had to be the focus of structural social work rather than class or gender or race only. It is interesting that a decade later the Canadian Association of Schools of Social Work includes in its Standards of Accreditation that social work programs must demonstrate that they have included oppression and anti-oppressive social work in their curricula.[3]

I have just completed a third edition that I have called *The New Structural Social Work* because it is sufficiently different from previous editions and because the economic, political, and intellectual context of social work is

---

[2] The first edition of Structural Social Work proved immensely popular because, in my view, it filled a large gap in the literature. Many, many social work practitioners and academics committed to fundamental social change and to social work practices that did not blame people experiencing social problems for their situations, and they were looking for workable progressive forms of social work.

[3] Several other books on progressive social work were published around the same time as the second edition of *Structural Social Work*. They included Jim Ife's *Rethinking Social Work: Towards Critical Practice* (1997) and *Human Rights and Social Work: Towards Rights-Based Practice* (2001); Peter Leonard's *Postmodern Welfare* (1997); Ben Carniol's third (1995) and fourth (2000) editions of *Case Critical*; Bob Pease and Jan Fook's *Transforming Social Work Practice: Postmodern Critical Perspectives* (1999); and Lena Dominelli's second edition of *Anti-Racist Social Work* (1997). By now there was a substantial body of literature on various schools of progressive social work.

also different today from what it was ten years ago. When I wrote the first edition of *Structural Social Work*, only a few social work programs in Canada (and elsewhere) might have had a single course on radical social work. Today, entire social work programs advertise themselves as structural or anti-oppressive or as some other variation of progressive social work.

Social Work in Australia

Any attempt to present a comprehensive overview of the development of social work in Australia is well beyond the scope of this paper.[4] Similar to North America and the United Kingdom, social work in Australia originated with the development of charitable organizations in the nineteenth and early part of the twentieth centuries. It began to become professionalized during the postwar period when training moved into the university sector. Two year programs were set up in the Universities of Adelaide, Sydney, and Melbourne in the early 1940s, and in the 1950s a significant number of Australians pursued Masters degrees in social work in the United States, mainly at Columbia, Smith College, Chicago University, and the University of Michigan (Lawrence 1976).

As well, a number of American social work educators began visiting Australian social work schools at this time bringing with them many American ideas about social work. The American influence meant that much emphasis was given to psychiatric or clinical social work, usually in a hospital setting or child welfare agency. Some Australian social work programs, such as the School of Social Work at The University of Melbourne, still retain strong linkages with American schools. Thus the major influence on Australian social work came from the United States whereby social work in Australia became dominated by therapeutic models of intervention influenced by psychodynamic theory and systems perspectives, as opposed to locating personal troubles within social structures (Martin, 2003). However, as Ife (1997, 391–92) notes, "[in] the earlier years of Australian social work, the British influence was especially strong, but by the 1960s gave way to a more American influence."[5]

Radical social work emerged in Australia with the publication of Harold Throssell's 1975 edited book, *Radical Essays in Social Work*. Contributing authors criticized the American-influenced social work profession as politically naïve, preoccupied with micro-level casework activity, and achieving professional status at the expense of the people they were supposed to serve. Following this book and others in the UK and the US, a reconceptualization of social work began to occur in some Australian schools of social work. One of these schools is located at the Royal Melbourne Institute of Technology

---

[4] For an overview of the early years of social work as a profession in Australia, see R. J. Lawrence (1965). For a succinct overview of contemporary social work and social welfare in Australia, see Jim Ife (1997).

[5] It has been my experience that there is a tendency by social work academics both in Canada and Australia in discussions to associate the US with a casework (therapeutic or clinical) approach, the UK with a social administration approach, and Canada, Australia, and New Zealand with approaches somewhere in between the two (David Cox 1997).

(RMIT). It has been a leader in Australia with respect to the development of progressive forms of social work and remains so today. Martin (2003) points out that the early influences on the development of progressive social work in Australia in general and at RMIT in particular were: (1) the 1970s Marxist critique of social work employed by the early radical social work school; (2) the developmental model of social work developed in Melbourne in the 1970s; (3) the structural approach to social work pioneered by the Canadian Maurice Moreau in the late 1970s and early 80s; and (4) feminist social work of the 1980s.

The developmental model of social work was devised by the Brotherhood of St. Laurence, a social agency working with the poor in Melbourne. The model is based on the belief that structural change is necessary to eliminate poverty. The Brotherhood replaced its casework service with a multidisciplinary approach where social work was only one of a range of services available to families and where the working relationship between social workers and service users was de-professionalized. The emphasis of the developmental model was placed on self-help, welfare rights, and social action (Benn 1981, cited in Martin 2003).

The work of Maurice Moreau had an enormous effect on social work education and scholarship at RMIT. Moreau had visited the School in the 1980s and shared his ideas and work with faculty and students. His 1979 article, "A Structural Approach to Social Work Practice" and a number of unpublished papers are still cited by RMIT faculty in their current writings about progressive and/or critical social work. When he returned to Canada, RMIT faculty (particularly Bob Pease and Wendy Weeks) remained in contact with Moreau and shared ideas in the area of structural social work. The structural approach was, of course, consistent with the development model discussed above.

The other early influence on the development of progressive social work at RMIT was feminist social work. Australian social work has had a feminist tradition since the 1970s where personal problems are defined as political and where the early forms of radical social work and the welfare state were criticized for being gender blind. One of the leading feminist social work writers in Australia was Wendy Weeks who was Director of the social work program at RMIT during the late 1980s before moving on to the University of Melbourne where she continued her prolific publication record in the area of women's issues, social policy, and social work. Wendy spent a significant part of her career in Canada as a faculty member in the School of Social Work at McMaster University before she returned to her native country of Australia. While in Canada, Wendy developed many of her feminist analytical skills and knowledge. She was also a friend of Maurice Moreau and was partly responsible for his visit to Australia.[6]

---

[6] Social Work faculty at RMIT have continued their development of critical social work theory and practice and have recently (2003) published a book, *Critical Social Work: An Introduction to Theories and Practices* in which they strive to amalgamate the earlier forms of critical social work and its materialist and modernist

Canadian Contributions (1995–Present)

I have already mentioned two people who contributed significantly to progressive social work in Australia: Maurice Moreau, who was a Canadian, and Wendy Weeks, who was a Canadian resident for a number of years. Before I elaborate on my own contribution there is one more Canadian who deserves special recognition for his contributions—Peter Leonard.

As I alluded to above, around the mid-nineties there was a group of Australian social work writers who seemed to abandon progressive social work theory and concepts in favour of what was, in my view, an individualistic and nihilistic form of postmodernism. I had such high regard for these people as writers that I began to question my own epistemological perspective. Consequently, I read volumes of postmodern, post-structural, and post-colonial literature along with what leading social work and social policy theorists were saying about these post philosophies. I discovered that postmodernism was not a homogeneous body of thought and that there were different kinds of postmodernism including a "critical" postmodernism. Writers such as Terry Eagleton, David Harvey, Nancy Fraser, Iris Marion Young, Ben Agger, and Peter Leonard were all working on the interstices of materialist philosophies and postmodernism attempting to retain the ideals of social justice, emancipation, and equality in a way that respects difference, diversity, and inclusion. Thus it was that I incorporated a critical postmodernism (and subsequently post-colonial theory and cultural studies) into my own conceptualization and writing of progressive social work, attempting to avoid totalizing belief systems and essentialisms, on the one hand, and politically-disabling fragmentation and witless-relativism, on the other.

I attempted to engage the postmodern social work adherents or puritans in debate and discussion, but was regularly dismissed or patronized as some outdated theoretical dinosaur who refused to let go of the past. Thus, I experienced the mid 1990s in Australian social work to be a time of theoretical intolerance with social work academics aligning themselves as either for or against postmodernism. There did not seem to be an in-between position during this time. In 1998, a conference was held at Deakin University where the invited international speakers were all writing in the area of postmodern social work. I was invited to chair the last panel presentation. I was not invited to present.

I recall that Peter Leonard was the show piece for the conference in the eyes of the organizers. He was a "social saint" among social worker academics in Australia because of his earlier development of Marxist and other forms of progressive social work. Organizers of the conference kept referring to him as a postmodernist because his recent work involved postmodern insights and a critique of critical social work. Because he was a mate of mine, I knew differently. I will never forget when Peter Leonard, after being introduced as a postmodernist, stated emphatically that he was not a postmodernist; that he

---

traditions with more recent critical postmodern ideas and epistemologies.

was still a Marxist even if he were holding onto his Marxism by his finger-nails. He used postmodernism, as he did post-colonialism, to inform his two most important sources of analysis—Marxism and feminism. I felt totally exonerated, but more importantly, because of Peter's theoretical declaration, the leading group of postmodern social work writers in Australia began to rethink their theoretical and ideological positions and eventually moved to a critical form of postmodernism, which they still use today. In other words, they dropped their total rejection of critical modernist concepts such as solidarity, social justice, and equality and are now attempting to deconstruct the problematic elements of these concepts along with such meta-narratives as Marxism, feminism, and socialism, but keep their essential social justice ideals.

The same year that the first edition of my book *Structural Social Work* was published, Jan Fook's *Radical Casework* was published in Australia. A Canadian social work academic, Bob Doyle, who had been working in Australia for several years and who taught with Jan Fook at LaTrobe University in Melbourne, began using my book in his courses and wrote a very favour-able review of it in *Australian Social Work* in 1994. My book was immediately adopted by many Australian social work instructors who were interested in progressive forms of social work and was used as a complementary text to *Radical Casework*.

In 1995, after receiving an invitation from Jan Fook and Bob Doyle to spend some time at LaTrobe University, I arranged for a sabbatical leave and went to Australia for the 1995-96 academic year where I was a visiting professor at the School of Social Work and Social Policy at LaTrobe University in Melbourne. The major part of my sabbatical plan was that I would collaborate with Jan Fook in further development of progressive social work, especially structural social work. Given her expertise in direct practice forms of radical social work and my own work in developing conceptual and theoretical frameworks of progressive social work at all levels, it seemed to me that it would be an ideal ideological and epistemological match.

Unfortunately, collaboration was not to be. Soon after I arrived and got settled in Melbourne, I met with Jan to discuss plans about researching and writing in the area of progressive social work. She informed me that she no longer subscribed to structural ideas, that she had "gone beyond them," and was now exploring postmodern concepts and critique along with their utility for social work. There was, at this time, a group of social work academics who, like Jan Fook, had renounced much of progressive social work because of its foundation in modernist concepts. Postmodernism has had much more of an impact on social work scholarship in Australia than it has had in Canada or in the United States.

Fortunately, however, there were still structural thinkers within the five social work programs that existed in the Melbourne area. I was fortunate to be invited to speak at each of these programs—a couple of them a number of times, including RMIT, which still based its program on feminist and structural principles although one of its leading theorists, Bob Pease (a friend of Maurice Moreau and Wendy Weeks). Pease was also in the process of renouncing structural social work in favour of postmodernism. For much of that year, I found myself discussing progressive (structural and feminist) social work with other structural thinkers.[7] I also used that year to read and discuss postmodernism and incorporated a major section of postmodern ideas and their application to progressive social work in the second edition of my book.

During my sabbatical year, I received a number of invitations from social work programs around the country to speak about structural social work. For example, I spent a week as the 1996 Distinguished Visiting Scholar at the Department of Social Work and Social Policy at Curtin University in Perth where I gave a series of public presentations and consulted with faculty on structural social work. Attending these lectures were faculty from other social work programs in Western Australia such as the pre-eminent critical social work writer in Australia at that time, Jim Ife[8] from the University of Western Australia, as well as Richard Hugman from Edith Cowan University, another critical social work writer. I also spent a week at the University of Queensland in Brisbane where I gave a few lectures on progressive social work. Bill DeMaria was a faculty person there at this time and was Coordinator of the Radical or Structural Social Work specialization. Bill, like many progressive social work faculty persons at that time, was alienated from much of the other faculty in his school. My visit helped to give some legitimation to the structural specialization Bill coordinated.

Following my sabbatical, I returned to my University in Canada (St. Thomas University in Fredericton) where I continued to work on the second edition of *Structural Social Work*. As a result of my interactions with my Australian colleagues, I included a significant section on postmodernism and its utility for progressive social work in this new edition. Also, at this time, a literature mainly from the UK was developing in the areas of anti-racist and anti-discriminatory social work. These areas seemed to me to be a logical extension of structural social work, so I included a new chapter in the second edition on anti-oppressive social work in which I argued that oppression had to be the focus of structural social work.

During the year back in Canada I was asked to apply for the position of Head (i.e., Director) of the Social Work Program at Victoria University. This university is located on the western outskirts of Melbourne in an industrial and impoverished area that is largely inhabited by the most recent groups of immigrant populations coming to Australia. Over 50% of the student population was from non-English speaking backgrounds and consisted mainly

---

[7] They included Bill Healy and Mark Furlong at LaTrobe, Philip Mendes and Heather Fraser at Monash University, Wendy Weeks at The University of Melbourne, June Allan and Martin Mowbry at RMIT, and Lis Starbuck at Victoria University.

[8] Jim Ife, although Australian born and having worked all his career in Australia, received an MSW from McGill University and was a student of David Woodsworth, a celebrated Canadian social policy scholar.

of students from Asian and Middle East countries. There were almost as many Muslims among the student population as there were Christians. I was successful in my application for the position, and so, in 1997, after twenty years at St.Thomas University, I left for "Down Under."

The social work program at Victoria University advertised itself as a "structural-feminist" social work and social policy program, but its curriculum was based only on a loose set of concepts, principles, and practices. My major tasks early on were to provide leadership in the area of structural social work with respect to revamping the program and developing the curriculum, and to shepherd the revamped program through accreditation by the Australian Association of Social Workers (AASW). These tasks were made manageable by a great group of colleagues and by students who, given their background, family situations, and experiences, appreciated an approach to social work that did not blame victims of oppression for social problems. My colleagues and I had many discussions about how while we were teaching about oppression, many of our students and their families had experienced and were experiencing oppression first hand, including torture and trauma in their homelands and long stays in refugee camps.

During my time at Victoria University, I finished the second edition of *Structural Social Work*, and wrote another book on progressive social work that focused on oppression and anti-oppressive social work, *Challenging Oppression: A Critical Social Work Approach*, which was published in 2002. This latter book was in many ways an extension of structural social work, but includes more postmodern material along with literature from critical or liberation psychology, cultural studies, and post-colonial theory. As with *Structural Social Work*, *Challenging Oppression* has been adopted by many social work programs, and has, I would argue, helped to shape progressive social work in Australia.

In 2002, I had decided to leave Victoria University so that I could devote myself to writing full-time. Coincidentally, I received two important invitations that year. First, I was asked by the editorial board of *Australian Social Work*, the major social work journal in Australia, if I would accept the position of editor (I accepted). Second, I was asked by the Head of the Social Work Program at The University of Melbourne if he could submit my name to the University's Board of Governors to be considered for the position of Honorary Professorial Fellow within the School of Social Work. I was awarded this position and so found myself in an office at The University of Melbourne surrounded by opulence (grand old buildings, beautiful landscaped grounds, and plenty of resources) and by an excess of social work conservatism. Someone once said to me that I must have felt like an arsonist at a fire chiefs' convention there, but in reality, I felt like a fire chief at an arsonists' convention.

While at The University of Melbourne, a number of Ph.D. students gravitated toward me because of my reputation as a critical social work theorist and as someone who could discuss with them certain ideas that no one else on faculty could. On the other hand, I never had one request from any faculty member to give a guest lecture in any of their classes. As Editor of *Australian Social Work*, I was able to help many authors incorporate structural variables into their analyses and research simply by suggesting that they look at certain progressive literature that touched on their subjects. As well, I ensured that no article was published that blamed victims for their situations or that was grounded in a personal deficiency explanation for social problems.

Conclusion

I consider myself to be most fortunate in being presented with a number of opportunities to make a contribution to social justice in Australia in the form of progressive social work scholarship and teaching. I was able to discuss my ideas at several schools of social work during my sabbatical year. I taught a structural approach to social work to several hundred students while I was head of the social work program at Victoria University for six and a-half years. I was the architect of the structural social work program at Victoria University. I completed writing two major progressive social work books while I lived and worked in Australia. I presented papers on progressive social work at several conferences around Australia. I was able to enhance and increase the structural content of the country's major social work journal while I was editor of *Australian Social Work*. However, it is must be noted that I probably gained more than I gave. Thanks to all my progressive social work mates in Australia, I have incorporated postmodern and post-colonial analyses into my scholarship and thanks to my wonderful students at Victoria University, I will always write from an anti-oppressive point of view. This kind of exchange is the hallmark of international social work.

Anybody I know who teaches outside the mainstream social work material always wonders if what they are doing is worthwhile and if it is making any kind of impact on students and, in turn, on the practice of social work. I have asked myself this question with respect to my students in Australia a number of times since I returned to Canada. This question was partially answered for me a few months ago when I received an email from a former student (from a working class background) who had tracked me down. The following is an excerpt from that email:

> As for my anti-oppressive practice, well it's something I'm always conscious of and reflective about. Its something I'm known for now, and despite having comments thrown at me like "You're so politically correct" (like as if that's a bad thing??? if that were what it was really even about) when I refuse to engage in degrading, disrespectful conversation about service users for instance, I stand strong. I have been able to afford this (along with the occasional refusal to implement policy that I see as oppressive) because I am good at what I do, and they know it. I know I've read somewhere about this? I've got a lot of work still to do, and inconsistency constantly knocks, but I critically reflect/deflect that too …

> Enough babble, you can tell I've become a social worker. You know I always say to people that it was so much more special having you here [at Victoria University in Australia], because it made the whole progressive social work thing real.

References

- Agger, Ben. 1989. *Socio(ontology):A Disciplinary Reading*. Urbana: University of Illinois Press.
- Agger, Ben. 1991. Critical Theory, Poststructuralism, Postmodernism: Their Sociological Relevance. *Annual Review of Sociology* 17: 105–31.
- Agger, Ben. 1992. *Cultural Studies as Critical Theory*. London: Falmer Press.
- Agger, Ben. 1998. *Critical Social Theories:An Introduction*. Boulder:Westview Press.
- Allan, June, Bob Pease, and Linda Briskman, eds. 2003. *Critical Social Work:An Introduction to Theories and Practices*. Crows Nest, NSW: Allen and Unwin.
- Bailey, Roy and Mike Brake, eds. 1975. *Radical Social Work*. New York: Pantheon Books.
- Barker, R. L. 1995. *The Social Work Dictionary*. 3rd ed. Washington: National Association of Social Workers.
- Benn, C. 1981. *Attacking Poverty Through Participation:A Community Approach*.Victoria: PIT Publishing.
- Boas, Philip J. and Jim Crawley. 1976. *Social Work in Australia: Responses to a Changing Context*. Melbourne:Australia International Press and Publications Pty. Ltd. in association with the Australian Association of Social Workers.
- Bolger, Steve, Paul Corrigan, Jan Docking, and Nick Frost. 1981. *Towards Socialist Welfare Work*. London: Macmillan.
- Carniol, Ben. 1979. A Critical Approach in Social Work. *Canadian Journal of Social Work Education* 5 (1): 95–111.
- Carniol, Ben 1987, 1990, 1995, 2000, 2005. *Case Critical*. Toronto: Between the Lines.
- Constable, R. and V. Mehta, eds. 1994. *Education for Social Work in Eastern Europe: Changing Horizons*. Chicago, IL: Lyceum.
- Corrigan, Paul and Peter Leonard. 1978. *Social Work Practice under Capitalism:A Marxist Approach*. London: Macmillan.
- Cox, David. 1997. Asia and the Pacific. In *International Handbook on Social Work Theory and Practice*, eds. N. S. Mayadas,T. D.Watts, and D. Elliott, 369–82. Westport: Greenwood Press.
- Cox, David and Manohar Pawar. 2006. *International Social Work: Issues, Strategies, and Programs*. London: Sage Publications.
- Dominelli, Lena. 1997. *Anti-Racist Social Work*. 2nd ed. London: Macmillan.
- Eagleton,T. 1996. *The Illusions of Postmodernism*. Oxford: Blackwell.
- Fook, Jan. 1993. *Radical Casework: A Theory of Practice*. St Leonards, NSW: Allen & Unwin.
- Galper, Jeffry. 1975. *The Politics of Social Services*. Englewood Cliffs: Prentice-Hall.
- Galper, Jeffry 1980. *Social Work Practice: A Radical Perspective*. Englewood Cliffs: Prentice-Hall.
- Jones, Chris 1983. *State Social Work and the Working Class*. London: Macmillan.
- Jones, Chris 1998. *Confronting Injustice and Oppression: Concepts and Strategies for Social Workers*. New York: Columbia University Press.
- Harvey, David. 1989. *The Condition of Postmodernity: An Enquiry into the Origins of Cultural Change*. Cambridge: Basil Blackwell.
- Healy, Lynne M. 2001. *International Social Work*. New York: Oxford University Press.
- Hokenstad, M. C., S. Khinduka, and J. Midgley, eds. 1992. *Profiles in International Social Work*.Washington: NASW Press.

- Hugman, Richard. 1998. *Social Welfare and Social Value: The Role of Caring Professions.* Basingstoke: Macmillan.
- Ife, Jim. 1995. *Community Development: Creating Community Alternatives—Vision, Analysis and Practice.* Melbourne: Longman.
- Ife, Jim. 1997a. *Rethinking Social Work: Towards Critical Practice.* Lance Cove: Addison-Wesley Longman.
- Ife, Jim. 1997b. Social Work in Australia. In *International Handbook on Social Work Theory and Practice*, eds. N. S. Mayadas, T. D. Watts, and D. Elliott. 383–407. Westport: Greenwood Press.
- Ife, Jim. 2001. *Human Rights and Social Work: Towards Rights-Based Practice.* Cambridge: Cambridge University Press.
- Kendall, K. A. 2000. *Social Work Education: Its Origins in Europe.* Washington: Council on Social Work Education.
- Langan, Mary, and Phil Lee. 1989a. Whatever Happened to Radical Social Work. In *Radical Social Work Today*, eds. M. Langan and P. Lee, 1–18. London: Unwin Hyman.
- Langan, Mary and Phil Lee, eds. 1989b. *Radical Social Work Today.* London: Unwin Hyman.
- Lawrence, R. J. 1965. *Professional Social Work in Australia.* Canberra: Australian National University Press.
- Lawrence, R. J. 1976. Australian Social Work: In Historical, International and Social Welfare Context. In *Social Work in Australia*, eds. Boas, and Crawley, 1–37. Melbourne: Australia International Press.
- Leonard, Peter. 1994. Knowledge/Power and Postmodernism. *Canadian Social Work Review* 11 (1): 11–26.
- Leonard, Peter. 1995. Postmodernism, Socialism and Social Welfare. *Journal of Progressive Human Services* 6 (2): 3–19.
- Leonard, Peter. 1997. *Postmodern Welfare: Reconstructing an Emancipatory Project.* London: Sage Publications.
- Longres, John. 1986. Marxian Theory and Social Work Practice. *Catalyst* 5 (4): 13–34.
- Martin, George. 1990. *Social Policy in the Welfare State.* Englewood Cliffs,: Prentice-Hall.
- Martin, Jennifer. 2003. Historical Development of Critical Practice. In *Critical Social Work: An Introduction to Theories and Practices*, eds. J. Allan, B. Pease, and L. Briskman. St. Leonard's: Allen & Unwin.
- Mayadas, Nazneen S., Thomas D. Watts, and Doreen Elliott, eds. 1997. *International Handbook on Social Work Theory and Practice.* Westport, CT: Greenwood Press.
- Midgely, J. 1995. *Social Development: The Developmental Perspective in Social Welfare.* London: Sage Publications.
- Midgely, J. 1999. Social Development in Social Work: Learning from Global Dialogue. In *All Our Futures: Principles & Resources for Social Work Practice in a Global Era*, eds. C. S. Ramanathan, and R. J. Link, 193–205. Belmont: Brooks-Cole.
- Moane, Geraldine. 1999. *Gender and Colonialism: A Psychological Analysis of Oppression and Liberation.* New York: St Martin's Press.
- Moreau, Maurice (n.d.). Practice Implications of a Structural Approach to Social Work. Unpublished Paper. University of Montreal.
- Moreau, Maurice. 1979. A Structural Approach to Social Work Practice. *Canadian Journal of Social Work Education* 5 (1): 78–94.
- Moreau, Maurice. 1990. Empowerment through Advocacy and Consciousness-Raising: Implications of a Structural Approach to Social Work. *Journal of Sociology and Social Welfare* 17 (2): 53–67.

- Mullaly, Bob. 1997. *Structural Social Work: Ideology, Theory, and Practice.* Toronto: Oxford University Press.

- Mullaly, Bob. 2002. *Challenging Oppression: A Critical Social Work Approach.* Toronto: Oxford University Press.

- Mullaly, Bob. 2007. *The New Structural Social Work.* Don Mills, ON: Oxford University Press Canada.

- Pease, Bob and Janis Fook, eds. 1999. *Transforming Social Work Practice: Postmodern Critical Perspectives.* St Leonards, NSW: Allen & Unwin.

- Pritchard, Colin and Richard Taylor. 1978. *Social Work: Reform or Revolution?* London: Routledge & Kegan Paul.

- Throssell, Harold, ed. 1975. *Social Work: Radical Essays.* St Lucia, Queensland: University of Queensland Press.

- Wagner, David and Marcia B. Cohen. 1978. Social Workers, Class and Professionalism. *Catalyst* 1 (1): 25–55.

- Watts, Thomas D. 1997. An Introduction to the World of Social Work. *International Handbook on Social Work Theory and Practice*, eds. N.S. Mayadas, T. D. Watts, and D. Elliott. 1–6. Westport: Greenwood Press.

- Williams, Fiona. 1989. *Social Policy: A Critical Introduction—Issues of Race, Gender and Class.* New York: Blackwell.

- Young, Iris Marion. 1990. *Justice and the Politics of Difference.* Princeton: Princeton University Press.

Chapter 11

Internationalizing Social Work in Canada: Working with Immigrants and Refugees

David Este

During the past 12 years, the majority of my research has focused on different aspects of the settlement and adaptation of newcomers in Canada. Some of the studies I have worked on include the examination of the health and well-being of immigrant and refugee children and youth, the experiences of immigrant men as fathers, affordable housing and immigrant seniors, factors influencing the child rearing practices of recently arrived immigrant women, and the acculturation of refugees from the Sudan. I have also participated in developing programs for immigrants and refugees primarily with the Calgary Immigrant Aid Society, The Mosaic Family Center, the Intergenerational Program, and Psychosocial Groups. I have engaged, in a limited way, in some direct social work practice activities with newcomers. I have co-facilitated a number of sessions in groups for newcomer men and counselled individual clients.

According to the 2006 Census data, 19.5% of Canada's total population was born outside of the country. Between 2001 and 2006, Canada's foreign born population increased by 13.6%. It is estimated that 1,110,000 immigrants came to Canada between January 1, 2001 and May 16, 2006. The top three countries of origin were China (155,051; 14%), India (129,140; 11.6%), and the Phillipines (77,880; 7%) (Government of Canada, 2007a). It is anticipated that the current intake levels (240,000–265,000) established by the federal government will continue or even increase given the low Canadian birth rate, the need for skilled workers, and the aging of the nations population (Government of Canada, 2007b). In 2006, a total of 251,649 newcomers were admitted as permanent residents. Of these individuals, 54.9% (138,257) were Economic Immigrants and their dependents, 28% (70,506) were in the Family Class, 12.9% (32,492) were designated under the Protected Persons Class, with 4% (10,223) being granted permanent resident status on Humanitarian and Compassionate grounds (Government of Canada 2007a).

Given these developments, it is highly likely that social workers, especially those working in large and mid-size urban centers, will have to address the needs of clients who are newcomers to Canadian society. While it is easy to simply conceptualize practice with newcomers as a process that deals with the acculturation experiences once newcomers arrive in Canada, it represents a very narrow lens in trying to understand the complex nature of the migration process. The primary purpose of this chapter, therefore, is to view social work practice with immigrants and refugees as a form of international social work. I begin with a discussion on the impact of globalization, and in particular the migration of people, on the practice of social work. Also included is an assessment of the American and Canadian social work literature relating to practice with immigrants and refugees. In the balance of the chapter, the argument is put forth that practice with newcomers in Canada is a form of international social work.

Globalization and Social Work Practice.

A critical determinant in ascertaining whether social work practice with immigrants and refugees in the Canadian context is a form of international social work is having clarity about what constitutes international social work. In reviewing the literature, various definitions have prevailed, Healy (2001) presents four dimensions of international social work action. These include: internationally related domestic practice; professional exchange; international practice; and international policy development. Of particular importance is the first dimension where Healy acknowledges the interface between international events and domestic social work practice. This relationship makes it difficult to separate the lives of newcomers into pre-migration and post-migration.

An emphasis on action and the well being of individuals is stressed by the International Association of Schools of Social Work (www.ifsw.org/en/p38000208.html): "The social work profession promotes change, problem solving in human relationships, and the empowerment and liberation of people to enhance well-being. Utilizing theories of human behaviour and social systems; social work intervenes at the points where people interact with their environments. Principles of human rights and social justice are fundamental to social work." An important commonality linking the last two definitions is the absence of geographic boundaries confining the practice of international social work. The emphasis is on the achievement of social justice regardless of location.

In Canada, most social work programs are shaped by local realities. As Lyons (1999, 110) has noted: "Social work has traditionally been seen as a local "culture" bound activity specific to a given time and place." On the other hand, several writers maintain that it is increasingly difficult for social work practitioners to ignore events that occur internationally as they affect local practice. Midgley (2000, 13) stresses the relationship between globalization and different aspects of social work practice: "Social work and social policy scholars who write about globalization are enhancing international awareness. By using this term, they remind their colleagues of the wider international forces that are shaping the world. They have also shown that international forces have a local impact, particularly on standards of living and social policies and programs."

Other writers (Healy 1996; Sherraden and Martin 1997) recognize that the migration of people is an integral component of international social work. Hokenstad and Midgley (1997, 2) state that "during the coming decade, members of groups of colour will become a majority in some states of the United States. Migration from South to North in Europe and from Asia to Oceania is increasing the heterogeneity of historically homogenous societies. Economic migrants along with political refugees produce cultural diversity that directly influences social work at all levels of practice."

Within Canadian society, there are several activities that social workers can perform in assisting newcomers. For example, they can provide information about the services immigrants and refugees can access in the community, including mainstream and immigrant service agencies. They can also serve as brokers for newcomers with other societal institutions such as the education system. In the eighties, Yelaja (1985, 350) identified the following social work objectives for practice with immigrants in Canada: (i) helping immigrants adjust to their new environments; (ii) preserving values of the culture of origin; and (iii) preventing racism or cultural stereotyping.

Based on earlier practices, however, it is quite easy to conceptualize the domain of practice with newcomers as a process of acculturation. While the issues that confront newcomers as they attempt to settle in Canada are important, it is also important to understand that the experiences immigrants and refugees have encountered in their countries of origin, and/or during their migration to this country, will influence their settlement experience and adaptation.

Ecological Practice

One way to extend practice beyond acculturation is to consider social work practice from an ecological perspective. An ecological perspective:

> accentuates the reciprocal relationships between the individual and the environment and the continuous adaptation of both the person and environment to each other and perceives society as being evolutionary and holistic. Within the ecological perspective human growth development constantly changes in relation to the social environment and the social environment changes in response to human factors. (Yelaja 1985, 29).

A second salient theme of the ecological perspective is the emphasis on the existence of stressors that are critical life issues: "Life stressors and associated stress include: difficult life transitions and traumatic life events; harsh social and physical environments; and dysfunctional interpersonal processes in families and groups (Yelaja 1985, ix).

In a recent article dealing with social work practice with immigrant children and their families, Segal contends that it is essential for social workers to use a person-in-environment perspective when working with newcomers. She states that practitioners, as part of the assessment process, must explore questions that focus on the reasons for leaving one's homeland; experience of migration; resources to function in unfamiliar environments and; receptiveness of the new host country (Segal and Nayada 2005, 564).

It is also imperative that social workers apply a macro perspective when working with immigrants and refugees. By only focusing on individual or family functioning, there is a strong probability that the messages being imparted to newcomers are negative in nature with the tendency of blaming these individuals for their circumstances. Such a position ignores structural and systematic barriers that contribute to the array of issues that newcomers encounter in trying to live in Canadian society. A narrow focus on acculturation is reinforced when one examines a list of the problems presented in the literature. Typically, it includes language barriers, role reversal in families, changes in socio-economic status, challenges in adjusting to the educational system, and loss of support systems.

Drachman (1992), who developed a "State of Migration Framework" (Appendix), asserts the critical importance of social workers' use of a person-in-environment perspective when working with newcomers. The framework is explicit in identifying the types of information and knowledge that are required in order to help newcomers adjust and adapt. Like Drachman, writers such as Pine and Drachman (2005) or Lum (1999) contend that social workers must understand the migration process from pre-migration to resettlement. Pine and Drachman (2005) developed a broader conceptual framework that can serve as a tool for social workers who work with immigrants and refugees. Building on Drachman's earlier model, this latest framework once again recognizes the intersection between a newcomers' experiences in her/his country of origin and the settlement process in Canada.

Roy and Montgomery (2003) in their work with immigrants in Québec also assert the importance of social workers having an understanding of the migration context. They developed "intercultural assessment guidelines," that are designed to provide an extensive portrait of a newcomer. One of the primary objectives is to "integrate the psychosocial dimensions of migration and exile into the assessment of intervention situations" (Roy and Montgomery 2003, 136). The guidelines include the following components: (i) migration context (e.g., pre-migration, post-migration, plans to return to home country, lifestyle in home country); (ii) immigration status; (iii) investigation into beliefs, world views, values; (iv) group memberships and use of this network; (v) definition of the situation (problem); and (vii) identification of areas of vulnerability.

Recently, I have engaged in a study with colleagues from the Centre for Addictions and Mental Health in Toronto exploring different aspects of the settlement and adaptation of Sudanese immigrants and refugees in Toronto, Calgary, and Brooks, Alberta. Working with members from the Sudanese community in Calgary and Brooks, I have come to understand the complex migration process. This includes gaining insight about the lived experiences of individuals from the southern Sudan and in particular how they have become victims of very strong forms of oppression and discrimination in their own countries. I have also been privy to information about how some of these individuals walked across miles of desert terrain to get to refugee camps in different parts of Africa where they spent part of their lives. Finally, I have become acutely aware of some the major settlement and adaptation issues members of this community have encountered in their efforts to integrate into Canadian society. Drachman's model and her later framework developed with Pine collectively provided me the tools to begin to understand these two Sudanese communities.

Strengths Perspective

A strengths perspective also helps to understand social work practice with immigrants and refugees as part of assessment and ongoing work with client systems. Weick, Rapp, Sullivan, and Kisthardt (1989, 352) maintain that the perspective serves as a corrective for the imbalance caused by the preoccupation with people's deficits and liabilities. A strengths perspective rests on an appreciation of the positive attributes and capabilities that people express and the social resources that can be developed and sustained.

When faced with the various challenges and barriers that newcomers face, social workers may be overwhelmed. As a result, it is important that we clearly appreciate that individuals will do better in the long run when they are able to identify, recognize, and use their strengths and resources in their environment. A basic concept associated with the strengths perspective is that people have survived to this point—certainly not without pain and struggle—by employing their will, their vision, their skills, and, as they have grappled with life, what they have learned about themselves and their world. We must understand these capacities and make alliance with this knowledge in order to help (Saleeby 1997, 302).

Employing a strengths perspective can be an inherent and vital dimension of the ecological perspective. In the case of Sudanese newcomers to Canada, for example, one of the critical assessment questions for "strengths" that can be posed, especially for those who migrated from the Southern Sudan, is how did they survive living under brutal conditions? Responses may provide practitioners with some indicators of the strengths possessed by members of this community. As social workers gain an understanding of the strengths possessed by newcomers and their respective communities, they are positioned to use these assets to empower individuals in developing strategies to address the issues that they face.

The following example illustrates how useful the strengths perspective can be used in working with immigrants and refugees. During the mid-1990s, Calgary became home to an increasing number of newcomers who resided in the former Yugoslavia. Some of these individuals came directly from their home country, while others ventured to the city after spending time in other locations in Canada. An immigrant service agency in the city, the Calgary Immigrant Aid Society (CIAS) was instrumental in establishing a series of programs for the former Yugoslavians under the agency's Mosaic Centre. The centre provides a wide range of services to Calgary's immigrant and refugee families with young children and adolescents.

One of the issues that surfaced from both pre-teens and teenagers from this community was their dissatisfaction with the school system in Calgary. The former Yugoslavia students maintained that they were not being intellectually challenged and secondly, the workload was far less than they were accustomed to in the former Yugoslavia. This desire for a more demanding educational curriculum was deemed a strength. As members of the program development team spoke with the parents of these youth, as well as the youths themselves, it became quite apparent that some type of intervention would be beneficial. Subsequently, staff of the agency, working with members of this community, helped to organize a Saturday educational program that addressed some of the gaps identified by the youth. The services were offered by the parents of the community rather than outside professionals. The agency was able to draw on communal strengths—the motivation, desire, and interests of the youth plus the knowledge and skills of the parents.

Culture

When working with immigrants and refugees, there is a general consensus within the social work literature, that practitioners should be knowledgeable about different cultures (Moore 1994; McPhatter 1997; Neukrug 1994; Ronnau 1994; Lum 1999). Olandi (1992, vi) defines culture as "the shared values, norms, traditions, customs, arts, history, folklore and institutions of a given people." According to James (2003) another important attribute of culture is recognizing that it is not a static entity: "Changes within a culture are due to global influences, the movement of people form one country and/or region to another and the interaction of various racial, ethnic and social groups" (James 2003, 202).

From my perspective, it is imperative for social workers to be aware of the shifting nature of culture as newcomers to Canada are highly likely to retain those parts of their culture they deem important while embracing certain aspects of "Canadian" culture—the essence of Canada's multiculturalism policy. Kirmayer and Minas (2000) maintain that there are positive notions of culture. It can be used to acknowledge the characteristics of groups as well as their needs and predicaments. Secondly, it can be used as a tool in identifying and using the strengths of individuals, families, or communities (Fong and Lum, 2001). One should not assume, however, that individual and community needs are fixed in nature. Needs change over time and service providers needs to make the necessary program changes to ensure that newcomers are receiving services that contribute to their health and well-being in a Canadian context.

Culture can also be used to form stereotypes resulting in interventions that may not be appropriate (Kirmayer and Minas 2000). Cultures are not unified, harmonious, seamless wholes that speak with one narrative voice (James 2003, 201). As a result, it is incumbent on social work practitioners who work with immigrants and refugees to recognize the inherent uniqueness of the individuals and families with whom they become engaged in their practice. Failure to adhere to this basic but important value premise may result in stereotyping or negative labels being attached to specific newcomer communities. Such behaviour may be an additional barrier or stigma that makes it difficult for newcomers to feel a sense of belonging to Canadian society.

There are negative consequences if social workers do not pay attention to the cultural backgrounds of immigrants and refugees (Williams 1997). A lack of understanding about the cultures of these clients and what impact culture has on their situations may serve as an obstacle in the social worker's ability to engage these individuals in a meaningful way. By not attempting to understand the clients' cultural reality, social work practitioners may force their own views on clients, with no recognition of the distinctive world view of the clients. By way of example, an area of conflict between the Sudanese community in Calgary and the local child welfare system is how Sudanese parents discipline their children. In a study I am conducting that examines the experiences of Sudanese refugee men as fathers, the following two narratives capture some concerns from the perspective of Sudanese men:

One of the challenges is that sometimes parents can be charged with negligence or mishandling or abusing their children even though children have started to threaten their fathers and mothers:

> Back home, the father is the only one to discipline them (the children). However, here we cannot discipline the children in the way they are in the mother country ... however, we have to respect the Canadian rules ... here it is difficult to control your children (Sudanese male) (Este and Tachble 2007).

It is important for social workers who work with this community to gain an understanding, not only of the disciplinary practices but also of the gender roles within Sudanese families and the behavioural expectations those parents have of their children. Failure to comprehend will lead to ongoing conflict between Sudanese families and the child welfare system.

Refugees

The international dimension of social work practice with newcomers is re-enforced when practitioners work with refugees. As Waxler-Morrison and her colleagues (2005) stress, social workers need to determine if their clients are refugees, as well as their category of refugee—convention refugees who are individuals who apply outside of Canada, or asylum seekers who apply from within. The distinction is important as their experiences in Canada vary. Some refugees leave their country of origins on an involuntary basis. Quite frequently they have suffered from some type of persecution and/or have witnessed severe forms of violence.

Lacroix, in a recent article, focused on social work practice with asylum seekers in Canada and stressed the need to: "understand the plight of asylum—to have a general understanding of the international context as it relates to asylum seekers, and the policies and practices that have been put in place (Lacroix 2006, 20). Another study explored the experiences of refugee women in war and abusive relationships. The comment of one participant was particularly poignant. She said: "They were really hitting me hard and I wasn't listening to what they were saying and they started to strip me of my clothes" (Lorenzetti 2006, 106). Kreitzer, in her research study concerning Liberian refugee women, also highlights the trauma experienced by women when fleeing Liberia and the affects of trauma on their lives in the refugee camp in Ghana (Kreitzer 1998; Kreitzer 2002).

As a result of the violence refugees have experienced or witnessed, they may suffer from post-traumatic stress disorder. Indicators of post-traumatic stress disorder may include recurring recollections of past trauma, recurrent dreams or nightmares, feelings of sadness, restricted affect, social numbness or withdrawal, memory impairment, and avoidance of activities that might trigger recollection of events. Individually and collectively these symptoms may impact on the ability of newcomers to successfully integrate into Canadian society.

Reunification

It is not uncommon for a parent or parents to move to Canada and leave other family members in their country of origin. Some of these separations are voluntary in nature while others are the result of the need to flee for fear of their lives. In both instances, once these individuals become settled, there is a desire to bring the rest of the family to Canada. Hence, family reunification frequently becomes a major priority for the newcomer. Known as sequenced migration (Yelaja 1985; Healy 2004), social workers may be instrumental in helping the entire family reunite, but the reunification may pose many challenges. In the case where children have joined a parent or parents, for example, the children may be strangers in the eyes of parents because the separation has been so long. Alternatively, the children may experience difficulties in adjusting to their new home.

As part of the reunification process, social workers in Canada will most likely need to understand the domestic migration policy and procedures, as well as those for countries that family members are leaving. Hence, once again this is a clear example of the intersection of domestic practice and the international domain. Healy (2004, 55) identifies two other patterns of family relationship that may prevail as consequences of international migration: "[Some] may live simultaneously in two countries, travelling back and forth between employment and family, with or without legal sanction. Still others, long resettled, plan to return some day to their country of origin and prepare for another round of leaving, transit, and resettlement perhaps creating new family separations in the process."

Family relationships result in a variety of challenges for social workers in their practice with newcomers, which include issues related to: divorce, child custody, support, and child visitation. The practice of remittance, whereby newcomers in Canada send money back to family members who have remained in the country of origin, also impacts immigrant families in their new country of residence (Healy 2004).

Conclusion

Social work practice with immigrants and refugees in Canada is a form of international social work. Knowledge of newcomer experiences in their home country, passage to Canada, continuing ties with family members in their countries of origin, and international events all affect the settlement and adaptation experiences.

By paying attention to the international dimension of newcomers' experiences, social workers can contribute in a positive manner to the settlement and adaptation of newcomers to Canadian society and be effective in dealing with the challenges of residing in a new country.

Appendix: Drachman Framework	
Stage of Migration	Critical Areas for Assessment
Pre-Migration and Departure	Social, political, economic, and religious factors
	Separation from family and friends
	Decisions regarding who leaves and who is left behind
	Act of leaving a familiar environment
	Life threatening circumstances
	Experiences of violence
	Loss of significant others
Transit	Perilous or saft journey of short or long duration
	Refugee camp or detention centre stay of long or short duration
	Act of awaiting a foreing country's decision regarding final relocation
Resettlement	Cultural issues
	Reception from host country
	Opportunity structure of host country
	Discrepancy between expectations and reality
	Degree of cumulative stress throughout migration process

References

- Chambers, N. and S. Canesan. 2005. Refugees in Canada. In *Cross Cultural Caring: A Handbook for Health Professionals*, eds. N. Waxler-Morrison, J. Anderson, E. Richardson, and N. Chambers. 2nd ed., 289–322. Vancouver: University of British Columbia Press.
- Drachman, D. 1992. A Stage of Migration Framework for Service to Immigrant Populations. *Social Work* 37 (1): 68–72.
- Drachman, D. and A. Paulino. 2004. Introduction: Thinking Beyond United States' Borders. *Journal of Immigrant and Refugee Services* 2 (1/2): 1–9.

- Este, D. and A. Tachble. 2007. *Fatherhood in the Canadian Context: Perceptions and Experiences of Sudanese Refugee*. Paper submitted in Sex Roles.

- Furuto, S. 2004. Theoretical Perspectives for Culturally Competent Practice with Immigrant Children and Families. In *Culturally Competent Practice with Immigrant and Refugee Families and Children*, ed. F. Fong, 19–35. New York: Guilford Press.

- Germain, C. and A. Gitterman. 1996. *The Life Model of Social Work Practice: Advances in Practice and Theory*. 2nd ed. New York: Columbia University Press.

- Government of Canada. 2005. *The Monitor-Year-End Figure for 2004*. Ottawa: Citizenship and Immigration Canada.

- Government of Canada. 2006. *The Monitor: Third Quarter Data 2006*. Ottawa: Citizenship and Immigration Canada.

- Government of Canada. 2007a. *Annual Report to Parliament on Immigration*. Ottawa: Citizenship and Immigration Canada.

- Government of Canada. 2007b. *Immigrants and Non-Permanent Residents*. Ottawa: Statistics Canada.

- Healy, L. 2004. Strengthening the Link: Social Work with Immigrants and Refugees and International Social Work. *Journal of Immigrant and Refugee Services* 2 (1/2): 46–47.

- Healy, L. 2001. *International Social Work: Professional Action in an Interdependent Work*. New York: Oxford University Press.

- Hokenstad, M. C. and J. Midgley, eds. 1997. *Issues in International Social Work: Global Challenges for a New Century*. Washington: NASW Press.

- James, C. 2003. *Seeing Ourselves: Exploring Race, Ethnicity and Culture*. 3rd edition. Toronto: Thompson Educational Publishing, Inc.

- Kirmayer, L. and I. Minas. 2000. The Future of Cultural Psychiatry. *Canadian Journal of Psychiatry* (45): 438–446.

- Kreitzer, L. 1998. *The Experiences of Refugee Women in the Planning and Implementation of Programmes at Buduburam Refugee Camp, Ghana*. Unpublished Master's Thesis. Calgary: University of Calgary.

- Kreitzer, L. 2002. Liberian Refugee Women: A Qualitative Study of their Participation in Planning Camp Programmes. *International Social Work* 45 (1): 47–58.

- Lacroix, M. 2003. Culturally Appropriate Knowledge and Skills Required for Effective Multicultural Practice with Individuals, Families and Small Groups. In *Multicultural Social Work in Canada: Working with Diverse Ethno-Racial Communities*, eds. A. Al-Krenawi and J. Graham, 23–46. Don Mills: Oxford University Press.

- Lorenzetti, L. 2006. *Family Violence and War: The Dual Impact of War Trauma and Domestic Violence on Refugee Women in Calgary*. Unpublished MSW Thesis. Calgary: University of Calgary.

- Lum, D. 1999. *Culturally Competent Practice: A Framework for Growth and Action*. Pacific Grove: Brooks/Cole.

- Lyons, K. 2006. Globalization and Social Work: International and Local Implications. *British Journal of Social Work* (36): 365–380.

- Lyons, K. 1999. *International Social Work: Themes and Perspectives*. Aldershot: Ashgate.

- McPatter, A. R. 1997. Cultural Competency in Child Welfare: What Is It? How do we Achieve it? What Happens Without It? *Child Welfare* 76 (1): 255–278.

- Midgley, J. 2000. Globalization, Capitalism and Social Welfare: A Social Development Perspective. *Social Work and Globalization* (Special Issue of *Canadian Social Work* 2(1) and *Canadian Social Work Review* 17): 13–28.

- Neukrug, E. 1994. Understanding Diversity in a Pluralistic World. *Journal of Intergroup Relations* 22 (2): 3–12.

- Olandi, M. 1992. Defining Cultural Competence: An Organizing Framework. In *Cultural Competence for Evaluations: A Guide for Alcohol and Other Drug Abuse Prevention Practitioners Working with Ethnic/Racial Communities*, ed. M. Olandi, i–viii. Rockville: Department of Health.
- Pine, B. and D. Drachman. 2005. Effective Child Welfare Practice with Immigrant and Refugee Children and Their Families. *Child Welfare* 84 (5): 537–562.
- Ronnau, J. 1994. Teaching Cultural Competence: Practical Ideas for Social Work Educators. *Journal of Multicultural Social Work* 5 (1): 29–42.
- Rowe, W., J. Hanley, E. Moreno, and J. Mould. 2000. Voices of Social Practice. In *Social Work and Globalization*, 65–87. Ottawa: Canadian Association of Social Work.
- Roy, G. and C. Montgomery. 2003. Practice with Immigrants in Quebec. In *Multicultural Social Work in Canada: Working with Diverse Ethno-Racial Communities*, eds. A. Al-Krenawi and J. Graham, 122–146. Don Mills: Oxford University Press Canada.
- Saleebey, D., ed. 2002. *The Strengths Perspective in Social Work Practice*. 3rd ed. Boston: Allyn & Bacon.
- Segal, U. and N. Nayada. 2005. Assessment of Issues Facing Immigrant and Refugee Families. *Child Welfare* 84 (5): 563–583.
- Sherraden, M. S. and J. J. Martin. 1994. Social Work with Immigrants: International Issues in Service Delivery. *International Social Work* 37 (4): 369–384.
- Waxler-Morrison, N., J. Anderson, E. Richardson, and N. Chambers, eds. 2005. *Cross-Cultural Caring: A Handbook for Health Professional*. 2nd ed. Vancouver: University of British Columbia Press.
- Weick, A., C. Rapp, W. P. Sullivan, and W. Kisthardt. 1989. A Strengths Perspective for Social Work Practice. *Social Work* 34 (4): 350–354.
- Williams, N. 1997. Personal Reflections on Permanency Planning and Cultural Competency. *Journal of Multicultural Social Work* 5 (1/2): 9–10.
- Yelaja, S. 1985. *Introduction to Social Work Practice in Canada*. Waterloo: Wilfred Laurier University Press.
- Yelaja, S. 1985. Concepts of Social Work Practice. In *An Introduction to Social Work Practice in Canada*, ed. S. Yelaja, 24–34. Waterloo: Prentice-Hall.
- Yelaja, S. 1985. Appendix A—Settings and Activities of Social Work Practice. In *An Introduction to Social Work Practice in Canada*, ed. S. Yelaja, 345–353. Waterloo: Prentice-Hall.

Chapter 12

Promoting Citizenship of Persons with Disabilities: Social Work and the Canada-Russia Disability Program

Don M. Fuchs

S ince the advent of glasnost and perestroika in the early 1990s, Russia has been undergoing a period of rapid tumultuous social and economic transformation. Over the past decade, I have had the opportunity to be a part of a Canada-Russia partnership working to create a more democratic, inclusive society arising out of the current period of major social reform. My involvement in this partnership has been focused on the development of social work education as a means for the promotion of social inclusion of persons with disability. I have worked closely with academics, non-government organizations and government partners in three diverse areas of Russia: Moscow, Stavropol, and Omsk.[1]

According to the World Bank, the Russian Federation has succeeded in significantly reducing its overall rate of Poverty (World Bank 2005a). However, the World Bank's recent poverty assessment indicates that this success in poverty reduction has been vastly unequal across the country and across population groupings (World Bank 2004, iv). The life expectancy of the Russia population has declined significantly over the past ten years. There has been an unprecedented increase in the spread of AIDS/HIV infection and major increases in the marginalization of youth (World Bank, 2005a). In addition, the overall expenditures on health, education, and social protection have been reduced significantly leaving large sectors of the population, particularly persons with disabilities, without the benefits and services essential for their access, participation, and social inclusion in the economic and social transformation that is occurring in the different regions of Russia.

This chapter examines the current factors that work against the full citizenship for persons with disabilities in Russian society and looks at the negative impact of the social exclusion of persons with disabilities on the social and economic development of Russia as a civil society. In addition, it provides a framework for viewing social work education as a form of social development intervention focused on fostering the social inclusion of persons with disability within a Russian civil society. Finally, it examines the application of the framework. Specifically, it reports on some of the major outcomes of the Canada-Russia Disability Program (CRDP) social work

---

[1] The information and observations in this chapter have been derived from my experiences as the director of the Canada-Russia Disability Program (CRDP). As a participant observer in this social development initiative, I have had the opportunity to observe some aspects of social and economic transformation processes and to learn about their impact on the Russian people and their communities.

stream intervention activities and describes the impacts they have had on fostering the social inclusion of persons with disabilities.

Context

There are many conflicting and paradoxical developments as persons with disability struggle for citizenship in Russian society. Rianovsky and Steinberg (2005, 650) argue that most Russians profess to value a "strong leader and a strong state over democratic institutions. Half of the population, according to a 2000 survey, insist that order is more important than personal freedom, and most believe that Russia's course in history cannot be the same as other countries, because Russia is distinguished by a unique way of life and spiritual culture."

However, Rianovsky and Steinberg (2005) also report that recent public opinion studies show deep skepticism about the utopian promise of state leaders. The young are more committed to democratic ideas and are impatient with the slow rate of reform. At the end of the 1990s, the overwhelming majority of the Russians believed they had lost more than they had gained from the changes over the decade since perestroika. In some respects, Russians have assimilated democratic values faster than governments have established democratic institutions (Rianovsky and Steinberg 2005, 651). Attitudes have varied since 1991 and "ambivalence is the most characteristic feature of public views" in such critical issues as democracy, markets, and westernizing reform. Also, there is increasing evidence of greater social exclusion and intolerance of many visible minority groups within Russian society (Brown 2004).

In recent years, robust economic growth and political stability in Russia have captured people's imagination. However, economic growth remains volatile and some argue that political stability has come at the expense of real democracy and social inclusion (Brown 2004, 8). In addition, income inequality, excessive concentration of wealth and disparate standards of living work against social cohesion and human development. Addressing social issues including health, social services, and education, has become a major concern. In the spring of 2004, the Putin government declared poverty as one of the most important challenges facing Russia (Brown 2004). However, since that declaration, the focus has shifted toward the maintenance of social stability and fighting terrorism (World Bank 2005a). At the core, Russia's challenge is to translate growth into a human and social capital base of healthy, educated, economically productive people, empowered to make choices in their lives, including political ones (Brown 2004).

The marginalization of persons with disabilities is a particularly acute issue, as the institutionally-based structures of services and benefits continue to be over stretched and under-resourced. The need for reform is evident in different ways. First, the effect of Russia's current programs and services for people with disabilities and psychiatric disorders has reinforced exclusion (CCDS 2002). The emphasis of state programs has been to respond to disabled persons' medical conditions in order to treat/fix/correct them or rehabilitate. Some persons with disabilities have been financially compensated for their isolation with monetary handouts. However, this approach has proven to be ineffective and the recent approval of new law (Bill 122) has increased the emphasis on medicalization and significantly reduced the number of individuals with disabilities who are eligible for pensions and other forms of financial assistance (World Bank 2005a).

Second, in spite of the reduction of allocations and restricted eligibility, approximately 98% of the Russian disability budget is still spent on pensions, financial assistance, and compensation (Russian Government Report 1999). Many people with disabilities experience periods of hunger and homelessness. However, given the limited number of paid work opportunities, attainment of disability status has actually become a short-term financial goal for many, regardless of the long-term ramifications. Hence, the system is doubly unsustainable. Not only are there constantly increasing numbers of people accessing fixed or decreasing public funds, but the loss of their participation in the labour force is having a negative impact on the overall economy of the country (World Bank 2005b). Virtually nothing is spent on rehabilitation and re-entry into society.

Third, professional and service models of addressing these issues are dated and ineffectual (Templeman 2001). Existing services are almost totally based on a "medical model" of disability, with very little evidence so far of a "social model" that recognizes not only the rights, but also the important role of people with disabilities in choosing their own future. In general, it can be said that people with disabilities are still seen as "patients" or "sick people" and are "objects of" (rather than participants in) rehabilitation (CCDS 2003). Fourth, there is, underlying the above, a pervasive social stigma of disability, particularly toward people with cognitive impairments and mental health disabilities (CCDS 2002). The exclusionary practices of existing programs serve to reinforce these negative stereotypes.

The tragic effect of these developments is encountered when meeting many of Russia's citizens with disabilities. Food is scarce as is satisfactory accommodation. Residential institutions are under-resourced, with inadequate furnishings, supplies, and medication. There also are virtually no supports for disabled people to return to society. Some groups, like war traumatized refugee families living in the North Caucuses' region, have little or no services available to help address the widespread evidence of post-traumatic stress disorder (CIDA 2003). Added to these concerns is a growing exodus of the skilled labour force from Russia to the United States and other countries (Brown 2004).

Emerging Role of Social Work

In Russia, there is a growing awareness of a need for social work as a profession to assist in building social capital and foster social development in the post-soviet society. The Ministry of Health and Social Development (formerly the Ministry of Labour and Social Protection) has been the driving force behind the development of social work. Social work is one of the fastest growing professions in Russia (Imbrogno 1994). Through her research, Templeman (2001) has found that social workers are developing new practice and research methodologies that help foster normal living conditions for families; detect emerging problems; prevent, eliminate, or moderate social and personal conflicts; and develop family communications skills, independence, or self-help capabilities. However, the social work roles remain ill-defined and can range from agency administration and skilled social service deliverery to instrumental functions such as delivering pension cheques, food, or forms of mobility assistance to the elderly and the disabled.

In addition to being part of one of the fastest growing professions in Russia, social workers are making significant strides in the development of national professional standards for social work education (Templeman 2001). Since 1991, a modern theory of social work in Russia has been emerging. The theory embraces the concept of prevention, the advancement from social assistance to self-help and self-protection, as well as the creation and provision of opportunities for personal development and some concepts of social development. Also, the social work profession is involved in social development activities, such as strengthening families and communities, revival of former Russian charity traditions, and cooperation between social services and the church. Increasingly social worker functions include: diagnosis, individual and family intervention, development of prevention and social therapeutic programs, agency management, consumer advocacy, and social protection (Tempelman 2001; Mardahaeve 2005)

Substance abuse is a serious problem and there are very limited services or trained professionals to address the need (CIDA 2003). There are also rapidly growing large scale problems with marginalized youth. Problems of drug addiction, AIDS/HIV, youth gangs, and youth crime are rampant. The Ministries of Justice and Social Protection have been extending their programs to include social development programs aimed at addressing these wide ranging social problems. Increasingly social workers, social work researchers, and educators are being called on to provide leadership (World Bank 2005). In addition, there seems to be an emerging consensus amongst both the government and the non-government sectors about the need for and importance of social workers to address the difficult social conditions within Russia (CRDP 2004).

Post-secondary institutions have been mandated by the Ministry of Labour and Social Development to provide social work education programs to build the professional capacity for fostering social policy and social service programs that provide much needed resources to the poor and the marginalized (CIDA 2003). Recently the Social Protection Ministry has extended this mandate to include the education of professionals to administer social programs and to foster community social development.

As a result of these government initiatives, formal training for social workers in Russia is expanding at an accelerating pace (Templeman 2001). However, the need for social workers to address the major issues resulting from the social and economic transformation is greater than the capacity to produce the trained social workers. This lack of capacity is greatly hindering the process of social development in Russia and contributes to marginalization and inequality (CCDS 2002).

In addition, there is a great need to broaden the mandate of health and social services to include social development components that are essential to the social and economic transformation that is occurring in Russia. Without appropriate social development strategies, there will continue to be more groups marginalized, social instability, and a reduction in a productive labour force (World Bank, 2004). The nature of the current social transformation in Russia necessitates the development of unprecedented partnerships between government, Universities, and NGOs to address the growing number of social problems. The social work profession and social work educators are emerging as major leaders in the transformative change efforts that are currently underway in the human services in the country (CCDS 2002).

Citizenship and Disability

To foster the social inclusion of persons with disability, it is important to understand the concepts of citizenship and civil society. They provide the bases for understanding the role of social work education in promoting social inclusion. Citizenship concerns the relationship of the state and the citizen, especially rights and obligations (Anheier 2001). A theory of civil society provides a rationale for understanding the relationship of "mediating institutions" between the citizen and the state. While citizenship and civil society are different—the former refers to state enforced rights and obligations and the latter focuses on groups in concert or opposition—they are empirically contingent. Civil society creates the groups and pressures for political choice and state legislation. Many ideas of citizenship originate in civil society rather than the state (Janowski 1998). Consequently, strong civil societies produce particular institutional structures that bolster citizenship. Society constructs much of the citizen–society discourse in terms of rights and obligations (Ward 2005). Weak civil societies will most often be dominated by the state or market sphere. Civil society consists of the public sphere of associations and organizations engaged in debate and discussion (Anheier 2001).

The issues of marginalization and social exclusion faced by the people with disability and other marginalized groups in Russian require a further expansion of our traditional understanding of the concept of citizenship. The United Nations (1984) declaration on the rights of persons with disabilities proclaims that citizens with disabilities must be "treated in all respects as valued members of our society, with full recognition of their contribution and full respect for their rights" (CCD 1999). Rights refer to entitlements of what citizens expect because they are members of a community. Responsibilities refer to the obligation to build and sustain a mutually caring society. In addition, full citizenship includes the rights of families and care-givers that provide long-term support for children, youth, or adults with a disability. "The right of these parents to a full life includes their status as parents with other children, as partners in a marriage or common-law union, as adults in or out of the paid labour market, as volunteers in community affairs, and as citizens wishing to participate in policy making and other political processes." (Government of Canada 1999, 15).

Unfortunately, as Russia moves toward a market economy, many of the universal rights of citizenship of persons with disabilities are being eroded. The institutional and financial supports are being reduced and eligibility criteria are applied selectively. The lack of accessible community based supports and services has fostered the further social exclusion of persons with disabilities from educational, employment, housing and transportation resources that are essential for full citizenship.

Citizenship and Social Development

The World Bank in its poverty reduction strategies indicates that social development promotes inclusive societies that recognize and protect human and civil rights and support the dignity of individuals and groups (World Bank 2004). It gives individuals and communities equitable access to economic opportunities by removing formal and informal social and cultural barriers. Social development also promotes effective, responsive, and transparent institutions, good governance and promotes the development of inclusive civil societies.

Midgley (1995, 25) defines social development as a process of planned social change designed to promote the well-being of the population as a whole in conjunction with a dynamic process of economic development. Important components of the definition are that it emphasizes process; prefers universal interventions that effect the total population, not just a segment or subgroup; and expresses well-being holistically. Midgley (2005) recommends three sets of intervention strategies to operationalize the social development approach: human capital development, social capital develop-ment and encouragement of self-employment or other productive employ-ment projects. Healy (2001) argues that participation, capacity building, equity, and inclusion are particularly important.

Civil society is the network of free associations through which people care for one another, build community, exercise influence on government, and stimulate commercial activity (Johnson and Wright 1998, 143). Civil society is the foundation and context for supporting, critiquing, and reforming the private economic sector, the public governmental sector and the social non-profit/nongovernmental sector. It is the communal infrastructure that underlies strong, public, private, and voluntary organization (Anheier 2001, 25). It represents a sphere of dynamic and responsive public discourse between the state, the public sphere consisting of voluntary organizations, and the market and public sphere consisting of voluntary organizations and the market sphere concerning private firms and unions (Janoski 1998, 12). This conception of civil society can be applied to all countries if they have private organizations between the state and the family (Janoski 1998 12–13). Social development intervention strategies represent a means for fostering the development of civil societies with inclusive models of citizenship.

Anheier (2001, 22) provides an operational definition of civil society as the sphere of institutions, organizations, and individuals located between the family, the state, and the market in which people associate voluntarily to advance common interests. He sees the relationship amongst civil society elements in the following manner: individuals shape organizations and pattern individual behaviour; individuals enact and shape institutions and form and use organizations; and organizations form out of institutions and provide vehicles for individual behaviour (Anheier 2001). This description provides a functional operational framework for the evaluation of the civil society development activities of the Canada-Russia Disability Project. It assists us in evaluating the impact of the social development efforts of social work education.

The International Association of Schools of Social Work (IASSW) indicates that social work education can foster the development of the capacity to build effective, inclusive, and accessible community service structures that nurture the development of the social capital necessary for social stability and economic development (IASSW 2004). The Association maintains that to have an effective social development strategy it is important to have a clear understanding of the concepts of civil society and citizenship. Social development interventions are guided by principles of human rights and social justice. They are directed towards fostering accessibility, participation, and social inclusion of marginalized groups within a civil society. Consequently they are most effective in promoting and working towards the full citizenship of persons with disability.

Canada-Russia Disability Program

Building on a model of full citizenship within a civil society, the CRDP has set out a program of action towards the reform of policies and practices in Russia affecting its most vulnerable populations, notably those with disabilities, but with wider application to at-risk children, frail elderly people and working age adults experiencing sustained distress. Consistent with a model of civil society, a tripartite model of engagement frames the various activities to be undertaken involving the voluntary sector, government, and institutions of higher learning. The model is built on a rights-based notion of full citizenship and civil society. It is premised on the success of previous work by the project partners in developing collaborative decision-making between service users, service providers, and university faculty and policy makers—approaches that cut across the chasms of traditional Russian planning and program implementation processes (CCDS 2002).

Program activities are clustered into four main components—education, alternative service model program development, policy promotion, and network development. All address social protection and health policies and practices to maximize the potential for change. Activities are undertaken in three regions of Russia: the North Caucasus region (centred in Stavropol), Middle Russia (centred in Moscow), and Northern Russia (centred in Omsk, Siberia).

The CRDP's social work stream central mission is to have social workers well prepared and engaged in activities that will improve social well-being structures and enhance individual, family, and community social functioning at local, national, and international levels. The social work education working groups in each region are striving to build the capacity of social work professionals in Russia to develop effective social policies, to do social work research, to undertake social development oriented social work practice, and to do fieldwork training of students. This is being done in a context of the newly approved national standards for social work curriculum.

To foster social development and increased social inclusion of persons with disabilities, the CRDP social work stream has used a set of principles adapted from the work of Johnson and Wright (Appendix). The principles guide the development of the partnerships and aim at building capacity and empowering persons with disability to participate in decision-making relating to their own lives and to increase their access to resources. To promote social development, Cheung and Meng (2004) indicate that social work education should be developed with an indigenous foundation, including a philosophical basis, theories, working principles and approaches, and study materials, since working with people calls for indigenous orientation and skills. As part of this process for indigenization, the CRDP social work stream has developed social work education working groups in each focal region to promote the "Russification" and localization of international social work education standards, scope of practice, and curriculum content.

The working groups in each focal region assist local social work educators to take into consideration social structures and development issues. They develop regional strategies in response to the economic, social, political, and psychological contexts in which social work practice occurs. Also, the regional working groups communicate with each other to solve problems, share information, and collaborate as they address the contextual issues in local institutions and communities. This enhances the national impact of the intervention.

To assist the social work profession in playing an effective role, the project staff have worked with local educators on defining and redefining the central focus, knowledge, and value base of social work practice in Russia. In the process of transferring knowledge and practice from a developed country such as Canada, staff work with local social work educators to redefine standards. The process has helped to modify and develop conceptual frameworks and methodologies rooted in a Russia socio-cultural practice context. The efforts are having a discernible impact on the development of social work practice, which is particularly apparent in the health and social service demonstration sites that have been set up through the CRDP in each of the regions. The project staff have been greatly assisted by the involvement of the disability consumer groups.

Conclusion

The rapidly changing political, social, and economic context in Russia presents a formidable challenge to the development of civil society. There is a movement to centralize the power of the state nationally and great pressure to overturn the democratic reforms to address threats of terrorism, social instability, and civil unrest (Brown 2004; N. Riasanosky and M. Steinberg 2005). The current trend of combining key government departments, resulting in the amalgamation of the national Ministries of Social Protection and Health under the newly formed Department of Health and Social Development, has resulted in the reduction of social services and benefits available for persons with disability.

Another challenge is that social work education is very new and is not based on curricula and approaches consistent with international standards. Education and training of community based professional practice in fields such as psychiatry, psychology, and education have been virtually absent. Few good models of community-based services exist, and appropriate legislative frameworks to assist transition from residential institutions to community-based services have yet to be framed. The CRDP social work stream intervention has made significant progress in the introduction of models of community-based health and social services across the regions. There is a great deal of resistance to change from entrenched and often corrupt government bureaucracies and post-secondary institutions.

While these challenges impact upon CRDP's targeted objectives, the flexibility within the program provides a narrow window for some innovative responses to changing needs and policies as they arise (World Bank, 2005). The decision by government to include health and social development under the auspices of one department can also be viewed as potentially beneficial to the accomplishment of the goals of the project. It may give rise to more influence, funding options and an overall higher priority being placed upon the promotion of community-based health and social services and an increase in opportunities for persons with disabilities. However, this initiative also must be viewed with guarded optimism as it increases tension between national and regional structures that could lead to a backlash and further centralization and control over resource allocation.

Over the past fifteen years, the Russian government has been largely responsible for stimulating the rapid development of the social work profession to provide the human resources necessary for the provision of community-based social services. It has also fostered rapid growth in post-secondary social work education.[2] Social workers and social work schools, in turn, have been called on to build the capacity to provide the personal, familial, and community supports necessary to assist in fostering the social inclusion of marginalized groups. Consequently there is great need to develop mechanisms and incentives to engage social work practitioners in the social work education process. The social work stream of the CRDP has been working in the three focal regions to improve collaboration among key stake holders to address the need.

The successful outcomes of the CRDP have been a result of the remarkable resilience of the Russian people under severe hardship and repression. The CRDP has demonstrated that the development of social work education can build the capacity for reform, innovation, and change in the delivery of health and social services. Furthermore, the results of the intervention illustrate the reformative and transformative capacity of social work and social work education in promoting civil society.[3] The use of innovative partnerships of non-government organizations, government, and universities in this process strengthens civil society, reduces oppression, and increases the social inclusion and participation of persons with disabilities. It also provides some checks and balances for monitoring and stimulating the development of effective social work programs to address the concerns of persons with disabilities.

Appendix: Principles of Civil Society Development

- **Participation.** This implies a strategy of listening to and involving local citizenry and leadership. It means organizing society so there is access to and influence on decision-making persons at all levels of society, in contrast to programs set-up and run only by professional elites.

- **Inclusion.** This means that no group or minority is excluded or left out. It requires democratic processes, equal treatment, and social justice.

- **Reciprocity.** This focuses on strengthening relationships to develop mutual support systems. It contrasts with the approach that identifies people in terms of their problems or deficiencies and then establishes programs to meet those deficiencies. This key principle differentiates a strategy of community building from one of social welfare.

- **Structural Change.** This affirms that change is more than motivating individuals. Its means recognizing and dealing with the social structures or habits within which personal behavior and consciousness are reinforced and assume meaning.

- **Cultural Appropriateness.** This affirms the integrity and importance of diverse cultural traditions and expressions as well as commonality at the root of all cultures. It implies a strategy in which diverse cultural expression are celebrated, renewed, and unified within communities.

---

[2] In the last decade I have been able to observe the geometric growth in the social work profession and commensurate growth in the number of post-secondary institutions providing social work education. Much of this has been directed by Russian State Social University, one of the major partners in the CRDP.

[3] The Russian Commission on Higher Education in Social Work has approved specializations in social work and disability. These specializations are beginning to provide the basis to build the capacity of the social work profession in many regions to address more effectively the needs of people with disabilities and to foster their social inclusion in Russian society.

- **Holism.** This supports strategies that link economic, political, cultural, and spiritual dimensions of local communities. It is based on the premise that values and affiliation move people and that a sense of belonging and meaning are as important as financial well-being.

- **Learning.** This calls for constant learning through critical inquiry. It implies a strategy that is self-reflective, evaluative, self-corrective, and based on actual results.

- **Action.** All the above principles are rooted in this one. It is the principle of human power—the ability of a community to act in concert. It is this principle that humankind accepts tradition, develops initiative, forms a community, connects to the world, and projects a future. Freedom, social justice, and distributive power are defined by and rooted in this principle. This is the principle that uses civil society developments as a strategy for human development (Johnson and Wright 1998, 144–145).

References

- Alexander, M. L. 2002. Disability Access and Inclusion Lens. Unpublished Monograph. Winnipeg, Manitoba.
- Anheier, H. K. 2001. *Civil Society: Measurement, Evaluation and Policy*. London: EarthScan.
- Barnes, C.,and G. Mercer. 2003. *Disability*. Oxford: Blackwell Publishing.
- Bothwell, R. 1998. Indicators of a Healthy Civil Society. In *Beyond Prince and Merchant: Citizen Participation and Rise of Civil Society*, ed. J. Burbidge, 249–262. New York: Pact Publications.
- Brown, M. M. 2004. Balancing Social and Economic Goals. *The Msocow Times* (March 18): 8.
- Bruyn, S. 2005. *A Civil Republic: Beyond Capitalism and Nationalism*. Bloomfield: Kumarian Press.
- Canadian Centre on Disability Studies. 2002. Canada-Russia Disability Program Proposal. Monograph Winnipeg: CCDS.
- Canadian International Development Agency. 2003. Russia Facts: *Programming Framework Annex 1 & 2*. Ottawa: Government of Canada.
- Chandhoke, N. 2003. *The Conceits of Civil Society*. New Delhi: Oxford University Press.
- Cheung, M. and Meung, L. 2004. The Self-Concept of Chinese Women and Indigenization of Social Work in China. *International Social Work* 47 (1): 109–127.
- Dixon, J., I. Weiss, and J. Gal. Professional Ideologies and Preferences: A Global and Comparative Perspective. In *Professional Ideologies and Preferences in Social Work: A Global Study*, eds. I. Weiss, J. Gal, and J. Dixon, 215–226. London: Praeger.
- Enns, H. and A. Neufeldt. 2003. *In Pursuit of Equal Participation: Canada and Disability at Home and Abroad*. Toronto: Captus Press.
- Epp, J. 1998. Core Values of a Civil Society. In *Beyond Prince and Merchant: Citizen Participation and Rise of Civil Society*, ed. J. Burbidge, 275-281. New York: Pact Publications.
- Gibson, J. L. 2003. Social Networks, Civil Society, and the Prospects for Consolidating Russia's Democratic Transition. In *Social Capital and the Transition to Democracy*, eds. G. Badescu and E. Uslaner. London: Routledge.
- Government of Canada. 1999. *A Framework to Improve the Social Union for Canadians An Agreement between the Government of Canada and the Governments of the Provinces and Territories*. Canada: Queens Press.
- Healy, L. M. 2001. *International Social Work: Professional Action In An Interdependent World*. Oxford: Oxford University Press.
- Ho, D. F. 1999. Indigenous Psychologies: Asian Perspective. *Journal of Cross-cultural Psychology* 29 (1).
- International Association of Schools of Social Work. 2004. *Global Standards for the Education and training of Social Workers*. IASSW, Adelaide Vienna.

- Imbrogno, S. 1994. The Emergence of the Profession of Social Work in the Russian Republic. In *Education for Social Work in Eastern Europe: Changing Horizons*, eds. R. Constable, and V. Mehta. Chicago: Lyceum Books.
- Johnson, A. and Wright, B. 1998. Civil Society in Romania: An Evolving Partnership. In *Beyond Prince and Merchant: Citizen Participation and Rise of Civil Society*, ed. J. Burbidge, 143–160. New York: Pact Publications.
- Janoski, T. 1998. *Citizenship and Civil Society: A Framework Of Rights & Obligations in Liberal, and Social Democratic Regimes*. Cambridge: Cambridge University of Press.
- Keane, J. 1998. *Civil Society: Old Images New Visions*. Stanford: Stanford University Press.
- Mayadas, N. S., T. D. Watts, and D. Elliott, eds. 1997. *International Handbook on Social Work Theory and Practice*. London: Greenwood Press.
- Midgley, J. 1981. *Professional Imperialism: Social Work in the Third World*. London: Heinenmann.
- Midgley, J. 1995. *Social Development*. London: Sage Publications.
- Midgley, J. 1997. *Social Welfare in Global Context*. Thousand Oaks: Sage Publications.
- Midgley, J. 1999. Social Development in Social Work: Learning from Global Dialogue. In *All our Futures: Principles and Resources for Social Work Practice in Global Era*, eds. C. S. Ramanathan and R. J. Lik, 193–205. Belmont: Brooks Cole
- Midgley, J. 2005. Development Theory and Community Practice. In *The Handbook of Community Practice*, ed. M. Weil, 153–168. Thousand Oaks: Sage Publications.
- Naidoos, K. and R. Tandon. 1999. The Promise of Civil Society. In *Civil Society at the Millennium*, ed. K. Naidoo. Hartford: Kumariam Press.
- Nimmagadda, J. and C. Cowger. 1999. Cross-Cultural Practice: Social Worker Ingenuity in the Indigenization of Practice Knowledge. *International Social Work* 42 (3): 261–276.
- Osei-Hwedie, K. 1993. The Challenge of Social Work in Africa: Starting the Indigenization Oricess. *Journal of Social Development in Africa* 8 (1): 19–30.
- Priestly, M. 2003. *Disability: A Life Course Approach*. Oxford: Blackwell Publishing.
- Ragab, I. 1990. How Social Work can Take Root in Developing Countries. *Social Development Issues* 12 (3): 38–51.
- Riasanosky, N. and M. Steinberg. 2005. *A History of Russia Since 1855*. Vol. 2. 7th ed. Oxford: Oxford University Press.
- Russian Federation, Ministry of Labour and Social Protection. *1999 Annual Report Situation of People with Disabilities in Russian Federation*.
- Templeman, S. 2001. Social Work in the New Russia at the Start of the Millennium. *International Social Work* 47 (1): 95–108.
- Ward, T., ed. 2005. *Development Social Justice and Civil Society: An Introduction to the Political Economy of NGOs*. St Paul's: Paragon Press.
- World Bank. 2002. *Transforming Growth, Neighbor, Nature and Future*. New York: Oxford University Press.
- World Bank. 2004. *Russian Federation Poverty Assessment*. Poverty Reduction and Economic Management Unit Europe and Central Asia Region. Monograph, New York: World Bank.
- World Bank. 2005a. *Russian Federation Reducing Poverty through Growth and Social Policy Reform*. Poverty Reduction and Economic Management Unit Europe and Central Asia Region. Monograph, New York: World Bank.
- World Bank. 2005b. *Russian Federation Economic Report*. Poverty Reduction and Economic Management Unit Europe and Central Asia Region. Monograph, New York: World Bank.

Part 4: Social Work Education

Chapter 13

Localizing Social Work: Bedouin-Arab of the Negev

Alean Al-Krenawi and John R. Graham

We have been working together for 15 years, having met in 1993 when we were Ph.D. students in social work at the University of Toronto. With common backgrounds as psychiatric social workers, and common interests in spirituality and social work, we wrote a journal article together combining our interests in historical (Graham) and Middle East (Al-Krenawi) research (Graham and Al-Krenawi 1996). That led to further research and to an ongoing collaboration that has been strongly anchored to Al-Krenawi's hometown of Rahat, Israel, the largest Bedouin-Arab village in Israel.

Over the last 15 years, we have written extensively about cultural mediation, divorce, family therapy, help-seeking processes, idioms of distress, polygamous family formation, and traditional healing; within Bedouin and other Arab communities in such countries as Egypt, Israel, Jordan, Palestine, and the United Arab Emirates. All of these concerns had in common an intention to make social work a better fit with the local knowledge of the communities with which we were working. These concerns have deep roots for both authors.

Before embarking on a Ph.D. program, Al-Krenawi had been a practitioner with his home community for 11 years. He had graduated with an MSW from the Hebrew University, and was deeply immersed in family therapy, psychotherapy, and other intervention approaches that had a strong intellectual legacy in North America and Western Europe. As a practitioner, he struggled continuously with the dissonance between his own western training, and the values and knowledge of his home community. Often this led to feelings of disjuncture and misunderstanding between client and worker, clients' frequent premature termination of service, and widespread ineffective service system delivery. Graham, for his part, had experienced similar difficulties in his own practice in a multicultural Canada and deeply appreciated the dilemmas Al-Krenawi had experienced.

Both of us knew enough about modern history to appreciate the distinct, culturally bound parameters in which social work had emerged; both understood the limited utility of social work with many of the world's diverse communities; and both had a strong worry that the social work profession was somehow aloof to these concerns, and was, as a result, frequently arrogant and hegemonic. Our work always intended to open dialogue between the global—which was social work, an internationally occurring profession—and the local customs and practices of the indigenous communities we worked with, particularly the Bedouin-Arab.

The Bedouin-Arab are historically nomadic and tribal people extending from northern Africa through the Arabian peninsula. Their livelihood traditionally depended on moving over vast terrains of land, and for whom goats, sheep, and camels were important commodities. They lived in the region prior to the establishment of Islam or Christianity as established religions. The Bedouin-Arab with whom we have worked are Muslim. As part of the Arab minority in the state of Israel, they have experienced dramatic and abrupt modernization, which has included official, state-sanctioned encouragement to live in villages. Recent exposure, for the first time in the community's history, to social work and other helping professions has been part of this modernization experience.

Localizing Social Work

This chapter summarizes three arguments we have been pursuing over the past 15 years in a number of published forums. The first, localization and related terms like indigenization, are long-standing concepts that require further theoretical rigour, and far greater currency of application (Al-Krenawi and Graham 2003a). The second, spirituality, is a viable, and potentially effective source of engaging with that recently rejuvenated movement to render social work relevant to the international communities in which it occurs: to indigenize, or (our preferred term) to localize, social work's knowledge base (Bradshaw and Graham 2007; Graham 2006). The third, scholarship regarding localizing social work, could also profitably involve case vignette insight (Al-Krenawi and Graham 2007).

We build the following claims on social work and social development research in the Middle East and the Global South[1] in general; and in particular, on the basis of our work in the Arab Middle East, a lot of which has concentrated on the Bedouin-Arab of the Negev, Israel. Research with which we have been involved in the Middle East has shed insight into sensitivity to such cultural anchors as Islam, group/collectivist context, and to such distinct cultural practices as blood vengeance, hakim mediation, and polygamous family formation. Many of these findings have been conveyed via case vignettes, using a variety of qualitative approaches, and ethnography especially. It should be said that spirituality, and Islam, have been an important current throughout. We suspect at least some of these analytical

---

[1] Like much terminology, the terms "Global North" and "Global South" obscure and neglect as much as they explain and illuminate. We therefore use them reluctantly, even though they are prevalent in development literatures, and are meant to replace earlier (and perhaps even more troubling) nomenclature such as developing/developed, and (from the Cold War) First, Second, and Third Worlds. By Global North, we mean those advanced industrialized countries, many (but not all) of which are in the Northern hemisphere, including the United States, Canada, and Western Europe; by Global South, we mean those countries in Asia, Africa, Central and South America, and elsewhere, that tend to be less industrialized and economically wealthy, and are more likely to be in the Southern rather than Northern hemisphere.

approaches have a basis of extrapolation to the cultural contexts of other parts of the world.[2]

We should probably introduce a further proviso. Since we have been working in the field of localization and social work for a while, a number of the preceding assumptions and proceeding arguments are highly personal. A lot of our early studies looked at various ways of understanding traditional healing in the Arab Middle East (among Dervish, Koranic healers, and others) in relation to professional disciplines such as social work (Al-Krenawi and Graham 1996ab, 1997ab, 1999bc; Graham and Al-Krenawi 1996). The research was strongly indebted to epistemologies other than our own, and indeed appeared not only in social work journals but in such disciplinary venues as anthropology, area studies, bereavement studies, family therapy, health sciences, psychology, psychiatry, sociology, and women's studies (Al-Krenawi and Graham 2005, 2004, 2003a, 1999abd, 1997a, 1996b; Al-Krenawi, Graham, and Sehwail 2002; Al-Krenawi, Graham, and Slonim-Nevo 2002).

Later, we moved into understanding Islam as a force in social work writ-large (Al-Krenawi and Graham 2000, 2003a), and to case studies regarding blood vengeance (Al-Krenawi and Graham 1997, 1999), polygamous family formation (Al-Krenawi and Graham 1999be, 2005, 2006; Al-Krenawi, Graham, and Al-Krenawi, 1997), and cultural mediation (Al-Krenawi and Graham 2001b). Our research was collaborative with Muslim communities in the Arab Middle East, particularly the Bedouin-Arab of the Negev, but also Arab communities in Palestine, Jordan, Egypt, the United Arab Emirates, and other parts of the Muslim world (Al-Krenawi and Graham 2006, 2005, 2004; Al-Krenawi, Graham, Dean, and El-Thabet 2004; Al-Krenawi, Graham, and Sehwail 2002, 2004).[3]

What is Localization? What Could It Be?

Our work has consciously attempted to provide a modest corrective to the dominance of voice and writings from outside the Muslim Arab Middle East. We have pointed out that much of social work's written, English-language knowledge base continues to be produced in the Global North, particularly its English language countries, but is consumed in the Global North and South (Al-Krenawi and Graham 2003a; Lyons 1999). Social work emerged in the Global North and was transplanted to the Global South during the interwar period as a product of what has been described (accurately, in our view) as "academic colonialization" (Atal 1981). After World War II, schools of social work in the Global South proliferated, with cultural assumptions, and with the predominance of professional writing, originating

---

[2] Comments on spirituality and international social work draw heavily from Graham (2006a, b). We are grateful to the editors of Arete: *A Professional Journal Devoted to Excellence in Social Work*, in which Graham 2006 appears, for permission to use sections from that work. Reference to case vignettes draws from Al-Krenawi & Graham, 2007, and the reader is referred to this chapter for elucidation.

[3] Al-Krenawi & Graham (2003a) is a summary overview.

in the North, profoundly influencing teaching, research, and practice in the Global South.

Many scholars in the Global South are clear on their commitment to disengaging from this colonial web. An article in the recently-inaugurated *Caribbean Journal of Social Work* discusses the region's oldest English-language school of social work, established in the 1940s in the aftermath of technical consultations from Great Britain, and strongly indebted to British social work training traditions. "Both lecturers and students are critical of the programme, especially the practice methodology area, for being too dependent on models derived predominantly from the United States and to a lesser extent from Britain and Canada" (Maxwell, Williams, Ring, and Cambridge 2003, 24).

Similar echoes are heard in a recent evaluation of social work education in Pakistan, which was established in the mid-1950s. Unlike the previous example, it owed more to the United Nations Technical Assistance Administration than to a British colonial heritage (which it nonetheless shared with the English-speaking Caribbean). To one observer, the originators of social work in Pakistan had always intended that practices would develop in such a way that they would become "appropriate for training of social workers in the cultural and social environment of Pakistan" (Rehmatullah 2002, 176).

Likewise, "the teaching of Western-based methodologies of social work was to be discouraged and replaced by indigenous methods evolved from practice in Pakistan" (Rehmatullah 2002, 176). To that end, "the task of developing Pakistani methods of social work, and producing Pakistani litera-ture would be undertaken and introduced in the universities in Pakistan" (ibid., 176). But the objectives of social work's founding mothers and fathers have "never been done" (ibid., 177). Indeed, "very little social work literature has been produced, and social work methodology of 'group work' and 'case work' are still being taught in the same manner as in 1954" (ibid., 177).

Some readers in the South, or who have journeyed internationally, would probably recollect similar stories from other parts of the Global South. We can think of many from our travels in Egypt, Jordan, Palestine, and Malaysia, among other countries. English language social work scholarship originating from the Global North can be profoundly influential upon the Global South. Most readers would probably be deeply concerned that there are instances in the Global South where social work's knowledge base is problem-ridden, needing to overcome a lot of its past and present limitations.

That concern has deep historic roots. Indeed, one of the earliest calls for the localization of social work practice occurred at the 1972 Annual Conference of the International Association of Schools of Social Work: "We have entered the era of indigenization—of indigenous development based on the needs and resources and the cultural, political, and economic landscape of each society—and the schools of social work are taking the lead, as they must, in carving out such new circumstances" (Stein, in Healy 2001, 35). Nearly 35 years later, the profession's success in indigenization has been sporadic and split along three lines.

First, some have advocated an internationalization of social work education, in which domestic and international curricula are no longer separated, but converge toward "a truly global perspective" (Asamoath, Healy, and Mayadas 1997; Kondrat and Ramathan 1996; Park 1999). Second, some insist upon a professional knowledge base that is more highly localized, and inevitably situated to immediate community concerns whether Aboriginal (Morrissette, McKenzie, and Morrissette 1993), African (Osei 1996; Schiele 1996, 1997; Swigonski 1996), Indian (Nagpaul 1993, 1996a, b), or other. And third, some scholars have proposed a multicultural approach to practice within their home countries that tries to adapt mainstream social work thinking to cultural, ethnic, and racial pluralism (Al-Krenawi and Graham 2003b; Dominelli 1997).

The process of rendering social work culturally relevant to the international communities in which it occurs has been fraught with problems of terminology. While some understand indigenization to mean a localization process that occurs only within indigenous communities worldwide—of which the Bedouin-Arab are one community—others see the term to be a synonym for localization with application to all communities, whether indigenous or not. Other terms, such as authentization, appear to us as awkward and uncommon to daily parlance (Bradshaw and Graham 2007). Because it has conflicting meanings, we have preferred the term localization to describe our work with Arab communities in the Middle East. These issues received preliminary exploration in a May 2006 conference, which produced a 2007 book on localization/indigenization in global contexts (Coates, Gray, and Yellowfeather 2007).

But all of these terms—indegenization, localization, authentization—have not benefited from fulsome exposure to insights from more sophisticated conceptions in other disciplines. It is useful, indeed, to analyse localization through anthropological and sociological theory on local versus globalizing knowledge (Antweiler 1998; Nathan 2004; Roach 2005); and to be aware that professional disciplines other than social work are also grappling with similar localization dilemmas (Atler 2005; Nathan 2004; Zifcak 2005). Future research could, and should, provide greater theoretical rigour to how social work scholars might look at localization, using these sorts of interdisciplinary lenses. Limits of space preclude fulsome analysis, allowing only three points from other disciplines to bear out for the time being. The first is that localization acts as a critical and reflexive response to globalization; those communities turning inward and developing decentralized, internal capacities may be understood to respond to the external forces of globalization (Brumann, 1998; Gilpin, 2001). The point has been long made in social work and allied helping professional literatures (Al-Krenawi and Graham 1996b); but its theoretical explications remain weak.

The second point is the diversity of terms used for local knowledge and its derivative categories (for further detail, see tables A–C). Anthropologists and related social scientists have used terms such as "indigenous knowledge," "local knowledge," "community knowledge," and "traditional knowledge" to capture the notions of "local" that are salient to our work and to that of other social work and allied disciplinary scholars working with diverse communities. Each term has specific meanings that often overlap with meanings of other terms and some common notions that appear salient to our work in the Arab world. Local knowledge may be anchored to small groups of people, and yet be widespread; practices may be integrated and implicit in community life and norms. Any knowledge system, like any community, is continuously evolving.

Local knowledge may be broken into several thematic fields (table B), and all are salient to understanding the cultures in which social work operates. Furthermore, forms of declarative knowledge, procedural knowledge, and complex knowledge are all essential to a community's knowledge base (table C). These vary over time and place; they interact with social work and may be mutually influencing; and yet they must never be objects of hegemonic "power over" by social work knowledge, theory, or practice. This leads to a third point: it is likewise probable, as table C suggests, that all forms of local knowledge—be they declarative, procedural, or complex—have some bearing on the localization project in social work. Holism is fundamental.

In social work, as in the social sciences generally, post-structuralist and postmodernist analysis is increasingly *de rigueur*, and in both, there is a discernable movement away from claims to objective truth or to universal models of practice (Leonard 1997). To some observers, postmodern and post-structuralist critiques call into question the project of seeking models (in the plural) of localizing social work. We are not certain that we would go this far, but we are sympathetic to those who critique the presumptuous claim to seek *a* model of localizing social work. There is much in postmodernist and post-structuralist theories that is helpful. Reality does not exist independent of human representations (Spiro 1992).

In other respects, we are not so sure about postmodernist assumptions. Lyotard and his followers, for example, claim that the grand, meta-narratives of modernity are exercises in futility (1984); yet we wonder if he and others might be oblivious to the possibility that this claim might be yet another (modernist even?) meta-narrative. In any case: meticulous scholars of most theoretical persuasions, postmodernist/post-structuralist or not, would agree that nuances, diversities, exceptions, and shades of grey may be the most important details to full understanding. A reasonable mandate for social work might be to try to come to terms with the diverse efforts at rendering social work sensitive to local understandings and practices, amongst social work clients, social work practitioners, and the agencies and communities in which both function.

At the same time, spirituality and case vignettes both offer fruitful means of appreciating local circumstances, of comparing innovations across trans-regional boundaries, and of determining those aspects that might have varying degrees of common ground and divergence across cultures and places. We think that scholars should try to seek such signposts—both culturally and analytically—that might be useful for research and practice; recent theory should inform, but should not make us shy away from, this mandate. Otherwise: there are dangers in being too aloof to practicalities, and to the need for concrete and declarative theory, contexts, and methods of application. Practitioners, and the communities with which they work, are very often practical people who deal with real life situations. And they need us to be practical, too.

Yet, the continued differentiation between multicultural practice and theory, on the one hand, and international practice and theory, on the other, obscures and neglects as much as it explains or illuminates (Al-Krenawi and Graham 1999c):

> There are important social, political, cultural, economic, and legal differences between multicultural practice in, say, North America versus domestic practice abroad. But many differences *also* occur between—and in some respects within—non-Western countries. And at the same time, there are many overlapping principles between practice within and outside the West. These, given the historic tendency to reify into "international" versus "multicultural" fields of interest, are either lost, or serve to reinforce a multicultural reference to one particular country, rather than transnational structures (Al-Krenawi and Graham 1999c, 271–2).

Political scientists, sociologists, and other scholars argue convincingly for the transformative capacities of globalization, where money, ideas, labour, and products move seamlessly across national boundaries (Graham, Swift, and Delaney 2007), and where time and place are increasingly compressed (Harvey 1989). Globalization may affect helping professions in relation to individual and collective identity, impact of economic inequalities on health and functioning, and through shaping of dissemination of knowledge itself (Kirmayer and Minas 2000). Many professions, such as psychiatry, predict that universalizing practices such as what is found in the DSM-IV, may become more relativistically sensitive to place and cultural background (Bhugra and Mastrogianni 2004). But with "ever greater numbers of people living in circumstances in which disembodied institutions linking local practices with globalized social relations organize major aspects of day to day life," dissonances may occur, in which individuals may be alienated from either, or both of, "localities and global space" (Bhugra and Mastrogianni 2004, 11).

Our work with the Bedouin-Arab of the Negev confirms some psychiatrists' supicions that globalization will probably not lead to cultural homogenisation worldwide (Kirmayer and Minas 2000). Such considerations are particularly important to the Bedouin-Arab community in the Negev, which is undergoing a remarkable period of change. Within a generation, Bedouin communities have been transformed from nomadism/semi-nomadism, to settlement, and from a time-honoured, agrarian economic base to growing participation in Israeli life. "In this clash between totalizing globalization versus localization, social work has a role to affirm an indigenous community's lived destiny, however subtle and dynamic particular cadences between globalization and localization might be. But only if its knowledge base and practices cultivate sensitivity to, and knowledge of, those cultural aspects that are of enduring importance to the minority community in question" (Al-Krenawi and Graham 1999c, 286).

Case Vignettes

Case vignettes that highlight particular approaches to localization are potentially fruitful venues for generating a more sophisticated theory and method. Case vignettes have long been used in social service and medical research and practice, and are perfectly well-established means of helping to assess the quality of care that may be available (Dale and Middleton 1990; Gibelman 2002). As previous work in the area points out, providers can be presented with vignettes of case material and asked to indicate what they would typically do in such a situation. Vignettes are easily administered, inexpensive, and account for case mix because everyone sees the same case. Case vignettes can be altered to differ by race or gender, and to examine disparities in service delivery. They can be used in social services research wherever there are accepted practice guidelines (Fihn 2000; McMillen, Proctor, Megivern, Striley, Cabasa, Munson, and Dickey 2005; Peabody, Luck, Glassman, Dresselhaus, and Lee 2000).

We suspect, too, that they can be used as a viable tool for generating knowledge in trans-regional, trans-cultural contexts: particularly if analytical points may be shifted from one culture/context to another unique culture/context. This can be seen in our recent works summarizing case study examples from our previous scholarship (Al-Krenawi and Graham 2003a, 2007). Limits of space preclude elaboration of our work on polygamous family formation, blood vengeance, cultural mediation, and traditional healing; each of which provides insight into how social work is practised very differently amongst the Arab communities with which we work, as compared to many practice situations in Canada (Al-Krenawi and Graham 1996ab, 1997ab, 1999abcd, 2001ab, 2003ab, 2004, 2005, 2006, 2007).

Spirituality in Social Work

Spirituality has been a major theme in the indigenization work we have undertaken. We have busied ourselves with understanding traditional healers such as the Dervish (Al-Krenawi and Graham 1996a, 1997b, 1999b; Al-Krenawi, Graham, and Maoz 1996) and Koranic healers (Al-Krenawi and Graham 1999d): learning from them, applying their methods and theories to social work in an effort at cultural sensitivity, and understanding the world on the spiritual (emic) grounds that they often function. We have written on Islam, on collective ways of knowing, and other things that, to us at least, are spiritual (Al-Krenawi and Graham 2000). To begin with, we like very much the Egyptian scholar Ibrahim Ragab's interest in retaining the best of social work (in its historic and contemporary senses) with the best that local communities might provide to a renewed knowledge base (1990, 1995).

The imperative to render a knowledge base locally and globally accessible is not mutually incompatible, for both may be, at this stage in our profession's history "necessary for understanding the complex articulation of global processes with local or regional conditions" (Smart 1994, 149).

Many scholars in the Global South consciously, and wisely, avoid wholesale rejection of knowledge from the North (Alatas 1995; Al-Krenawi and Graham 1996–2007). The key, in our view, is to have those centres of power in the North come together with communities (scholars, the public, civil society, and social service communities) in the South in a way that is non-hegemonic, collaborative, and mutually enriching to participants and to the discipline's knowledge. Processes that are mutually respectful, and non-hierarchical, nicely align themselves to long-established principles that embrace cooperative or participatory inquiry (Heron 1996; Heron and Reason 2001; Park 2001). Research in nursing and allied disciplines is conclusive regarding the reciprocal knowledge base that occurs when students in one country learn from those in another (Ekstrom and Sigurdsson 2002). Global South scholars, such as Friere in community development (1970), or Gutierrez in liberation theology (1971), have been profoundly transformative of methodologies and analytical assumptions in the Global North and South. Both, it needs to be emphasized (and not coincidentally), are highly relevant to the agenda of internationalizing social work.

And here—at least for the part of the world in which we have been conducting research into international social work, the Muslim Arab world—spirituality is a most useful venue for rendering social work more culturally sensitive, and for indigenizing the knowledge base. As we argue in another venue: the social work profession in North America needs to move beyond its own geographically-bound anchors and understand spirituality in international terms (Graham 2006). Scholarship from the Global North continues to influence the Global South. And we have—replete with charts and longitudinal analyses of the literature—made arguments that Global North journals should encourage scholars in the Global South to publish in Global North journals on spirituality topics from a Global South perspective.

There may be instances where scholars in the Global North could be invited to collaborate in that dissemination (Bradshaw and Graham 2007; Graham 2006). This is not to preclude other complementary imperatives: publishing in journals and other venues situated in the Global South; reading, appreciating, and better integrating into knowledge bases (in the North and South) from these Southern sources; and appreciating multiple means of knowledge production, of which journal articles are merely one, albeit important form. Further writings, beyond the parameters of the present article, could rightly elaborate on these other vital matters. Future research, also beyond the parameters of the present paper, could certainly consider strategies for dialogue within the Global North. For there are many sectors in the North, be it religion, creed, theology, socio-economic class, sexual orientation, race, ethnicity, geography, or other parameters, represent-ing voices that are not always soundly present in mainstream social work writing. And they could form useful alliances within the North, comparable to the North-South alliances that the present paper advocates. In these respects, and in the respects for which we are arguing, reciprocal knowledge production will lead to something much better, and richer, than what might occur in the limited hands of scholars, concepts, and journals oriented too much to current epistemological power bases within the North (Graham 2006).

Conclusion

The two authors have been working in the area for 15 years and have come to a few provisional conclusions. We are all custodians of a social work knowledge base: scholars, practitioners, and in our mind, consumers and the broader public, too. Ours should be a community of mutual expertise. To this end, we should seek the opposite of Melanie Klein's notion of a paranoid schizophrenic position: where those who disagree with you are inevitably, eternally, the enemy; where the Other is evil and must be destroyed either electorally or with a laser sword (Salutin 2005, A15). Rather, the Other could, and should be loved, elevated, and be the person from whom we can learn more about our approach to social work had we not been touched by them. Being open to different, and sometimes competing perspectives is essential. We are often at our creative best when we are at the edges of our own disciplines, the edges of our own knowledge bases (Landry 2005, 13).

Unfortunately, as in other disciplines, social work has its share of scholars and practitioners who are not always in tune with these possibilities. We can sadly think of examples of social work scholarship that are highly derivative, others that say little that is new, and others that are acutely intent on shutting down what they perceive to be previous, and outdated modes of under-standing the social world: a sort of our way or the highway approach to life and scholarship that is antithetical to deeper discernment. Occasionally, all three weaknesses present themselves in one scholar or scholarly output. Open, inclusive dialogue, even for talking professions such as social work, may be a hard slog. It requires humility of disposition, confidence of position, and openness of mind, all of which are not as common as one might like (Graham 2008).

But press on we must; not just for our own purpose, nor for the sake of a professional discipline whose period in history may one day come to an end, perhaps in the lifetime of some readers of this book chapter. Our focus must remain on an imperative that has everything to do with a manifest imbalance of power between the South and the North; and our great potential, in response, to commit to another level and type of social justice. "Anti-colonial approaches," "cultural sensitivity," and "cultural competence" involves a dialogue between the local (community) and global (social work) knowledge systems, ensuring that local knowledge is not over-whelmed by the global forces of social work. Social workers are key to this enterprise, to ensure that this dialogue between social work and local community knowledge occurs, and that intervention and knowledge be as sophisticated and helpful as possible. Those who believe the world is globalizing lay equal claim to the increasing extent and importance of the rapid movement of ideas, people, and the commensurate flattening of geographic boundaries (Friedman 2005; Lyons 1999; Saul 2005). To the end of greater inclusive social work knowledge and theory, the current chapter argues the case for attention to spirituality and case vignettes. These are modest means of achieving greater representation, and may provide greater insight into that recently coined concept of "localizing" social work.

Table A: Diversity of Terms for Local Knowledge and Various Connotations (Antweiler 1998)	
Term, Synonyms	**Meaning, Salient Aspect, Implicit Significance, Antonym**
Indigenous Knowledge (internationally the most widespread term)	culturally integrated knowledge; knowledge of small, marginal/non-western groups
Endogenous Knowledge	of internal origin, as opposed to exogenous or external knowledge
Native Knowledge/Expertise	implies knowledge of a natural character, closeness to nature
Local Knowledge	knowledge rooted in local or regional culture and ecology
Sustainable Knowledge	sustainable within the natural and cultural environment
Traditional Knowledge	handed down, old, oral (implying static, low-level of change)
Autochthonous Knowledge	on internal origin, culturally integrated
People's Knowledge	broadly disseminated knowledge, knowledge as potential for political resistance, as opposed to elite knowledge
Folk Knowledge, Folk Science, Folk Competence	traditional, rural (in industrial societies)
Little Tradition	tends to denote oral knowledge, as opposed to great tradition
Community Knowledge	related to small social units
Cultural Knowledge, Cognition (in the restricted sense)	culturally integrated and practice oriented
Ethnic Knowledge	related to an ethnic "we" group (ethnicity)
Culturally Specific Knowledge	specificity, singularity, particularity
Ethnoscience (used here to denote local knowledge; previously used to denote the field of research)	scientific (systematic) character (e.g., ethnobotany, ethnosociology, ethnomedicine, ethnopharmacology, ethnoepidemology)
(cultural) Knowledge System (superseded "ethnoscience")	systematic character, generating rules (if X then Y) and structures

(cultural) Belief System, (cultural) Meaning System	Means the same as "knowledge system," but implies a less scientific character
Science of the Concrete	based on that which actually exists and is visible
Experiential Knowledge	as opposed to theoretical knowledge, speculation
Experimental Knowledge	trial and error, as opposed to controlled experiment
Farmers' Knowledge	knowledge relating to the farm as an economic unit
Peasant Knowledge	as opposed to elite knowledge; implies experiences of dependency

Table B: Various Thematic Fields of Local Knowledge (Antweiler 1998, 473)

1. Environmental Knowledge, environmental cognition.

   Knowledge on the natural environment (e.g., plants, animals, ecosystems, natural disasters).

   Knowledge on the anthropogenically modified environment (e.g., risks, management of tropical soils, agroecological knowledge).

   Knowledge on the social and political "environment" (neighbourhood groups, structures of the dominant group, state structures, development projects).

2. Agricultural knowledge (cf. 1.2 above)

3. Medical Knowledge (e.g.,medicinal knowledge, health knowledge, diagnosis, and therapy).

4. Indigenous Technical Knowledge

5. Organizational and management knowledge, including knowledge on conflict management (e.g.,legal knowledge).

6. Knowledge on persons, structures, and relationships within the own society (social cognition).

Table C: Forms of Local Knowledge (Antweiler 1998, 474)

General Forms of Knowledge	Examples
1. Declarative Knowledge 1.1 Factual Knowledge	animals, plants, temperature, social status, prices, salaries, administrative levels
1.2 Categorical Knowledge	categories of organisms, colours, kinship, development project types
2. Procedural Knowledge 2.1 General Process/Rules	farming calendar, religious calendar, environmental crises, household cycle, development project cycle
2.2 Specific Process (scripts, schemes, plans)	everyday routines (e.g., greetings and farewells, natural resource management, ritual sequences, project request schema)

3. Complex Knowledge (concepts; belief systems/ knowledge systems)	cosmology, therapies, models of honour, of marriage, of justice, cropping systems, decision making procedures

References

- Al-Issa, I., ed. 2000. *Al-Junun: Mental Illness in The Islamic World*. Madison, CN: International Universities Press.
- Al-Krenawi, A., J. R. Graham, and B. Maoz. 1996. The Healing Significance of the Negev's Bedouin Dervish. *Social Science and Medicine* 43 (1): 13–21.
- Al-Krenawi, A. and J. R. Graham. 1996a. Social Work Practice and Traditional Healing Rituals Among the Bedouin of the Negev, Israel. *International Social Work* 39 (2): 177–188.
- Al-Krenawi, A. and J. R. Graham. 1996b. Tackling Mental Illness: Roles for Old and New Disciplines. *World Health Forum* 17: 246–248.
- Al-Krenawi, A., J. R. Graham, and S. Al-Krenawi. 1997. Social Work Practice with Polygamous Families. *Child and Adolescent Social Work Journal* 14 (6): 444–458.
- Al-Krenawi, A. and J. R. Graham. 1997a. Nebi-Musa: A Therapeutic Community for Drug Addicts in a Muslim Context. *Transcultural Psychiatry* 34 (3): 377–391.
- Al-Krenawi, A. and J. R. Graham. 1997b. Spirit Possession and Exorcism: The Integration of Modern and Traditional Mental Health Care Systems in the Treatment of a Bedouin Patient. *Clinical Social Work Journal* 25: 211–222.
- Al-Krenawi, A. and J. R. Graham. 1999a. Conflict Resolution Through a Traditional Ritual Among the Bedouin-Arabs of the Negev. *Ethnology: An International Journal of Cultural and Social Anthropology* 38 (2): 163-174.
- Al-Krenawi, A. and J. R. Graham. 1999b. Gender and Biomedical/Traditional Mental Health Utilization Among the Bedouin-Arabs of the Negev. *Culture, Medicine, and Psychiatry* 23 (2): 219–243.
- Al-Krenawi, A. and J. R. Graham. 1999c. Globalization, Identity, and Social Work Practice: What Can we Learn from the Perspective of Working with Bedouin-Arab Peoples? In *Globlization: Challenges and Responses*, ed. S. T. Ismael, 271–286. Calgary: Detselig Press.
- Al-Krenwai, A. and J. R. Graham. 1999d. Social Work and Koranic Mental Health Healers. *International Social Work* 42 (1): 54–66.
- Al-Krenawi, A. and J. R. Graham. 1999e. The story of Bedouin-Arab Women in a Polygamous Marriage. *Women's Studies International Forum* 22 (5): 497–509.
- Al-Krenawi, A. and J. R. Graham. 2000. Islamic Theology and Prayer: Relevance for Social Work Practice. *International Social Work* 43 (3): 289–302.
- Al-Krenawi, A., J. R. Graham, and A. Izzeldin. 2001. The Psychosocial Impact of Polygamous Marriages on Palestinian Women. *Women and Health* 34 (1): 1–16.
- Al-Krenawi, A., V. Slonim-Nevo, Y. Maymon, and S. Al-Krenawi. 2001. Psychological Responses to Blood Vengeance among Arab Adolescents. *Child Abuse and Neglect* 25: 457–472
- Al-Krenawi, A. and J. R. Graham. 2001a. Polygamous Family Structure and its Interaction with Gender: Effects on Children's Academic Achievements and Implications for Culturally Diverse Social Work Practice in Schools. *School Social Work Journal* 25 (3): 1–16.

- Al-Krenawi, A. and J. R. Graham. 2001b. The Cultural Mediator: Bridging the Gap Between a Non-Western Community and Professional Social Work Practice. *British Journal of Social Work* 31 (4): 665–686.

- Al-Krenawi, A., J. R. Graham, and M. Sehwail. 2002. Bereavement Responses Among Palestinian Widows, Daughters, and Sons Following the Hebron Massacre. *Omega: Journal of Death and Dying* 44 (3): 241–255.

- Al-Krenawi, A., J. R. Graham, and V. Slonim-Nevo. 2002. Mental Health Aspects of Arab Adolescents of Polygamous/Monogamous Families. *Journal of Social Psychology* 142 (4): 446–460.

- Al-Krenawi, A. and J. R. Graham. 2003a. Principles of Social Work Practice in the Muslim Arab World. *Arab Studies Quarterly* 26 (4): 75–91.

- Al-Krenawi, A. and J. R. Graham, eds. 2003b. *Multicultural Social Work with Diverse Ethno-Racial Communities in Canada.* Toronto: Oxford University Press.

- Al-Krenawi, A. and J. R. Graham. 2004. Somatization Among Bedouin-Arab Women: Differentiated by Marital Status. *Journal of Divorce and Remarriage* 42(1/2): 131–143.

- Al-Krenawi, A., J. R. Graham, Y. Dean, and N. El-Thabet. 2004. Cross National Study of Attitudes Towards Seeking Professional Help: Jordan, United Arab Emirates (UAE) and Arab in Israel. *International Journal of Social Psychiatry* 50 (1): 92–104.

- Al-Krenawi, A., J. R. Graham, and M. Sehwail. 2004. Mental Health and Violence/ Trauma in Palestine: Implications for Helping Professional Practice. *Journal of Comparative Family Studies* 35 (2): 185–209.

- Al-Krenawi, A. and J. R. Graham. 2005. Marital Therapy for Muslim Arab Couples: Acculturation and Reacculturation. *The Family Journal: Counseling and Therapy for Couples and Families* 13 (3): 300–310.

- Al-Krenawi, A. and J. R. Graham. 2006. A Comparison of Family Functioning, Life and Marital Satisfaction, and Mental Health of Women in Polygamous and Monogamous Marriages. *International Journal of Social Psychiatry* 52(1), 5-17.

- Al-Krenawi, A. and J. R. Graham. 2007b. Localizing Social Work with Bedouin Arab Communities in Israel: Limitations and Possibilties. In *"Indigenization" and Indigenous Social Work Around the World: Towards Culturally Relevant Social Work Education and Practice*, eds. J. Coates, M. Gray, and M. Yellowfeather. London: Ashgate Press.

- Alatas, S. F. 1995. The Sacralization of the Social Sciences: A Critique of an Emerging Theme in Academic Discourse. *Archives de sciences socials des religions* 40 (91): 89–111.

- Antweiler, C. 1998. Local Knowledge and Local Knowing: An Anthropological Analysis of Contested "Cultural Products" in the Context of Development. *Anthropos* 93 (4/6): 469–494.

- Asamoath, Y., L. M. Healey, and N. Mayadas. 1997. Ending the International-Domestic Dichotomy: New Approaches to a Global Curriculum for the Millennium. *Journal of Social Work Education* 33 (2): 389–401.

- Atal, Y. 1981. *Building a Nation: Essays on India.* Delhi: Abhinav.

- Atler, J. S. 2005. *Asian medicine and globalization.* Philadelphia, PA: University of Pennsylvania Press.

- Boddy, J. 1989. *Wombs and Alien Spirits: Women, Men and the Zar Cult in Northern Sudan.* Wisconsin: University of Wisconsin Press.

- Bradshaw, C. and J. R. Graham. 2007. Localization of Social Work Practice, Education and Research: A Content Analysis. *Social Development Issues* 29 (2): 92–111.

- Brumann, C. 1998. The Anthropological Study of Globalization: Towards an Agenda for the Second Phase. *Anthropos* 93: 495–506.

- Bhugra, D. and A. Mastrogianni. 2004. Globalisation and Mental Disorders: Overview with Relation to Depression. *The British Journal of Psychiatry* 184: 10–20.

- Coates, J., M. Gray, and M. Yellowfeather, eds. *"Indigenization" and Indigenous Social Work Around the World: Towards Culturally Relevant Social Work Education and Practice.* London: Ashgate Press.

- Crapanzano, V. 1973. *The Hamadsha: A Study in Moroccan Ethno-Psychiatry.* Berkeley: University of California Press.

- Dale, J. and H. Middleton. 1990. Factors Influencing General Practitioners' Management of Psychosocial and Physical Problems: A Study Using Case Vignettes. *The British Journal of General Practice: The Journal of the Royal College of General Practitioners* 40 (336): 284–288.

- Dominelli, L. 1997. *Anti-Racist Social Work.* London: Macmillan Press.

- Ekstrom, D. N. and H. O. Sigurdsson. 2002. An International Collaboration in Nursing Education Viewed Through the Lens of Critical Social Theory. *Journal of Nursing Education* 41 (7): 289–294.

- El-Islam, M. F. 1982. Arabic Cultural Psychiatry. *Transcultural Psychiatric Research Review* 19 (1): 5–24.

- Fihn, S. D. 2000. The Quest to Quantify. *Journal of the American Medical Association* 283: 1740–1741.

- Friedman, T. L. 2005. *The World is Flat: A Brief History of the Twenty-First Century.* New York: Farrar, Straus and Giroux.

- Freire, P. 1970. *Pedagogy of the Oppressed.* New York: Plenum.

- Gibelman, M. 2002. Treatment Choices in a Managed Care Environment: A Multi-Disciplinary Exploration. *Clinical Social Work Journal* 30 (2): 199–214.

- Gilpin, R. 2001. *Global Political Economy: Understanding the International Economic Order.* Princeton, NJ: Princeton University Press.

- Graham, J. R. 2006. Spirituality and Social Work: A Call for an International Focus of Research. *Arete: A Professional Journal Devoted to Excellence in Social Work* 30 (1): 63–77.

- Graham, J. R. 2008. Who am I? An Essay on Inclusion and Spiritual Growth Through Community and Mutual Appreciation. *Journal of Religion, Spirituality, and Social Work* 27 (1/2): 1–14.

- Graham, J. R., A. Al-Krenawi, and C. Bradshaw. 2000. The Social Work Research Group/NASW Research Secti on/Council on Social Work Research: 1949–1965, an Emerging Research Identity in the American Profession. *Research on Social Work Practice* 10 (5): 622–643.

- Graham, J. R. and A. Al-Krenawi. 1996. A Comparison Study of Traditional Helpers in a Late Nineteenth Century Canadian (Christian) Society and in a Late Twentieth Century Bedouin (Muslim) Society in the Negev, Israel. *Journal of Multicultural Social Work* 4 (2): 31–45.

- Graham, J. R., K. Swift, and R. Delaney. 2007. *Canadian Social Policy: An Introduction.* Toronto: Prentice Hall. Third edition.

- Gray, M. 2002. Cross-Cultural Practice and the Indigenization of African Social Work. *Social Work/Maatskaplike Werk* 38 (4): 324–336.

- Gutierrez, G. 1971. *A Theology of Liberation.* Maryknoll, NY: Orbis.

- Hancock, G. 1989. *Lords of Poverty: The Power, Prestige, and Corruption of the International Aid Business.* New York: Atlantic Monthly Press.

- Harvey, D. 1989. *The Condition of Post-Modernity.* Oxford: Blackwell.

- Healey, L. 1999. International Social Work Curriculum in Historical Perspective. In *All our Futures: Principles and Resources for Social Work Practice in a Global Era*, eds. R. J. Link, and C. S. Ramanathan, 14–29. New York: Brooks Cole.

- Healy, L. 2001. *International Social Work: Professional Action in an Interdependent World.* New York: Oxford University Press.

- Heron, J. 1996. *Co-Operative Inquiry: Research into the Human Condition*. London: Sage Publications.

- Heron, J. and P. Reason. 2001. The Practice of Co-Operative Inquiry: Research "With" Rather Than "On" People. In *Handbook of Action Research: Participative Inquiry and Practice*, eds. P. Reason, and H. Bradbury, 179–188. Thousand Oaks: Sage Publications.

- Kennedy, J. 1967. Nubian Zar Ceremonies as Psychotherapy. *Human Organization* 26 (4): 185–194.

- Kirmayer, L. J. and I. H. Minas. 2000. The Future of Cultural Psychiatry: An International Perspective. *Canadian Journal of Psychiatry* 45: 438–446.

- Kondrat, M. E. and C. S. Ramathan. 1996. International Perspectives and the Local Practitioner: An Exploratory Study of Practitioner Perception of and Attitudes Toward Globalization. *Social Development Issues* 18 (2): 1–17.

- Landry, C. 2005. *The Creative City: A Toolkit for Urban Innovators*. London: Earthscan.

- Leonard, P. 1997. *Postmodern Welfare*. Thousand Oaks: Sage Press.

- Lyons, K. 1999. *International Social Work: Themes and Perspectives*. Aldershot: Ashgate Arena.

- Lyotard, J. F. 1984. *The Postmodern Condition: A Report on Knowledge*. Minneapolis: University of Minnesota.

- Maxwell, J., L. Williams, K. Ring, and I. Cambridge. 2003. Caribbean Social Work Education: The University of the West Indies. *Caribbean Journal of Social Work* 2: 11–35.

- McMillen, J. C., E. K. Proctor, D. Megivern, C. W. Striley, L. J. Cabasa, M. R. Munson, and B. Dickey. 2005. Quality of Care in Social Services: Research Agenda and Methods. *Social Work Research* 29 (3): 181–191.

- Midgley, J. 1981. *Professional Imperialism: Social Work in the Third World*. London: Heinemann.

- Modesto, K. F., A. J. Weaver, and K. J. Flannelly. 2006. A Systematic Review of Religious and Spiritual Research in Social Work. *Christianity and Social Work* 33(1): 77–89.

- Morrissette, V., B. McKenzie, and L. Morrissette. 1993. Towards an Aboriginal Model of Social Work Practice: Cultural Knowledge and Traditional Practices. *Canadian Social Work Review/Revue Canadienne de Service Social* 10(1): 91–108.

- Nagpaul, H. 1993. Analysis of Social Work Teaching Material in India: The Need for Indigenous Foundations. *International Social Work* 36 (3): 207–220.

- Nagpaul, H. 1996. *Modernization and Urbanization in India: Problems and Issues*. Jaipur & New Delhi: Rawat.

- Nagpaul, H. 1996. *Social Work in Urban India*. Jaipur & New Delhi: Rawat.

- Nathan, D. 2004. *Globalization and Indigenous Peoples in Asia: Changing the Local-Global Interface*. Thousand Oaks: Sage Publications.

- Noble, C. 2004. Social Work Education, Training, and Standards in the Asia-Pacific Region. *Social Work Education* 23 (5): 527–536.

- Okasha, A. 1999. Mental Health Services and in the Arab World. *Eastern Mediterranean Health Journal* 5 (2): 223–230

- Osei, H. K. 1996. The Indigenisation of Social Work Practice and Education in Africa: The Dilemma of Theory and Method. *Maatskaplike-Werk/Social-Work,* 32 (3): 215–225.

- Park, P. 2001. Knowledge and Participatory Research. In *Handbook of Action Research: Participative inquiry and practice*, eds. P. Reason and H. Bradbury, 81–90. Thousand Oaks: Sage Publications.

- Park, K. S. 1999. Internationalization: Direction of Social Welfare Policy Education in the Future. *Arete: A Professional Journal Devoted to Excellence in Social Work* 23(2): 33–45.

- Peabody, J. W., J. Luck, P. Glassman, T. R. Dresselhaus, and M. Lee. 2000. Comparison of Vignettes, Standardized Patients and Chart Abstraction: A Prospective Validation Study of Three Methods for Measuring Quality. *Journal of the American Medical Association* 283: 1715–1722.

- Ragab, I. A. 1995. The Middle East and Egypt. In *International Handbook on Social Work Education*, eds. N. S. Mayadas, T. D. Watts, and D. Elliott, 281–304. Westport: Greenwood Press.

- Ragab, I. A. 1990. How Social Work Can Take Root in Developing Countries. *Social Development-Issues* 12 (3): 38–51.

- Rehmatullah, S. 2002. *Social Welfare in Pakistan.* London: Oxford University Press.

- Roach, S. C. 2005. *Cultural Autonomy, Minority Rights, and Globalization.* London: Ashgate.

- Salutin, R. 2005. Proud despite the facts. *The Globe and Mail* (March 18): A15.

- Saul, J. R. 2005. *The Collapse of Globalism: And the Reinvention of the World.* Toronto: Viking.

- Schellenberg, J. A. 1996. *Conflict Resolution: Theory, Research, and Practice.* Albany, NY: University of New York Press.

- Schiele, J. H. 1997. The Contour and Meaning of Afrocentric Social Work. *Journal of Black Studies* 27 (6): 800–819

- Schiele, J. H. 1996. Afrocentricity: An Emerging Paradigm in Social Work. *Social Work* 41 (3): 284–294.

- Smart, B. 1994. Sociology, Globalisation and Postmodernity: Comment on the Sociology for one World Thesis. *International Sociology* 9 (2): 149–159.

- Spiro, M. E. 1992. Cultural Relativism and the Future of Anthropology. In *Rereading Cultural Anthropology*, ed. G. E. Marcus. Durham: Duke University Press.

- Swigonski, M. 1996. Challenging Privilege Through Afrocentric Social Work Practice. *Social Work* 41 (2): 153–161.

- Wong, Y. L. R., S. Cheng, S. Y. Choi, K. Ky, S. LeBa, K. Tsang, and L. Y. 2003. Deconstructing Culture in Cultural Competence: Dissenting Voices from Asian-Canadian Practitioners. *Canadian Social Work Review* 20 (2): 149.

- Zifcak, S. 2005. *Globalisation and the Rule of Law.* New York: Routledge.

Chapter 14

Promoting Social Work Education in Ukraine

Brad McKenzie and Nina Hayduk

Winnipeg is home to a large population of Ukrainian people, many of whom immigrated from Lviv, and other regions in western Ukraine, and originally settled in the north end of the city. From early settlement, Ukrainian social and cultural organizations emerged to provide forms of mutual aid and to promote ethnic solidarity and support. One of the key organizations was the Manitoba branch of Ukrainian Canadian Social Services (UCSS). Although its role in the provision of services has diminished over time, it has remained a source of support for new immigrants and has played a role in providing material support to those in need in Ukraine.

In 1992, shortly after Ukraine became an independent state, one of us (Brad McKenzie) attended an international conference on foster family care in Budapest with the then president of the local chapter of UCSS. Social work was virtually an unknown profession in Ukraine at the time, and UCSS was particularly interested in promoting a role for social work in the "new Ukraine." As a beginning step, the organization sponsored three individuals from Ukraine to the conference. Informal discussions at the conference led to an invitation to spend time in Ukraine to meet with individuals and organizations interested in the development of the social work profession; a six week volunteer placement was organized in 1994. Although the event was hosted by the Kyiv Mohyla Academy, volunteers met with a variety of government, university, and community organizations to provide lectures and promote greater awareness about the profession of social work and social work education.

In 1995, a Master of Social Work (MSW) Program was initiated at Kyiv Mohyla Academy with funding from the European community. Canadian attention shifted to Lviv, the hub of western Ukraine, with a population of more than 800,000 and no social work education program on the radar screen. The breakup of the Soviet Union had created new opportunities for the advancement of democracy, but the economic and social conditions for most Ukrainians had deteriorated by the mid-1990s, and there was a growing interest in developing new responses to social issues. The Vice-Rector of International Relations, and members of the English Language department at Lviv Polytechnic National University, led by Nina Hayduk, had some knowledge of social work, and expressed an interest in collaborating in the development of a social work program. Back home, the Canadian Centre on Disability Studies (CCDS), a Winnipeg-based research and development organization with Henry Enns as its executive director, expressed interest in a jointly sponsored initiative that would establish both a social work education program and a community-based service model to respond comprehensively to the needs of disabled people. Based on these commitments, a partnership group consisting of a university and a community-based voluntary organization in each country was established. Development work proceeded with separate meetings in each country and communication updates through the internet.

The first application for funding to the Canadian International Development Agency (CIDA) in 1996 was unsuccessful. Feedback suggested the need for building greater political support in Ukraine both at the city and national levels. With collaboration from colleagues at Lviv Polytechnic National University, a community needs study was undertaken to better understand local priorities and begin a dialogue with government and voluntary sector agencies about the broad goals of the project. Government and community respondents were enthusiastic about the initiative, and some of these individuals became important allies in promoting support for the initiative at the national level. In 1997, the president of UCSS and Brad McKenzie returned to Ukraine. Along with their Ukrainian partners, they met with key government officials, notably within the Department of Education, to gain official support for the project. Following this visit, a new proposal was drafted that was submitted to CIDA in the fall of 1998. In the spring of 1999, the $2.34 million project to develop an undergraduate social work education program at Lviv Polytechnic National University and to strengthen community-based services for persons with disabilities was approved.

This chapter describes the development of the social work program within the Department of Sociology at Lviv Polytechnic National University and the unique nature of its partnership with community-based disability organizations. As well, the quality and sustainability of the initiative following the end of CIDA funding in the fall of 2003 is examined.[1] The initiative brought together four key implementing partners. These were: the Faculty of Social Work of the University of Manitoba (the lead agency); the Winnipeg-based Canadian Centre for Disability Studies (CCDS); a consortium of community-based disability organizations in Lviv operating under the auspices of the Lviv Independent Living Resource Centre; and Lviv Polytechnic National University (the main host partner). The goal of the project was to: promote civil society and social change through the development of social work education; support community-based social services, including a special focus on disability organizations; and develop a partnership between the university and social service organizations.

There were two components to the project. The objective of the first, and largest, component was to develop a sustainable social work education

---

[1] Brad McKenzie was the director of the initiative, known as the *Reforming Social Services: Canada-Ukraine Project*, and Nina Hayduk became the head of the new Social Work Program at Lviv Polytechnic National University after completing her MSW at the University of Manitoba.

program with ongoing participation from the community at Lviv Polytechnic National University. Between 1999 and 2003, a four year Bachelor of Social Work (BSW) program was developed, and 140 social work students were admitted to the program. This program was accredited in 2003. Although CIDA funding for the project ended in 2003, the program not only has been continued, but also has established a Master of Social Work program. The MSW program was accredited in 2005. The BSW program, which is based on a generalist model, has more social work instructional hours than the typical Canadian program and 800 hours of field instruction time. The MSW program includes both direct practice courses and courses pertaining to planning and social policy. Each student in the graduate program must complete a research focused thesis. During the four year CIDA sponsored project, more than 250 agency staff participated in professional development courses in social work sponsored by the social work component.

The objective of the second component was to build a strong consumer-based advocacy and service organization for disabled people based on the independent living philosophy. This involved a partnership between the Lviv Independent Living Resource Centre (LILRC) and CCDS. This objective reflected the need to transform both the ideology and service paradigm based on marginalization, stigmatization, and the institutionalization of persons with disabilities in Ukraine to a model consistent with the independent living paradigm. In fact, a more enlightened approach had been initiated in Ukraine by a number of organizations affiliated with the LILRC, and the second component of the project was designed to build on these strengths. By 2003, the LILRC had a well-developed organizational structure, a service model based on support, self-help, and advocacy, and had become an influential local and national advocate for the rights of the disabled.

Although the two components were guided by somewhat different objectives, the synergy between the two components, including joint management of the project, had several benefits. For example, the university became an important partner in initiatives designed to promote accessibility, and disability organizations became field education sites. They supported the project in obtaining a more accessible building for the new social work program, and became active participants in the development of the social work curriculum, including the design of a special course on social work and disability issues. In effect, the partnership between the social work education program and the disability community, which was a central feature of the project at inception, became a model for the extension of university-community partnerships throughout the implementation phase of the social work component of the project. There has been a dramatic growth in social work education in Ukraine over the past decade, and the Social Work Program at Lviv Polytechnic has become one of the three university-based programs (other programs include Kyiv Mohyla University and Uzhgorod University) to play a leadership role in the development of the profession in Ukraine (Bridge 2002).

Challenges

The development of the social work profession and a more progressive approach to social services in Ukraine has faced a number of challenges. First, growing social problems have not been matched by concomitant growth in state-sponsored social welfare measures. Under the Soviet system, a broad social safety net had been established through employment policies, and publicly provided education, health care, and pension provisions. Although both the economic and social welfare system created under state socialism prior to 1991 was unsustainable, Ukraine has experienced more difficulties in the transition to a market-oriented economy than many other eastern European countries. Unemployment increased after independence and remained high throughout the 1990s; the GDP declined for much of the decade, and poverty and inequality increased (Kalachova 2002). Low wages and pensions were eroded by high inflation, and lower government revenues, coupled with inefficiencies and corruption, have not only made it difficult to address old problems, but have also contributed to new problems.

Thus the stigmatized treatment of marginalized groups, including the disabled, has been slow to change. Most children in out-of-home care live in overcrowded and inadequately equipped residential institutions (World Organization Against Torture (OMCT) 2002). Moreover, the number of orphans and children lacking parental care doubled during the 1990s to more than 100,000 and there has been a significant growth in the number of disabled children (United Nations Country Team (UNCT) 2002, 24). Other significant problems include the growth in street children, young offenders, HIV/AIDS, and the trafficking of women and children abroad (OMCT 2002).

A second challenge was the underdeveloped non-government social service sector. There was almost no voluntary social service sector in Ukraine prior to independence; however, the 1990s witnessed a rapid growth in the number of voluntary organizations attempting to respond to newly identified social needs. International assistance has provided support to a growing number of initiatives in selected sectors; for example, by 1999, Lviv developed a number of progressive programs in the disability field, and some early efforts to provide new services to children had emerged. However, these, and most other non-government organizations, are under-funded, and services are poorly coordinated.

The lack of collaboration between the state and voluntary sectors is a continuing problem, and work with the voluntary sector presents a dilemma. On the one hand, non-government organizations contribute to progressive social change because they are willing to respond proactively to local needs rather than await approval from a highly centralized and frequently unresponsive administrative structure. On the other hand, reliance on this sector alone encourages the off-loading of social services essential to equity. Although some projects are developed with international assistance, and make a short-term contribution to social reform, many are not sustained after project funding has ended. In the case of locally initiated NGOs, the inability to secure government funding or raise funds locally makes these organizations primarily dependent on volunteers. Although there are several notable success stories, most local NGOs make an insignificant contribution to social service reform.

A third challenge was the absence of social work as a profession and the limited range of social services provided to individuals and families. Social issues that were not defined as the state's responsibility under communism were not officially recognized and therefore were not addressed in an open manner (Constable and Mehta 1994). Under these circumstances, the role and function of social work in Eastern European countries was often delegated to families, and to women in particular (Mayadas, Watts, and Elliott 1997). When families could not deal with problems, the state was forced to intervene, and union or party officials were responsible for filling the gap between "officially proclaimed and actual social rights" (Lorenz 1994). Most social service activities were confined to regulatory functions, such as the distribution of financial support or actions pertaining to child protection, with a strong social control orientation. In 1999 there was no social work education program in Lviv; the profession's closest allies were psychology, sociology, and social pedagogy. Within the human services, there was a strong emphasis on specialization. Themes such as the integration of policy and practice and the "generalist" were met with skepticism. Yet the nature and scope of social problems made it apparent that the profession's role as an advocate for progressive social change would depend on its ability to transcend approaches focusing on the micro-environment and an over-emphasis on specialization.

Finally, there were questions about the extent to which universities would embrace an applied profession with an extensive commitment to field education. Questions also existed as to whether the university would make the necessary adaptations to curriculum policies and procedures to accommodate a different model of education. For example, there was a need within the university to allocate sufficient time and credit for the field practicum component within a curriculum that was already overburdened with courses and instructional hours. Field education was a major challenge for other reasons. First, there were no professional social workers within the service delivery system who could provide field supervision or instruction to social work students, and the role of the social worker within social agencies was not yet clearly defined. As well, social agencies had limited resources, and the ability to support student learning was a challenge even where there was a personal or agency level commitment to the goals of field instruction.

Conceptual Framework

It has been argued that social work can make a major contribution to emerging social reform efforts in eastern Europe (Constable and Mehta 1994); however, Midgley (1981) notes that the uncritical application of western models of social work practice and education based on an elitist belief that social work has a universally relevant methodology and an international professional identity represents nothing less than a form of professional imperialism. At the same time, approaches that are introduced without adequate efforts to include a social change agenda based on a critique of the cultural and socio-economic realities of the recipient country, may relegate such approaches to the margins of any social reform movement.

There was a need, then, to ensure the availability of qualified service providers who could promote international standards of practice for the profession (Edwards, Roth, Davis, and Papeskee 2000), but the introduction of international perspectives had to be combined with information and discourse about local needs and knowledge. Wilson and Whitmore (2000) note that the potential contribution of social work to meaningful international development will be enhanced by a strong commitment to the process of "accompaniment," which incorporates principles of partnership in "working with" local people in building social capital. At the more global level, Healy (2001) supports a social development framework in enhancing the ability of social work to play an influential role in global social change.

Early dialogue with university officials and agency staff in Lviv indicated a strong commitment to reform, a willingness to alter university policies to meet the requirements of a new social work curriculum, and community support for a new profession that would promote progressive social change and provide opportunities for ongoing professional training for staff already employed in the social services. Both the consumer oriented disability group, who had a vision of a new type of professional in the helping services, and agency staff became advocates for a generalist model of undergraduate social work education and a new, more participatory approach to learning. While it was recognized that curriculum building and instruction in the early stages would draw extensively on western models of social work education common to Canada, principles and strategies were adopted to ensure adequate attention to the incorporation of local experiences and knowledge, particularly as the project matured. From the beginning, the two universities agreed that the transition from knowledge transfer to a more collaborative model of knowledge development would be based on principles associated with social development and the indigenization of knowledge.

Historically, international partnerships have been primarily unilateral in that information flowed from professionals in the more developed country to the recipient nation. Development, in such partnerships, involved the transfer of western models of education and practice, without consideration of cultural differences and the appropriateness of these methods in addressing the nature and scope of social problems in different parts of the world. As dissenting voices emerged both from inside and outside developing countries, a more thoughtful approach to international collaboration has emerged, which now measures effectiveness by the appropriateness of responses to local needs and their service delivery systems, as well as the degree of equality and reciprocity within these partnership arrangements.

Social development was selected as the model for project implementation in this case since it embraces a participatory approach to capacity building. However, ambiguity about the meaning of social development complicates the application of a social development approach. After the second world war, the concept was used to convey a dual focus on both economic and social development, and Midgley (1995, 23) reiterates this orientation in his definition of social development as a "process of planned social change designed to promote the well-being of the population as a whole in conjunction with the dynamic process of economic development." He contrasts social development with other approaches to social welfare such as philanthropy, social work, and social administration because social development focuses on developing opportunities as opposed to dealing with individuals through rehabilitative or personal service responses. Curiously, social development is identified as a distinct field of practice rather than a conceptual framework that might guide the practice of social work.

Midgley (1995) notes that the preoccupation with micro level practice and social pathologies within social work may limit the degree to which the goal of "social work as social development" can be achieved. He also situates economic development as an aspect of social development. This is similar to the concept of community development as this has evolved from a multidisciplinary body of practice theory and knowledge in the international context. The definition of community development as a model that includes community economic development has become more common, even in Canada, in recent years (Frank and Smith 1999). However, it lacks a social work emphasis on policy change and connecting policy to practice inherent in the definition of social development. Tucker Rambally (1999) argues that social development is primarily concerned with social justice, and the development and transformation of social structures to ensure social justice. Economic development may fail to address issues of equity, and Campfens (1996) notes that the goal of social development is to promote the well-being of people. Issues of social justice, equity, and well-being are core elements of social development that shape the approach to, or critique of, economic development within any particular context.

Social development in international social work has also been associated with efforts to link micro and macro levels of practice (Asamoah, Kealy, and Maydadas 1997), respond proactively to issues of globalization, and reinforce social work principles associated with empowerment, social and economic justice, capacity-building and problem solving with individuals, families, groups, and communities (International Federation of Social Workers, 2000). Early planning meetings between stakeholders in both countries were used to establish this model as a general framework for project development, and to address immediate issues, such as curriculum development and student recruitment.

The importance attached to principles associated with the project's social development framework served to guide decision-making at the different stages of project development: strategic planning, operational planning, and implementation. This framework included a commitment to empowerment, and this is essential to the sustainability of new time limited international development projects. Thus the project was conceptualized as a process that involved more extensive knowledge and human resource transfers to project activities in Ukraine in the early phase of implementation, a collaborative form of partnership during the middle to late stages, and the transfer of full power and control by the final stage. In the final stage, and following the formal conclusion of the project in 2003, it was recognized that Canadian partners would be used more as consultants who acted in response to requests for assistance from Ukrainian partners.

In adopting social development as a framework for the design and implementation of the *Reforming Social Services: Canada-Ukraine Project,* project planners recognized the following principles:

- the need to incorporate a critique of approaches to economic development that are unresponsive to underlying principles of social justice;
- a primary focus on capacity-building for social welfare reform and models of education and community development that could realize this goal;
- the importance of both institutionally-based and community-based training to capacity-building;
- the need to build an undergraduate educational model that incorporated participatory approaches to learning, the development of critical analytic skills, and a generalist model of education where linkages between policy and practice were emphasized;
- the importance of fostering collaborative approaches to education and social action, particularly between the university and social service agencies and among the government and non-government sectors, with the goal of developing a more responsive range of community-based services; and
- an emphasis on indigenization, where both Ukrainian and Canadian partners share in decision-making about the nature and scope of social work knowledge and approaches to be transferred, with particular attention to how these interact with local culture, values, needs, economics, and political realities.

It was recognized that curriculum development and adaptation are ongoing and that the process will be shaped, in part, by interactions with community agencies and organizations. Partnership development with community agencies was recognized as important to sustainability and to the general goal of social change. These partnerships provided ongoing support for maintaining and growing the new social work education program. Agencies, including field placement organizations, would become potential employers of graduates. Community partnerships would also lead to service innovations, and, through the engagement with students and new graduates, potential change in institutional practices by enhancing the quality and effectiveness of services.

Curriculum Building Partnerships

The initial curriculum for the social work program reflected an adaptation of the model at the University of Manitoba, with its emphasis on the generalist and a commitment to approximately 800 hours of field instruction. This decision followed a community consultation phase that involved a visit to Canada for key university staff and advisory committee members, a needs survey of community agencies, and a series of community meetings. The process confirmed support for the proposed model of social work education and a commitment on the part of local agencies to host students during their field education. The consultation phase also clarified the need for a significant investment in field education training for agency staff who would supervise social work students, and highlighted the interest of staff in ongoing training designed to improve their own capacity to deliver supportive, family-centred services.

As a result, three course modules, each nine days in duration (160 hours of instruction in total) were designed and delivered to agency staff selected from both the government and non-government sectors. There was a dual focus to the training: to prepare agency staff for responsibilities related to the supervision of social work students and to enhance staff capacity for the delivery of quality social services. This certificate program, designed and delivered in 2000–01, was evaluated following the first year (Rudy 2002). Based on results that confirmed the success of the model, the course was offered in each of the three following years. Canadian staff provided almost all instruction during the first year, but by the end of the project, a shared model of instruction involving both Canadian and Ukrainian staff had evolved.

This course was critical to the development of community partnerships and graduates from the course became agency supervisors for students during their field placement experiences, as well as community advocates for the program. A number of the graduates from the course have become involved as members of the advisory committee to the program or as guest lecturers in social work courses. Agency participants in the course also successfully advocated for additional community workshops that were sponsored by the project on more specialized topics such as mediation, interventions related to family violence, and fund-raising strategies.[2]

---

[2] An important aspect of building university-community partnerships is direct involvement in research and development activities. This activity was encouraged through the provision of small development grants to community agencies. In turn, these agencies worked collaboratively with the university, including students, in developing service innovations or undertaking research projects on topics such as family violence. Curriculum development has been an evolutionary process. In the early stages, the program was designed around generalist principles, and new courses on anti-oppression, social development, feminist perspectives, and community development were introduced. An innovative approach to curriculum development was the

Efforts to build partnerships with community agencies was essential to the success of the program, but it was also recognized that the engagement of qualified Ukrainian social work faculty were also important to long-term sustainability. Although the project design phase recognized that most social work courses in the early implementation stage would be taught by visiting instructors, Ukrainian instructors had to be recruited or trained to assume social work faculty roles. One strategy was the sponsorship of four candidates for advanced social work education conditional on their commitment to return and teach in the program.[3] Other instructors have been recruited from allied professions and sociology. Some of the program's own graduates are now employed as junior lecturers in the program. Ukrainian instructors now teach all courses in both the BSW and MSW programs, although Canadian instructors may teach an occasional course as a visiting instructor.

Planning for sustainability required attention to factors other than the development of a core of well qualified instructors. Student demand for the program has remained high since program inception, and considerable attention was devoted to the design a quality curriculum. Curriculum issues were addressed by involving Canadian instructors in teaching courses during the early cycle of courses and then producing course manuals, in collaboration with Ukrainian instructors, to guide future teaching. External strategies to build sustainability involved ensuring a long-term commitment to the program by the University and building relationships with community groups and agencies as advocates for the program. The University's commitment, which was established with ongoing support from key advocates within senior administration, was symbolized with the allocation of a permanent building to the new Department of Sociology and Social Work during the second year of the project.

Professional and Community Change

The promotion of progressive professional and community change involved several activities. First, it was hypothesized that student involvement in agency activities through their field placements would support the adoption of innovative practices if this was combined with professional training for field supervisors that encouraged them to support students in promoting such practices. Evaluation activities, undertaken at the end of the project, found evidence that this expectation had been met in a number of organizations (Faculty of Social Work, University of Manitoba, 2003). Second, faculty involvement in community issues, including community

---

approach used to design content for a course on Social Work and Disability Issues. This course was designed by the Disability Component of the project and taught by an instructor proposed by this component. Although early attention in all courses was given to the inclusion of Ukrainian materials and examples, the amount of Ukrainian content has expanded considerably over time. This is a result not only of the increase in Ukrainian social work publications, but also research reports produced both by faculty and students on local social issues. These materials are an important element in indigenizing the curriculum.

[3] Two of these instructors received their MSW degrees at the University of Manitoba and two completed the MSW program at Kyiv-Mohyla Academy. One has since completed her Ph.D. and the other three faculty members are engaged in Ph.D. studies. All are currently teaching in the program.

research, work with disability organizations, and the initiation of a new association focused on the promotion of mediation, has helped to promote a social reform agenda. At the national level, the faculty played instrumental roles in advancing a more progressive model of social work education through conference presentations and involvement in curriculum development, including the joint sponsorship of a conference on the development of models for social work education. Third, the provision of ongoing workshops and training was designed to support this general objective.

One of the more significant contributions to the community was the design and delivery of the *Innovations in Social Development* course, which was provided in three modules, each two weeks in duration, to approximately 30 agency staff from the government and non-government sectors. Staff were selected for the course in dyads, based on a proposal to develop and evaluate an innovative social service project over a one-year period of time. In addition to classroom instruction on planning, managing, and evaluating a new project, participants received ongoing supervision and support from two supervisors (one from Ukraine and one from Canada) and small grants, if required, to meet essential expenses during the implementation phase of their projects. Twelve projects, including projects related to family violence, youth addictions, and offender rehabilitation, were successfully launched during the year-long course, but one unanticipated result was the development of ongoing partnerships between participants from different organizations, including those from the government and non-government sectors. One example of an activity emerging from this initiative was the formation of a committee to lobby the mayor on the need to support social service innovation and foster more collaboration, including shared space among state and voluntary sector organizations.[4]

Evaluation

Funding for the project from the Canadian government concluded in 2003. The results documented in the final report to CIDA (Faculty of Social Work, University of Manitoba, 2003) indicate the achievement of major outcome objectives and related project outputs consistent with the model of social development. However, the sustainability of the social work education model was re-examined in early 2006, using a modified case study approach consisting of a review of current social work literature in Ukraine, critical personal reflections on the effects of the program and focus group interviews and discussions with representatives from four primary stakeholders: agency-based field instructors, the Advisory Committee to the Social Work Program, social work instructors, and social work students near the end of their program of studies. Selected interviews were completed with key

---

[4] The course has now been modified and included as a core requirement with the MSW Program. Project proposals developed by some of the students during the course have been revised and developed as new community-based initiatives.

informants from other universities who were involved with the Social Work Program in matters such as accreditation and the evaluation of students.

There is a growing body of literature on social work in Ukraine, and a number of these publications, including two doctoral dissertations by Ukrainian scholars (Hayduk 2005; Mykytenko 2005), reflect efforts to adapt the transfer of knowledge emerging from the project to the Ukrainian context. Drawing on the project's experience, Savka (2005) documents the influence of social work on social policy development in Ukraine, and its relationship to democracy and civil society. He notes that the profession's influence on social policy is oriented to social change and this differs markedly from state initiated social policies that are preoccupied with regulatory functions and the rationing of scarce resources. These observations reinforce the importance of integrating policy and practice content within the emerging models of social work education in Ukraine.[5]

Interviews with individuals and focus group participants in the case study were designed to elicit general comments on the Social Work Program, its students, and its relationship with the community. Respondents were invited to comment on both strengths and weaknesses. These results provide feedback on the social development model used in the planning and implementation of the project, including future challenges. Four themes identified in the following summary emerged from the data. They are based on underlying concepts or topics that capture the general focus of comments from respondents.

Theme 1: Development of the Profession

Respondents noted the growth in recognition of social work as a distinct profession in Ukraine since 1999. Conferences sponsored by the project on *Reforming Social Services in Ukraine (2002)* and *Models of Social Work Education (2003)* were cited as examples of initiatives that helped to promote this recognition. New educational standards that have developed in Ukraine, partly in response to these conferences, now place greater emphasis on the integration of theory and practice and the connections between policy and practice. These conferences were also important to knowledge development among participants, as noted in the following comments:

- The conference *Reforming Social Services in Ukraine* developed my understanding of the front line social worker as a policy maker. (Advisory Committee Member)
- The conference *Models of Social Work Education* made it possible to bring together different models of social work education, one of these being the Canadian one specifically. The opportunity to get exposure

---

[5] A number of course manuals and related publications were produced during the project and these have been widely disseminated as teaching and resource materials. These include a manual on mediation (Zurawsky and Hayduk 2004), an English-Ukrainian dictionary of social work terminology (Zurawsky, Baybakova, and Hayduk 2004), and a manual on social work practice (Klos and Mykytenko 2005). As well, a manual on field instructor training has been published.

to the advanced experiences in the area of professional training of social workers was like "skimming the cream" from the best. (Social Work Instructor)

- For me the opportunity to participate in the *Reforming Social Services in Ukraine* conference was a chance to hear about social work theory and practice in Canada where social work is a developed profession. (Field Instructor)

Despite these positive developments, many challenges remain. There are no specific doctoral programs in social work in Ukraine, and standards for social work education are still considered as a specialized discipline within the field of Sociology. Although there are now approximately thirty university or college programs in Ukraine involved in the education and training of social workers, national educational standards are not yet used in a proactive way to promote the development of more progressive models of social work education. As well, local governments lack a good understanding of social work and the social services remain critically underfunded.

Theme 2: Model at Lviv Polytechnic National University

The social development perspective associated with the program was regarded as a strength, and courses on international social development, community development, and human rights and anti-oppressive practice were specifically identified as examples of this framework. The focus on the integration of policy and practice, both within the program and in courses organized around fields of practice such as health, disability issues, and child welfare, were described as reflecting social development principles. The student-centred participatory approach to learning and the focus on integrating theory and practice were highly valued by both students and instructors:

- What I really like about our program is the possibility to take part in group activities in class, and discuss things. (Social Work Student)
- The interactive approach to learning that we apply allows for bringing field experiences into the class. (Social Work Instructor)

The participatory approach to learning can be contrasted with the more didactic, lecture-focused model of education that still remains quite dominant in Ukraine, and it was argued that this model encouraged the integration of theory and practice.[6] Another aspect of partnership identified was the continuing support of individuals from the University of Manitoba after the official termination of the project. This assistance has included consultation around curriculum development for the MSW program, and ongoing roles as visiting instructors and workshop leaders.

---

[6] The role of the community as a partner in the ongoing development of the program, which was one of the assumptions of the original model, is captured in this statement from a member of the Advisory Committee: "I appreciate the opportunity to discuss at our Advisory Committee meetings both the students' involvement at our agencies and the way the program is responding. This provides the feeling of being supported and being supportive at the same time."

Other reflections about the model were voiced during the interviews. It was noted, for example, that the Social Work Program at Lviv Polytechnic National University (LPNU) continues to play a significant role nationally. For example, the program's curriculum materials have been used in the development of national educational standards for social work; as well, other universities have used the program as a model in developing their own program. Second, the ongoing student exchange program with the University of Manitoba has provided opportunities for mutual learning among students in both countries. By 2006, nine Ukrainian students and three Canadian students had participated in one term study exchanges, and the exchange program is currently being expanded to graduate students and students from other disciplines. Finally, the model of education developed in social work is being used as a prototype for the development of a specialized program of study within Sociology.[7]

Although these comments illustrate the positive reputation associated with the program, the real test of any model of social work education is the quality of its students. In that respect, social work students from LPNU won second and sixth prizes in the National University Students' Contest in Social Work in 2005, and the Head of the State Examination Commission in Lviv made the following observation in 2006: "The quality of your graduates is incredibly high. I draw this conclusion by comparing your graduates with the graduates of other higher educational establishments in Lviv where I've been involved as a member of state examination commissions in recent years."[8]

Despite the success associated with the ongoing implementation of the educational model, respondents also identified future challenges. The quality of learning opportunities in some field agencies is uneven, and in part this is a reflection of inadequate resources and the related quality of social services within these agencies. The Social Work Program itself is also under-resourced, and instructors, who have very high teaching loads, are unable to adequately respond to community demands for professional workshops and training.

Theme 3: Social Service Reform

Social service reforms, a long-term goal of the *Reforming Social Services: Canada-Ukraine Project,* must be assessed against Ukraine's general progress related to economic and social development over the past decade. Although some recent changes can be identified, economic growth has been quite limited and investment in the social services has failed to keep pace with growing social problems or respond adequately to growing inequality.

---

[7] The national reputation of the program is reflected in the observation made by a Professor of Sociology from Kyiv and members of the Accreditation Review Commission: "The social work education model at your department is very well developed. It is a pattern to follow."

[8] The model's initial connection to disability organizations remains strong and courses on disability issues, with input from this community, continue to be taught in both the undergraduate and graduate programs. Several disability organizations are used as field placement sites, and a number of students with disabilities have been admitted to the program.

Nevertheless, at a smaller and more localized level, the program's contributions have been significant.

Faculty within the program have provided leadership in the development of new service responses, including mediation, foster family care, and rehabilitation services for offenders. As noted by a social work instructor, "the instructors of our department take an active part in the development of new social services. This often occurs through their involvement as field instructors, joint projects with agency staff or through projects that receive special funding." Two graduates are now teaching in the program and the program is playing an important role in promoting collaboration among government and non-government organizations.

Students also brought new, creative ideas for the improvement of social services to their field agencies, and some of the graduates are now working as social worker staff or volunteers with community agencies. In one case, two graduate students were actively involved in the development of a new self-help organization to provide assistance to citizens in dealing with housing and other consumer related problems. In another case, a graduate student completed a research project on HIV/AIDS for a government agency and was hired by the agency following her graduation. In still other cases, students in their field placement settings were identified as knowing how to work with children and parents, and instrumental in work with crime prevention among minors.[9]

Although the contributions social work can make to social services is becoming better understood, the level of awareness among social agencies and the general public about the essential role of social services to community well-being is still not well recognized. A prevailing problem is the limited number of designated social work positions within community social agencies and the low salaries paid to social workers. In response to these issues, the Community Advisory Committee to the Social Work Program has undertaken strategies aimed at creating greater awareness about social work and the social services, and encouraging social agencies to designate new positions for social workers within their organizations. As well, increased involvement from agency representatives in the selection and orientation of new social work students will help to promote continuing agency investment in graduates from the program.

---

[9] This summary is reinforced by evaluative comments like the following:

• The topics of your students' MSW theses are always of particular interest as they are of an applied nature and in response to pressing needs in our community. (Professor of Sociology and Member of State Examination Commission at LPNU)

• We think highly of your social work students as they know how to work with disabled children. Your students are proactive and change oriented, enthusiastic, willing to apply their advanced knowledge and skills in practice and gain new social work practice experience. (Agency representative)

• We are trying to involve as many social work students from Lviv Polytechnic as we can because they are highly knowledgeable and progressive. We have eight social work students at our agency, and one of your recent graduates has already been employed here as a staff member.(Agency representative).

Theme 4: Training Human Services Staff

Two major certificate programs were developed and delivered to community-based staff under the auspices of the *Reforming Social Services: Canada-Ukraine Project.* These were the professional development course for field instructors and the course on Innovations in Social Development. In addition, a number of shorter workshops and training opportunities were provided.[10] In the past few years there has also been a growing demand from the field for a part-time or distance educational social work program that would enable staff working in community agencies to complete studies leading to a degree in social work.

The establishment of the Research Resource Centre at the Department of Sociology and Social Work during the last year of the project has facilitated the provision of some short-term community workshops and provided some support to faculty engaging in research and development projects. However, the high teaching load of faculty reduces the program's capacity to respond to requests from the community for certified professional development programs or a distance education degree program in social work.

Conclusion

The historical connection between Ukrainian people in Lviv and Winnipeg was a factor in events that led to the initiation of this project. The connection made it easy to recruit social workers of Ukrainian heritage, or others committed to international social justice, to travel to Ukraine to teach and provide other project-related services without being fully compensated for their time. The project implementation group consisted of a core of six individuals from Ukraine and eight Canadians. It was the vision and commitment of this group that made the difference in the project.

A commitment to social justice and social development principles as an organizing framework for the project also helped to establish a common vision, but it was the personal relationships among individuals in both countries that sustained this vision and contributed to the results reported in the previous section. Of particular significance has been the enduring nature of these relationships long after the expiration of project funding. Although this is exemplified by the continuing collaboration between the authors of this chapter, it is not limited to us. For example, other Canadian members of the core implementation team have returned to Ukraine to provide community-based workshops on several occasions since 2003, and

---

[10] These were highly valued, as illustrated by the following responses, and there have been several requests to re-establish these programs.
• My participation in the delivery of professional development courses together with our Canadian colleagues was a way to personally acquire new social work knowledge and experience. (Social Work Instructor)
• My involvement as a participant in the professional development training delivered by the project went beyond my expectations. Along with exposure to advanced knowledge in social work, the training was an effective way of bringing the community together. (Advisory Committee Member)

the collaborative partnership between the two universities has expanded to include other individuals.[11]

In the early development stage there was a tendency to adopt Canadian service and educational models without a full recognition of their limitations, but over time a more critical stance to Canadian experiences in curriculum building has evolved. Canadian experiences are regarded as valuable, but these are screened for appropriateness through criteria, such as community needs, organizational context, cultural traditions, and individual and community assets prior to application. International development initiatives also affect the host country and experiences from this project have been instrumental in internationalizing the social work curriculum at the University of Manitoba. The effects on one's own commitment to social justice, both locally and globally, is also transformed.

In this project, the social development framework, with its emphasis on participatory approaches and partnerships, was a useful guide in re-conceptualizing an approach to international social work education that included a more critical examination of western models. In a review of project accomplishments in 2002, McKenzie, Rudy, and Hayduk noted that, although ongoing feedback from students and field instructors confirmed the general benefits associated with the curriculum, much remained to be done to ensure the sustainability of the social work education model at Lviv Polytechnic National University. These authors also noted that success would be influenced by participatory partnerships that had been developed among key advocates within the university, local community agencies, government, and other universities.

In the early stage, there was greater reliance on Canadian expertise and the type of partnership was largely consultative. By the third year of the project a more collaborative model of partnership had evolved and this was characterized by more input from Ukrainian stakeholders into curriculum development and direct responsibility for teaching a number of courses in the program. In the final year of the project and beyond, a locality development model of social development was established where primary authority and responsibility for the program was assumed by Ukrainian stakeholders. Although this case study has documented the enduring nature of the partnership between the social work programs in the two universities, consultative assistance and support provided by the University of Manitoba is now provided in response to specific requests from Ukrainian partners.

The developmental stage of the project has been matched by increased attention to the indigenization of the curriculum over time. Thus local knowledge and cultural practices are now commonly used to shape the approach to analysis and intervention within courses. However, core content and competencies still reflect a generalist model of social work education,

---

[11] Nina Hayduk, the Head of the Social Work Program, has played a key role in the development of the social work program at Lviv Polytechnic National University and in promoting the profession of social work in Lviv and elsewhere in Ukraine.

even if that model has been shaped by Ukrainian context and realities. For example, structural analysis includes a critical view of state authority as this has been exercized in Ukraine, and the multiple and overlapping nature of oppression includes recognition of gender, ethnic minorities, and the loss of civil society that was an outcome of state socialism in the Soviet era. One of the most important challenges is rebuilding a sense of civil society where public participation is encouraged and where a sphere of institutions and voluntary organizations, located between the family, state, and market, provide opportunities for individuals to exercise the right of citizenship. The project's connection to and support of local voluntary and community organizations, including disability organizations, and the inclusion of core content on community development within the curriculum, have promoted this development in small but significant ways.

References

- Asamoah, Y., L. Kealy, and N. Mayadas. 1997. Ending the International-Domestic Dichotomy: New Approaches to a Global Curriculum for the Millennium. *Journal of Social Work Education* 33 (2): 389–401.
- Bridge, G. 2002. Sustaining Social Work Education in Ukraine: The Second Phase. *European Journal of Social Work* 5 (2): 139–147.
- Campfens, H. 1996. Partnerships in International Development: Evolution in Practice and Concept. *International Social Work* 39 (2): 201–223.
- Constable, R. and V. Mehta. 1994. *Education for Social Work in Eastern Europe: Changing Horizons.* Chicago: Lyceum.
- Edwards, R., M. Roth, R. Davis, and L. Popescu. 2000. The Role of Global Collaborative Efforts to Develop Romania's Child Protection and Social Work Education Systems. *Social Work and Globalization* (Special Issue of *Canadian Social Work* 2 (1) and *Canadian Social Work Review* 17: 162–183).
- Faculty of Social Work, University of Manitoba. 2003. *Reforming Social Services: Canada-Ukraine Project.* Final Report submitted to Canadian International Development Agency. Winnipeg: University of Manitoba.
- Frank, F. and A. Smith. 1999. *The Community Development Handbook.* Hull: Minister of Public Works & Government Services Canada.
- Hayduk, N. 2005. *Profesijna pidhotovka sotsial'nykh pratsivnykiv do zdijsnennia poserednytstva (na materialakh SSHA i Kanady).* (Professional Training of Social Workers to Apply Mediation (Based on American and Canadian experiences). Ph.D. Thesis. Kiev: Academy of Pedagogical Sciences of Ukraine.
- Healy, L. 2001. *International Social Work: Professional Action in an Interdependent World.* New York: Oxford.
- International Federation of Social Workers. 2000. *Definition of Social Work.* Berne: IFSW.
- Kalachova, I. 2002. *Poverty and Welfare Trends in Ukraine over the 1990s.* (Background country paper). Florence: UNICEF Innocenti Research Centre. www.unicef-icdc.org/research/ESP/CountryReports2002_02/Ukraine01.pdf.
- Klos, L. and N. Mykytenko. 2005. *Navchal'nyj posibnyk: Vstup do praktychnoji sotsial'noji roboty (na prykladi vyvchennia dosvidu Ukrajiny i Kanady* (Manual: Introduction to Social Work Practice (based on experiences in Ukraine and Canada). Lviv: Lviv Polytechnic National University.
- Lorenz, W. 1994. *Social Work in a Changing Europe.* London: Routledge.

- Mayades, N. S., T. D. Watts, and D. Elliott, eds. 1997. *International Handbook on Social Work Education.* Westport: Greenwood Press.

- McKenzie, B., D. Rudy, and N. Hayduk. 2002. *Partnerships for Social Development Reform in Eastern Europe: A Canada-Ukraine Initiative in Social Work Education.* Paper presented to International Association of Schools of Social Work Conference. Montpellier, France (July 14–19).

- Midgley, J. 1981. *Professional Imperialism: Social Work in the Third World.* London: Heinemann Educational Books.

- Midgley, J. 1995. *Social Development.* London: Sage Publications.

- Midgley, J. 2000. Globalization, Capitalism and Social Welfare: A Social Development Perspective. *Social Work and Globalization* (Special Issue of *Canadian Social Work* 2 (1) and *Canadian Social Work Review* 17: 13–28).

- Mykytenko, N. 2006. *Profesijna pidhotovka sotsial'nykh pratsivnykiv u Kanads'Kykh universytetakh* (Professional Training of Social Workers at Canadian Universities). Draft Ph.D. Thesis. Lviv: Ukraine.

- Nimmagadda, J. and C. Cowger. 1999. Cross-Cultural Practice. *International Social Work* 42 (3): 261–276.

- Rudy, D. 2002. *Evaluating Professional Development Training for Field Instructors in an Undergraduate Social Work Program in Ukraine.* Master's Practicum. Faculty of Social Work. Winnipeg: University of Manitoba.

- Savka, V. 2005. *Do pytannia pro systemu instrumentiv sotsial'noji polityky v demokratychnomu suspil'stvi* (The Issue of the System of Social Policy Instruments in a Democratic Society). www.democracy.kiev.ua/publications/collections/conference_2005/section_17.

- Seidle, F. 1995. *Rethinking the Delivery of Public Services for Citizens.* Montreal: Institute for Research on Public Policy.

- The World Organization Against Torture (OMCT). 2002. *Rights of the Child in Ukraine.* Geneva: OMCT. www.omct.org/pdf/cc/UkraineEng.cc.pdf.

- Tucker Rambally, R. 1999. Field Education in a Developing Country: Promoting Organizational Change and Social Development. *International Social Work* 42 (4): 485–496.

- Tunney, K. and R. Kulys. 2004. Social Work Field Education as Social Development: A Lithuanian Case Study. *Social Work in Mental Health* 2 (2/3): 59–75.

- United Nations Committee on the Rights of the Child. 1995. *Concluding Observations of the Committee on the Rights of the Child: Ukraine.* http://umn.edu/humanrtns/crc-ukraine95.htm.

- United Nations Country Team (UNCT). 2002. *Ukraine: Common Country Assessment,* Kiev: UNCT. www.un.kiev.ua/en/countryteam/docs/CCA_en.pdf.

- Wilson, M. and E. Whitmore. 2000. *Seeds of Fire: Social Development in an Era of Globalism.* Halifax: Fernwood.

- Zurawsky, A., I. Baybakova, and N. Hayduk. 2004. *English-Ukrainian Terminological Dictionary-Directory in Social Work.* Lviv: Lviv Polytechnic National University.

- Zurawsky, A., and N. Hayduk. 2004. *Posibnyk: Model'protsecu poserednytstva: Kontseptsiji, metody i pryjomy* (Manual: Mediation Process Model: Concepts, Methods, Techniques). Lviv: Lviv Polytechnic National University.

Chapter 15

Framework for Social Work Education: Indigenous World View

Betty Bastien

This chapter presents an indigenous conceptual framework that draws on Aboriginal theories and Blackfoot concepts to illustrate the knowledge and practices necessary in social work to affirm indigeneity and structures that will support the recovery process of indigenous well-being and identity. If social work, including international social work, is to meet the needs and aspirations of the healing movement of indigenous peoples, it must work from an Indigenous world view. The world view and practices of Indigenous cultures contain the necessary knowledge and skills required to respond to the fragmentation not just of Indigenous peoples, but of humanity in general, and to heal the separation from the world in which we live as human beings.

Indigenous people struggle on a daily basis for their collective survival and quality of life, inherent in the struggle for the protection and preservation of their way of life. As an example, one of the patterns that is significant among indigenous population is poverty; they are more likely to be poor, life expectancy is 10–20 years less than the national average and infant mortality can be three times greater. In addition, malnutrition and communicable disease continue to affect large populations. Also, indigenous people have less access to education and are subjected to curricula designed for other cultural groups that ignore their own history, knowledge, and values (Eversole et al. 2006, 2–3). The United Nations have also stated that worldwide indigenous peoples continue to be disadvantaged in every aspect of their lives, including the violation of human rights such as forced displacement and the confiscation or denial of access to their communal or individual property (Eversole et al. 2006, 3–4).

In the mid 1980s, the United Nations Sub-Commission on Prevention of Discrimination and Protection of Minorities defined Indigenous communities, nations, and peoples as "having an historical continuity with pre-invasion and pre-colonial societies ... and are determined to preserve, develop, and transmit to future generations their ancestral territories, and their ethnic identity, as a basis of their continued existence as peoples" (Eversole et al. 2006, 5). The historical cultural continuity of the Blackfoot people can be observed in the oral traditions held in their ceremonies and sacred text. The ceremonies embody their collective identity and relationships to ecological balance necessary for the collective survival.

The preservation and protection of Indigenous peoples and their cultures begins with an understanding of their critical and tenuous position in the world structure. It is estimated that 300 million people in the world are indigenous who belong to 5,000 indigenous groups. These small-identified collective groups bring a diversity of knowledge, education, and practice to the world community. Along with their high mortality, their knowledge systems, languages, and practices are disappearing. Without support from the educational systems of the world universities, these knowledge systems, which hold hope for balance, peace and healing, will disappear.

An ideology of progress and development has, in the past, ascribed these knowledge systems as useless. However, as the global community is faced with a growing scarcity of resources and energy, an alternative paradigm for sustainable resource development is emerging. The emerging paradigm may look toward the indigenous population for the knowledge that can create balance between human populations and the ecology required for collective survival.

Traditional Indigenous knowledge is the process and practice of being in the present; the Indigenous self or identity, in the Blackfoot (*Siksikaitsitapi*) and other Indigenous world views, emerge through the integration of roles and responsibilities that are constituted by, and maintain, cosmic and natural alliances. This way of being in the universe creates ontological responsibilities that occur in the context of the good heart, the moral and ethical responsibilities of maintaining balance and peace. Knowing one's alliances is the active participation with the natural world. The inclusiveness, diversity, collaboration, and transformational aspects of Indigenous social work go beyond the classical western conception of reality in general, and its conceptions of nature and knowledge production in particular.

Background

The Eurocentric world view has impacted the lives of Indigenous peoples of Canada for 500 hundred years. It has been able to dominate and control Aboriginal people through its economic force, technology, and science, which have fuelled the unrestrained exploitation of natural resources. A central part of this world view is the belief that science and technology can fix any negative consequence of progress. Although the industrialized countries, in general, enjoy a quality of life that has been unprecedented in history, the levels of poverty and oppression among Indigenous populations are also unprecedented.

Because of the resource crisis, critical issues have surfaced in discussions on ecological sustainability and international justice. Indigenous cultures, as the prophecies have foretold (Peat 1994), embody knowledge systems that can address the crisis of the fragmentation of our relationships. This healing process begins with critical self-reflection. It is an inner journey to the heart, which takes its starting point with the question "Who am I?"

The struggle for First Nations in Canada is navigating cultural continuity in the face of the Indian Act and Sec 91, 24 of the *British North American Act* that created, and perpetuates, political dependency, economic marginalization, and cultural degradation. It is estimated that prior to European settlement, 18.5 million Aboriginal people lived in North America, with two million of these in Canada. By the turn of the twentieth century it is thought that up to 99% of the continent's Aboriginal people had been wiped out (Churchill 1998). Currently, Aboriginal people still make up only 5% of Alberta's population and 3% of Canada's population (Statistics Canada 2004).

The policies and practices created by the *Indian Act* have normalized violence, abuse, and neglect in First Nation communities and families. Children were removed to residential schools, in a dehumanizing practice of stigmatization and isolation. Generation after generation were humiliated and repeatedly violated. The implementation of the *Indian Act* and its subsequent policies (such as the *Child Welfare Act*) resulted in dependency, poverty, and unemployment. The multigenerational impact of oppressive and traumatic experiences was criminalized and pathologized.

These practices, in turn, have had genocidal consequences for the cultural continuity of First Nations. They involve the following three factors:

1. Violence targeted at a viable group of people large enough to undermine the capability to self-perpetuate and the defence of their own identity.

2. Deprivation of resources necessary to continue the struggle of self-determination.

3. Destruction of their spiritual foundations and, at the same time, attacking their psychological, spiritual and social beliefs, and values.[1]

Decades of cumulative violence have constructed a social reality in which experiences of trauma and prejudice have shaped Indigenous peoples' orientation to the world and their interpretation of their relationship experiences. The bottom line has been genocide. The objectification and dehumanization lasting several generations in Canada and the United States has created a reality that continues to perpetuate itself through key constructs based in colonial and supremacist thinking. Central social, political, economic, and spiritual constructs are premised on ideologies of race, individualism, competition for scarcity, and blaming and pathologizing victims. Scientific knowledge and research are instrumental in giving this particular social construction power and legitimacy while obscuring and normalizing ongoing violence.

The violence is exemplified as follows:

- The *Indian Act* created reservations with the category "Indian" based on the assumption that it was necessary to civilize the heathens, a stigmatization process in which Indigenous peoples are considered not quite human.

- 80% of First Nations' children were affected by religious indoctrination.

---

[1] Chrisjohn summarizes these practices in the following manner: (1) the volume of violence has been large enough to undermine the will and resilience of the sufferer, and to terrorize them into surrender to the superior power and into acceptance of the order it imposed; and (2) the group has been deprived of resources necessary for the continuation of the struggles (Chrisjohn et al. 1994, 30).

264 / Part 4: Social Work Education

- In 1920, under the *Indian Act*, children were forcibly removed from their families and communities and became de facto political prisoners or hostages.

- In 1930, under the *Indian Act*, parents were criminalized for their refusal to send children to schools—schools in which children suffered high levels of sexual and physical abuse and neglect and were subjected to an identity number system.

"Residential schools were [eventually] replaced by ... child welfare ... in a second attempt to ensure that the next generation of Indian children was different from their parents" (Armitage 1993, 131). The number of Indigenous children in the child welfare system is about four times greater than that of non-Aboriginal children (Berry and Brink 2004). Statistics from the Prairie Provinces reveal even greater proportions of Aboriginal children in care.

In Alberta, about 38% of children in care are Aboriginal and in Saskatchewan and Manitoba the number of Aboriginal children in care is estimated to be up to 70% (Blackstock and Trocme 2005). According to Indian and Northern Affairs Canada, the number of on-reserve registered Aboriginal children in care increased by over 150% between 1995 and 2003. The child welfare system continually argues for more resources, but without structural and substantive change, the constant request becomes an irritant that further escalates the intolerance for Aboriginal people in social programs.

Challenge

Survivors of the genocidal history challenge the professions in the human services to reconnect the fragments of their Indigenous world, heal their sense of self, and revise history so that they can make meaning of their present symptoms in light of past events (Atkins 2002). Recovery occurs when the survivor develops a new schema for understanding what happened and thus can integrate new experiences. Long-term trauma involving threats to survival is commonly conceptualized as a post-traumatic stress syndrome,[2] a rather recent field of research with a dearth of information on Indigenous populations (Bastien et al. 2003).

Social work is culture bound. Responses to the traumatic history of Indigenous peoples and its transgenerational impact were, and continue to be, developed within the epistemology and ontology of the colonizing paradigm from which social work generally derives its knowledge and skills. However, it must be understood that survivors in First Nation communities are now developing a new schema[3] in order to understand past events. Recovery for Indigenous people requires that it begins with affirming their Indigenous

---

[2] The literature has gleaned from experiences such as the Jewish holocaust, survivors of war, refugees, survivors of domestic violence, survivors of totalitarian control, religious cult survivors, and (political) hostages. Little consideration has been given to peoples who continue to survive in a colonial environment.

[3] Schema refers to the completion of principles that summarize the human mind's intrinsic ability to process new information in order to bring up to date the inner schemata of self and the world.

identities; thus allowing for a new understanding of the past, outside the socially constructed reality of the colonizer, so that they can begin to create a future based on their own values.

The distinctive qualities constituting Indigenous selves or identities must become central to the discussion of recovery, healing, and social work practice. This identity is dependent upon the meaning and purpose of relationships. Relationships are the essence of how one identifies the self and relates to the world; it is the context in which the self is understood. Relationships are the essence of one's identity. These relationships become the focus for an Indigenous social work practice; relationships are at the heart of health and social integration.

Indigenous people have understood the universe to be an indivisible whole that only recently has been seen by physicists in this way. It is this indivisible wholeness of the universe that is the source of Indigenous spirituality. Spirituality is a way of life based on ontological responsibilities that are constituted by the interdependence and interconnectedness of the universe. Indigenous peoples share responsibility for the balance of these interconnections and interdependences. They emulate the workings of the universe that are referred to as natural laws of the universe, (i.e., the way the universe functions). It is the collective responsibility of Indigenous peoples to work with the universe for peace, balance, and survival.

New findings about the nature of reality are summarized as "everything is intimately present to everything else in the universe. In other words, material objects are no longer perceived as independent entities but as concentrations of energy of the quantum field. The universe is more accurately described as a quantum field that is present everywhere in space and yet in its particles aspect has a discontinuous, granular structure" (Atleo 2004, xiii–xiv).

Blackfoot Experience

In the Blackfoot world view, relationships are sourced from the ontological responsibilities that form the connections. Identity or self is constructed through an intricate system of collective responsibilities that are all inclusive in their orientation to each other, family, community, nature, and the universe. These responsibilities embody the meaning of life, the purpose of existence, and the structure and order of the universe. Relationships begin with a "good heart" and are the measure of health and social functioning. The self is located in place (ecology). The point of harmony with the kinship system of alliances is characterized by affinity and balance. Relationships are timeless and by their nature determine the continuity of life.

Spirituality, in this context, is a connection with *Ihtsipaitapiiyopa,* a source of life. Life is the broadest of terms that includes "all of time" and "everything that is." A relationship to an organic all-inclusive universe has no divisions or separations, such as: thought vs. speech; being vs. doing; living a private or individual life vs. a public or communal life. It is being one with the whole and being one with the spiritual nature of life, the source of life, and "all that is." *Natosi* (Sun) is the greatest manifestation of this understanding, it is both a spiritual and physical manifestation of the life source, *Ihtsipaitapiiyopa*. In this respect it is much easier to understand that the *Sun* is a life source for the planet and must be respected for the great kindness and generosity of the gifts bestowed on the planet for our collective survival. I will use these concepts to illustrate a framework for social work practice.

The theory of affinity begins with *Kimmapiiyipitsinni,* which refers to a way of being that imbues kindness, compassion, and generosity. This way of being is the nature of the source of life, *Ihtsipaitapiiyopa*. This understanding is based on centuries of observation, understanding, and experience with an organic universe. In western terms, the theory of what holds the universe in balance and the nature of these connections is of what the universe is made of. Compassion and generosity are the orientation of the universe. They are the heart centre of the *Niitsitapi* (Indigenous peoples') way of life. The power of the universe resides in love and compassion.

Language

Language is the expression of culture's relation to the world. It is the mirror in which a group or society conceptualizes and experiences relationships. It is also the articulation of the group's knowledge systems, identity, values, and responsibilities. Language, from an Indigenous viewpoint, articulates and calls into the present knowledge and responsibilities that will guide the recovery process and survival practices for the collective health of the Nations. The respect for the interdependence of life within the Indigenous paradigm is the path toward the integrity required for balance. It begins with the inner worlds of the people themselves, affirming Indigenous identity. Cultural integrity is the foundation for any recovery process.

Language embodies epistemologies and pedagogies. It describes and reflects the potentialities of humanity and defines limitations. Human consciousness carves out concepts through which the interpretation of the world is expressed and perpetuated. Through language, humans ascribe themselves specific characteristics or articulate their understanding of the essence of being human. This process creates human constructs about the nature and function of humanity. Each cultural world view is an articulation of an understanding of what the nature of the human being is.

Indigenous world views and languages have the common elements of interdependence and interconnections. Each cultural group, however, has its own language that addresses cosmic responsibilities of balance as stewards of the land, in Blackfoot it is expressed as *Ihpo Kiitomohpiipotokoi* (collective ontological responsibilities). The collective responsibility of balance and harmony is premised on being in good relationships with others and the world in which we live. The traditional knowledge of living in peace and honouring the processes of balance with others has been transferred through the generations by grandparents.

Language is the connection to the good heart, to the good path, the red road. It connects us with a world that shapes and guides the processes for maintaining ontological responsibilities. Language guides the human development process, the social relations that guide the orientation toward balance. It reflects the philosophical system of the people. It evokes and describes the relational perspective that is a mirror of the sacred world (Bastien 2004, 127). It contains the meanings ascribed to existence and describes the purpose of relationships, as well as the responsibilities inherent in these connections; it provides a way of making sense of the world (Bastien 2004, 129). Because language guides the epistemological and pedagogical practices, it is instrumental in creating knowledge and understanding of where Indigenous people came from and who they are in the present.

Interdependent reality, from an Indigenous world view, provides guidance for health and survival. Language embodies the connections, relationships, responsibilities, and cosmic alliances necessary for balance of *Siksikaitsitapi* (Blackfoot speaking peoples). The oral tradition is a way of connecting with the spiritual alliances. Language carries our breath and with it the connections to the teachings. The experiences of the ancients can be simultaneously experienced in the present. Indigenous languages are necessary for cultural continuity and for survival.

Framework

Striving for peace and good relations with ancestors, alliances, and life is then referred to as ceremony. Being mindful of, and responsible for, wellness and health of all is inherently ceremony. This means understanding that the well-being of all is a collective sacred responsibility and is the essence of the purpose for living. Spirituality and gatherings are the cornerstones for affirming knowledge systems for health and wellness.

Spirituality is the source for strengthening the alliances of kinship responsibilities for a sustainable and thriving community. It means forging new alliances, kinships, and coming to know relatives through the good heart. Spirituality means taking the respectful care of family, elder, children, parents, and grandparents. Respect means striving to preserve the sacred nature of all relationships that life holds for everyone and everything and between everyone and everything. It is "all my relatives" of the Nation, it is the continuity of respect for life.

Gatherings renew and revitalize the communal values and the affinity of kinship systems. They are the traditional method for bringing together and promoting the collective knowledge and wisdom, much like a research project. Gatherings expand responsibilities and collective action. They revitalize the traditional ways for strengthening the affinity of collective and family ties, affirm and use knowledge building, decrease external dependencies, and develop Indigenous-style leadership and practices, and, finally, create sources of knowledge for their recovery.

The following four Blackfoot constructs illustrate the collective ontological responsibilities of Indigenous peoples. They are organic or holistic and encompass the physical and spiritual worlds of *Siksikaitsitapi*. In other words, they are all-inclusive in their relation to life. Their application is contextual and, like the snowflake, no two circumstances are the same—thus usage and application of terms are dependent upon the experience expressed. The four are:

1. *Isskanaitapsi*, meaning "relationships, self in others."
2. *Pommaksinni*, meaning "transfers, interrelationship of life, transgenerational transfer of knowledge."
3. *Ihtaaohkoitapiyo'p*, meaning "gifts, the reciprocal and interdependent nature of the universe."
4. *Kaamotaani*, meaning "survival, balance among all things, practice, thought; the organic nature of the universe provides structures and processes to maintain balance." (Bastien 2004).

1. Isskanaitapsi

Isskanaitapsi, the fact of interrelatedness and relationships, means that life is purposeful and all-inclusive. This understanding of the cosmic organic nature of the universe, how it works and how we are related as relatives, is at the core of Indigenous people's survival. The wisdom of traditional knowledge and custom manifests the understanding that everything is relationships and relatedness. It is at the very centre of Indigenous people's identity.

In other words, the nature of the self, "self in others," *isskanaitapsi*, links the self with the universe and provides us with responsibilities, roles, and rules of conduct that strengthen the collective nature of the universe, i.e., the collective nature of our communities, the work place, the family, and ourselves as *Siksikaitsitapi*. The collective nature of Indigenous cultures is an affirmation that the universe works as a whole, it is an indivisible universe. Indigenous peoples live in concert with this understanding through their ceremonies.

The concept of maintaining balance and good relations means honouring and working with the dynamic power of the universe. It is the fervent, passionate being one with all our relations. Being one with life, and the life source, constitutes integrity. It means living for goodness, health, and the well-being of all. It is the understanding that every thought, word, and action of self has implications and influences the relationships with the universe. As given to *Siksikaitsitapi*, our language and ceremonies reveal the intricate interrelationship of our decisions and the impact they have on the world in which we live.

The understanding that the universe works in a collective or organic manner denotes the gift of contributing to the existence or activity of others. It means being of service to others and manifesting in the collective well-being of family and community. It refers to working together for the same mutual benefit in community efforts. The collective or communal holistic nature of Indigenous cultures creates this way of being. Collective support is seen as providing strength to the powers of the universe and is understood to be the source of life, of well-being, peace, and harmony. Culture and social organization are premised on strengthening these relations—all can live. For example, at Sundance, if you go up with your teepee, people will come out of their lodges to help. Community and family support each other to address the adversity and oppression of poverty, justice, and social agencies.

Each person relates to the collectivity or wholeness of the tribe through this way of being. It demonstrates the intricate responsibility contained within the reciprocal and indivisible nature of the universe. People have a gift, which, as it is put into service for the tribe, contributes to the collective and the continuity of the group. Individuals may be gifted with song, medicines, creativity, and insight. These are gifts that make the circle.

2. Pommaksinni

Pommaksinni or knowledge transfers are the way of passing and transferring knowledge, it is a way of life. In an all-interconnected universe it is the reciprocal nature of giving and receiving that supports and strengthens the life source. All knowledge and knowing is understood to be transferred.

Pommaksinni means giving away one's knowledge of strengthening the source of life. It is the process of giving and receiving within the spiritual and material culture. It includes connecting with alliances through ceremony; receiving names that connect one to the ancestors and relatives; the retelling of stories that are the traditional knowledge of the ancients; and receiving the advice, support, and guidance of the grandparents. It is in the transfers that a way of life and the connections between generations has continuity. Giving in transfers is not perceived as losing something, but as giving life to others so they, too, can understand the gift and collective responsibility of strengthening and renewing life. At a gathering, one of the ceremonial grandfathers said: "Traditions, as they have been taught to us through our ancestors and through the ceremonies, are the most accurate at this time; as opposed to other forms of knowledge." (Delaney, personal communication, 2003)

According to *Siksikaitsitapi*, a fundamental aspect of the cosmic universe is reciprocity, which is experienced in *Aipommotsspisyi'p,* the practice of ceremonial transfers. As a *Siksikaitsitapi* word, *Aipommotsp* means, "we are transferred, it was given, or passed on." It is the process of passing on the reciprocal responsibilities that ensure the continuity of the *Siksikaitsitapi* way of life. The natural law of reciprocity can be observed in everyday customs and activities, such as the giving of gifts, tobacco for offerings, the sharing of food, and always greeting each other.

Transfers connect us to the alliances and ancestors since time immemorial. They ensure the continuance of *Siksikaitsitapi*. As one ceremonialist said:

"Our life is transferred to us." Transfer is the way knowledge is passed on; it is the way to maintain balance among all our relations. The ceremony maintains the connection with *Ihtsipaitapiiyo'p*, the Source of Life.

It is our responsibility, in the *Siksikaitsitapi* way, to give back what we have been transferred. It is not the way of the people to sit with or keep that which has been given to you. For example, those who have received an education return and give it back to the people. The *Siksikaitsitapi* way, our way, the *Niitsitapi's* way, is to help, to assist, and then *Ihtsipaitapiiyo'p* will help us. We have to try hard and work hard. It is good *Ihtsipaitapiiyo'p* will help (Bastien 2004, 141–142).

The connections constitute our identity. They ensure our continuity and survival.

3. Ihtaaohkoitapiyo'p

Ihtaaohkoitapiyo'p is the giving and receiving of gifts for human and spiritual maturity.

Striving for meaning, the universe is ever unfolding its gifts. Everything in life and the universe is a gift. The gift of life exists in an all inclusive organic universe. Everything has a purpose and contributes to the interconnecting source of life. The universe is an intricate kinship system from which knowledge is gleaned. The understanding of interdependence and interconnectedness is the context for the kinships relationships in an all-inclusive universe.

The connections among these kinship systems are premised on the potentiality of a life giving source. It is in the anticipation that life and the relationships within are life giving. Life is perceived in a world as a source of gift giving. Gift giving is synonymous with giving life or strengthening life through gifts. Gifts are considered anything that promotes and strengthens the life source or spirituality. The source of life permeates the world, therefore everything has the potential for giving gifts. Receiving the abundance of gifts of the universe is dependent upon one's perceptions and interactions with life. For example, to have good health is a tremendous gift, it is abundance in one's life. The kindness and support of relatives is perceived to be one of the greatest gifts in life. Gifts from the source of life are in our daily lives and are often taken for granted, such as kind, supportive, and affirming words from colleagues. Humility and gratitude are central to this orientation to humanity.

4. Kaamotaani

Kaamotaani refers to the fact that someone or a group has successfully overcome grave challenges, imbalances, and adversity. *Kaamotaani* can be translated as "survival," and can be used to refer to overcoming specific challenges in life, such as rites of passage and having life births or such adversities as illness, accidents, losses, and misfortune. It refers to the mindfulness and receptiveness to the challenges and obstacles of life. Implicit in the term is an understanding of the ways to address these challenges and adversities of life.

Indigenous cultures have recognized the delicate nature of life. Their cultural practices have been developed to strengthen life and they work with the universe on strengthening life. They understand that the balance of life and death is fragile. It was once said that the braiding of the hair was a constant reminder of the delicate balance of life; each sunrise is acknowledged as the renewal of life; no day is ever the same, and each is received as the gift of renewal and it is celebrated. Adversity is also a part of life, it is nothing to be avoided, it is a natural part of one's development, and the culture is equipped to support individuals during the known adversities of life, such as child birth, illness, and death.

The uncertainty of life and the constant motion of energy are at the very heart of balance. This orientation to maintain and strive for balance meant that it was necessary to come to know the natural order of the universe and emulate that order through a cultural expression from which we can glean this orientation to life through language. The elders say: The language speaks to us about who we are ... we have not lost our culture. It is we who are lost. The grandparents said to me: If you have listened you will not come across anything in you lives you can not overcome ... if you come across a challenge and you cannot work with it ... you have not listened.

The following is an example of one of the principles of ethical practice that support the social organization and responsibilities of First Nations. *Ainnakowa* (respect) means striving to preserve the natural or sacred state of the universe. Cultural protocol and customs are the manifestations of this mission. Respect is contextual and as tribal members mature they understand that intuition is the best indicator for how to be respectful. This way of being is constantly mindful of the interrelatedness and interdependence of our relationships. For example, by learning to respect the natural world one becomes knowledgeable about the inherent properties of plants and their contribution to the survival of the group. Learning to maintain harmony with particular medicines is the outcome of respecting the properties of plants. This example can be extended to any relationship that contributes to the collective identity.

Social Work Education

Social work education informs anti-oppressive practice through the principles of inclusiveness and diversity. Moreover, the pursuit for self-determination is paramount. Therefore, without question, social work education and practice must include the historical and contemporary structural practices of oppression, including the central assumption constructed by the colonial ideologies regarding the identity and cultural context of Canadian Indigenous peoples' experience.

Two aspects are urgent for Indigenous-based social work:

1. Community capacity—restoring independence and connectedness of First Nation communities. A focus on the resiliency of the First

Nations must be a priority in policy, (i.e., protecting children and their families by mutually reinforcing, restoring, and promoting the interdependence and connectedness of families and communities and reaffirming collective responsibilities). This means strengthening the extended family and kinships systems by promoting, affirming, and sustaining good relations through cultural protocols. Kinship relationships, premised on the cultural ontological responsibilities, are the processes, which alter and interrupt the colonial beliefs and practices of violence and trauma. To do otherwise, will only maintain and support the destructive practices constructed by colonial realities.

2. Developing community and cultural competencies for cultural continuity. Elders have always been the protectors of the sacred knowledge that sustains and strengthens life. They have an integral role in teaching and practice. Indigenous pedagogy must be central to the curricula for indigenous populations. It presupposes an experience of unity, the collective knowledge of interdependence and interconnectedness, furthermore, it comes from within, living the knowledge. Therefore, it requires the collective consciousness of unity that is premised on capabilities of humanity to transcend and transform.

Indigenous social work practice affirms Indigenous identities in a context that not only reconnects Indigenous peoples to a holistic and nurturing universe, but more importantly, it connects their humanity with the essence of their relationship with each other, honouring the interconnectedness and interdependence of the life structure and essence. It provides a context for healing that is not based on deficiency but on the human species' intrinsic essence of completeness and unity. Any social work practice that attempts to address the consequences of a genocidal history needs to take an Indigenous world view as its starting point.

References

- Armitage, A. 1993. Family and Child Welfare in First Nation Communities. In *Rethinking Child Welfare in Canada*, ed. B. Wharf, 131–171. Toronto: McClelland & Stewart.
- Atkins, J. 2002. *Trauma Trails. Recreating Song Lines*. Melbourne: Spinifex Press.
- Atleo, R. E. 2004. *Tsawalk A Nuu-chah-nulth Worldview*. Vancover: UBC Press.
- Bastien, B. 2004. *Blackfoot Ways of Knowing: The Worldview of the Siksikaitsitapi*. Calgary: University of Calgary Press.
- Bastien, B., J. W. Kremer, R. Kuokkanen, and P. Vickers. 2003. Healing the Impact of Colonization, Genocide, and Racism on Indigenous Populations. In *The Psychological Impact of War Trauma on Civilians: An International Perspective*, eds. S. Krippner and T. M. McIntyre, 25–37. Westport: Praeger Publishers.
- Berry, S. and J. Brink. 2004. *Aboriginal Cultures in Alberta: Five Hundred Generations*. Edmonton: The Provincial Museum of Alberta.
- Blackstock, C. and N. Trocmé. 2005. Community-Based Child Welfare for Aboriginal Children: Supporting Resilience through Structural Change. In *A Handbook for*

Working with Children and Youth: Pathways to Resilience across Cultures and Contexts, ed. M. Ungar, 105–120. Thousand Oaks: Sage Publications.

- Chrisjohn, R. D., S. L. Young, and M. Maraun. 1994. *The Circle Game: Shadows and Substance in the Indian Residential School Experience in Canada.* Penticton: Theytus Books.

- Churchill, W. 1998. *A Little Matter of Genocide: Holocaust and Denial in the Americas: 1492 to Present.* Winnipeg: Arbeiter Ring.

- Eversole, R., J. A. McNeish, and A. Cimadamore. 2006. *Indigenous Peoples and Poverty: An International Perspective.* London: Zed Books.

- Peat, F. D. 1994. *Lighting the Seventh Fire: The Spiritual Ways, Healing, and Science of the Native American.* New York: Birch Lane Press.

- Statistics Canada. 2004. Aboriginal Peoples of Canada. Accessed October 23, 2005. www12.statcan.ca/english/census01/products/analytic/companion/abor/canada.cfm.

Marquis Book Printing Inc.

Québec, Canada
2009